Intelligence in an Insecure World

Second Edition

Intelligence in an Insecure World

Second Edition

PETER GILL AND MARK PHYTHIAN

polity

First published in 2012 by Polity Press

Polity Press
65 Bridge Street
Cambridge CB2 1UR, UK

Polity Press
350 Main Street
Malden, MA 02148, USA

ISBN-13: 978-0-7456-5278-8
ISBN-13: 978-0-7456-5279-5(pb)

A catalogue record for this book is available from the British Library.

Typeset in 9.5 on 13 pt Swift Light
by Servis Filmsetting Ltd, Stockport, Cheshire
Printed and bound in Great Britain by
the MPG Books Group

For further information on Polity, visit our website: www.politybooks.com

Peter Gill: for Pen

Mark Phythian: to my parents, Vic and Mary Phythian

Contents

Figures, Tables and Boxes

Figures

Tables

Boxes

Preface to the Second Edition

We commented in the preface to the first edition that intelligence is never far from the news headlines, and that continues to provide the context for this revision. We have sought to update the whole text but have also made some larger structural changes to reflect major developments in the study of intelligence. First, we have included a separate Introduction in which we describe the main developments in intelligence studies (IS) and try to assess the state of the art ten years after 9/11. Chapter 1 surveys the evolution of intelligence and considers how we define the term. One of the main developments discussed here is the extent to which scholars and practitioners are now challenging the model of the intelligence 'cycle' that has provided the bedrock for IS since serious studies began in the mid-twentieth century. The structure of chapter 2 remains essentially intact as we develop a conceptual framework for the study of intelligence. Chapter 3 provides an updated review of some of the main intelligence organizations both inside and outside the state as intelligence networks have continued to grow in scale and scope in recent years.

Chapter 4 examines the main methods of information gathering or collection. One of the main changes reflects the increasing significance of agencies accessing electronic information left by everybody in their daily lives; the other examines in much greater detail the major controversy generated by the US policy of extraordinary rendition of people suspected of being 'terrorists'. The kidnap and torture of 'enemies' in the search for information has a long and infamous history in intelligence, but its application on a global scale under the name of 'international co-operation' has raised major legal and ethical questions. Chapter 5 deals with the analysis of information, the development of 'intelligence' and its dissemination. The analytical failures in relation to weapons of mass destruction (WMD) in Iraq have led to much soul-searching in western intelligence agencies, and we examine that issue here as well as the attempt to make use of Web 2.0 technologies in order to enhance information sharing and analysis. We have 'upgraded' what was the final section of this chapter on action and policy into a more detailed consideration in chapter 6. In particular, this enables us to give due attention to perhaps the most significant development in security intelligence – the rapidly increasing use of unmanned aerial vehicles (UAVs or drones) not just for purposes of monitoring or watching but also for killing those targeted.

Chapter 7 in the first edition was a case study of the intelligence 'failure' with respect to Iraq, and we still consider that here, but as part of a more general consideration both of how 'failure' is perceived and analysed and of its causes. The core of chapter 8 remains the issues of democratic control, but we have included a longer consideration of the question of how intelligence comes to be 'democratized' in former authoritarian regimes. We discuss also two cases in the UK which bring together a number of the book's themes. Both Binyam Mohamed and Rangzieb Ahmed found themselves subjected to torture in foreign jails with the apparent collusion of British intelligence agencies. Their cases illustrate starkly the challenge facing all of us in seeking to maintain some semblance of democratic control over enhanced intelligence networks. As before, chapter 9 seeks to draw our conclusions.

Our continuing involvement in seminars, workshops and conferences over the past few years, in which we have discussed many of the themes to be found here, leaves us even more indebted to others than hitherto and we apologize to anyone who thinks they should be in the following list but has been omitted! We express our particular gratitude to: Michael Andregg, Rubén Arcos, Annika Bergman-Rosamond, Bob Brecher, Stefan Brem, Tom Bruneau, Marina Caparini, Marco Cepik, Antonio Díaz, Rob Dover, Eduardo Estevez, Stuart Farson, Mike Goodman, Dan Gressang, Michael Herman, Claudia Hillebrand, Peter Jackson, Loch Johnson, Ian Leigh, Steve Marrin, Cris Matei, Gustavo Matey, Dan Mazare, Jon Moran, John Nomikos, Sir David Omand, Andrew O'Neil, Jim Pfiffner, Gabriel Sebe, Shlomo Shpiro, Andrei Soldatov, David Strachan-Morris, Dennis Töllborg, Mike Warner, Thorsten Wetzling, Aidan Wills and Jim Wirtz (also for the whisky in Istanbul!). Many thanks to Pen Gill and Diane Evans, who have continued to be very supportive despite their own challenging lives at the chalkface. We are also grateful to Louise Knight and David Winters at Polity for their encouragement to prepare this new edition, and to Fiona Sewell for her excellent copy-editing.

Figures 3.1 and 3.2 and some portions of chapter 3 were previously published in an article 'Not just joining the dots but crossing the borders and bridging the voids: constructing security networks after 11th September 2001', *Policing & Society*, 16,1 (2006), pp. 26–48 (http://www.tandfonline.com) and are reproduced here by permission of Taylor & Francis.

As ever, remaining errors are our responsibility alone.

Peter Gill and Mark Phythian, January 2012

Abbreviations

Abbreviations are spelled out in full when they first appear. Those that appear at more than one point are listed here.

7/7	7 July 2005 London suicide bombings
9/11	11 September 2001 suicide attacks on New York, Washington, DC
ACLU	American Civil Liberties Union
AWACS	airborne warning and control system
BW	biological warfare
CBW	chemical and biological weapons
CCR	Center for Constitutional Rights (US)
CIA	Central Intelligence Agency (US)
CoE	Council of Europe
COINTELPRO	Counter Intelligence Programs (FBI, 1950–1960s)
CSE	Communications Security Establishment (Canada)
CSIS	Canadian Security Intelligence Service
CTC	Counter Terrorism Command (UK)
CTC	Counterterrorism Center (US)
CTG	Counterterrorist Group (EU plus)
DCI	Director of Central Intelligence (US, 1947–2004)
DHS	Department of Homeland Security (US)
DIA	Defense Intelligence Agency (US)
DIS	Defence Intelligence Staff (UK)
DNI	Director of National Intelligence (US, since 2005)
DoD	Department of Defense (US)
EP	European Parliament
EPIC	Electronic Privacy Information Center (US)
FBI	Federal Bureau of Investigation (US)
FEMA	Federal Emergency Management Agency (US)
FRU	Force Research Unit (UK)
FSB	Federal Security Service (Russia)
GCHQ	Government Communications Headquarters (UK)
GRU	Main Intelligence Directorate (military intelligence, Russia)
HMIC	Her Majesty's Inspectorate of Constabulary (UK)

HUMINT	human intelligence
IAEA	International Atomic Energy Agency
ICT	information and communication technology
IMINT	imagery intelligence
INR	Bureau of Intelligence and Research (US State Department)
IR	international relations
IS	intelligence studies
ISA	Intelligence Services Act 1994 (UK)
ISC	Intelligence and Security Committee (UK)
ISI	Inter-Services Intelligence (Pakistan)
JIC	Joint Intelligence Committee (UK)
JSOC	Joint Special Operations Command (US)
JTAC	Joint Terrorism Analysis Centre (UK, since 2003)
JWICS	Joint Worldwide Intelligence Communications System (US)
KGB	Committee of State Security (Soviet Union)
MASINT	measurement and signatures intelligence
MI5	Security Service (UK)
MI6	Secret Intelligence Service (UK)
NCCL	National Council for Civil Liberties (now Liberty, UK)
NCIS	National Criminal Intelligence Service (UK)
NCTC	National Counterterrorism Center (US)
NGO	non-governmental organization
NIC	National Intelligence Council (US)
NIE	National Intelligence Estimate (US)
NSA	National Security Agency/National Security Advisor (US)
NSC	National Security Council (US)
ODNI	Office of the Director of National Intelligence (US)
OEV	Operation Earnest Voice (US)
ONE	Office of National Estimates (US)
ORCON	originator control (the 'control principle')
OSINT	open source intelligence
PDB	President's Daily Brief (US)
PHIA	Professional Head of Intelligence Analysis (UK)
PIRA	Provisional Irish Republican Army
PMC	private military companies
PROTINT	protected information
PSC	private security companies
RCMP	Royal Canadian Mounted Police
SIGINT	signals intelligence
SIRC	Security Intelligence Review Committee (Canada)
SIS	Secret Intelligence Service (also known as MI6, UK)
SOCA	Serious Organized Crime Agency (UK)
SSCI	Senate Select Committee on Intelligence (US)

TECHINT	technical intelligence
UAV	unmanned aerial vehicle
UDA	Ulster Defence Association (UK)
UNSCOM	United Nations Special Commission (on Iraqi WMD)
WMD	weapons of mass destruction

Introduction: The Development of Intelligence Studies

We thought it would be useful to include a new Introduction in this edition reflecting on the state of intelligence studies (IS). It is twenty years since Wesley Wark did something similar in his introduction to a special issue of *Intelligence and National Security* that was based on papers delivered at a conference in Toronto in 1991. Wark identified eight approaches to the study of intelligence: the research project; the historical project; the definitional project; the methodological project (applying social science concepts to intelligence); memoirs; the civil liberties project; investigative journalism; and the popular culture project.[1] Since then, we have seen steadily, at times rapidly, growing interest in and discussion of intelligence matters that has been driven not only by the pressure of events but also by greater academic research and increased teaching of relevant subjects. As we shall see, the term 'intelligence studies' is used advisedly since all those who have commented on its development agree that the field is multi- if not inter-disciplinary. This may reflect the relative youth of the field – until 1990 people outside the US will only have talked of 'intelligence history' – but it is also a strength. Many academic disciplines now contribute to IS by bringing their disciplinary concepts and methods to the party, and this is important in demystifying the study of intelligence. In its early days writing was dominated by ex-practitioners and the impression given was that intelligence was a unique human activity. But intelligence is, at heart, an organizational activity and, with its special features such as secrecy, can be studied as such.

This survey is not intended to be a comprehensive review of the field but summarizes what seem to us to be the major currents in research. The recent growth in IS is reflected in a number of interesting articles examining the state of IS in various countries and languages. To a greater or lesser extent, the recent articles build on Wark's categories. Drawing on Wark, Scott, Kahn, Rudner, Denécé and Arboit, and Matey, we identify four main areas of work: research/historical; definitional/methodological; organizational/functional; and governance/policy.[2] The *research/historical* project continues to be dominant, at least outside the US, where the IS community has always been larger and more diverse. In the UK what has sometimes been described as the 'British school' of IS reflects not just the strength of the British community of historians but also that the two twentieth-century world wars provided much of the original raw material, as the strength of official secrecy ensured little on peacetime intelligence emerged before the 1990s and made the study of contemporary intelligence developments almost impossible. Academic writings based in part on released archives were supplemented by 'insider' accounts and memoirs of former practitioners, official histories, 'usually reliable sources' in which intelligence officers found willing journalists and writers such as Chapman Pincher and Nigel West to make their views public, and more critical accounts from writers such as Stephen Dorril.[3] Since the 'open government' initiative launched by Prime Minister John Major's administration in the early 1990s started to bear fruit, releases of files from the National Archives have accelerated, at least from MI5 and GCHQ, if not MI6.[4] There has been much more academic work, for example, by former intelligence official Michael Herman, Richard Aldrich on UK/US co-operation in the Cold War and GCHQ, Phil Davies on MI6 and whistleblower contributions.[5] To celebrate their one hundredth anniversaries in 2009, both MI5 and MI6 commissioned official histories,[6] with all the potential and limitations that official sanction implies.[7] In some cases unofficial histories based on 'liberated' archives have been written, such as the collaboration between Christopher Andrew and Vasili Mitrokhin on KGB material.[8] Finally, we would refer to the trove of information available in the reports of inquiries into intelligence on Iraq and 7/7 that we discuss in chapter 7.

David Kahn talks of a rebirth of French intelligence literature since the early 2000s, mainly regarding the Cold War and facilitated by new archive releases,[9] though Eric Denécé and Gérald Arboit note that IS is only in its infancy in France: intelligence has been viewed pejoratively and academics have approached it in a fragmentary fashion. They note the lack of a French intelligence culture and, very differently from the UK, that it is seen primarily as a domestic phenomenon – the problem of the 'enemy within'. Intelligence in France has been mistrusted since the Dreyfus affair and is still seen as subservient to political interests. Until the 1990s there were only memoirs and journalistic writings; even academic writing on French intelligence tended to be by foreigners, though subsequently academic output of history and other research subjects has increased.[10]

For Kahn the German intelligence literature is less extensive than the Francophone.[11] He notes the creation after reunification of the office for the administration of the Stasi archives, known as Gauck-Behörde; many volumes have been published and access to personal files is provided for victims and families.[12] The German literature is also primarily historical, and the International Intelligence History group meets mainly in Germany and has published the *Journal of Intelligence History* since 2001. Gustavo Matey's discussion of IS in Spain is more normative in tone but notes a similar increase in interest since the end of the Cold War. Earlier IS was dominated by history and military studies, reinforced by books on intelligence scandals in the 1980s and 1990s. Matey suggests there are four broad main approaches to IS in Spain: the historical-military, the journalistic, the economic, and the international relations (IR)/political science (including philosophy and law).[13]

Of course, the largest community of intelligence scholars is in the US, where historical research has also played an important part in the development of the field. Whereas in most countries history dominates, however, in the US it has been complemented by other concerns. Although the study of intelligence everywhere is hindered by the ubiquity of secrecy, as Jim Wirtz notes, compared to elsewhere, Americans are remarkably open about discussing intelligence processes.[14] He suggests this 'culture of openness' derives from a number of factors: the tradition of official post mortems into intelligence failures – there have been ten official inquiries into Pearl Harbor; investigations into intelligence 'scandals', such as those during 1975–6 into CIA and FBI operations and in the 1980s into the Iran–Contra affair; official use of classified information to justify policy – most recently and infamously, Colin Powell's highly misleading presentation on Iraq to the UN Security Council in February 2003; serial commissions and inquiries into how to 'fix' the US intelligence community; and leaks, of which the 2010 WikiLeaks case was on an especially massive scale.

Martin Rudner notes that out of 1,800 research chairs in Canadian universities, there is not one in IS.[15] Nevertheless, in many respects the scholarly and research community in Canada is better developed than in any other country outside the US. This can be seen in the very active Canadian Association for Security and Intelligence Studies (CASIS), whose annual conference exceeds in size and interest anything that could be organized currently in Europe. There have been similar motivations for historical research to those in the US, including investigation of scandals – McDonald and O'Connor – edited work on historical archives such as those on *RCMP Security Bulletins* by Greg Kealey and Reg Whitaker,[16] and Wesley Wark's official history of the community – long completed but as yet unpublished because of opposition from one of the agencies.

The US contribution has been greater when it comes to the second project: *definitional/methodological*. Reflecting the youth of the field, definitional debates are still taking place.[17] While these seem overly pedantic to some, and others may well prefer the well-known 'duck' definition, these debates matter to the extent that they reflect serious questions of clarifying what is to be studied and why. For example, one key question is whether 'intelligence' should be defined purely as an information or knowledge process or whether it is also a power process involving policy and action. We take the latter view, but there are those who prefer the former (see chapter 1). Another important question is prompted by Wilhelm Agrell's observation that 'if everything is intelligence, then nothing is intelligence':[18] is 'intelligence' any different from the 'knowledge management' that is the bedrock of all state and corporate activities? If the answer is 'yes' then we must be able to specify what is different about intelligence. Similarly, what, if anything, is the difference between the intelligence process and the more general 'risk-assessment' process that accompanies everything from business takeovers and foreign investment to organizing school trips for children? We discuss these questions in chapter 1.

Before the 1990s, some researchers were already seeking to apply concepts from elsewhere in the social sciences to understanding intelligence, to explain its successes and failures – especially the latter – and to examine intelligence organizations and processes, especially with the normative aim of improving them.[19] The central concept of 'cycle' or process was developed as a mechanism for analysing how intelligence worked, or not, at various 'levels' – individual, organizational, societal (see further discussion in chapter 2). As we have noted, much consideration has been given to the issue of 'failure', starting with Betts' classic article,[20] which arguably provides a theoretical handle on our subject equivalent to the 'causes' of war in IR.[21] More recently, more researchers have applied other social science concepts; for example, Michael Herman, Phil Davies and Amy Zegart deploying ideas of organizational process; Gill using 'information control';[22] and our use of 'surveillance' as an underlying concept for the study of intelligence (see chapter 2). The main point is that intelligence is a pre-eminently social and political phenomenon and, therefore, there is no need for IS to reinvent the wheel.

Most of the historical work discussed above was essentially descriptive, but it provides the basis for the third project: the *organizational/functional*. Looking at the potential population of intelligence agencies that might have been written about, it is striking that some have received much more coverage than others. Probably reflecting the historical interest in international politics and war, foreign intelligence agencies are best covered, especially those gathering human intelligence and also involved in covert operations. More ink has probably been spilt on the CIA than on any other agency in the world.[23] Why is this? The analytical directorate of the CIA provided a home for many intellectuals who, on retirement, took the opportunity to reflect on and contribute to the debates about the study of intelligence and intelligence reform. The operational side of the CIA, on the other hand, provided much of the material for discussing the more kinetic side of intelligence throughout the Cold War and after. Domestic agencies have received less coverage, although the counterintelligence efforts of the FBI under J. Edgar Hoover have been much written about.[24] Outside of liberal democracies, agencies such as the Soviet KGB and GDR's Stasi combined foreign and domestic intelligence duties which were best described in the context of their respective 'counterintelligence' states.[25]

Apart from largely descriptive histories of agencies and the occasional attempts to explain how they function in terms of organizational processes that we referred to above, another goal of this project is the normative one of improving agency performance in terms of effectiveness and, hopefully, propriety. The balance between these goals is likely to be determined by the context. Where agencies are deemed to have failed, such as in the US in not preventing the 9/11 attacks, there has been great concentration on the inability of the FBI and CIA to co-operate. Efforts are likely to concentrate on recruitment and training – more people with broader language skills and cultural understanding of 'the other' must be recruited – and seeking organizational and/or technical solutions to problems of information sharing. Within the broader context of 'democratizing' agencies in former authoritarian regimes, emphasis has been placed on increasing the professionalism of intelligence officials. This involves replacing loyalty to a party or ideology with that to a notion of national security and public safety that reflects a genuine assessment of a country's needs rather than merely the security in office of a specific faction. Though the existence or not of such professionalism is a factor that normally distinguishes between intelligence agencies in democratic and authoritarian regimes, agencies in some 'older' as well as 'newer' democracies have had to reassess the ethical component of professionalism in the wake of the extraordinary rendition scandal. A range of scholars, some ex-practitioners, have discussed these issues,[26] and the issue is considered throughout this book.

Given the fact that, compared with the rest of state bureaucracies, intelligence agencies have segregated themselves behind walls of secrecy, if their own methods of working were to change it would need to be because of their own internal dynamics. However, few organizations change themselves easily and, if reform or regression takes place, it is very likely to be the result of external pressure from other, government or civil society, actors. This relationship is the subject of the fourth project: *governance/policy*. This might be summarized in the questions: 'What impact does intelligence have on government, and what impact does government have on intelligence?' The first of these is part of the intelligence process referred to above. While much intelligence that is developed within agencies may go no further, the reason that states fund intelligence at all is so that they are better informed. Therefore, one central aspect of the literature, especially in the US, is the extent to which intelligence does or does not actually affect government policy. In the wake of the Iraq weapons of mass destruction (WMD) controversy, of course, there has been much study of the reverse: when policy determines what is defined as 'intelligence'. We discuss this in chapter 7. Not surprisingly, more of the work on this project has been conducted by IR and legal scholars. For most of the twentieth century the answer to the question of how much control and oversight of intelligence agencies was exercised by elected governments was: 'Not a lot.' But since the mid-1980s, a great deal more attention has been given to these questions, both in the older democracies where scandals about the abuse of intelligence have led to reforms, and in post-authoritarian states where more democratic intelligence architectures have been constructed.[27]

Most of this governance literature to date, following on the historical research into single countries and single agencies, is concerned with issues of control and oversight of *state* intelligence. Current developments throw up new challenges for future research, however. First is the rapid growth of corporate intelligence represented mainly by the increased role of private security and military companies working on contract for governments or companies. While much of this work is clearly related to security as conventionally defined, much of it will also be in the area of 'economic intelligence', which has received less attention in the Anglo-American literature than in the more recent European literature, as we saw above in the cases of France and Spain. A second key area is international intelligence collaboration. The earliest work here discussed the post-war UKUSA Signals Intelligence Agreement between the US, UK, Australia, Canada and New Zealand,[28] but there is little literature on this question, mainly because it is one that all countries and agencies keep very secret. New urgency has been injected into the subject by the post-9/11 surge in collaboration, mainly at the behest of the US, vis-à-vis the perceived global threat of terrorism and the subsequent controversies around rendition and torture. Current arrangements for the control and oversight of international intelligence co-operation are, to put it mildly, underdeveloped.[29]

Finally, we come to the question: at whom is IS aimed? Within UK universities there are some courses in intelligence for undergraduates that usually reflect the interests of a specific member of staff and sit within broader courses on IR and politics. The main increase in security-related courses since 9/11 has been in 'terrorism' – for example, within law, criminology and IR – some of which may well include aspects of intelligence. Paul Maddrell's 2003 survey of IS at UK universities identified twelve universities with an undergraduate module in some aspect of intelligence, studied by *c.*1,000 students.[30] We should note that different academic courses have different emphases: on the one hand, there are those seeking to advance the social science analysis of security intelligence as a social and political phenomenon – which is what we set out to do in this book; on the other hand, there are courses with a higher training component aimed at those already working in intelligence or hoping for such a career.

The oldest example of the latter, and the most extensive programme for undergraduates, is found in the US at the private university at Mercyhurst, where courses were developed specifically for those looking for a career in intelligence. In 1995 a non-profit Centre for Intelligence Research and Training was created to go after contracts, collaboration and grants, in part to give students experience of working with open sources through internships with companies such as Kroll. After 9/11 both the availability of jobs in the public and private sector and those willing to take them increased dramatically: the US intelligence community initiated a 'Center of Academic Excellence' programme in 2005 that involves ten US universities.[31] These are also mainly private – there is more resistance on the campuses of public universities to teaching intelligence.

Outside of the US, most courses are at postgraduate level. As part of the Spanish 'intelligence culture' project, Rey Juan Carlos III University in Madrid established a National Intelligence Centre and in 2005 established a Chair of Intelligence Services and Democratic Systems. In 2006 an Institute of Intelligence for Security and Defence was set up at Carlos III University in Madrid. These initiatives are sponsored as part of a broader 'intelligence culture' project by the Spanish intelligence service, the Centro Nacional de Inteligencia (CNI). The first cohort of thirty graduates on the MA in intelligence analysis was taught by the two universities in 2009–10. There are still only six UK universities with specific postgraduate courses in intelligence – Aberystwyth, Birmingham, Brunel, Buckingham, King's College London and Salford – and something like 120–50 students. The most recent additions to this list – Brunel and Buckingham – market themselves more explicitly towards existing practitioners or those who are aiming for a career in intelligence, while Salford deploys distance learning for part-time students already employed in military intelligence. Part of the programme at King's has been developed in response to the Butler Report's recommendations for reform of analyst training.[32]

This brief survey indicates that IS represents a healthy and growing activity of great relevance to contemporary security governance. At the same time IS faces continuing challenges. First, Anglo-American authors and subject matter continue to dominate the Anglophone literature. Take, for example, the eight volumes published by Praeger (*Strategic Intelligence*, 5 volumes, 2007), Routledge (*Handbook of Intelligence Studies*, 2007, and *Intelligence (Critical Concepts in Military, Strategic and Security Studies)*, 2010) and Oxford University Press (*The Oxford Handbook of National Security Intelligence*, 2010), all edited by Loch Johnson, which collectively can be regarded as the best guide to the state of the art. Some authors appear in more than one of these, but there are over 219 authors of the 205 articles; 75 per cent of the authors are US-based (94 per cent of the authors are US, UK or Canadian) and roughly 68 per cent of the articles concern US intelligence alone. Even allowing for recent history and the size of their respective intelligence and university sectors, we suggest this shows we are only slowly moving away from the Anglo-American-centrism that characterized the early development of IS. As we have seen in this Introduction, there are increasing communities of scholars elsewhere and it is important that their work be recognized within the IS mainstream. Single-country studies still constitute the bulk of historical and current work; they provide the bedrock for IS, but we suggest a globalized world and increased intelligence co-operation cry out for more comparative work so that we can avoid simplistic assumptions about the relevance of the US or UK experience to countries with very different economic, political and social conditions.[33] In writing this revised edition we would have liked to draw more on literature other than the US and UK, but the significance of intelligence developments, especially regarding counterterrorism, has militated against that.

In several European countries there is an explicit attempt to construct an 'intelligence culture' which reflects post-reform openness and seeks to develop not just increased awareness of the importance of a 'democratic intelligence' but also greater readiness by academics and other professionals to lend their expertise to the intelligence community.[34] In two countries, Romania and Spain, reformed agencies themselves sponsor these efforts through journals, conferences and academic courses; for example, *Inteligencia y seguridad: Revista de análisis y prospectiva* first appeared in 2006. Relations between intelligence agencies and academic institutions have not always been easy; indeed, relations between operations people and analysts *within* agencies have often been fraught. Discussing the CIA in its earliest days, Roger Hilsman noted: 'And they [practitioners] distrust the research man – they see the researcher as a long-haired academic, poring over musty books in dusty libraries far from the realities of practical life.'[35] And it does not seem that much changed in the following half century: in her analysis of the CIA's contribution to the 9/11 failure, Amy Zegart found that Directorate of Operations (DO) officers still viewed analysts with disdain:

> So deep was the divide between DO officers and analysts that when the Counterterrorist Center was first created (in 1996), DO personnel assigned there requested additional safes and procedures to keep their information out of the hands of the analysts working alongside them, despite the fact that the Center was designed to foster precisely this kind of collaboration between analysts and collectors and everyone held the same level of security clearance.[36]

So it is hardly surprising that there is even greater mistrust from the practitioner community towards (even short-haired) academics and, as Scott notes, in many countries there is minimal contact and what does occur is fraught with suspicion.[37] This has a clear impact on the numbers of academics prepared to contemplate research into intelligence:[38] there is now much archival material for historians to examine but accessing more current material is still impossible (unless revealed by an agency's own website, inquiry or whistle-blowers). Many officials will not want to be interviewed and obtaining large research grants is much harder than in more conventional areas of 'political science'. However, the study of intelligence remains a fascinating intellectual experience with very important potential for the quality of security governance, and the new, though still partial, openness provides many research opportunities.

In addition to research, there is also clearly a place for academics to use their expertise to advise agencies, but this poses a dilemma for scholars that is analogous to that of the correct distance between intelligence professionals and policymakers: if it is too distant then the former have little or no influence; if it is too close then their independence may be compromised. Scholars must consider the implications of their work: in some circumstances it may not be appropriate – for example, the American Anthropological Association examined concerns over the involvement of anthropologists in the US Army's Human Terrain Teams in Afghanistan and Iraq. The Association concluded that the programme's goals – research, data collection, sources of intelligence and a counterinsurgency tactic – were potentially irreconcilable and incompatible with disciplinary ethics and practice.[39] Practitioners turned academics are in a unique position to develop interesting and relevant courses, but academic rigour must not be sacrificed to the desire to attract paying students. IS will lose legitimacy if it is seen merely as a vehicle for agencies to recreate themselves, or for former practitioners to recount 'war stories'. Thus academics should never see themselves as any more than 'critical friends' of the agencies.

Given how we see the state of IS we seek to propose in this book a framework for an inter-disciplinary subject that has hitherto been ill-defined. Discussing the significance of John le Carré's 1974 novel, *Tinker Tailor Soldier Spy*, the novelist William Boyd commented: 'Non-fiction accounts of the secret service are highly interesting but only for obsessives or former operatives, I would suggest, in the way that books about steam engines are fascinating only to train-spotters.'[40] By applying the tools of social science to the study of intelligence, we realize we run the risk of providing evidence in support of Boyd's argument, but we hope that we shall not only make the subject interesting, but also show its relevance to security governance in general and encourage professionals to reflect on their policies and practices.

CHAPTER ONE

What Is Intelligence?

Introduction

This chapter poses a seemingly straightforward question: what is intelligence? However, once we attempt to define intelligence, it soon becomes apparent that, as a concept, it is as elusive as the daring fictional agents who have cemented it in the popular imagination – partly because any worthwhile definition needs to go beyond the idea that it is solely about 'stealing secrets'[1] to embrace the full range of activities in which intelligence agencies engage and the purposes underpinning these.

Our starting point should be to recognize that intelligence is a means to an end. This end is the security, including the prosperity, of the entity that provides for the collection and subsequent analysis of intelligence. In the contemporary international system, states are the principal customers of intelligence and the key organizers of collection and analysis agencies. However, a range of sub-state actors, political, commercial and criminal, also perceive a need to collect and analyse intelligence and guard against the theft of their own secrets. In the contemporary world, this need even extends to sports teams. For example, ahead of the November 2003 rugby union world cup final against hosts Australia, the England team swept their changing room and training base for electronic surveillance equipment, concerned that in 2001 espionage had allowed an Australian team to crack the codes employed by the British Lions, helping secure their dominance in line outs and go on to win the series.[2] Allegations of spying or espionage have also been a feature of Formula 1 motor racing and yacht racing via allegations of attempts to steal yacht designs.[3] In high-value team sports there is a clear incentive to uncover and understand the secrets that produce a competitive edge.

Indeed, once we define it in terms of security it becomes clear that intelligence is an inherently competitive pursuit. Security is relative, and therefore the purpose of intelligence is to bestow a relative security advantage. Moreover, as discussion of sports espionage suggests, security is a broad concept which goes beyond preventing military surprise or terrorist attack. In Britain, the *Statement of Purpose and Values* of the Security Service (MI5) talks of protecting 'national security and economic well-being'.[4] The Canadian Security Intelligence Service (CSIS) defines one of its priority areas as countering activities by foreign governments that 'may be detrimental to Canada's scientific and technological developments; that may harm our country's critical economic and information infrastructures or that may affect our military, commercial interests, and classified government information'.[5] In other words, a key dimension of security is preserving relative economic advantage and, from there, advancing it through the collection of financial and commercial intelligence on competitors – whether foreign states or sub-state actors such as competitor companies.

Ideally, intelligence will enhance security by bestowing on the wise collector, perceptive analyst and skilled customer a predictive power on which basis policy can be formulated. However, intelligence is often fragmentary. As a process it has been compared to the construction of a jigsaw puzzle. It begins with few pieces in place and although more may be collected over time, allowing for a progressively fuller picture to be constructed gradually, the analyst can never be sure whether all of the necessary pieces have been collected or some come from an entirely different puzzle. Unlike a conventional jigsaw, intelligence has no box to provide a picture of what the complete puzzle should look like. This is a matter for analysts' (and customers') judgement.[6] As a consequence, customers need to be aware of the limits of intelligence if it is to be most effective as a basis of policy. This was the clear message contained in gently admonitory passages in the UK Butler Report, which arose out of the apparent intelligence failure over the question of Iraq's WMD, discussed more fully in chapter 7. The Butler Report warned that:

> These limitations are best offset by ensuring that the ultimate users of intelligence, the decision-makers at all levels, properly understand its strengths and limitations and have the opportunity to acquire experience in handling it. It is not easy to do this while preserving the security of sensitive sources and methods. But unless intelligence is properly handled at this final stage, all preceding effort and expenditure is wasted.[7]

Similarly, the 2004 Flood Report into Australia's intelligence agencies warned that while its customers would like intelligence to possess the characteristics of a science, and despite the benefit of decades of technological innovation, it stubbornly remains more of an art:

> In so far as it seeks to forecast the future, assessment based on intelligence will seldom be precise or definitive. This is particularly so when it seeks to understand complex developments and trends in future years. Greater precision is sometimes possible in relation to intelligence's warning function – highlighting the possibility of a specific event in the near term future . . . But even in this field, precision will be hard to achieve. Intelligence will rarely provide comprehensive coverage of a topic. More often it is fragmentary and incomplete.[8]

The Concept of the Intelligence Cycle: Help or Hindrance?

In defining 'intelligence', we need to recognize that it is an umbrella term – a fact that renders precise definition problematic – covering a chain or cycle of linked activities from the targeting and collection of data (only half-jokingly defined by former US Senator Daniel Patrick Moynihan as 'the plural of anecdote'[9]), through analysis to dissemination and the actions, some covert, which can result.[10] The intelligence process has traditionally been explained by reference to the concept of the intelligence cycle, typically held to comprise five stages:

- planning and direction,
- collection,
- processing,
- all-source analysis and production, and
- dissemination.

For example, figure 1.1 shows how the CIA explains the intelligence process.

Intelligence collection – the subject of chapter 4 – involves accumulating the raw information that will be fed into the analytical process, either via open sources such as newspapers, books and official (government) publications or via secret human sources and whatever technical sources the intelligence agency has at its disposal. It is worth bearing in mind that these can vary widely from state to state and at sub-state levels. Not all intelligence agencies possess the technological capabilities or reach of western, Russian or Chinese state intelligence agencies. Processing can include technical issues such as transcribing and translating intercepted telephone conversations and verifying the reliability of information. Analysis is the process of determining what the information 'means'. This is the crucial stage in the production

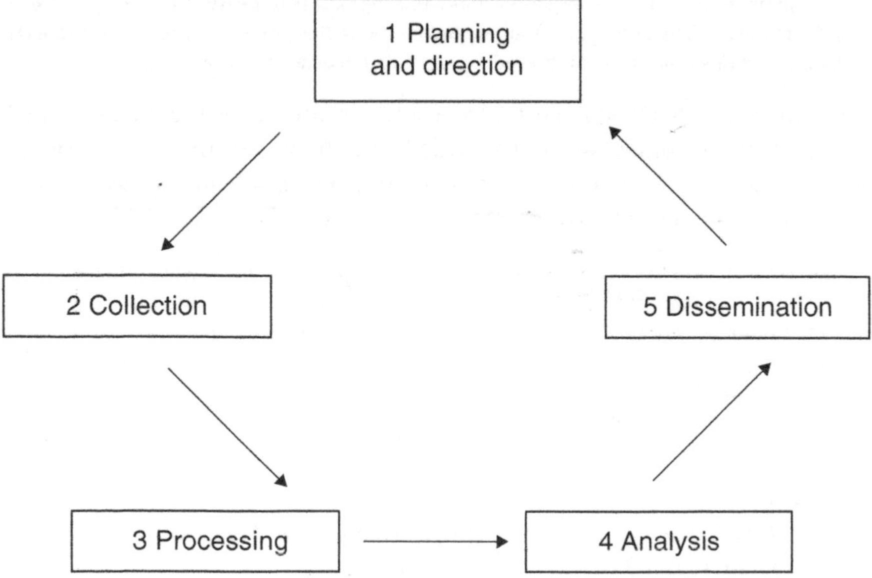

Source: http://www.odci.gov/cia/publications/facttell/intelligence_cycle.html

Figure 1.1 *The intelligence cycle*

of intelligence, for it is the analytical process (examined in more detail in chapter 5) that transforms the information, however acquired, into usable intelligence.

The CIA defines this stage of the intelligence process as involving:

> the conversion of basic information into finished intelligence. It includes integrating, evaluating, and analyzing all available data – which is often fragmented and even contradictory – and preparing intelligence products. Analysts, who are subject-matter specialists, consider the information's reliability, validity, and relevance. They integrate data into a coherent whole, put the evaluated information in context, and produce finished intelligence that includes assessments of events and judgments about the implications of the information.[11]

The language employed in the finished product is crucial. In a field which deals with estimates and probabilities, it is essential to convey accurately to the policymaker the degree of certainty underpinning judgements. It needs to be calibrated according to a commonly understood scale. Unfortunately, no such scale exists, a fact exposed by inquiries into intelligence on Iraq's WMD. As Sherman Kent wrote, the language used should 'set forth the community's findings in such a way as to make clear to the reader what is certain knowledge and what is reasoned judgment, and within this large realm of judgment what varying degrees of certitude lie behind each key statement'.[12]

In recent years the utility of the concept of the intelligence cycle has been called into question. Like all models, it is a simplification of a more complex reality. While useful as a means of introducing the different stages of the intelligence process, the notion of a *cycle* fails to capture fully the fact that the end product of intelligence is an assessment designed for the customer that the customer then uses in formulating policy or operations. It feeds into and has the capacity to alter the very environment in which information was collected and analysis undertaken. The concept of a cycle cannot, in other words, capture the dynamic nature of intelligence's impact on the external environment. An alternative way of viewing the intelligence process in order to capture this dynamic fully is to adopt the concept of a system that includes feedback, as in the 'funnel of causality' (figure 1.2).[13] Moreover, the funnel shape indicates the point that not all information is necessarily translated via analysis into policy; much is filtered out.

Another problem with the concept of the intelligence cycle is that it invariably begins with direction from policymakers. The largest collectors of intelligence permanently cast their nets wide, sweeping up all information within their reach. The breadth of this sweep has implications for what we understand 'targeting' to mean. Notwithstanding this, targeted collection responds to international developments, but this response – the determination of the information to be targeted – is usually the business of intelligence managers, because it is they who are aware of the gaps in existing knowledge. As Arthur Hulnick has argued: 'Filling the gaps is what drives the intelligence collection process, not guidance from policy makers.'[14] Understanding intelligence in

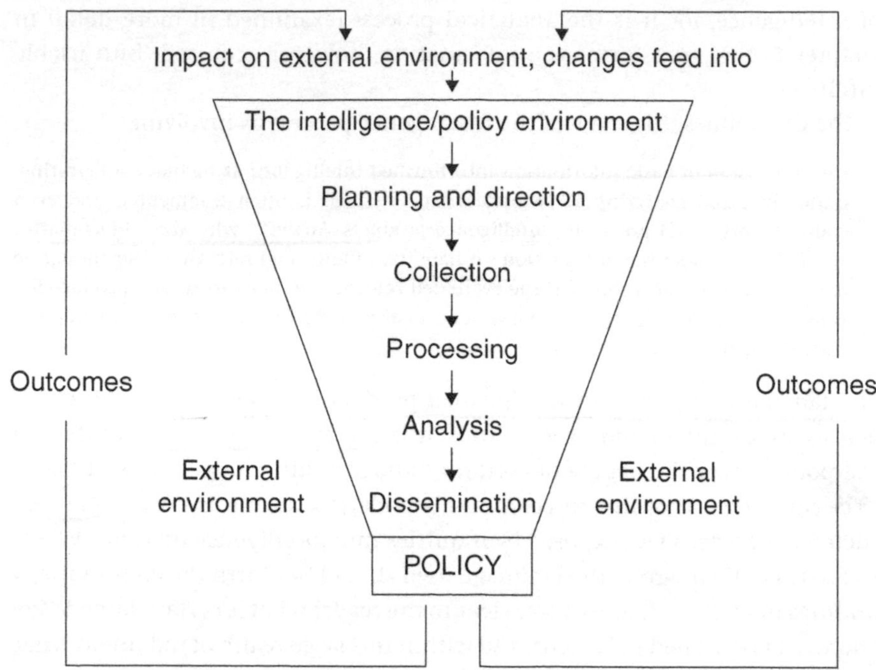

Figure 1.2 *The intelligence process*

terms of uncertainty and risk calls this aspect of the intelligence cycle into question for similar reasons.[15]

The precise arrangements by which priorities are established for agencies vary; for example, in the UK the Joint Intelligence Committee (JIC; see further in chapter 3) establishes the 'requirements' for MI6 and Government Communications Headquarters (GCHQ), but MI5 retains autonomy in determining its own priorities. After 9/11 it formally allocated some institutional resources to looking ahead for 'emerging threats' (see table 3.1 below), but this does not seem to have survived renewed emphasis on counterterrorism after 7/7, and Eliza Manningham-Buller, Director-General from 2002 to 2007, later admitted that the Service had not been very successful in this task.[16]

The idea that intelligence agencies await and then respond to policymaker direction is one that is most relevant to liberal democratic contexts, and is an extension of the principles governing civil–military relations in established democracies. Outside of this context, intelligence agencies may enjoy greater degrees of autonomy in determining targets and direction. For example, in the former GDR, the Stasi clearly enjoyed a considerable degree of autonomy in determining targets, to the extent that it has been discussed in terms of representing a 'state within a state'.[17] In its early years a foreign intelligence agency – the KGB – played a key role in setting its agenda. Even in formal democracies, intelligence agencies can operate with a significant degree of autonomy – for example, Inter-Services Intelligence (ISI) in contemporary

Pakistan, and the Servicio de Inteligencia Nacional (SIN) in Peru under spy chief Vladimiro Montesinos.[18]

Beyond issues around targeting and collection, the concept of the intelligence cycle suggests that the collection and analytical functions are sequential, that the latter can only begin once the former is complete. This is not the case, and in practice collection and analysis occur broadly concurrently. The cycle concept also rests on the implicit assumption that policymakers await objective analysis before deciding on a course of action. This assumption has been criticized by several commentators in the wake of the Iraqi WMD case. For example, Stephen Marrin has argued for an alternative understanding of the relationship between intelligence analysis and decision-making where, 'rather than start with the intelligence analyst, it starts with the concepts and values being pursued by the decision-maker which determine the meaning and the relevance of the intelligence analysis that is provided to them'.[19]

Hence, it is wrong to think, as the intelligence cycle seems to imply, that policymakers wait for the analytical product before embarking on an action. They may well seek intelligence analysis that matches and supports an existing policy or policy preference. If they don't get it they may ask for further analysis – or even question analysts personally, as Vice President Dick Cheney did in relation to US intelligence on Iraqi WMD in the lead-up to the 2003 Iraq war. We will return to this issue when we discuss the concept of politicization in later chapters. For now, the key point is that the contemporary intelligence process might, in David Omand's words, be 'best thought of as an interactive network rather than a cycle'.[20]

The intelligence cycle concept also omits a core intelligence function: covert action. Intelligence is not simply passive. Some intelligence agencies, such as CSIS in Canada, are charged just with advising government, but many are called upon to implement the policy response arising from their own collection and analysis. There is, though, a debate as to whether covert actions are a part of the intelligence process or actually represent a separate realm of activity.[21]

While some authors see covert action as intrinsic to intelligence, others characterize it as an 'allied activity', somewhat separate from the core business of intelligence.[22] Hence, for Michael Herman: 'Intelligence is information and information gathering, not *doing* things to people; no-one gets hurt by it, at least not directly. Some agencies do indeed carry out covert action, which confuses the ethical issues, but this is a separable and subsidiary function.'[23] However, the extent and regularity of recourse to covert actions, and the nature of these, help to define the wider security and intelligence culture and, to an extent, reflect the form of government intelligence agencies serve.[24] In this respect, separation of covert action from intelligence is artificial. Indeed, as we shall see in chapter 4, gathering information of itself may have an impact on the target. More broadly, if police or security agencies do not act in some way on the basis of intelligence, or at least consider its implications for their policies and practices, then one might ask, what is the point of intelligence?

Covert action also raises the question of the relationship between ethics and intelligence. The question of ethics does not relate solely to covert responses based on intelligence, but also to covert methods of collection where these involve, for example, communications interception, deception, blackmail, the use of 'honeytraps' and threats, kidnapping and/or torture. The question of 'spying on friends' raises its own ethical issues. Nevertheless, it is with regard to covert operations that ethical issues are most acute, and the higher covert responses ascend up what has been termed the 'ladder of escalation', the more acute they become.[25]

While, in contrast to the CIA, MI5's mission is centred on domestic security, its role, as presented on its website, clearly does embrace covert actions to frustrate entities considered hostile and/or threatening. The role of MI5, it tells us, is:

- *Investigating* suspect individuals and organisations to obtain, collate, analyse and assess secret intelligence relating to the threats. This requires us to gather intelligence and manage information effectively.
- *Acting* to counter the sources of threats, compiling evidence that enables us to bring suspects to justice.
- *Advising* the Government and others to keep them informed of the threats and advises on the appropriate response, including protective security measures; and
- *Assisting* other agencies, organisations and Government departments in combating threats. We contribute to the collective work of the UK's National Intelligence Machinery and form partnerships with other organisations in the UK and abroad.[26]

Covert actions, then, are fundamental to intelligence collection and counter-intelligence (discussed below). It seems artificial to exclude the possibility of covert actions as a policy response from models of intelligence activity when these are carried out or funded by intelligence organizations and use secret intelligence methods in pursuit of policy objectives.

This is, however, an evolving area. Whilst during the Cold War such actions were covert so as to provide deniability and avoid destabilizing the prevailing 'balance of terror',[27] the situation is somewhat different in the post-Cold War, post-9/11 world. Here, intelligence 'actions' can be overt as well as covert, or can even fall somewhere in between. Armed US Predator drone strikes on al-Qaeda suspects inside Pakistan, Yemen and Somalia provide a good example. These are not avowed by the CIA, which carries them out. But neither can their occurrence be denied. Hence, in the contemporary international environment it is perhaps more accurate to speak of 'actions' rather than simply 'covert actions'. These will be the subject of chapter 6.

One final thought on the idea of the intelligence cycle before we move towards a focus on how best to define 'intelligence': the intelligence cycle was designed to describe the intelligence production process. In a contemporary liberal democratic context, should oversight and accountability be factored into it? At the time the cycle concept was first used, oversight was conducted (to the extent that it was at all) by policymakers, who sat at the end point of the cycle. Today, however, few would accept a situation where oversight of intelligence in a liberal democratic context resided solely in the hands of the executive. Given this, and bearing in mind David Omand's suggestion that the intelligence process today might 'best be thought of as an interactive network rather than a cycle', should that interactive model not reflect (not to say, require) the input of and interaction with overseers? We shall return to the question of oversight and accountability in chapter 8.

A Definition of 'Intelligence'

As an area of academic inquiry, intelligence is still in its infancy. Existing definitions of intelligence can generate as many questions as answers. In the CIA's in-house intelligence journal, *Studies in Intelligence*, Michael Warner has pointed out that despite a long history, even in the early years of the twenty-first century 'we have no accepted definition of intelligence'. This has led to problems, because 'intelligence . . . is defined anew by each author who addresses it, and these definitions rarely refer to one another or build off what has been written before. Without a clear idea of what intelligence is, how can we develop a theory to explain how it works?'[28]

As Warner points out, there are many competing definitions of intelligence. In the 1947 US National Security Act, 'foreign intelligence . . . means information relating to the capabilities, intentions, or activities of foreign governments or elements thereof, foreign organizations, or foreign persons'.[29] The definition arrived at by the Brown–Aspin Commission in 1996 showed that governmental thinking about how intelligence can best be defined had not evolved much despite the passage of fifty years and vast increases in budgets: 'The Commission believes it preferable to define "intelligence" simply and broadly as information about "things foreign" – people, places, things, and events – needed by the Government for the conduct of its functions.'[30]

The definition offered by Loch Johnson, that intelligence is 'the knowledge – and, ideally, foreknowledge – sought by nations in response to external threats and to protect their vital interests, especially the well-being of their own people',[31] represents an advance. This definition brings the security purpose centre-stage, and also introduces the vital ingredient of *prior knowledge*. If intelligence is worth having it is because analysis will provide customers with prior warnings of potential developments (that is, potential surprises) affecting their security or relative advantage. However, this definition does not distinguish between the collection of targeted information and the subsequent analysis that frames it, thereby providing decision-makers with policy options.

At the end of his discussion of the definitional poverty surrounding intelligence, Michael Warner offered his own definition: 'Intelligence is secret, state activity to understand or influence foreign entities.'[32] But this is frustratingly incomplete. It risks elevating a feature of intelligence – secrecy – above its purpose. There is no explicit reference to the purpose of intelligence as lying in security, nor is there any reference to the essential element of providing foreknowledge. Moreover, it is a very *American* definition, in that its focus is on *foreign entities*, reflecting political debates at the time of the creation of the CIA and the basic American suspicion of secret police activity at home, thus ignoring a significant sphere of potential intelligence activity.

Is secrecy essential to a definition of intelligence? Warner goes so far as to suggest that, 'Without secrets it is not intelligence.' We also think that secrecy is important to intelligence. A lack of secrecy endangers the comparative advantage sought from the intelligence. If a target is aware that information is being collected on it, that knowledge could impact on the process by allowing the target to feed (dis)information into it, or adopt other countermeasures. Even knowledge of the range or balance of sources that inform assessments could allow a target to attempt an assessment of the state of this intelligence, and engage in counterintelligence activities aimed at affecting the conclusions drawn. Clearly, analysis must also be secret, however much the information that feeds into it is open source.[33] However, secrecy also raises key issues of legality, morality and accountability. It creates an unchallengeable political space for its customers, because they base their actions on supposedly superior analysis. Because this is secret it is denied to others and so cannot easily be challenged.[34]

Jennifer Sims has written of intelligence as 'the collection, analysis, and dissemination of information for decision makers engaged in a competitive enterprise'. This definition gives a prominence to the competitive dimension of intelligence with which we agree. For Sims intelligence 'is a process by which competitors improve their decision making relative to their opponents. Whether in business, politics, or sports, the purpose of intelligence is the same: to obtain better information than opponents do about relevant plans, capabilities, rules, and terrain through directed and often secretive learning.'[35]

To summarize the discussion thus far, any definition of intelligence needs to make reference to the following factors:

- It is more than merely information collection.
- It covers a range of linked activities.
- It is security-based.
- It aims to provide advance warning.
- It is required because of a competitive environment, so the gains being sought are relative ones.
- It encompasses the potential for covert actions.
- Secrecy is essential to the comparative advantage being aimed for.

We can bring these factors together to form our own definition of intelligence:

> *Intelligence is the umbrella term referrin[illegible] – from planning and information collection to analysis and disseminatior[illegible]nd aimed at maintaining or enhancing relative security by providing forewarn[illegible]ential threats in a manner that allows for the timely implementation of a preventive policy or strategy, including, where deemed desirable, covert activities.*

The need for counterintelligence arises out of this logic. Because the intelligence requirement has its origins in the competitive nature of the international, commercial, sports etc. environments, all must guard against the attempted theft of their secrets (including knowledge of the means by which they are collected) by others, and must assume that all others will attempt to enhance their security by doing so. Actors do this via counterintelligence. This can be both defensive and offensive. The former is reactive and involves blocking attempts to steal secrets by vetting employees, securing communications and guarding identities. The latter is proactive and typically involves various degrees of deception, including strategic deception, as in the Second World War British deception operation Mincemeat[36] and Saddam Hussein's policy of leading his neighbours and potential adversaries to believe that he retained some non-conventional weapons capability after the 1991 Gulf War. It also includes running agents inside target organizations or states, from where they can misdirect or disrupt operations. Clearly, then, counterintelligence can involve covert action, strengthening arguments for considering this as a part of 'intelligence'. We will return to this theme in our discussion of secrecy and resistance in the next chapter.

Intelligence is a dynamic process. Hence, any definition should be adaptable and so capable of reflecting this dynamism and the ongoing debate about how intelligence should be understood. In this context, Michael Warner has argued that our definition above of intelligence 'cannot be regarded as dispositive, unfortunately, due to its focus on the defensive uses of intelligence (to wit, the emphasis on "security" can be seen to neglect the offensive or aggressive uses of intelligence to gain or expand power).'[37] This is a significant point, and to accommodate it we have adapted, and shortened, our original definition, whilst retaining the original's core premises. In this adaptation, we term intelligence:

> *the mainly secret activities – targeting, collection, analysis, dissemination and action – intended to enhance security and/or maintain power relative to competitors by forewarning of threats and opportunities.*[38]

There is a sense in which an emphasis on the intelligence function of states and the consequent intelligence competition between them can lead us to view international affairs through the state-centric and security-driven emphases of neo-realist analyses of IR. From this perspective, there is no real need for a separate body of definitional and particularly theoretical work on intelligence, because the operation of state intelligence agencies is no more than a logical expression of the broader neo-realist reality that states are the core actors in international politics, searching for security in an anarchical and inherently competitive environment.

There are likely to be limits to the extent to which neo-realism can form the basis of a theoretically informed understanding of intelligence.[39] As David Omand has pointed out in a UK context: 'Measured by the proportion of effort, British secret intelligence is now no longer principally concerned with the activities of potentially hostile nations, but much more concerned with the activities of non-state actors, especially terrorist groups.' This leads him to question whether we even require the concept of a (state) adversary in discussing intelligence.[40]

At the same time, however, it is worth noting that the 2010 UK National Security Strategy, while listing international terrorism at the top of its prioritization of risks and including major accidents or national hazards (such as a flu pandemic or flooding) in the same top tier, also included hostile attacks upon UK cyberspace by other states and large-scale cybercrime, as well as 'an international military crisis between states, drawing in the UK and its allies as well as other states and non-state actors'.[41] Clearly, then, intelligence operates in an environment characterized by a wide range of potential risks and considerable uncertainty. Perhaps, in this context, the most appropriate theoretical approach to intelligence is one that explains its relationship to concepts of risk and uncertainty? Suitably forewarned of the complexities that confront us in this area, we shall turn our attention to the theoretical landscape in chapter 2, and consider the intelligence process more conceptually within the broader context of social science. First, however, we sketch out the manner in which intelligence as we know it today has evolved.

Evolution

Today's global intelligence networks (as discussed in chapter 3) are a product of the Cold War era. However, just as students of terrorism can trace the antecedents of terrorism back to the activities of the Sicarii of Palestine (AD 66–73) and then the Assassins,[42] and students of warfare the early use of chemical weapons to the use of pitch and sulphur to create toxic fumes during the Peloponnesian War,[43] so too the rise of intelligence as a means of providing security can be traced back to antiquity and before.

Indeed, enterprising scholars have gone so far as to trace the practice of intelligence collection back to the Bible, beginning in the Old Testament when 'the Lord spake unto Moses' telling him to send spies into Canaan, raising the awkward theological question of why those blessed with omniscience require the espionage assistance of mere mortals. Spies and agents appear elsewhere, from Delilah to Judas. In the early fourth century BC, the Chinese general Sun-Tzu recognized that 'A hundred ounces of silver spent for information may save ten thousand spent on war', and wrote in *The Art of War* of the importance of advance intelligence. Intelligence also plays a role in Thucydides' account of the Peloponnesian War.[44]

Just as in Aristotle's model of political development, where constitutional change followed military innovation, so we would argue that developments in intelligence follow from the emergence of threat situations, either real or perceived. Historically, awareness of or a perception of vulnerability[45] – what might be termed the 'security deficit' – can be linked to developments in intelligence designed to improve preparedness to meet that threat. Because the bigger an actor is, the more it stands to lose, and the more it can invest in preventive intelligence to safeguard its relative advantage, the most advanced intelligence networks are found in the wealthiest players in any given state or corporate segment of concurrent global intelligence contests.[46]

With the rise of the modern state system, intelligence requirements became more permanent, collection and analysis began to assume a more professional character and the stakes became larger, focused on the protection of the state and the monarch at its head. In Britain, the development of systems of intelligence was rooted in the protection of the crown and the uncovering of plots against it. Following the excommunication of Queen Elizabeth I by Pope Pius V in 1570, the threat increased, and so an intelligence effort that up to that point had been configured to uncover domestic treason suddenly required a continental dimension. This was provided by Sir Francis Walsingham, the queen's Secretary of State from 1573. Walsingham's spies targeted Catholics to uncover potential threats to the Queen, and amongst his successes may be counted advance knowledge of Spanish plans to send an Armada against England.[47] With Walsingham's death and the passing of this threat, intelligence atrophied, but nonetheless later revived to deal with crises relating, for example, to Jacobite plots and instability in the American colonies.

Throughout the sixteenth century, French intelligence was developing in parallel – for example, with the establishment in 1590 of the Poste aux Lettres, employing resealing experts alongside early analysts to open, read and then reseal private letters. Similarly, as soon as postal services started in the UK, governments started to intercept mail, relying on the traditional royal prerogative power.[48] Given the threatening environment into which it emerged, it should come as little surprise that the newly independent United States soon saw the benefit of intelligence. In 1790 George Washington established a Contingency Fund of which Congress had only limited oversight.[49]

In the nineteenth century, industrialization, the creation of a large urban working class, large-scale immigration, and the dissemination of doctrines and ideas challenging the existing order increased the significance of intelligence on internal threats to order. In Britain, threats ranged from those posed by Fenians, leading to the creation of the Metropolitan Police Special Branch,[50] to those of anarchists. In the US, an anarchist, Leon Czolgosz, shot dead President McKinley. In Russia, revolutionary activity would culminate in the overthrow of the state.[51]

It was the spectre of war in Europe at the beginning of the twentieth century that provided the incentive for the further development of modern state intelligence agencies. In Britain, this was a need highlighted by the Boer War, and finally given form by the establishment of a Secret Service Bureau in 1909, in the midst of German spy fever.[52] No sooner was the First World War over than a new threat – Bolshevism – was identified to justify the continuation of institutionalized intelligence, to be formally divided into MI5 and MI6, whose most famous agent of the period, Sidney Reilly, cemented his reputation for derring-do against the Soviet Union.[53] There certainly was a concerted post-war Soviet effort to gain intelligence on the intentions of those powers such as Britain that had displayed so much hostility to the newly formed Soviet state.[54] Counterintelligence aimed at this effort, subsequently joined by the lesser imperative of needing to keep the indigenous fascist right under surveillance, constituted MI5's main workload during the twenty years' crisis of the inter-war period. The exposure of the Arcos affair in 1927, and the defection and debriefing of Soviet intelligence officer Walter G. Krivitsky, gave MI5 a good idea of the scale of the Soviet operation.[55]

In Russia, foreign intelligence collection under the Czars had been rudimentary, and may be said to have contributed to the debacle of the Russo-Japanese War. Lenin's creation of the Cheka was meant to go some way towards rectifying this, and secure the Soviet state and its leaders by gaining intelligence on internal and external threats to the state. Doing so involved the Cheka in eliminating many (one estimate puts the figure killed as a result of Cheka counterintelligence at 250,000 by 1925) and imprisoning many more in camps in Siberia and similarly remote outposts of the Soviet land mass. While some historians have seen the Cheka as an outgrowth of Leninist ideology,[56] the Soviet Union, as revolutionary regimes invariably are, was born into a world containing powers hostile to it. The creation of the Cheka was a reflection of the perceived vulnerability of the new state in the international system rather than any specific branch of Leninist ideology. This is true to a greater or lesser extent of all states created as a consequence of revolution or war, whether Cuba after 1959, Vietnam after reunification in 1975 or Iran after 1979.[57]

Since the 1920s, intelligence agencies had been intercepting the communications and breaking the codes even of allies. Yet liberal sensitivities were still in evidence: the US Secretary of State Henry Stimson tried to halt US interceptions by closing its Black Chamber with the immortal words, 'Gentlemen do not read each other's mail.'[58] In a similar vein, consider former Director General of MI5 Sir Percy Sillitoe's account of the Klaus Fuchs case:

> I would like to point out that MI5 is not a supernatural organization. I have sometimes felt that many people, not knowing accurately what its methods are, have come to expect that its representatives must all be endowed with a sixth sense. The fact is that there was absolutely no valid reason why anyone's suspicions should reasonably have been aroused about Fuchs . . .
>
> Given then, that we had never had any grounds for suspecting Fuchs, what should we

> have done? Should we have, all the same, arranged for him to be shadowed night and day? In that case we should have had logically to follow the same procedure in the case of all the other apparently quite innocent men who were engaged on secret work – and their number was fairly large . . .
>
> Apart from the obvious practical impossibility of employing such tactics, inevitably some of the scientists would come to sense or somehow suspect that they were being watched. And then you would have a violent outcry, for these men, ninety-nine percent of whom would be entirely blameless, would, very reasonably, protest most strongly. Their lives would have become a nightmare once they realized that their every action was being spied upon.[59]

However, the Fuchs case, the whole question of atomic espionage, and the successful Soviet testing of an atomic bomb well in advance of the US's most pessimistic estimates all served to make the sense of threat both greater and more immediate than ever before. Sillitoe's strictly constitutionalist approach would soon be unrecognizable as the intelligence world became the arena where the Cold War was at its most intense, and the sense of threat was held to justify stretching the bounds of the ethically acceptable.

It was against this background that, in the UK, cinema appeared to bring the world of intelligence into the open. In the wake of the Fuchs, Burgess and Maclean scandals, the construction of the Berlin Wall and the Cuban Missile crisis, the emergence of James Bond – armed and gadget-laden successor to Sherlock Holmes, Richard Hannay and Bulldog Drummond – came to represent all that the British public wanted to know, and because of the operation of the D-Notice system, all they were likely to discover, about intelligence.[60] The filmic version of James Bond gave the impression of being rooted in reality by virtue of loosely mirroring Cold War antagonisms. It also left audiences predisposed to believe in individual villains with a global reach. In this respect, Osama bin Laden was preceded by a cast that included Dr No, Blofeld, Zorin, Stromberg, Drax et al.

The Bond films eschewed a focus on the mundane world of signals intelligence (SIGINT) and analysis for the high-octane world of covert operations. In the Cold War-era films in the series there is no sense of ambivalence or doubt – Bond would not have made sense or worked at the box office in the desired way if he had been anything less than an inveterate cold warrior, confirming for the watching public the necessity of Cold War struggle, the evil ingenuity of the enemy, and the global role that Britain's intelligence services afforded it.[61] In short, through Bond, intelligence was feel-good, reassuring and, of course, invariably successful. To demonstrate that this fiction could be mistaken for reality, we need look no further than KGB defector Oleg Gordievsky, who has claimed that the Central Committee of the Soviet Communist Party watched Bond films, that the KGB requested that he try to obtain the devices used by Bond in the films, and that Bond helped shape the Soviet leadership's perception of British intelligence.[62]

While the British public has remained intrigued by the secret world of intelligence ever since, this fascination has been qualified and shaped by a continual stream of allegations concerning the behaviour and penetration of the intelligence services. The Burgess and Maclean defections, the Profumo affair and the defection of Kim Philby (which occurred concurrently) all produced bestsellers, testimony to the British public's appetite for spy stories. But they were just the beginning. Writers like Chapman Pincher, described by historian E. P. Thompson as 'a kind of official urinal in which, side by side, high officials of MI5 and MI6, Sea Lords, Permanent Under-Secretaries . . . and others, stand patiently leaking in the public interest',[63] popularized the intelligence exposé, the best known being his Peter Wright-informed account of the case against former MI5 Director General Sir Roger Hollis, *Their Trade is Treachery*. This was followed up with further bestsellers offering slight variations on the theme.[64] More significantly, by the 1970s MI5's focus on the 'enemy within' led to allegations concerning a wide range of dubious domestic activities, ranging from the targeting of the leadership of the Campaign for Nuclear Disarmament and National Council for Civil Liberties (NCCL)[65] to a range of questionable activities in Northern Ireland,[66] its alleged role in the 1984–5 miners' strike,[67] and the involvement of MI5 officers in a plot to undermine Labour Prime Minister Harold Wilson, as recounted by Peter Wright in *Spycatcher*.[68] Neither did the revelations end with the Cold War. During the late 1990s, two disaffected young officers in MI5 and MI6, David Shayler and Richard Tomlinson, spoke out about dubious practices including domestic political surveillance and an alleged MI6 plot to assassinate the then Libyan leader, Colonel Gaddafi.[69]

This stream of revelations has resulted in a pronounced ambivalence in attitudes towards the intelligence services – attraction to the James Bond myth co-existing alongside a degree of scepticism and mistrust. Reflecting this, the distinguished historian Bernard Porter opened his 1989 history of political espionage in Britain with the observation that:

> All evidence in this area is undependable. That means that even if we were able to see the official record, it might not help. It also means that we cannot rely on the evidence we are able to see. The reason for this is that all spies and secret agents are liars, trained in techniques of deception and dissimulation, who are just as likely to fake the historical record as anything else. This is why the first rule for the reader of any book about secret services, including this one, is *not to trust a word of it*. It could all be lies and disinformation; not on the part of the writer necessarily, but on the part of the sources he is gullible enough to believe.[70]

Since Porter wrote this, of course, official intelligence archives have become available at an increasing rate in Britain and scholars have made much use of them. Nevertheless, it is important for researchers in the archives to remember that they 'have no external guarantee that what is preserved there is necessarily an analogue of reality'.[71]

Meanwhile, the emergence of highly differentiated strategic environments in different regions of the world encouraged the development of intelligence structures on markedly different lines. The national security state that arose from the early-to-mid-1960s in Latin America saw, with US encouragement, the principal threat to the nation as deriving from an enemy within funded and inspired by Moscow.[72] Accordingly, intelligence in these states was oriented primarily towards internal security. South Africa's international isolation during the apartheid era, combined with its perception of encirclement by pro-Moscow southern African states, contributed to the almost unique characteristics of its security services.[73] While John Dziak developed the term 'counterintelligence state' to describe how Lenin and his successors in the USSR devoted maximum effort to the destruction of domestic and foreign opponents,[74] we can see how the term might also be applied to other states.

In a different context, Israel's perception of an acute threat to its very existence is essential to any understanding of the centrality of intelligence to the Israeli state, which ended the twentieth century spending more per head on intelligence than any other country. Indeed, some of Israel's success in the 1948 War of Independence was attributable to the role of intelligence, in part relying on structures which pre-dated the establishment of the state and were intended to facilitate the immigration of Jews in the face of restrictions applied by the British. In 1951 Mossad was added to the existing intelligence structure, modelled on the recently created CIA and designed as an arm of the executive branch that answered directly to the office of the Prime Minister. While the intelligence community played a role in providing intelligence that led to the pre-emptive launch of the Six Day War of 1967, it failed in 1973 to provide clear warning of the Egyptian and Syrian surprise attack. Clear evidence of war preparations existed (a movement of Egyptian troops towards the Suez Canal, Egyptian appeals for blood donors, etc.) but the intelligence community's analysis of the raw intelligence led them to conclude that this was Arab disinformation.[75] In more recent years, intelligence has focused on careful monitoring of the intentions of Arab states, particularly Iraq and Syria, towards Israel; monitoring the Iranian nuclear programme and intervening on occasion (to which we return later); and dealing with the more immediate internal security problems associated with the Intifada, including the rise of an indigenous extreme religious right critical of any accommodation over the Occupied Territories, and one of whose number, Yigal Amir, assassinated Prime Minister Yitzhak Rabin in 1995. A key concern has been to counter the flow of suicide bombers from the Occupied Territories. Countermeasures have included targeting Hamas, Hizbullah, the Popular Front for the Liberation of Palestine (PFLP) and Islamic Jihad leaders for assassination.

Israeli intelligence has been distinctive in the degree of its proactive approach to dealing with threats once identified and dealing in retribution (from the capture of Adolf Eichmann in 1960, through the tracking down of the Black September terrorists, the assassination of Arab scientists in Europe in the 1980s, the kidnapping of Mordechai Vanunu, etc.), which does not require sensationalizing in any way. Unfortunately, serious study of the Israeli intelligence community has been hampered by accounts that mix reality with less reliable but more marketable accounts of derring-do, and which also suffer from failure to treat sufficiently the context in which that community operates.

Following the collapse of the Soviet Union, the erstwhile enemy against which the CIA was to protect the US, a debate emerged as to whether there was further need for the agency, led inside the US by national politicians such as Daniel Patrick Moynihan and public intellectuals like Theodore Draper.[76] In essence this was a combination of a coda to the Church and Pike investigations of the mid-1970s,[77] prompted by new revelations concerning Cold War-era covert operations in the Third World, and a liberal reaction rooted in the traditional American opposition to unnecessary secrecy. Defenders of the need for a national foreign intelligence agency took refuge in metaphor, conceding that the Cold War dragon might have been slain but that, as Director of Central Intelligence (DCI) James Woolsey characterized it at his 1993 confirmation hearings, the US was now confronted by a jungle containing 'a bewildering variety of poisonous snakes'.[78] One path that post-Cold War intelligence would take soon emerged in the form of a heightened focus on economic espionage, with tales of CIA agents attempting to bribe French officials to learn about the French position at the World Trade Organization, electronic surveillance of Japanese officials during a car import dispute and so on. At the time, US commentators were at pains to stress that this was not a one-way street, warning that: 'France possesses a well-developed intelligence service, one of the most aggressive collectors of economic intelligence in the world. Using techniques often reminiscent of the KGB or spy novels, the French in recent years have planted moles in US companies such as IBM, Texas Instruments, and Corning.'[79] Indeed, US companies have been a primary target of state-directed industrial espionage, one 1996 survey ranking China, Canada, France, India, Japan, Germany, South Korea, Russia, Taiwan, the UK, Israel and Mexico as the lead perpetrators.[80] Prior to the events of 9/11, some analysts saw a more globalized world as dictating that market intelligence would become a lead intelligence requirement. For example, Gregory F. Treverton applied the idea of the 'market state' as successor to the 'territorial state', confidently arguing that: 'The era of the "territorial state" is passing away, and probably has been for a century. The change was obscured, though, by this century's preoccupation with particular, and particularly aggressive, territorial states.' In this brave new world the business of intelligence, as it were, concerned the questions: 'which government's reserves are lower than it has admitted? Which respected finance minister is about to resign? Which government doesn't have the stomach for raising interest rates to defend its currency? Secrets are relevant to answering these questions, many of them puzzles. They are good targets for intelligence.'[81]

Post 9/11 analyses, however, would suggest that the authors of these accounts drank too freely at the well of globalization (Treverton even went so far as to suggest that John Mearsheimer's fairly uncontroversial thesis that the nation-state and national interests were 'alive and well' was 'a provocative argument'[82]), and that while economic espionage will continue to have an important role to play, so too will more fundamental and enduring intelligence questions of state security, war and peace. Hence, while US SIGINT may well still target Japanese industrial concerns, it was also involved in the high politics of spying on the UN Security Council delegates from Angola, Cameroon, Chile, Bulgaria, Guinea and Pakistan during the period leading to the 2003 war in Iraq[83] and, as the WikiLeaks revelations showed, on the office of the UN Secretary General, Ban Ki-moon.[84]

Does Intelligence Matter?

To what extent have state expenditures on, and obsession with, intelligence actually made a difference? As Richard Aldrich has noted,[85] it remains the case that most diplomatic histories eschew detailed consideration of the role of intelligence. Key histories of the early Cold War and national security state in the US, such as those by the eminent historians Michael Hogan and Melvyn Leffler, devote little space to the intelligence dimension of their subjects, all suggesting that the relative significance of intelligence is more limited than the agencies themselves profess to believe.[86] Military historian John Keegan has suggested that the importance of intelligence in warfare has been overestimated.[87] Indeed, a number of commentators – such as Phillip Knightley and Stephen Dorril – have argued that the achievements of intelligence are exaggerated or illusory, while another, Rhodri Jeffreys-Jones, has gone so far as to offer an interpretation of the operation and maintenance of the US intelligence services as amounting to little more than a highly successful confidence trick.[88] In this vein, Knightley recalled a 1994 conference in Germany, 'attended by a panel of spymasters from east and west. I challenged them to name a single important historical event in peacetime in which intelligence had played a decisive role. No one could do so.'[89] It is also worth noting in this respect that while the Soviet Union and eastern bloc countries invested heavily in intelligence and counterintelligence, the official Marxist line was that intelligence could not determine the course of history.[90] Neither did their heavy investment in intelligence enable them to maintain influence abroad or prevent the collapse of their parent states.[91]

How important, then, was intelligence to the course of Cold War history? As Michael Herman has noted, it was certainly extensive, constituting, 'a central element of the Cold War, on both sides; never before was intelligence so extensive, institutionalized and prized in peacetime'. But extent is not the same thing as influence. As Herman recognizes, it will be for subsequent generations of historians to provide answers to the more specific kinds of question he has himself posed: 'whether intelligence made a difference [?] Did it produce better knowledge and understanding, and a safer world? Or was it playing out and intensifying the Cold War as a self-serving game between opposing intelligence agencies? Did it contribute to its own *déformation professionelle*, demonizing the enemy and exaggerating threats in a destabilizing way?'[92] Alternatively, might it not be argued that the mutual interpenetration of hostile powers actually enhanced security by reducing the possibility that one could surprise the other? These questions essentially build on the question set by intelligence historian Robin Winks. 'Academics generally work in an environment that respects knowledge for its own sake,' Winks argued, 'and merely knowing, rather than acting upon what one knows, is sufficient reward for many academics.' What is necessary is also to ask the 'effectiveness' question: 'So what?'[93] In turn, John Lewis Gaddis used this as a point of departure in his essay on the study of intelligence, warning of the need to go beyond the 'fascination of dealing with what was once surreptitious, sneaky, and sly'.[94] Even now, are we able to provide any firm answers to Winks' question?

One person who has offered an answer to these questions is the former head of the CIA's Soviet Counter Intelligence Division, the prize Soviet spy Aldrich Ames, himself the son of a career CIA officer. Ames has argued that:

> The espionage business, as carried out by the CIA and a few other American agencies, was and is a self-serving sham, carried out by careerist bureaucrats who have managed to deceive several generations of American policymakers and the public about both the necessity and the value of their work. There is and has been no rational need for thousands of agents working around the world, primarily in and against friendly countries. The information our vast espionage network acquires is generally insignificant or irrelevant to our policymakers' needs . . . Frankly, these spy wars are a sideshow which have had no real impact on our significant security interests over the years.[95]

There is, of course, a significant degree of special pleading involved here, and there is far too much that remains unknown for such sweeping assertions to be accepted. Where the role of intelligence has been factored in to key events of the last century, it can be seen to have affected the nature of events if not necessarily their outcomes.[96] In particular, historians await access to SIGINT decrypts, which will add substantially, and maybe alter, our understanding of key historical events.[97] There is also the difficulty of how to measure success or influence in the intelligence field. How, for example, is the 'security blanket' aspect of intelligence to be measured? How is the deterrent effect to be assessed? It could be argued that in a Cold War context, intelligence success or failure can be measured best by reference to the confidence intelligence brought, and to the things that did not happen as a consequence of intelligence actions, or even its mere existence.

Moreover, there is the problem identified by Richard Betts, wherein 'particular failures are accorded disproportionate significance if they are considered in isolation rather than in terms of the general ratio of failures to successes; the record of success is less striking because observers tend not to notice disasters that do not happen'.[98] This picture is complicated a little more by Avi Shlaim's observation that if an act, for example a terrorist act, cannot be carried out because intelligence agencies have uncovered it in time to allow effective countermeasures to be put in place, then there is the possibility that the 'success of the intelligence services would have been expressed in the falsification of its predictions', raising questions about the accuracy of the initial analysis.[99] It is complicated further still by the fact that in an operational environment characterized by recent significant failure, intelligence agencies are likely to act more cautiously both in their drafting of analyses and in their subsequent presentation to the customer, more readily advocating countermeasures through identification of a threat which, for reasons of self-preservation, they dare not fail to flag up. Moreover, as we noted above, intelligence agencies are bureaucratic entities and as such have a vested interest in continuation of threat – their budgets are umbilically linked to levels of threat – and so, while at times willing to trumpet successes in ongoing campaigns, they have been more reluctant to acknowledge the successful end of campaigns. For example, in October 2002 DCI George Tenet sought to explain partially the CIA's apparent failure to anticipate the events of 9/11 by reminding a congressional committee that in the previous decade Congress had cut the CIA's budget by 18 per cent in real terms, leading to a 16 per cent reduction in employees across the board.[100] In this wilderness of mirrors, it is tempting therefore to conclude that it is virtually impossible to measure success or failure.[101]

With the post-Cold War, post-9/11 shift away from an overwhelming focus on state-based threats to one that attaches a higher priority to the transnational terrorist threat, however, it is possible to measure some kinds of success. Unlike in the covert world of Cold War espionage, where successes remained secret while failures could become all too public, successful intelligence-led operations can today lead to arrest, the laying of criminal charges, trial and conviction. Hence, for example, in the UK the successful prosecution that resulted from Operation Crevice – the operation to prevent the realization of the plot to explode bombs in multiple targets, including the Bluewater shopping centre in Kent and the Ministry of Sound nightclub in London – led to life sentences for five defendants. Operation Overt, which targeted the post-7/7 plot to explode a number of transatlantic aircraft departing from the UK using liquid bombs, was a further success. However, this case also illustrates the challenge of gathering sufficient intelligence to bring about a successful prosecution whilst balancing this requirement against the risk that if unchecked the plot might succeed. In this case, at the first trial of the defendants in 2008 none was convicted of plotting to bring down aircraft. At their retrial in September 2009 three defendants were found guilty of plotting to do so on a majority verdict. Three further defendants were acquitted of the main charge. They were found guilty of conspiracy to murder at a further retrial in July 2010.[102]

On this basis, though, it is possible to construct a number of indicators of intelligence agency success:

- predictive success – analysis leading to timely warning, facilitating prevention (i.e. of surprise);
- successful criminal prosecution;
- absence of predictive failure;
- maintenance of customer trust;
- maintenance of public trust;
- maintenance of effective partnerships with allied intelligence agencies; and
- maintenance or enhancement of the customer's relative advantage.

It is often noted that the failures of intelligence services, especially to prevent 'surprise' attacks, are very well known, whereas their successes are unknown because they cannot be publicized, except in the event that people are prosecuted in court. Otherwise we have to rely on what former officers tell us, and history tells us that we should treat their claims with caution. However, according to the former MI5 Director General, in the period after 9/11 until her retirement in April 2007, MI5 successfully disrupted twelve plots and failed on three occasions: Richard Reid, the 'shoe bomber', in December 2001; the 7/7 bombings in London in 2005; and the attack two weeks later (21/7), when the bombs on underground trains and a bus failed to explode.[103]

Identifying threats, then, has been the business of intelligence agencies. Yet, as intelligence practitioners themselves confess and as the Flood Report again reminded us, intelligence is not a science; rather, it is an art. This fact is not a consequence of reliance on any particular collection method, or because of a *lack* of unprocessed information. More of a particular type of input will not alter the basic fact that intelligence can only deal in probabilities, and that the range of variables that can be generated by human interaction or introduced by different, subjective analyses of a given situation will always serve to limit the utility of intelligence work and limit its predictive power to well below 100 per cent.[104] Hence, despite impressive budgets the world's most high-profile intelligence agency, the CIA, has failed to anticipate a catalogue of momentous developments and acute disasters, key amongst any listing of which would have to be the construction of the Berlin Wall and the collapse of the Soviet Union. Two further fundamental intelligence failures – to anticipate the December 1979 Soviet invasion of Afghanistan or the August 1990 Iraqi invasion of Kuwait – can be attributed confidently to failures in analysis rather than failures brought about through an absence or lack of information. The case of Afghanistan additionally raises the question of intelligence agencies gearing assessments to what their customers may be thought to want to hear, or at least avoiding headlining an analysis that would be unwelcome – a subject to which we shall return in chapters 6 and 7. To illustrate the kinds of pressures involved, with regard to the case of Afghanistan in 1979, a CIA analysis concluded that:

> it would be unfair not to acknowledge the pressures on intelligence either to express more certainty – justified by evidence – or to engage in safe hedging. Clearly, at a

> time when détente was being challenged and the SALT II treaty appeared to be in a life-threatening status with the Senate, allegations that Moscow was about to engage in yet another Third World aggression barely two years after what was regarded as its proxy intervention in Ethiopia was not something most US policy officials wanted to see casually aired.[105]

More devastatingly for the US, while recognizing the existence of a threat, the FBI and CIA failed in a variety of ways to appreciate the *nature* and *scope* of the threat posed by al-Qaeda, from the linkages between al-Qaeda and the 1993 World Trade Center bombing led by Ramzi Yousef up to and including the significance of a meeting in Malaysia in 2000, where al-Qaeda members and two of the 9/11 hijackers came together. Moreover, the evidence suggests that the agencies failed to convince politicians, whose Cold War mindset determined that they saw threats as emanating from states, particularly China, rather than non-state actors.[106] With the benefit of hindsight, Senator Richard C. Shelby of Alabama, the senior Republican member of the Senate Select Committee of Intelligence, expressed a general exasperation at the scale of the failure when he complained that: 'If you tie the general warnings together, and you put all of the bombings and attacks of the 90's together, then combine it with last summer's failures, it should have, in my judgment, had the bells ringing, all the way up. But it didn't.'[107]

Still, failures will occur, such as that to prevent the so-called 'underpants bomber', Umar Farouk Abdulmutallab, from boarding a Northwest Airlines flight from Amsterdam to Detroit on Christmas Day 2009, despite clear intelligence that he might pose a threat – including that volunteered by his own father to two CIA officers in the US Embassy in Abuja, Nigeria – and the inclusion of his name on the 550,000-long Terrorist Identities Datamart Environment list maintained by the US National Counterterrorism Center (NCTC). US President Obama called the incident a 'systemic failure' which was 'totally unacceptable'.[108]

Conclusion: Towards a Theory of Intelligence?

In this opening chapter we have defined intelligence as a process of gathering and analysing information with a view to providing forewarning and shaping policy so as to protect or enhance relative advantage. Conducted largely in secret, intelligence has the clear potential to do good by increasing public security, but also has the potential to do great harm by trampling on human rights. Therefore, as citizens we need to be prepared to ask the kind of questions that we will now go on to explore in greater detail in the rest of the book. Why is intelligence conducted? Who does it? How do they do it? What are its limits? How can it be controlled so that it does more good than harm? Chapter 2 sets out a theoretical basis for consideration of these questions by discussing what we should expect from a theory of intelligence. What should it be able to tell us? Is its purpose to provide a model that can be applied to direct us to the most important questions and generate answers that explain intelligence outcomes? Should it do so within the framework of liberal-democratic norms and expectations? What is the relationship between our definition of intelligence and a theory of intelligence?

CHAPTER TWO

How Do We Understand Intelligence?

Introduction

This chapter identifies the central conceptual and theoretical issues that we must confront in order to enhance our ability to understand and explain intelligence processes, including their role in contemporary governance. To some, this may seem a rather tedious exercise – why not just get on with examining the more interesting and exciting aspects of intelligence? This is tempting but would be ultimately futile: there is a wealth of literature that does nothing but describe the real or imagined 'facts' of intelligence scandals but, taken overall, it adds up to a highly coloured and distorted view of intelligence and its relation to government and the state. Practitioners, for their part, may well complain that conceptual discussions will not necessarily lead directly to improvements in the performance of intelligence. But we would argue that such discussions can indirectly affect practice through better-informed public debate, awareness and self-reflection among customers and decreasing ignorance in the academic world.[1] Therefore our objective in this chapter is to discuss basic issues of theory and method and suggest a framework for research into intelligence that will assist anyone who seeks to understand intelligence.

In the previous chapter we defined intelligence as *the mainly secret activities – targeting, collection, analysis, dissemination and action – intended to enhance security and/or maintain power relative to competitors by forewarning of threats and opportunities.* We need to be concerned with concepts and theory in any field of studies because of their indispensable role in generating and organizing knowledge. The need is greater when studying intelligence because, especially in Britain,[2] historical accounts have always constituted the main literature. The memoirs of former intelligence officers, the reconstruction of past episodes from released official files and the emergence of official histories provide the raw material for the hitherto 'missing dimension' of historical studies.[3] The theoretical assumptions behind this work tend to be those of the IR school of 'realism', so that the 'great game' was played out between states, threats could be objectively measured and the 'truth' of what happened discovered by the accumulation of oral and written evidence. More broadly, the study of intelligence within IR has been situated mainly within realist or neo-realist analyses because the core concern of them all is security, notwithstanding national and regional variations in the ways in which security is defined.[4]

In the US greater efforts have been made to 'theorize' intelligence at the organizational level, especially the relation between 'intelligence', 'secrecy' and 'policy' including covert action, but these efforts are often too enmeshed in the debates around the specific organization of the US intelligence community to move towards more generalizable findings.[5] David Kahn recently set out principles that, he argues, a theory of intelligence should offer in explaining the relation between intelligence and policy, but they remain too narrowly focused on the issue of states and war for our purposes.[6] We need to examine theoretical issues more explicitly if we are to move beyond 'story-telling' and lay the groundwork for more systematic and comparative explanations of intelligence in different social and organizational contexts.

What kind of theory is most likely to be productive? The mainstream within Anglo-American social science since the 1950s has been behaviouralism with the following significant features: general law-like statements can be induced from empirical research and observation of social systems; political behaviour displays regularities; as in the natural sciences, appearance and reality are the same; and neutral 'value-free' research is possible. Knowledge claims are then tested by subsequent research and confirmed, modified or abandoned in the light of the findings.[7] This approach has its roots in positivism based on 'foundationalist' ontology; that is, the 'real world' exists independently of our knowledge, our knowledge of this world is developed by observation and the aim of social science is to generate explanations of what 'is', not to be concerned with philosophical or normative questions of what 'ought' to be. Positivism incorporates a powerful preference for quantitative research and the ultimate goal is prediction.[8]

The Critique of Positivism

Positivism and behaviouralism have been subject to numerous criticisms. Some can be reiterated *a fortiori* with respect to studying intelligence. Theory cannot be developed simply by accumulating observations of 'reality' but itself plays a part in determining what are relevant 'facts'. Whether or not we agree with the proposition that 'all the most important questions about society are empirical ones, as are the most important answers',[9] an approach relying solely on induction cannot suffice; to embark on research *about* the intelligence process (or analysis *within* it[10]) without some prior conceptual framework, model or theory is to invite death by drowning or, at least, mental collapse in a deep sea of information.[11] Of course, this fate is routinely avoided, but only because of the *implicit* frameworks we employ. For the study of intelligence to become systematic, we must be more explicit about our frameworks; to do otherwise is at best naïve or at worst dishonest if our work is based on the presentation as 'scientific' of assumptions that are actually highly value-laden and contestable. To pursue the watery metaphor, as analysts we must remember Graham Allison's crucial point that we *select* the ponds in which we fish.[12]

Behaviouralism is inadequate because it requires 'observability' as a criterion for evidence and 'actors' who cause events (see further below on agency and structure). The intelligence literature is replete with accounts of individuals who claim to have had a great impact on events, either in the formation and operation of agencies or as agents working for some agency (and sometimes for several). Such historical accounts are a rich source of material but, of themselves, can provide only part of the basis for more general statements about intelligence processes. Any attempt to devise a theory of intelligence is doomed if we can theorize only on the basis of what we can observe, whether or not it is from 'official' sources. For example, during Lord Justice Scott's 1992–6 inquiry into UK arms sales to Iraq, a British civil servant sought to defend the practice of providing answers to parliamentary questions that were less than complete by suggesting that: 'Of course half a picture can be accurate.'[13] Bearing in mind Porter's admonition in the last chapter that we should not 'believe a word of it', the problem for the student of intelligence is to know the extent to which the partial pictures we develop are accurate. Compared with other areas of governance, and, according to our definition, secrecy being a significant feature of intelligence processes, we shall never be able to theorize in a way that behaviouralists would regard as methodologically credible.

The critique of positivism has been developed into a range of 'post-positivist' approaches.[14] One major strand of post-positive thinking is feminism, though this follows a number of different routes, including liberal, radical and Marxist. Although some feminists share a positivist approach by arguing that certain aspects of the nature and experience of women are universally 'true', others point to the different experiences of women as mediated by class, ethnicity, culture and sexuality.[15] There has been little direct feminist study of intelligence *per se*,[16] but more critique of the state-centric definitions of 'security' deployed in traditional IR. The connection between states and sovereignty, backed up by the state's claim to the internal monopoly of legitimate violence and readiness to use force externally in pursuit of its interests, has led to national or state security becoming the central analytical concern. The steady entrenchment of patriarchal norms through the process of state formation marginalizes the experience of many women for whom (in)security means something quite different: 'A more comprehensive view of security, which begins by asking what, or who, most threatens particular groups of people, will disrupt any notion of "national security", for the greatest threats to people's security in many cases are local state agents or military personnel, or "home men who are constructed as soldier-protectors of the very people they endanger.'[17] To the extent that most intelligence literature has 'spun off' from IR's concern with state or national security, it is equally vulnerable to this critique.

The Challenge of Postmodernism

Postmodernism represents the most radical departure from positivism. Since intelligence is about the production of knowledge, with agencies operating at the cutting edge of deploying new information and communication technology (ICT), it seems entirely appropriate to explain it with an approach to social theory that itself emphasizes the significance of new information technologies in reshaping and subverting 'modernist' methods of generating knowledge. But postmodernism goes much further in its radical epistemological claim that there is no single rationality by which knowledge can be generated; there are no means of establishing 'truth' that transcend the location of the observer and so there can be only competing 'discourses' or ways of representing or narrating events. For example, James der Derian notes the relative under-theorization of intelligence and argues that what there is is too positivistic in its attempt to 'discipline' global disorder. Rather, he suggests, what is needed is a 'meta-theory' that would take into account the fact that 'ambiguous discourse, not objective truth, is the fluctuating currency of intelligence'. The indeterminacy of what is seen or heard, aggravated by encoding, decoding and, possibly, deception plus the gulf between what is said and what is meant, requires an approach rooted more in rhetoric than in reason. This approach – intertextualism – 'aptly covers the field of intelligence, where there is no final arbiter of truth, meaning is derived from an interrelationship of texts and power is implicated by the contingent nature and ambiguity of language and other signifying practices'. Further, the texts to be analysed are not just the 'factive' ones of national security studies but also the 'fictive' literature of international intrigue that 'produce meaning and legitimate particular forms of *power* in their relation to each other'.[18]

For his part, Andrew Rathmell identifies five 'core' postmodern themes: the end of grand narratives; the end of the search for absolute 'truths'; the fracturing of identities; increased blurring of boundaries between both approaches to explanation and states, cultures etc.; and the emergence of the knowledge economy, with its implications for organization shifts from hierarchies to networks. He goes on to relate these to contemporary shifts in the intelligence business: first, the collapse of the 'grand narrative' of the Soviet threat and its replacement by a variety of rapidly changing and loosely organized targets such as transnational organized crime, proliferation and terrorism. Second, unlike the 'objective reality' of the Cold War, intelligence now does not even know 'if there is a single objective reality out there'.[19] Third, individual and collective identity is challenged, technologically by the development of human/machine systems, organizationally by doubts as to for whom intelligence is being produced – is it states, corporations, non-governmental organizations? – and by the collapse of old certainties about who is on whose side and with respect to what. Fourth, the previously impermeable boundaries within the intelligence community and between it and outside (state and private) organizations are dissolving in the face of the decline in the state's monopoly of expertise and consequently greater interchanges of personnel and technologies. Fifth, the knowledge economy has hastened the demise of 'factories' for the production of intelligence just as much as it has elsewhere in commerce and government.[20] Rathmell suggests that the key implications of all this for intelligence organizations are that they should acknowledge their essential nature as a knowledge industry with the concomitant delayering, embrace horizontal knowledge networks and accept change as 'dynamic, non-linear and accelerating'.[21]

Now, there is much here that can be agreed upon. Behaviouralist methods cannot readily capture the uncertainties, complexities and ambiguities of the world, and this applies to the work of intelligence as much as to those studying intelligence. Both groups do seek 'facts' that others wish to keep secret and also make judgements about others' intentions, but the object of the exercise is not necessarily to discover 'truth'. Intelligence analysts seek knowledge with a degree of certainty sufficient to satisfy and inform those who wish to act upon it; academics are not seeking 'truth' but knowledge with a degree of reliability that will satisfy peer reviewers and standards of 'intersubjectivity'.[22] Thus while a central part of the postmodern critique is that there are no objective 'truths' towards which the social analyst can seek to progress, it is not at all clear that intelligence (or its scholars) assumed there were.[23] Indeed, one of the reasons for the tension between intelligence professionals and policymakers is the very fact that the former deal in ambiguities and probabilities as they develop 'estimates', and recoil from the certainties that the latter wish to hear in their attempts to persuade mass publics as to the rightness of their cause. As noted in the last chapter, intelligence is more art than science and, like art, is about nuance. Politicians distrust nuance.[24]

But there is something of the counsel of despair in der Derian's argument: yes, making sense and explaining the world of intelligence is very difficult for all the reasons he enumerates, and any scholar who claimed to have ascertained the 'truth' of it would be a fool. But it is far from clear that his alternative methodology would improve our understanding. The fictional literature of intelligence, some of which we referred to in chapter 1, may well serve useful purposes (aside from simple enjoyment) when it is a vehicle for the description of events that could not be recounted as 'fact',[25] and for its ability to explore and reveal aspects of life as do art and fiction in general. But it would be highly misleading if we concluded that James Bond represented a typical MI6 officer and, taken literally, might lead to the absurdity of Baudrillard's claim that the first Gulf War was not 'real'.[26] Rather, our purpose must be to seek ways of understanding and explaining intelligence, including by way of analysing texts, believing that useful knowledge (that which has some real existence beyond the text) can be ascertained and made use of by those seeking to improve the human condition.

More recently, Hamilton Bean has deployed postmodernist approaches to intelligence to argue that a dominant discourse of 'organizational culture' has enabled both scholars and managers to avoid the painful implications of holding individuals accountable for intelligence failures, such as 9/11. Bean notes there has been much useful postmodernist work on organizations, and he seeks to 'encourage more critical examination of the interconnections and distinctions between systemic forces and individual judgment and decision making'.[27] We agree absolutely with that aim but it is not clear why postmodern approaches are required to achieve it. Rather, as we suggest below, we need to analyse the interaction of agency and structure and the 'nesting' of these within each other at various 'levels' (see figure 2.1 below). Hatlebrekke and Smith also deploy discourse analysis to argue that the source of intelligence failure resides not 'in strict technical confines of the intelligence cycle, but *primarily* in the cognitive processes among intelligence analysts and among those who receive the intelligence product'. But their subsequent analysis identifies a range of factors that contributed to the 9/11 failure, including erosion of programme management in the National Security Agency (NSA), failure to adapt to new technology, inadequate linguistic capacities, and inability to adapt agencies' structures to recognize the interaction of foreign and domestic terrorist threats. These authors then conclude: 'In summary, these areas demonstrated, *among many other things of course*, the existence of discourse failure.'[28] It does not appear that this conclusion supports the initial contention as to the 'primary' role of discourse and cognitive closure as problems within intelligence. Of course, scholars have identified similar lists of factors – involving aspects of both agency and structure – for many years.

Although postmodern*ism* may be of limited help to us, we do need to pay attention to key elements of postmodern*ity* as a description of the social and political conditions at the start of the twenty-first century, notably postindustrialism and globalization.[29] It is important, however, to consider just what is new here: it seems to us that there are some continuities which caution against any wholesale ditching of modernist methods. For example, the extent to which the threat emanating from the Soviet Union during the Cold War was represented as an 'objective reality' reflected not only Soviet capacities and actions but also the success of specific organizational and political interests in institutionalizing that representation.[30] To the extent that this actually misconstrued what the Soviet Union was seeking to achieve, it was poor intelligence that can be blamed on a number of factors such as politicization, 'mirror-imaging', 'groupthink', deception or some toxic brew of them all.[31] It may well be that, in the more fluid conditions of post- or late modernity, the intelligence business has become even more complex, but it does not necessarily follow that our criteria for judging its effectiveness or otherwise have been transformed, as appears to be the postmodernist claim.

The decline of state sovereignty may well be a central feature of postmodernity but national security remains the last refuge of the spook. Paradoxically, or perhaps not, as the greater fluidity of global change and relationships seems to demand the recognition by intelligence that it is just another knowledge industry, the concomitant increase in perceptions of insecurity since 9/11 see it acquiring yet more special powers for the penetration of privacy and maintenance of secrecy for its operations.[32] Rathmell's argument reflects a particular period when the attempt to replace the Cold War with a 'grand narrative' around transnational terrorism and organized crime failed to convince. However, the contemporary centrality of the 'global War on Terror' (notwithstanding the fact that the phrase has been dropped from official narratives, as we write the US drone war has been extended from Pakistan to include Yemen and Somalia) and overt concern with the nuclear activities of Iran and North Korea and the intelligence activities of China demonstrate the continued relevance of older themes. Competition and co-operation between states and corporations will dominate developments in intelligence for the foreseeable future. In generating our own signposts for this future and the tools with which we examine intelligence, we agree with Rathmell that postmodern perspectives capture some elements of the contemporary intelligence environment, but we do not accept that they provide a satisfactory theory for explaining it.

Critical Realism: Neither Positivist nor Postmodernist

In seeking to further the task of theorizing intelligence, it will be most fruitful to identify a path that avoids the major pitfalls of both positivism and postmodernism. Neither is able to develop knowledge that leads to understanding or is generalizable beyond the particularities of time and place. We must make our theoretical considerations explicit if for no other reason than intellectual honesty. 'Value-free' social science is impossible because analysts are embedded within the socio-political context that is the subject of their study. Since analysts cannot claim 'value-freedom' for their findings, they must acknowledge what their value-assumptions are in order that their arguments can be evaluated in that context. Analysts cannot claim superiority for their views simply because they occupy a privileged 'scientific' viewpoint from which to observe, but they can make their reasoning, methods and sources transparent to others so that the validity of their arguments can be judged.

Thus our objective is to establish some principles upon which progress can be made rather than arguing for the necessary superiority of any particular conceptual framework; ultimately choice will be finalized on the basis of the personal beliefs and objectives of the analyst. There is some 'reality' in the world[33] but the process of understanding it requires critical self-reflection on *how* we understand. Thus, theory and empirical work are inextricably linked:

> theory is a guide to empirical exploration, a means of reflecting more or less abstractly upon complex processes of institutional evolution and transformation in order to highlight key periods or phases of change which warrant closer empirical scrutiny. Theory

> sensitizes the analyst to the causal processes being elucidated, selecting from the rich complexity of events the underlying mechanisms and processes of change.[34]

Neither deduction nor induction alone is adequate in social science: we do not 'discover' new events but we do discover new connections and relations that are not directly observable and by which we can analyse already known occurrences in a novel way. This creative process of redescription or 'abduction' is what investigators or doctors do as they test out different hypotheses or diagnoses.[35] By applying alternative theories and models in order to discern connections that were not evident, intelligence scholars are doing what, as we shall see throughout the book, good intelligence analysts do. But in doing so, neither group is merely describing reality as if through a clear pane of glass: they are seeking to make sense and thus actively 'create' the worlds of intelligence, government and IR.[36] David Kahn has argued that: 'Intelligence has been an academic discipline for half a century now. Almost from the start, scholars have called for a theory of intelligence. None has been advanced. Although some authors entitle sections of their work "theory of intelligence", to my knowledge no one has proposed concepts that can be tested.'[37] It should be clear from our discussion that it would be futile to search for the 'testable concepts' that Kahn's positivist view of theory would demand but that the process of abduction can further the development of intelligence theory.

Thus 'critical realism' seeks to avoid the hobbling effect of both positivism and its anti-foundationalist critics. It distinguishes elements of reality that are relatively unchanging and exist independently of the scientific process from those that change more frequently, being produced (socially constructed) as part of the scientific process.[38] Further, with positivism, it believes that causal statements can be made while, against positivism, it accepts that not all social phenomena can be observed and therefore research must also seek out underlying mechanisms of events.[39]

Agency and Structure

This is a central methodological issue in exploring causal processes. Agency refers to action based on free will so that 'actors' have some degree of choice or autonomy. Note that actors may be individual or collective – political analysis contains many references to groups, classes or states as actors. Analyses that emphasize the role of agency (sometimes to the exclusion of any role for structure) are referred to as 'intentionalist'. For example, Dennis Wrong argues that 'intentionality' is the indispensable defining characteristic of 'political power'.[40] By comparison, structure refers 'to the fact that political institutions, practices, routines and conventions appear to exhibit some regularity . . . over time'.[41] Sociologists are more likely to define structure in terms of class, ethnicity, gender and sexuality. While these may be 'deeper' structures than institutions and practices, the central point is that they provide the context or arena within which people do or do not act. Our object is not to explore the long-running debate between the proponents of intentionalism and structuralism as *alternatives*.[42] There is nothing 'essential' about the distinction: the (in)actions of any individual actor can only be understood within a range of structural contexts (group, organizational, social) and the constraints that these impose. For example, if our focus is on a specific organization such as the British Cabinet, then we need to understand both its impact as a structure within which people and colleague groups interact – that is, within which bureaucratic politics[43] occurs – and as an agent acting within the broader context of state and society. In this way, actors at different 'levels' of intelligence can be seen as 'nesting' within each other (see figure 2.1 below).[44]

In a further refinement to the basic agency–structure relationship, Jessop suggests the incorporation of strategy. Thus agents are reflexive, capable of thinking strategically about their situation and reformulating their interests within the existing structural constraints. These, in turn, are not determined absolutely but operate selectively and are always related to the situation of specific agents.[45] Thus, certain strategies will be favoured over others – the environment is not a level playing field. Outcomes are not structurally determined but, over time, certain outcomes are more likely to occur than others. This 'strategic-relational' approach can be summarized in the following way: the strategic actor makes (explicit or intuitive) choices within the strategically selective context that imposes limits on behaviour. The strategic action that results then produces some direct effect on the structural context (though it may be very slight and not as intended) and provides some potential for the actor to learn.[46]

Thus, the analysis of intelligence can proceed best if agency and structure are viewed as existing in a dialectical relationship. Therefore the task for the analyst of intelligence becomes to develop a way to generalize about both how people understand and are thus influenced by their structural context and how their strategic actions (or inactions) impact upon that context. The context may be either empowering or constraining and actions may amend or reinforce it. For example, at a micro level we might examine how intelligence officers view procedural rules and laws. Whether they view them as empowering or constraining will have some effect on their conduct – their original intention to act in a given situation may be reinforced, they may decide to act differently within the rules, act outside of the rules or not act at all. In turn, these (in)actions may have (short- or long-term) implications for the rules – they may be seen as providing useful legal protection for officers, as unwieldy, or as so restrictive as to require amendment.

Elsewhere, with colleagues, we edited a collection of national studies of intelligence in which we asked contributors to analyse how different regime types interacted with their strategic environment (an amalgam of strategy and structure).[47] In his review of the collection, Michael Warner suggested that 'technology' be added as a third independent variable, and he subsequently developed the argument that strategy, regime and technology can be used to explain the character of intelligence 'systems'.[48] This parallels closely our argument: available technologies are a key element of the structural context for regimes, but may be varied. Thus, regimes (agency) vary in terms of factors such as form, culture and organization and develop strategies in the light of their basic orientation, motives and objectives, which are, in turn, constrained by technology (structure), including their location, resources, mode of production and social formations. In implementing their strategies, regimes may succeed or fail in achieving their objectives and, in the process, their structural constraints may increase or decrease. There may also be some feedback into the nature of the regime itself – it may even collapse – but the dialectic between these three variables is clear.

Intelligence as Surveillance: Knowledge and Power

Returning to our central concern, we shall adopt *surveillance* as the core concept because of its importance in explaining modern governance, including the behaviour of agents and the development of structures. Though social theorists such as Dandeker, Giddens and Foucault discuss it in different ways, there is a core of similarity in their definition of surveillance as constituted by two components: first, the gathering and storing of information and, second, the supervision of people's behaviour. In other words, it is concerned with knowledge and power. This is not exactly a novel idea in the study of intelligence. In 1952 Roger Hilsman commented: 'Intelligence on the one hand and policymaking and action on the other are separated physically, organizationally, chronologically, functionally, and by skills – separated in every possible way. The question is whether this division of labor is a wise or even valid one.'[49] Whatever the answer to this from the perspective of the practitioner, we would argue that, if we want to understand how intelligence works, then we must study this relationship: 'Much of the study of intelligence concerns the relationship between power and knowledge, or rather the relationship between certain kinds of power and certain kinds of knowledge.'[50]

In contemporary western social theory, surveillance is seen as the central aspect both of the establishment of modern 'sovereign' state forms[51] and of the more recent decline of sovereignty as it is replaced by 'governance' (or, for Foucault, 'governmentality'[52]), including the concomitant recognition of the significance of private forms of governance. Furthermore, studies of non-western societies show that surveillance is similarly central there: its philosophical basis may be crucially different, for example, rooted in the rejection of individualism, but its core goals – understanding and control – are constants.[53] So, not surprisingly, global surveillance is argued to be an intrinsic part of the general economic restructuring of capitalism that is referred to as globalization,[54] and post-9/11 developments have served only to accelerate this already existing trend.[55] We defined our interest in chapter 1

as the generation of knowledge in conditions of secrecy that
formation and implementation of security policy; this is essen
of the more general surveillance that constitutes contemporary

Producing knowledge

Information gathered can be classified as one of two main types:
and offensive. The object of the former is to identify one's own (personal, organizational or societal) vulnerabilities and the risks or threats emanating from either external or internal sources in order to defend oneself. 'Risks' and 'threats' might be distinguished in various ways: one of us has argued that it is useful to retain the traditional meaning in intelligence of threats as emanating from malign intent while risks derive from unintentional events such as floods or pandemics;[56] the other sees threats as being more imminent than risks, and distinguished by the conjunction of capability and intent.[57] For practitioners, a third idea will be familiar, that is, the risk assessments concerning the safety of officers and public carried out prior to an intelligence operation.[58] Whatever the preferred concept, the analysis normally seeks to calculate two main dimensions: the magnitude of the risk or threat and the likelihood of its occurrence. The object of 'offensive' information is to bring about change. An individual may take either intentional or habitual action to bring about some improvement in personal prospects or feelings of security, an organization might perceive the need to develop new markets (in the private sector) or improve its performance (in the public sector), while states may seek information with a view to the maintenance of public order or acquisition of new territory. There are also significant 'grey areas' of intelligence. For example, in economic intelligence the efforts of states to gather information on competitors within the context of market economies may be defined as offensive (in terms of increasing market share) or defensive (in terms of domestic jobs).

Information gathering takes place in two broad ways (discussed in more detail in chapter 4): either openly through the collation of already published material and relatively passive 'environmental scanning' ('overt'), or through more aggressive techniques of penetrating the secrecy and privacy of others ('covert'). The first of these may be conducted more or less self-consciously and the amounts of potentially relevant material available on any issue are prodigious and, thanks to the Internet, readily available. Covert information gathering requires the commitment of greater resources. Expertise in the gathering of information held covertly by others is significant within 'intelligence' but covert information should not be reified, because it is not *necessarily* more useful than open source information and may only be comprehensible in the context of material from open sources.

What is to be done with information gathered? It is useful to draw the common distinction between 'information' and 'intelligence': the latter is produced by a process of analysis or evaluation of the former. Again, this process may be more or less conscious: in the case of individuals, the act of obtaining some information is often accompanied immediately by an intuitive evaluation of its meaning and significance based on the credibility or otherwise of its source and substance. On other occasions a more explicit process is undertaken in which we are forced to confront information from various sources that does not apparently 'make sense'. This is where the process of abduction identified earlier is so important. Analysis can never be reduced to induction, the simple accumulation of data; it requires also creative reasoning to compare the utility of different frames of interpretation – what is sometimes called alternative analysis.[59] Even in organizational settings those involved in collecting information will often immediately evaluate its meaning if only to decide whether further information needs to be sought, as we saw in chapter 1. 'Facts' do not 'speak for themselves'; analysis is the crucial process through which appearances are subjected to critical scrutiny.

Memory plays a key role in this collection/analysis cycle: again, this is a feature that exists at all levels. What is or is not consigned to an individual's conscious memory is itself subject to a highly complex process involving not just the significance of the information but also the will to remember. Evaluation is carried out with respect to, for example, the veracity of sources and the consistency or otherwise of fresh information with what is already in the 'store'. One of the characteristics of the bureaucracies that came to signify the emergence of modern state forms was the maintenance of records that could provide the basis for greater consistency of decisions over time. In specialized intelligence agencies 'the files' represent the formal organizational memory that provides the structural context for current analysis. Yet organizational memories also have an informal dimension and, to the regular frustration of those who would reform and reorganize bureaucracies, intelligence or otherwise, organizational subcultures persist, fuelled by employees' memories, preferred ways of working and reluctance to entrust everything known to the files.

Exercising power

Collection and analysis processes may or may not be followed by 'action'; the crucial connection between 'knowledge' and 'power' (or, 'intelligence' and 'policy') being provided by the dissemination of intelligence. If the 'knowledge problem' is believed to have been solved, then what can be done about the threat, the vulnerability or the ambition? Can the 'power problem' be solved? In considering this, it is useful to identify two broad theoretical streams with respect to power. The first, sometimes referred to as the 'sovereign' view of power, is principally concerned with the power that one agent may exercise over another in a 'zero-' or 'constant-sum' relationship. The second stream is more concerned with agents' ability to facilitate things, that is, with the 'techniques' of power, and sees power as more widely dispersed in society rather than concentrated in 'sovereign' states or individuals. As such, power may facilitate as well as repress and therefore is 'non-zero-' or 'variable-sum'.[60] Again, the point is not that one of these streams is superior to the other; it is that the analyst needs to be aware that power is contingent and may be manifested as either constant- or variable-sum.

Dissemination may take several forms but what they all have in common is the link with power. Even the simple decision to pass 'intelligence' on to another person or organization will have consequences for power. We must distinguish between situations in which the intelligence disseminated is believed to be true, and thus may persuade because it is accepted on trust, and those in which the intelligence is believed to be misleading, in which case 'deception' or 'manipulation' are more appropriate terms.[61] But whether believed to be true or not, intelligence is itself a *form* of power: 'knowledge *is* power'. Indeed, dissemination may not be necessary in order for knowledge to have an impact: by the 'law of anticipated reactions' someone may act in a particular way as a consequence of anticipating how other participants would react were she or he to behave otherwise.[62] More generally, the same idea is at the core of the argument that surveillance breeds self-regulating subjects: the principle of the Panopticon is that those surveilled base their behaviour on their understanding that they *may be* under surveillance. Thus they regulate their own behaviour despite their ignorance as to whether they actually *are* under surveillance at any particular time.[63] This creates difficulties for analysis since no observable behaviour on the part of those wielding power may be necessary; another illustration that understanding based entirely on empirical work will only ever be partial, if not actually misleading.

Otherwise, information is not so much a form of power in itself as a resource which can support the exercise of other forms of power, such as material or coercive. This is the more common view that intelligence provides the basis for policy or decisions: that people, organizations and states, if they are to act 'rationally', will do so after canvassing fully the alternative courses of action open to them and their costs and benefits. Of course, as the voluminous decision-making literature indicates, rational action is really only useful as an 'ideal-type' against which practice might be measured. Various phrases have been used to describe the messier realities of the relation between information and action: for example, 'bounded rationality', 'garbage can' model and 'incrementalism'.[64] Key to these is 'selectivity', whereby a combination of prior assumptions and limited resources means that we are very rarely willing or able to conduct a full canvass of potentially relevant information.

Indeed, as noted earlier, there can be significant tension between the conditional conclusions in intelligence and politicians' craving for certain answers. Policy tends to be formulated deductively from first principles or grounded in ideology. Intelligence is produced abductively by evaluating the information gathered against alternative hypotheses. When they meet the contest is uneven: 'When intelligence clashes with policy preference, intelligence loses; when information runs up against power, information is the casualty. Indeed, when information is countered by perception or, more accurately, conception, evidence is discounted.'[65] In practice, therefore, the 'normal' knowledge–power connection will be reversed so that the urge to act pre-exists the search for information, and the significance of what is collected will be judged in terms of its ability to support a chosen course of action rather than to inform it. Here, the relation between knowledge and power is like that of lamppost and drunk: to provide support not illumination. As we shall see in chapter 7, just such a relationship characterized the use of intelligence by US and UK administrations in the lead-up to the invasion of Iraq in 2003.

Secrecy and resistance

There are two additional variables permeating the knowledge–power relation at the centre of security intelligence. The first is secrecy, as we explained in chapter 1. Apart from the sheer complexity of modern society, another reason why 'knowledge problems' exist lies in the conscious effort that individuals, organizations and states make to keep their affairs secret. Individuals' privacy rights are contained in human rights declarations and conventions because privacy is seen as indispensable to people's dignity and autonomy. Corporations seek the same privilege via notions of commercial confidentiality that are written into contracts with employees and also present a significant bulwark to the work of outside regulators. At the level of states, current ideas of 'official secrets' developed alongside modern state bureaucracies but may be traced back further to the notion of *arcana* in pre-modern religious states.[66] Thus, once open sources are exhausted, the privacy of subjects presents an obstacle to surveillance that provokes a whole panoply of covert gathering techniques. But secrecy is not just significant as a barrier to surveillance; it permeates aspects of the process itself. Security requires the protection of information gathered, methods and the identity of sources by means of elaborate internal procedures, including the restricted circulation of documents on a 'need-to-know' basis. But the consequent limitation on the availability of information can, in turn, hinder the free flow of ideas and quality of analysis. Secrecy may also apply to power: some actions, such as most arrests, make no sense unless carried out with an element of 'surprise'. But there are other, more controversial examples where actions are taken secretly in the hope that responsibility can be disguised or 'plausibly denied'.

The second variable is resistance. Secrecy is one form of resistance: attempts to maintain personal privacy or business confidentiality are forms of resistance to the efforts of others to collect information. But if privacy fails then lying and deception are other forms of resistance. Evaluation or analysis is, in turn, an attempt to resist the attempt of others to mislead. Resistance to other forms of power such as coercion may well take on a more physical aspect but often these will be intertwined with the use of information. The central point here is that the relation between surveillance and its subjects is dialectical: efforts at gathering information and wielding power (in whatever form) will provoke greater or lesser attempts to resist. 'Blowback' – when the unintended consequences of information and other covert operations damage the initiator of the operations – is a particular example of 'resistance'.[67] If resistance succeeds then fresh approaches to surveillance may be deployed, and so on.[68] Taken together, secrecy and resistance are the key variables in counterintelligence. The more competitive intelligence is, the more an agency has to protect itself against the actions of rivals, such as obtaining access to its information, suborning its employees, compromising its information security or planting misinformation. Secrecy, vetting and protective security of personnel and buildings are just some of the ways in which the intelligence operations of others are countered.

Levels of surveillance

The social sciences (indeed, sciences in general) are characterized by increasing specialization. It is far from clear that this is entirely beneficial: as research and analysis focus on very narrowly defined issues or problems, it sometimes feels as though we acquire ever more information about less and less. We specialize in ways that, not surprisingly, mirror the most obvious divisions in the world we study. So, for example, reflecting the dominance of the nation-state since the seventeenth century, political science is dominated by national studies, sub-national studies, IR and comparative politics (as between nations).[69] Most IS reflects this dominance and we suggest that is more helpful to talk in terms of 'levels' of intelligence if we are to encompass the full field of our interest.[70]

Specifically, we suggest that five distinct levels may be deployed in order to organize our thinking about the key issues and appropriate analytic strategies. They are:

- individual,
- small group,
- organizational,
- societal, and
- inter-societal.

These are convenient because they are commonly used categories that require distinct study. But we must not forget that this is an analytical device; these social 'levels' actually co-exist within great complexity.[71] Yet this establishes a framework for the analysis of intelligence that will enable us to identify variables that are peculiar to just one level or common to several.

States clearly depend as much on internal as on external security for their wellbeing, but most writing on intelligence at the national or 'macro' level has concerned external intelligence within the context of international relations.[72] This was established a half century ago when Sherman Kent reflected on the agenda for post-1945 US 'strategic intelligence' and excluded from his discussion internal or police intelligence.[73] We suggest this is no longer tenable, if it ever was. The blurring of boundaries between intelligence disciplines and attempts to 'join the dots' invalidate the analytical isolation of foreign or military intelligence from domestic. Also, there are discussions as to the possibility of organizing intelligence at a transnational level.[74] Initially, this was limited to the discussion of transnational sharing agreements[75] – a much enhanced concern since 9/11 – but now includes consideration of how intelligence can support multilateral peacekeeping[76] and international organizations such as the International Atomic Energy Agency (IAEA).[77]

Surveillance is equally central to the 'meso'-level body of literature that has sought to explain, more specifically, how intelligence 'works' (or not) in organizations. All organizations spend some resources on seeking information about the environment within which they operate, though in many this will not be specifically organized or even referred to as 'intelligence'. Even the most humble organizations will engage in information gathering regarding their strengths, weaknesses, opportunities and threats (SWOT analysis) and those of their competitors, and will then seek to translate the findings into action aimed at better achieving their goals. But the concern here is with a more specific subset of the literature that is concerned with the examination of various 'INTS' – foreign, military, security, criminal, environmental, economic, business – and how they contribute to the goal of increasing *security*.

At the 'micro' level of individuals (cognitive psychology) and small groups (social psychology) there are extensive literatures on the processes involved in information gathering, problem solving and decision-making. For example, cognitive psychology is characterized by an 'information processing' approach that makes much of the computer metaphor. The means by which information acquired via the senses is transformed into experience is described as 'perception', which, according to some, is direct or 'bottom-up' while for others – constructivists – it is indirect or 'top-down'; it 'occurs as the end-product of the interactive influences of the presented stimulus and internal hypotheses, expectations, and knowledge, as well as motivational and emotional factors'.[78] 'Attention' is the term used to refer to the selectivity involved in processing; again, this may be 'top-down' when determined by the individual's goals rather than directly in response to the external stimulus. Memory involves both structure and the processes operating within the structure: encoding, storing and retrieval. This 'knowledge' has to be organized or categorized in a way that is economical yet sufficiently detailed to be informative, and may be 'represented' internally or mentally as well as externally through language – for example, speaking, writing or drawing. The object of this thinking and reflection is to plan and solve problems by creativity, discovery, reasoning, judgement and decision-making.[79] In terms of our overall argument, it is significant to note that, even in this self-proclaimed 'hardest' of the social sciences, processes of selectivity and 'construction' demonstrate the limits of behaviouralism.

Thus, we might safely assume that the desire for information is ubiquitous among individuals, groups, organizations, states and societies. Faced with uncertainty, risk and feelings of insecurity, or in search of some other goal, all human entities face a 'knowledge problem'[80] and seek information that (they hope) will reduce uncertainty, enabling them to address their vulnerabilities and advance their interests. This search is necessarily selective: complete scanning is unrealistic (which, as discussed above, is why rational actor theories can exist only as ideal-types) and therefore the criteria guiding the search are crucial.

Conclusion: A Map for Theorizing and Researching Intelligence

Any community of scholars and researchers shares certain assumptions about the way in which knowledge claims in their field are generated. As a result of academic specialization and/or personal taste, some people choose to spend more time concerned with conceptual and theoretical issues while others prefer to 'get their hands dirty' with empirical work. The democratization of intelligence in many countries beginning in the 1980s and the accompanying avalanche of released files and papers, not to mention the increased tendency of former officers to write their memoirs, has given an extraordinary boost to scholarship in the field. However, this has been based more on an urge to provide some historical accounting for the past – the 'missing dimension' – than to reflect on how we study and write about intelligence. This is entirely understandable: in former authoritarian regimes the unearthing of intelligence secrets has been a painful but necessary part of making political progress, and even in liberal democracies it has contributed to reforms intended to reduce the likelihood of future abuses of state power.

So the production of detailed historical accounts is a necessary part of intelligence scholarship, but we need to move beyond this if we are to develop understandings and explanations of intelligence that transcend particular times and places. The theoretical assumptions that precede research are too often implicit and thus disagreements between scholars and practitioners may be generated as much by different assumptions as by different empirical findings. Therefore, we must be explicit about the conceptual frameworks and theoretical assumptions we use. We have argued that the behaviouralist paradigm that has dominated Anglo-American social science since the early 1960s is inadequate, if for no other reason than that the insistence on 'observability' is entirely disabling to the study of intelligence. Yet we argue against switching wholesale to an interpretist approach. This can seem very tempting when trying to make sense of the 'wilderness of mirrors' that is intelligence. Indeed, the dichotomies of appearance and reality are precisely what the intelligence business is about. Hence any approach to theory must include an important place for the social construction of knowledge. We have emphasized issues of security and secrecy and identify the central significance of the unknown (and possibly unknowable) in analysing intelligence. But to deny that there are any 'realities' independent of our research efforts is to disable ourselves in a different way, leaving us enmeshed in endless debates as to how we might describe the world with no chance of proceeding further. We should heed the cautionary tale that is postmodernism, but must not allow this 'modish apparition'[81] to immobilize us.

We suggest that understanding and explanation can best be furthered by the self-conscious development of a reflexive critical theory. This proceeds by the interplay of theoretical approaches and empirical studies. The object is to produce 'knowledge' that is applicable beyond particular time/space dimensions and that can serve the purposes of all those concerned with intelligence. Whether what we produce counts as 'knowledge' will be determined by the judgements of the scholarly and professional communities. In practice, their concerns are different, but there is no necessary incompatibility between 'theory' and 'practice' in intelligence: laws, techniques, policies and practices are all informed by theoretical assumptions; better that they be explicit and generally accepted than implicit and highly debatable once exposed. The point is that we seek to ensure that intelligence is conducted in proper and efficacious ways. Reflexive consideration of the role of intelligence in society is required: intelligence is the handmaiden of public and private political power with potentially great consequences for people's lives. Theory must be developed in such a way that it does not become a simple apologist for that power.

Of course, work of different degrees of abstraction interests people in different positions and with varying concerns, but this makes it all the more important that there is some core understanding that is acknowledged as establishing basic principles of knowledge upon which more specific studies, reconstructions, policies and explanations can be built. We have suggested that the core concept be *surveillance*, understood in terms of the two components of *knowledge* and *power*. This is the best place to start because there is already considerable work regarding its significance at all levels of society from the micro to the macro, and it includes everything in which we might be interested. Yet it needs narrowing down to our field of interest, that is, *intelligence*. This can be distinguished from the generality of surveillance by the characteristics of *security, secrecy and resistance*.

Figure 2.1 summarizes the argument so far by means of a map for theorizing about and researching intelligence. Our *research focus* is the *intelligence process* (see chapter 1). The left- and right-hand columns indicate that intelligence needs to be studied in the light of differences between times (*historical dimension*) and places (*spatial dimension*). Studies of single agencies and countries at particular times are important both in their own right and as potential building blocks for broader, comparative work. The *research elements* correspond to the 'levels' of analysis identified earlier in this chapter: each provides the context for, and is influenced by, the actions and dispositions of those 'below'. Put another way, each element acts as an 'agent' with respect to the level above it and as a 'structure' for the level below. Note also the concept of 'emergence': phenomena or actions at any one level cannot be explained simply by analysing processes or properties at lower 'levels'. New causal

Historical dimension	**Research element**	**Research focus: intelligence process**			**Theoretical approaches**	**Spatial dimension**
↑	Context (a): trans-societal	International relations; transnational corporations; international co-operation and sharing agreements; peacekeeping			Macro (a): realism, international political economy, constructivism	↑
	Context (b): societal	Social organization: values, traditions, forms of organization and power relations, e.g. types of regime, property ownership, governance			Macro (b): hierarchies, markets, networks; realism, idealism, constructivism; social divisions	
Nature of regimes through history and of transition between regimes	Setting: organizational	**Sectors of intermediate social organization:**			Meso: bureaucratic politics; profit maximization; risk minimization; organizational cultures	1 Study of intelligence at different 'levels': local/ regional 2 Comparative studies
		State: departments, agencies	Corporate: profit-making corporations	Non-state sovereignty: neighbourhood, community associations, non-governmental organizations		
	Situated activity: small group	Face-to-face activity in small work groups, associations etc.			(a) Social psychology; 'groupthink'	
↓	Self: individual	Self-identity and individual's social experience			(b) Cognitive psychology	↓
Research techniques	Taking 'slices' across levels and sectors; applying theoretical approaches to case studies such as comparisons between states, regime transitions, intelligence 'successes' and 'failures'; modifying those approaches in the light of research findings; and so on					

'Historical dimension', 'Research element' and 'Research focus' are derived from Derek Layder, in *New Strategies in Social Research* (Cambridge: Polity, 1993), p. 72. 'Sectors' and 'Spatial dimension' are derived from Peter Gill, 'Not just joining the dots but crossing the borders and bridging the voids: constructing security networks after 11 September 2001', *Policing and Society*, 16,1 (2006), pp. 26–48, and are discussed further in chapter 3. 'Research techniques' is derived from Berth Danermark, Mats Ekstrom, Liselotte Jackson and Jan Ch. Karlsson, *Explaining Society* (London: Routledge, 2002), pp. 101–5.

Figure 2.1 *A map for theorizing and researching intelligence*

factors and mechanisms emerge at each level – the whole is greater than the sum of the parts.[82] The *theoretical approaches* identified in figure 2.1 are to illustrate the range that already exists within social science and can be deployed by scholars and researchers. Our choice of theoretical approach will depend largely on the 'level' of our analysis but, in order to develop our discipline, analysts must test out alternative approaches with a view to identifying those that are most fruitful. Theory performs a number of tasks;[83] here it can be used to generate propositions that can then be researched.[84] Analysts will use various *research techniques* as they focus on different levels of intelligence processes in order to produce the detailed empirical work we need, but individual case studies must be conducted with an awareness of the larger picture. We know already how important are the mutual interactions between these 'levels': for example, how the organization of intelligence agencies reflects broader issues of political culture and regime type,[85] how the formal bureaucratic organization of agencies clashes with the working preferences of officers in specialized groups. The specific need to examine organized intelligence *sectors* beyond the state is discussed in detail in chapter 3.

The consequences of the use and abuse of intelligence are clearly profound; the years since 9/11 have seen unprecedented levels of public controversy regarding intelligence. If academics are to make a serious contribution to better explanation, understanding and public education on the key relationships of intelligence to politics, security and governance, law and ethics, their work must be based on an appreciation of central theoretical issues. Then they will be able to speak truth unto power and not simply find themselves conscripted as and when power finds it convenient.[86]

CHAPTER THREE

Who Does Intelligence?

Introduction: Security Intelligence Networks

Most writing on intelligence has been concerned with state agencies – as we noted in the last chapter, this is hardly surprising given the state-centrism of IR and, with respect to internal security, the central concern with the impact of state surveillance on citizens' rights and liberties. While states remain the central actors with respect to security intelligence, we must now include an analysis of corporate and other non-state security agents as part of the general shift towards 'security governance'. This has been in progress for some time: as the Cold War ended, Fry and Hochstein noted that in future: 'Intelligence activities would involve formally a network of units where sovereignty is dispersed among non-governmental actors, international organizations and corporations, and pay due attention to the worm's eye view of the world, i.e., the view from the streets.'[1] And so, according to Peter Singer, it has come to pass: 'the state's role in the security sphere has now become deprivileged. The start of the twenty-first century has begun to see the Weberian monopoly of the state slowly break down.'[2]

Noting the current 'pluralization' of security governance, partly through privatization but also because of the role for private concerns enabled by property law, Johnston and Shearing argue for the adoption of a nodal (network-based) rather than state-centred conception of governance. They identify four sets of governmental nodes: state, corporate, non-governmental organizations (NGOs) and the informal or voluntary sector.[3] Yet, although security *intelligence* is central to security *governance*, Johnston and Shearing say very little explicitly about the role of intelligence. To understand the non-state, non-corporate sector, we would suggest following Michael Warner in identifying 'sovereignties'. He builds on Adda Bozeman's observation that often the state is not the decisive intelligence actor, and suggests that we must study the various paramilitary groups, tribal militias, liberation movements etc. who are willing 'to use violence to hold or gain control over people, resources, and territory'.[4] However, the willingness to use force does not mean that it is the only form of power that sovereignties will deploy (see further discussion in chapter 6).

At root, the idea of networks is 'of informal relationships between essentially equal social agents and agencies'.[5] Both informality and 'essential equality' are, indeed, significant in security networks: informality because this is how they have developed in the first place – as links made between security agents for the sharing of information – and 'essential equality' because, in contrast to the ranks of formal super- and sub-ordination in police and other security organizations, what matters in a network is that you are trusted and have information with which to trade. However, neither of these tells the whole story: on the one hand we see the slow but steady development of *formal* networks between security agencies via treaties and formal legal agreements and, on the other, some agencies and some agents are clearly more equal than others in their ability to structure networks and operate within them. Security does not depart from the general rule that networks 'link up different places and assign to each one of them a role and a weight in the hierarchy of wealth generation, information processing and power making that ultimately conditions the fate of each locale'.[6] For example, national wealth is a key factor in understanding different intelligence systems[7] in terms of not only their independent capacities to conduct surveillance but also their ability to trade intelligence with other states.

One reason why networks are potentially most useful for the study of developments in security intelligence is that they provide an umbrella concept for comparative study. In what has become a commonly deployed device, it has been suggested that markets, hierarchies and networks represent the three dominant modes in which social life is co-ordinated.[8] Applying this idea to security we can see how *markets* are the organizational logic for corporate providers of private security and *hierarchies* for traditional state policing. What, however, is the underlying model for the provision of security by sovereignties? This is contingent on circumstances; for example, if security is provided by NGOs and voluntary groups of citizens, the answer can be found in what Leishman describes as the *communitarian* orientation in policing that has been most pervasive in Asia,[9] although aspects have been 'borrowed' by police elsewhere. To be sure, this is a very wide category that can incorporate neighbourhood watch schemes, victim support, Guardian Angels and, at the extreme, vigilantism.

But where do *networks* fit in? Although *individual* security providers are likely to be located quite clearly within a market, state or collaborative model, we may well find *elements* of two or all three different models within any single provider, such as a public police force whose dominant strategy is 'community policing' and which charges citizens for services such as policing sporting events. The strength of networks is that they can map the multifarious connections *between* security agencies whatever the precise mix of market, hierarchy and collaboration they embody. Further, it can be suggested that networks are the most general category of co-ordination:[10] the market resembles a security network of firms in price competition and their customers; hierarchy is a network of bureaucratically organized public police and intelligence agencies; and sovereignties will work through various family, clan or contractual networks. Within paramilitary, militia or criminal groups, voluntary collaboration will often be overlaid by elements of hierarch order to provide internal discipline.

Mapping Networks

It has been suggested that:

> Network analysis, by emphasizing relations that connect the social positions within a system, offers a powerful brush for painting a systematic picture of global social structures and their components. The organization of social relations thus becomes a central concept in analysing the structural properties of the networks within which individual actors are embedded, and for detecting emergent social phenomena that have no existence at the level of the individual actor.[11]

Figure 3.1 is an attempt to draw a picture or map of the 'territory' within which police and security intelligence networks develop. This territory is as much symbolic as physical now – as much greater use is made of information and intelligence in order to support traditional policing of people and spaces, so there have been major developments in the policing of information flows themselves.[12] Ironically, perhaps, our endeavours to understand security networks mirror those facing intelligence analysts when they map criminal or terrorist networks. For all of us, providing structural maps is a complex but essential prerequisite to attempts to explain how networks operate and why. Drawing a map is the relatively easy part – what is much harder is moving

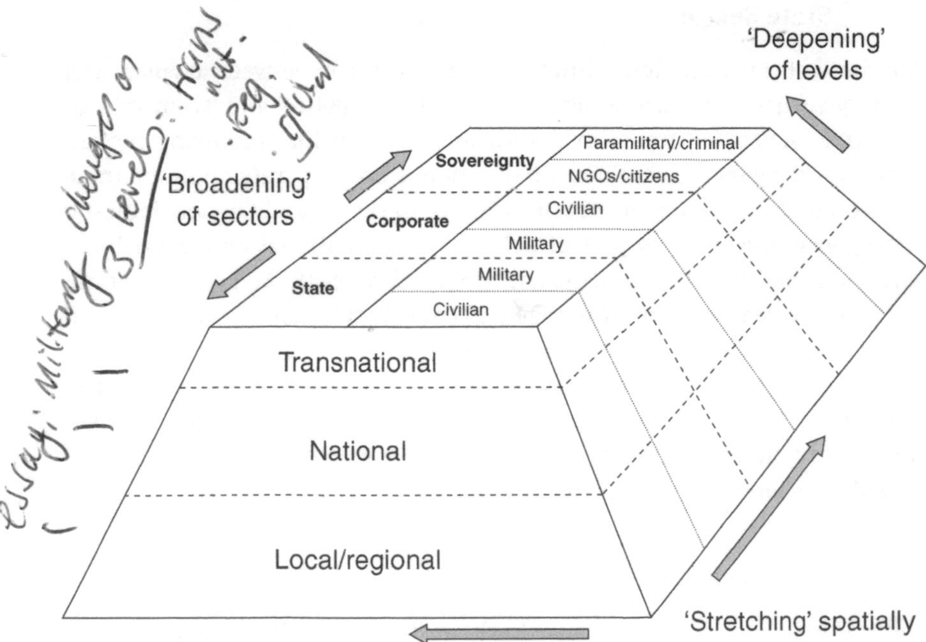

Source: Adapted from Gill, 'Not just joining the dots', p. 29

Figure 3.1 *Security intelligence networks*

beyond metaphor to analyse the extent to which the network structure is an independent variable distinct from simply the actions of individual actors.[13] As Jean-Paul Brodeur has pointed out, public and private police agencies generally go about their business in relative ignorance of each other and outsourcing is not synonymous with networking.[14]

Globalization – the process that describes the current territory for policing and security intelligence – has had a profound impact on intelligence agencies, including what they are expected to do and how they can do it in the face of much-altered perceptions of threat, the communications revolution and shifting perceptions of how the agencies should operate.[15] It manifests itself along three dimensions: a 'deepening' of levels so that there is increased interaction between local and transnational developments; second, a 'broadening' of sectors that are involved in governance; and, third, spatial 'stretching' so that developments in one part of the globe can have immediate and worldwide impact.[16] Contemporary security networks operate within and across all three dimensions, but it is the second on which we concentrate.

The three main sectors identified in figure 3.1 coincide with the organizational models discussed above: the state (organized in bureaucratic hierarchies), corporate security (competing in markets) and non-state, non-corporate sovereignties. There are, of course, subdivisions within each of these sectors.

State Sector

The most obvious division within the state sector is between civilian and military agencies, the former usually divided into 'police' and 'security' and the latter into the separate services. Various patterns for organizing civilian security intelligence exist: the main question is how separate domestic intelligence should be from mainstream policing. In the US and Canada domestic intelligence developed as part of policing at the national or federal level, with both the FBI and Royal Canadian Mounted Police (RCMP) having special sections devoted to counterintelligence, counter-subversion and so on. UK police also developed 'special branches' with similar functions, but the main internal security agency since 1909 has been MI5. However, the police/security distinction has become more blurred recently because of the police's own embrace of 'intelligence-led policing' and deployment of techniques of surveillance long used by security intelligence.

Police intelligence

Police intelligence developed only slowly in the UK: specific criminal intelligence squads were established first in London after the Second World War and by the mid-1970s all forces and their constituent divisions had some criminal intelligence capacity, though it was often poorly developed. Regional criminal intelligence offices were created in 1978 to complement the work of the regional crime squads, and in the 1990s the National Criminal Intelligence Service (NCIS) was formed from the merger of police regional offices, Customs personnel and civilian analysts. Also in the early 1990s, arguably when faced with the discrediting of then current crime control policies, the notion of 'intelligence-led policing' was promulgated with the intention of intelligence techniques being applied not just to organized but also to volume crime. To reinforce this, a National Intelligence Model was published in 2000.[17] NCIS was superseded by a Serious Organized Crime Agency (SOCA) in 2005, which, in turn, is to be replaced by a National Crime Agency in 2013. In the US it is not always easy to disentangle the development of police intelligence aimed at 'political subversion' from that aimed at 'rackets' or organized crime: in the main urban centres anti-radical 'Red Squads' were established in the wake of the 'red scare' of 1919–20, and during the 1950s squads targeting 'organized crime' were established. The similarities derived from the common ideological pedigree; that is, threats of subversion, corruption and organized crime were believed to emanate from ethnic and foreign conspiracies that required special powers for covert investigation.[18]

Police intelligence with a more specifically political and security emphasis started earlier in the UK with the establishment of Special Branch in the London Metropolitan Police in 1883 in response to Irish Republican bombings, but it was the 1960s before all forces formed their own special branches. Their key feature in the UK is that, while they are part of their parent police force in terms of budget, recruitment and direction, their day-to-day activities are determined largely independently from other policing objectives and mainly by current Security Service priorities. Branches vary widely in size: in general they are largest in those forces with significant ports (especially those serving Ireland, since the port units were responsible for the surveillance of travellers to and from Britain) while in many forces they are quite small. Their official functions are summarized in guidelines issued by the Home Office, first published in 1984 when controversies around the activities of special branch officers at the time of the miners' strike and the peace movement prompted the House of Commons Home Affairs Committee to conduct the first parliamentary inquiry. Updated since, these guidelines identify the role of the branches as 'primarily to acquire intelligence' both to meet local policing needs and to assist MI5 and MI6 in their role of protecting national security.[19] The mandate now refers mainly to counterterrorism, although branches used also to have a role in assessing threats to public order.

In the wake of the 1992 decision that MI5 would take over from the Metropolitan Police the lead role in countering Irish Republican terrorism in Britain, and of the Provisional Irish Republican Army (PIRA) ceasefires later in the 1990s, it appeared that there would be a move to integrate special branches more thoroughly into criminal investigation divisions, but any moves in this direction did not survive 9/11. A review of special branches conducted by Her

Majesty's Inspectorate of Constabulary (HMIC) in 2002 confirmed the semi-detached status of special branches in terms of the security requirements of their work, and the continuing significance of MI5 in providing training and co-ordination.[20] Following publication of this report the government announced, as part of a broader paper on counterterrorism powers, that it was establishing a specific post to oversee national co-ordination of special branches and regional special branch intelligence cells.[21] Further spurred by the 7/7 bombings in London, the Metropolitan police merged the Anti-Terrorist Branch and Special Branch to create a new Counter Terrorism Command (CTC) that acts as the lead national police counterterrorism agency in co-ordinating the work of local police and liaison with MI5 and foreign police forces.

CTC also manages the National Co-ordinator for Domestic Extremism (NCDE), which is made up of three units: a National Public Order Intelligence Unit that seeks to develop countrywide intelligence and maintain a database; a National Domestic Extremism team who co-ordinate investigations and operations; and a National Extremism Tactical Coordination Unit who advise companies and other organizations on countermeasures. In essence 'domestic extremism' is the new 'subversion' – a concept which, while never a crime in the UK, provided the umbrella under which surveillance of many people was conducted during the Cold War.[22] According to the Association of Chief Police Officers (ACPO): 'The term is generally used to describe the activity of individuals or groups carrying out criminal acts of direct action to further their protest campaign. These people and activities usually seek to prevent something from happening or to change legislation or domestic policy, but attempt to do so outside the normal democratic process.'[23] However, as with subversion before it, much of the surveillance is of people who may act 'outside the normal democratic process' in the eyes of police but still are committing no crime. Particular controversy erupted in the UK in January 2011 with the revelation that at least four undercover police officers had infiltrated environmental protest groups in Britain and may well have acted as *agents provocateurs* (see further discussion in chapter 6).

Domestic security intelligence

The size of MI5 increased significantly during the two twentieth-century world wars and reduced between them. The onset of the Cold War meant that MI5 remained nearer the wartime level and from the 1970s onwards the number of personnel was around 2,000, of whom about one in six were case officers and analysts, with the rest technical and administrative. It was not until 1989 that a statutory mandate was passed. This was prompted by a series of events including media allegations of MI5 malpractice, revelations of Cold War spies such as Anthony Blunt, and the government's failed attempt to prevent the publication of *Spycatcher*, written by Peter Wright, a former MI5 Deputy Director. Finally, there was the realization in Whitehall that a case pending before the European Court of Human Rights (ECtHR) concerning the surveillance of people working at the (then) NCCL was almost certain to succeed in the light of developing jurisprudence that intrusive surveillance must be authorized by legislation and citizens must have a mechanism for the redress of grievances against security agencies.[24]

In the 1989 Security Service Act, the function of MI5 is described as:

> the protection of national security and, in particular, its protection against threats from espionage, terrorism and sabotage, from the activities of agents of foreign powers and from actions intended to undermine parliamentary democracy by political, industrial or violent means. It shall also be the function of the Service to safeguard the economic well-being of the United Kingdom against threats posed by the actions or intentions of persons outside the British Islands.[25]

In 1996 'support of the prevention and detection of serious crime' was added.

As a consequence of the greater openness regarding security intelligence matters in the 1990s, we now have more official information regarding the allocation of resources to different areas of the mandate: in 1993 the first public announcement and press conference of a new Director General of MI5 – Stella Rimington – was followed by the publication of a corporate brochure that was updated in 1996 and 1998. Now, the information is updated regularly on the website: www.mi5.gov.uk. While reading table 3.1, it needs to be remembered that about 10 per cent of MI5's budget is consumed by protective security advice to government and private firms who are either engaged in

Table 3.1 UK security service: major areas of work (%)

Area	1990/1[a]	1995/6[a]	1998/9[b]	2002/3[c]	2004/5[d]	2009/10[e]
Counter-espionage	50.0	–	24.4	14.6	11.5	3.3
(and) counter-proliferation	–	(25.0)	4.2	4.5	2.3	1.1
Counterterrorism	37.5	72.0	63.1	68.5	77.0	95.6
International	*20.0*	*33.0*	*26.8*	*37.1*	*50.6*	*79.3*
Irish (and other domestic)	*17.5*	*39.0*	*36.3*	*31.5*	*26.4*	*16.3*
Counter-subversion	12.5	3.0	–	–	–	–
Serious crime	–	–	8.3	9.0	4.6	–
Emerging threats	–	–	–	3.4	4.6	<0.5

Counter-proliferation first appeared in 1995/6 and was combined with counter-espionage.

Source: [a] *MI5 The Security Service*, 2nd edn (London: HMSO, 1996), p. 17
[b] www.mi5.gov.uk, accessed 22 May 2001
[c] www.mi5.gov.uk accessed 19 June 2003
[d] www.mi5.gov.uk accessed 25 June 2005
[e] https://www.mi5.gov.uk/output/major-areas-of-work.html, accessed 16 June 2011

security and defence contracting and/or perceived to be otherwise vulnerable. The figures in the table have been adapted to take that into account.

Even as the Cold War drew to a close, in 1990/1 counter-espionage was still the main target and counter-subversion – as with special branches, the most controversial part of the mandate – was still a significant activity. In 1995/6 counter-espionage was counted with counter-proliferation as part of the new discourse of post-Cold War threats. Counter-subversion had almost disappeared while resources devoted to counterterrorism had doubled, reflecting the fact that MI5 had taken over lead responsibility for Irish Republican terrorism in 1992. In 1998/9 counterterrorism work had declined somewhat as a result of the ceasefire in Northern Ireland. Work supporting NCIS and the police with respect to organized crime featured for the first time after the 1996 addition to the mandate. Since 9/11 there has been a significant increase in resources allocated to international terrorism, and in 2004 the Home Secretary announced that MI5 was to increase by 50 per cent over the next three years.[26] This would be rapid growth for any organization to absorb in so short a time; for one in which recruitment procedures are particularly lengthy because of vetting requirements, it represented a major challenge. Furthermore, there was clear tension between the need for rapid recruitment of, say, linguists, on the one hand, and the risk of the organization being infiltrated by those it was targeting, on the other. By 2010 MI5 was almost entirely a counterterrorist agency.[27]

In the US, as a law enforcement agency, the FBI has always struggled to face in several different directions. Director J. Edgar Hoover's development of domestic political intelligence programmes from the 1930s onwards led to massive scandal after his death and the Bureau reoriented towards white-collar and organized crime in the 1970s, though it retained responsibility for counterintelligence.[28] In May 2001, despite some rhetoric about the importance of counterterrorism, FBI budget allocations reflected concerns with gun crime, drugs trafficking and civil rights.[29] In the wake of 9/11 fundamental criticisms were made of the Bureau; mainly that, as an agency that saw its primary goal as making cases against people who might then be prosecuted, it was simply unsuited to intelligence work aimed at the prevention of terrorist attacks. Other criticisms made of the Bureau were of its chronically inadequate ICT and inability to conduct all source analysis.[30]

The Bureau was apparently in the grip of sclerosis in which following agreed procedures took priority over imaginative investigative work, to the extent that, it was argued, possible chances to prevent the 9/11 attacks were lost. For example, Zacarias Moussaoui, possibly the 'twentieth hijacker', was detained as a visa over-stayer in Minneapolis in August 2001 after suspicions arose as to his behaviour at a flight school. FBI agents wanted to search his laptop computer but FBI headquarters ruled that there was insufficient 'probable cause' to apply to the US Attorney's Office in Minneapolis for a warrant. In order to obtain a warrant under the Foreign Intelligence Surveillance Act, the FBI would have needed to show that Moussaoui was an 'agent of a foreign power'. Relevant information was sought in London and Paris but substantial disagreement remained between Minneapolis agents and FBI headquarters: accusations from the latter that the former were exaggerating the threat reportedly brought the comment from a Minneapolis agent that he was 'trying to keep someone from taking a plane and crashing into the World Trade Center'. DCI George Tenet was briefed on Moussaoui in August but drew no connection between him and the other increased threat reporting during the summer of 2001.[31] This, and other examples, has been used as a reason for dismantling the so-called 'wall' erected between law enforcement and intelligence gathering after the Hoover-era abuses exposed in the 1970s but, arguably, the problem was less an issue of the inappropriateness of legal standards to counterterrorism and more one of over-bureaucratization of decision-making procedures.[32] Rapidly dismantling these protections in the wake of 9/11 runs the risk that history repeats itself – the FBI concentrates surveillance on people whose politics may be in opposition to US policy and/or specific Middle Eastern regimes but who pose no *security* threat. There have been regular allegations that precisely this is occurring; for example, the Justice Department's Inspector General has investigated reports that the Bureau was monitoring anti-war and environmental organizations only on the basis of their exercise of first amendment rights. The Inspector General's report in September 2010 absolved the Bureau of this charge but criticized it for starting investigations on weak factual predicates, continuing investigations longer than necessary and retaining information inappropriately.[33]

Interestingly, similar criticisms that police agencies are unsuited to security intelligence work were made by the McDonald Commission in Canada when it investigated wrongdoing by the RCMP and provided the basis on which the civilian CSIS was created.[34] The issue of whether the US should follow the same path has certainly been on the agenda but the 9/11 Commission recommended against it.[35] However, although efforts were under way to refocus the FBI away from 'law enforcement' and towards counterterrorism, including redeploying CIA personnel to advise the Bureau on establishing its new Office of Intelligence,[36] the process has been fraught: seven people headed counterterrorism in the five years after 9/11 and, although the number of analysts and linguists increased as resources were shifted from crime and corruption investigations, the emphasis remained on preparing cases for prosecution rather than developing preventive intelligence.[37] The tension remains between the US desire to pursue a vigorous intelligence and military 'war' against terrorism and the FBI's position as a rule-governed law enforcement agency in a country deeply suspicious of 'political policing'. A major successful home-grown attack in the US could well be the trigger for the creation of a US-style CSIS or MI5.

The FBI is formally located within the Justice Department, which also contains the Drug Enforcement Administration (DEA) – another agency much involved in intelligence. Four of the other five national civilian intelligence agencies are located in, respectively, the Energy Department (covering, for example, nuclear proliferation); the Bureau of Intelligence and Research (INR) in the State Department, which draws on classified diplomatic reporting; the Treasury Department (covering *inter alia* taxation and money laundering); and the CIA. The newest kid on the US domestic intelligence block is the Department of Homeland Security (DHS), established in the wake of 9/11. The language with which it was launched suggested the DHS would have a major intelligence role, but no existing agencies were subject to reorganization and it became essentially a consumer rather than a producer of intelligence. A number of the departments incorporated into the DHS – Coast Guard, Customs, Immigration and Naturalization – had their own intelligence collection divisions but the new arrangements did not really address the problem of intelligence sharing identified by the 9/11 Commission. Much of the DHS's own work involves the mining of large databases of travellers and trade (see further below, pp. 96–7) as well as disseminating what it receives at the federal level to states and localities. Such risk assessments cover areas beyond terrorism – though the DHS performed very badly in the face of Hurricane Katrina – and elements of an intelligence 'cycle' can be seen in their work, but it is doubtful that it is useful to see the DHS as a whole as an 'intelligence agency'.[38]

Foreign intelligence

As we showed in chapter 1, in the popular imagination, intelligence work centres on foreign intelligence agencies conducting espionage and covert operations against real or imagined enemies. Academic work, too, has concentrated on this aspect as intelligence has been seen as part of the IR story, and therefore it is hardly surprising that probably the best-known intelligence agencies in the world are the US CIA,[39] MI6 in the UK[40] and the Soviet KGB.[41] The main difference between the agencies is that the last of them conducted both foreign and domestic intelligence and was the central element of what John Dziak called the Soviet 'counterintelligence' state.[42] Although both the CIA and MI6 have on occasions become involved in their respective domestic politics, these were of an entirely different order to the ubiquity of the KGB in Soviet life and, perhaps, the role of its Russian successor, the Federal Security Service (FSB).[43]

The CIA was established by the National Security Act 1947 as the successor to the wartime Office of Strategic Services (OSS). Originally intended as an agency primarily for the collection and analysis of foreign intelligence, it quickly developed two main functions: one for analysis and the other for covert operations. It is the latter that is mainly responsible for the agency's reputation – for good or ill – as the agency was in the forefront of US postwar policy to contain communism behind the Iron Curtain. The agency was embroiled in all the accompanying political controversies in Central and South America – including the abortive invasion of Cuba in 1961 at the Bay of Pigs, subsequent attempts to assassinate Fidel Castro with Mafia assistance,[44] and the successful attempt to destabilize the elected government of Chile in 1973 that led to the killing of President Salvador Allende and the installation of the Pinochet dictatorship.

More recently, it was the analytical side of the agency that fell into disrepute as its estimates of Iraqi WMD turned out to be entirely inaccurate (as discussed in chapter 7).[45] By comparison, MI6 managed to remain within the shadows, at least until 2003. Indeed, until 1992 its existence outside of wartime was not even officially acknowledged by the government. In a more relaxed government environment after the fall of Margaret Thatcher, with the end of the Cold War and encouraged by the fact that the sky had not fallen in when the Security Service Act 1989 was passed, the government under John Major passed the Intelligence Services Act 1994 (ISA), which provided statutory mandates for both the Secret Intelligence Service (SIS) and its SIGINT partner, GCHQ (see further below) and also established the Intelligence and Security Committee (ISC) to oversee the agencies. (The ISC is discussed in chapter 8.) However, the ISA presaged no heady rush into the sunlight by MI6 – it was October 2005 before it launched its own website, available in French, Spanish, Russian, Chinese and Arabic as well as English, incorporating brief information on the agency's role, relevant legislation, available careers and a potted history (www.sis.gov.uk). This has since been upgraded to include a 'virtual tour' and a more 'corporate' presentation but does not yet include a special section for children as does the CIA (www.cia.gov). Up to a point, CIA and MI6 self-descriptions are analogous: they both gather information with respect to threats to national interest and conduct operations to pre-empt or disrupt these threats. Where they differ is in the role of analysis. The CIA describes this as one of its three missions whereas MI6 refers to the recruitment of three main Operational Officer roles: case officers for agent-running, targeting officers and reports officers. The last two clearly do involve analytical skills, but not specifying analysis reflects the different US and UK systems for the production of national-level assessments that we discuss below.

Signals intelligence agencies

Complementing the domestic and foreign intelligence agencies in those countries wealthy enough to afford the major investment involved are what are usually referred to as SIGINT agencies. The US NSA[46] and GCHQ[47] both have offensive and defensive functions: the first is the interception of the communications of others (states, armies, companies, etc.) and the second is 'information assurance' – protecting the state's own communications from interception and disruption by others (www.nsa.gov; www.gchq.gov.uk). Historically, they have developed out of code-breaking efforts in wartime, and ng the Cold War represented the cutting edge of technological developts in cryptography. Partly for this reason, at least until the 1980s they ceeded in remaining even less visible than their domestic intelligence and foreign human intelligence (HUMINT) equivalents: 'No Such Agency' was the NSA's nickname in the US. Whereas during the Cold War the agencies had one central target – Soviet military capabilities – they have now been enlisted into the surveillance of other, more mobile, security threats: terrorism, proliferation and organized crime; for example, Scott Ritter, the former UN weapons inspector in Iraq, has provided a fascinating account of how SIGINT was deployed to counter Iraqi deception.[48] The current counterterrorism context symbolizes the increasing merger of foreign and domestic intelligence as, for example, GCHQ is as much involved in Bradford and Birmingham as in Kabul and Kandahar.[49] The sheer volume of communication potentially overloads the ability of the agencies to process information, despite developing sophisticated tools for selecting messages of interest, while digitization, fibre optics and commercial encryption make interception harder. Governments attempt to ameliorate this problem by gathering and storing everything they can gather – an issue we discuss more fully in the next chapter.

Military intelligence

Formally, military intelligence is concerned with the conduct of tactical and strategic intelligence in support of military operations. The more broadly these are defined the more likely it is that military intelligence will spill over into the surveillance of civil society and political life. Military agencies have the broadest functions in regimes that could be characterized as 'national security states' (see chapter 1) and have been involved in the surveillance of their own civilians as much as, if not more than, potential foreign enemies. In the early 1980s internal security surveillance was still the main task of military intelligence agencies in a number of Latin American and Eastern European regimes, but it has also been carried out in democratic regimes – for example, illegal operations carried out in the US by the army in the guise of counterintelligence.[50] Since the 1980s one aspect of the democratization of intelligence in former authoritarian regimes has been to replace military with civilian agencies, for example, in Brazil.[51] Currently, there is concern that, to the extent that fears of terrorism are defined as a 'War on Terror', there is a risk of military agencies again becoming too significant in civil society.[52]

In the US after 9/11 a Counterintelligence Field Office was set up in the Defense Department to gather information in the US, contrary to a longstanding ban on domestic operations by the Pentagon. After controversies aroused by its monitoring of anti-war groups, the Office was disbanded in 2008 while some of its functions were transferred to the Defense Intelligence Agency (DIA).[53] Another consequence of 9/11 was that the Pentagon became much more assertive in gathering HUMINT abroad, an area of work that was traditionally the job of the CIA. While this could be justified in war zones such as Afghanistan and Iraq on the grounds of providing intelligence to troops, the establishment of Military Support Teams in many embassies indicated some broader militarization of foreign policy.[54] Another indicator of this is the rapid growth of the Joint Special Operations Command (JSOC), which has as many as 25,000 members with their own intelligence division, drones, reconnaissance planes and even satellites. Deployed primarily in Afghanistan and Iraq – but also elsewhere – for killing al-Qaeda operatives, it is also estimated to have imprisoned and interrogated ten times as many suspected terrorists as the CIA. Currently it also assists US domestic agencies in their work with the Mexican government on drug and border issues.[55]

In the UK and US, state military intelligence is basically organized within each service plus some mechanism for joint assessments; in the UK, for example, the Defence Intelligence Staff (DIS) provides a central assessment process for military intelligence. In the US the parameters of organization are similar but complicated by the sheer size and extreme fragmentation of the military and intelligence establishment. There are nine national intelligence organizations within the Defense Department, including one for each of the four Services; the DIA, which both runs military espionage agents and provides assessments, like the DIS in the UK; the National Reconnaissance Office (NRO), with responsibility for spy satellites; and the National Geospatial-Intelligence Agency (NGA), which interprets satellite imagery and prepares world maps.

The latest kid on the US military intelligence block is Cyber Command, established in May 2010 and increasingly duplicated elsewhere; for example, Iran announced the founding of its cyber-command in June 2011.[56] As with SIGINT before it, the objective in the US is both to defend military information networks and to conduct military operations, both cyber and forceful, in order to try to ensure freedom of action for the US and allies.[57]

Central security and intelligence assessments

One of the paradoxes facing those countries wealthy enough to maintain a variety of different intelligence agencies collecting information by different technical and human methods is how to make sense of the masses of information and possible competing analyses that result. For example, both India and Japan[58] have a JIC modelled to some extent on that of the UK (see below) while in the US the National Intelligence Council (NIC) is a small group of analysts, some drawn from outside government, who prepare National Intelligence Estimates (NIEs) from the combined efforts of all the agencies.[59]

In the UK the collection agencies send their product both directly to customers (if they believe it important enough) and to the JIC structure in the Cabinet Office.[60] This represents the main instrument for determining collection priorities and providing a national assessment of what is gathered. The JIC consists of the heads of the three intelligence agencies (MI5, MI6 and GCHQ), the head of defence and intelligence at the Foreign Office, the chair of DIS, and senior representatives from the Ministries of Defence and of Trade and Industry, the Treasury and the Home Office. Other departments attend the weekly meetings when necessary.

Insight into the workings of the JIC and its assessment staff was provided by witnesses to the Hutton Inquiry and the reports of the ISC and Butler inquiries. The then chair of the JIC, John Scarlett, described the basic JIC process to Lord Hutton: 'raw intelligence' is issued by the collection agencies together with their evaluation to customers in the policy departments and to relevant JIC assessment staff. The actual work programme for staff is set by an interdepartmental group chaired by the chief of the assessment staff responding to requests from policy departments. An initial draft of an assessment is prepared by the relevant staff officer based on her or his own expertise and contacts in Whitehall. This is circulated to interested parties for comments and then goes before a formal meeting of an interdepartmental Current Intelligence Group (CIG). Chaired by a deputy head of assessment staff, this group agrees a new draft for recirculation and, after any further changes, presentation to a full meeting of the JIC. After any further changes that JIC 'almost always' makes, the approved assessment is circulated. As well as the text that seeks to answer the questions raised by the sponsors, the assessment includes a section for 'key judgements' in which the JIC states its formal view on the central questions posed within the broader context of other JIC assessments, open sources and so on.[61] One consequence of the Butler Report's conclusions regarding the perceived failure of intelligence over Iraq was the appointment of a Professional Head of Intelligence Analysis whose role was to enhance the quality of analysis through developing capabilities, methodology and training. This role is now performed by the chair of the JIC.[62]

Immediately after 9/11 a Counter-Terrorist Analysis Centre (CTAC) was established, staffed mainly by MI5.[63] Review of these arrangements was still under way when the Bali bombing occurred in October 2002 and provided further rationale for a Joint Terrorism Analysis Centre (JTAC), which started operating in June 2003. This had more staff from agencies other than MI5: mainly from MI6, GCHQ and DIS but with others from the Foreign and Commonwealth Office, Home Office, police, Cabinet Office, Office of Nuclear Safety and Department of Transport Security Division (TRANSEC). JTAC sought to overcome the problems of information sharing in the normal fashion of 'task forces' by ensuring that each representative had access to their home agency's database. JTAC does provide trend reports but its main focus is setting threat levels and issuing warnings.[64]

The structure for national security and intelligence policymaking in the UK was given a significant overhaul by the coalition Conservative–Liberal Democrat government formed in May 2010. At the apex is a National Security Council (NSC) of ministers that meets weekly and is attended by the heads of intelligence agencies if necessary. The NSC has a Committee for Threats,

Hazards, Resilience and Contingencies whose remit includes intelligence policy and performance. This committee approves intelligence requirements and priorities as developed by the JIC.[65]

There have been problems with the co-ordination of both intelligence and security assessments in the UK, but compared with those in the US they are nothing. The central structural flaw at the heart of the US intelligence structure was the designation of the CIA Director as also the DCI with the role of co-ordinating intelligence. But the DCI was never able to 'co-ordinate' the Department of Defense (DoD), which controls the lion's share – about 80 per cent – of the US intelligence budget, and is institutionally bound to see the main function of intelligence as support for the military. This flaw was exposed by both the 9/11 and Silberman-Robb commissions (see further discussion in chapter 7). Following their recommendations,[66] the Intelligence Reform and Terrorist Prevention Act 2004 established an Office of the Director of National Intelligence (ODNI) with greater formal authority over the fifteen intelligence agencies. But the DNI still faces the problem of having no control over the Pentagon, and none of the first three directors served more than two years. Although there have been some improvements in co-ordination, such as agencies recognizing each other's 'badges', there remain competing views on whether the ODNI has achieved much or whether it has just added an extra layer to an already congested federal intelligence architecture.[67]

Like JTAC in the UK, the NCTC was established in the US in 2003 as a 'fusion centre' providing all-source analysis of terrorist threats. The NCTC has 500 personnel drawn from sixteen departments and tasks collection and analysis by other intelligence community agencies and networks. But it is difficult see how these changes have reduced the possibilities for confusion. The NCTC, CIA and DIA now all have analytical responsibilities regarding international terrorism while the FBI's Counterterrorism Division and Homeland Security share analytical work for domestic terrorism. On top of this, of course, is the myriad of interagency groups and other 'fusion centres' (see below) seeking to co-ordinate across the broader and highly fragmented law enforcement community at federal, state and local levels.[68]

Corporate Sector

In the corporate sector there is a wide range of security providers.[69] These are divided into civilian (or security) and military in figure 3.1 since some companies are fairly clearly one or the other but others operate within both sectors. The distinction between private security companies (PSCs) and private military companies (PMCs) is less significant than it was in the 1990s but reflects, respectively, primarily defensive or offensive roles, even if they merge in conflict zones.[70] Not only does private sector security provision have a very long history but, more importantly, it has been for the direct benefit of states as well as corporate clients. Pinkerton, for example, provided not just 'low policing' functions of guarding corporate clients but also 'high policing' surveillance of labour activists and intelligence activities on behalf of the government during the US Civil War.[71] There is now an extensive literature on private security in general,[72] but less on the extent to which 'intelligence' is a specific part of these activities.[73]

Corporate security tends either to be organized in specialist departments or provided by outside contractors. The security sector has seen a wave of mergers and acquisitions in recent years; for example, in July 2004 Securicor and Group 4 merged as G4S, whose joint turnover in 2010 was £7.4 billion. Both groups were best known for their provision of technical security systems and guarding and patrolling services but they offer a very wide variety of technologies, consultancy and personnel, all of which incorporate elements of security intelligence, to government and business in 120 countries.[74] Securitas, founded in Sweden in 1934, embarked on an aggressive acquisition policy in the 1990s, taking over well-known firms such as Burns International and Pinkerton. The main services offered by Securitas are specialized guarding, mobile security services, monitoring, consulting and investigation.[75] Pinkerton still offers more specialist investigation and intelligence services, including undercover operations and covert surveillance, to both the public and private sectors in the context of risk assessments, fraud investigation, due diligence and so on.[76]

Military Professional Resources Inc. (MPRI) was founded in 1987 by eight retired military officers and is engaged primarily in military contracting but with law enforcement expertise also. In 2000 it was acquired by the L-3 Communications Corporation, a major US defence contractor. MPRI is not large in terms of number of employees – 5,000 – but draws its workforce on a contracting basis from a database of more than 40,000 former military and other personnel.[77] It was involved in south-eastern Europe in training both the Bosnian and the Croatian armies and is generally credited with carrying out, at one remove, the US policy of neutralizing the Serb military in the mid-1990s.[78] Control Risks Group, founded in 1975, appears to bridge the civilian and military sectors, offering government and corporate clients a range of services including political and security risk analysis, investigations, pre-employment screening, crisis management and information security. Political and security risk analysis offers 'a bespoke service' for investors on emerging markets, country risk forecasts and travel advice. Business intelligence offers due diligence investigations into potential partners and forensic accounting.[79]

In the post-9/11 world, perhaps the most high-profile of these security sector organizations has been Blackwater.[80] This company was founded in 1997, although its work for the US government only began to expand after 9/11. In 2001 it had federal government contracts worth US$737,000, but by 2006 this had shot up to a figure of US$593.6 million, giving a total value of federal government contracts of over US$1 billion for the 2001–6 period.[81] The spur to this was the company's involvement in Iraq, beginning with Coalition

Provisional Authority Administrator Paul Bremer's August 2003 decision to award Blackwater a no-bid contract to protect US officials. By 2006, Blackwater was authorized to have in excess of 1,000 staff in Iraq. However, its role was often controversial, partly reflecting the legal grey area in which it operated. Blackwater personnel were regularly killed, and at times shot at Iraqis with little apparent discrimination.[82] The WikiLeaks revelations suggested that rather than make Iraq safer, the extensive use of PSCs was actually adding to the insecurity. For example, the *New York Times* recounted one episode from March 2005 in which:

> a small battle erupted involving three separate security companies. At a notoriously dangerous checkpoint on the main road to the Baghdad airport, a cement truck entered a lane reserved for Department of Defense vehicles. A guard from Global, a British company, fired a warning shot, and when a man initially identified as an Iraqi opened the door and tried to flee, guards from a tower started firing, too. The man dropped to the ground. Then members of an Iraqi private security team parked nearby also opened fire, shooting through the chest not the driver but a worker from DynCorp International, an American security company. When the truck driver was finally questioned, he turned out to be a Filipino named José who worked with yet a third company, KBR, the American logistics and security giant. The conclusion drawn from this chaos was, 'IT IS BELIEVED THE DRIVER ENTERED THE DOD LANE BY ACCIDENT.'[83]

In the wake of serial controversies, in 2009 it was announced that Blackwater was changing its name to Xe Services LLC. It continued to work closely with the CIA in Afghanistan and Iraq (so closely that Blackwater personnel reportedly took part in rendition flights and elsewhere loaded missiles onto Predator drones prior to their operation), to the extent that the boundary between providing security for CIA missions and being a partner in them became blurred. As one former CIA officer put it: 'There was a feeling that Blackwater eventually became an extension of the agency.'[84] The line separating defensive security from offensive partnership was all the more easy to cross given the high degree of secrecy that attached to these operations.

The only country for which we have a systematic overview of this sector is the US. According to Tim Shorrock, by 2006 about 70 per cent of the estimated US$60 billion spent by the government on foreign and domestic intelligence was outsourced to contractors. He identifies four main periods of development: the privatization revolution that started during the Reagan administration but reached fruition under Clinton; the leap in defence outsourcing in the late 1990s; the surge in intelligence spending negotiated by then DCI George Tenet at the turn of the century after a decade of cuts; and the post-9/11 expansion. Technological innovation was a key element in this as commercial developments in encryption, ICT etc. outpaced government innovations and coincided with the post-1991 downsizing. Thus, by the turn of the century, Shorrock argues, the institutional memory of the US intelligence community resided in the private sector.[85] We shall consider the implications of this for democratic control in chapter 8.

'Sovereignty' Sector

Outside of the state and corporate sectors in what is often referred to as 'civil society', there are many organizations which gather information as they seek to wield influence or power. The US Federation of Scientists provides a very useful resource for research into intelligence, including an index of almost 400 'para-states', some nice but mainly nasty, which would qualify under our heading of 'sovereignties'.[86] Of course, not all of these will be implicitly or explicitly 'para-states' inasmuch as they are challenging the legitimacy of the state. For example, some NGOs need to be included since they have a crucial presence in areas of insecurity and carry out their work in conjunction with state agencies. Personnel involved in aid, migration or peacekeeping functions may well find themselves, knowingly or unknowingly, part of security intelligence networks. Individuals and voluntary groups are involved in local security networks in various ways; for example, 'gated' communities – either horizontal on private estates or vertical in apartment blocks – may buy in the services of a private contractor or establish watch schemes to mobilize collective community resources. From a different perspective, Deibert identifies the development of citizen intelligence networks from the merging of NGOs, activists and computer hackers.[87] Communities based on family, clan, tribe or shared cultural beliefs and practices may also provide the basis for organizing security.

The issue of citizens deploying self-defence can be quite controversial – witness the debate in the UK as to just how much violence householders should be permitted to use on intruders – but there is less ambiguity when it comes to individuals involving themselves in information gathering. For example, Crimestoppers, in both the UK and the US, is an innovation by which individuals who provide information anonymously leading to an arrest or conviction may be paid a reward, funded by the private sector.[88] After 9/11 US Attorney General John Ashcroft sought to introduce a programme called TIPS whereby millions of American workers would involve themselves in reporting suspicious behaviour or people, but the scheme foundered on a wave of opposition. Yet some still envisage a much wider role for citizens than merely that of self-defence. Robert Steele argues vigorously for a 'citizen-centred intelligence' on the grounds that the public – the 'intelligence minutemen of the twenty-first century' – can only rely on themselves, not on elites, to protect their interests.[89] Some people apparently need little encouragement: it is estimated that about forty citizen militias voluntarily patrol US borders with Mexico and Canada.[90]

Finally, we need to acknowledge the place of illegal organizations. These may be paramilitary groups, criminal organizations, liberation movements or some mixture of all three. Their 'intelligence' activities will be more or less formal depending on circumstances and their size, but are likely to include targeting and surveillance as well as basic counterintelligence measures against infiltration by undercover police or informers.

Cross-Sectoral Networks

Networks might develop within and/or between any of these three dimensions. States or corporations will often appear to be the 'dominant node' or partner in a security network but Johnston suggests that, in general, the most productive view to take is of 'a changing morphology of governance in which partly fragmented states interact with commercial, civil and voluntary bodies both within and across national jurisdictional boundaries'.[91] Similarly, Deibert identifies 'transnational networks of citizen activists weaving in and around the traditional structures of state interaction'.[92] Security companies and NGOs themselves maintain intelligence capacities in network form as they operate globally and within specific nations and localities, that is, as a form of multi-level governance. The development of 'local security networks' between agencies both public and private and citizen groups[93] provide clear examples of cross-sectoral networks, and other examples can be found at regional, national and transnational level. Some 'networks' may be little more than a euphemism for state police and security officials also acting as 'corporate' or 'citizen' vigilantes. For example, up to 200 Italian police and former intelligence officials were under investigation in 2005 having set up a private security firm called the Department for Anti-Terrorist Strategic Studies, specializing in counterterrorism. Allegedly, they maintained their own weaponry and accessed Ministry of Interior databases.[94]

Illegal sovereignties may, on occasion, be involved in networks with legal organizations, for example, if state agencies wish to 'subcontract' illegal operations because of the risks they run if exposed. This may involve just information gathering but, far more controversially, state agencies might subcontract *covert action*; for example, the use by the CIA of organized crime to attempt to assassinate Castro in the 1960s, the deployment of 'death squads' by authoritarian regimes in several Latin American countries[95] and the 'collusion' between British intelligence and loyalist paramilitaries in the assassination of Republicans in Northern Ireland (see chapter 5). At different times any of these may be agents of state intelligence and therefore be part of a broader network of security governance.[96] More broadly still, the very social and insurgent movements against which state agencies deploy may actually be created by the actions and inactions of state and corporate powers – if not directly, then in the sense that those movements are reacting to the impact of the conditions created or sustained by the powerful.[97]

Clearly there must be some shared interest in order to bring the actors into the network in the first place. It is not difficult to identify the interest shared by many western states and corporate security providers, summed up as it is by the neo-liberal preference for market provision of security (along with all other services) subject to steering by states. The clearest example of this is post-9/11 when, according to Shorrock, the ideology of an intelligence–industrial complex was born from a blend of patriotism, national chauvinism, fear of the unknown and old-fashioned war-profiteering.[98] Harold Greenberg notes that there are 30,000 companies with DHS contracts and some of these, such as the failed border security programme SBInet, have led to nothing more than 'expensive boondoggles'.[99] But the actual nature of relationships must be subject to empirical validation and conflicts may occur between nodes within networks. These will arise for a variety of reasons. Within the state sector, for example, agencies have different mandates and objectives that sometimes overlap but sometimes do not; corporations may agree to some joint project but they are also in a competitive relationship. Conflicts will be resolved depending on the relative power of the actors; in some cases they may lead to some restructuring of the network.[100]

In all of this we must not forget the impact on security networks of those who are their objects; as we have seen, groups who are the primary targets of security may, under certain conditions, become part of the network. Similarly, the way in which targets react to attempts at information gathering and repressive action may have an impact not just on specific operations but also on the form of the network as it has to adjust further.[101] This is a particular manifestation of the point we made in chapter 2 – that resistance is an integral part of intelligence.

But conflict within networks is not the only reason they are far from 'seamless' – to the great frustration of authorities and practitioners. The organizational boundaries between intelligence agencies (represented in figure 3.1 as dotted or broken lines between sectors and levels) interrupt the flow of information; although borders may be transformed or blurred they will remain, even if redefined. Also, the traditional 'border maintenance' conducted by hierarchies ensures the ubiquity of 'bureaucratic politics' and will remain a structural barrier to network flexibility. But as well as being blocked at the borders, information may just locate in voids where no agency has an immediate interest or adequate resources to analyse or otherwise deal with it.[102] The sheer quantity of security data within information systems far outstrips their capacity to analyse it. Therefore a more accurate image of figure 3.1 would be as an 'exploded' diagram that incorporates both the borders between agencies operating in whatever sector, level or space and the voids into which information 'disappears' (figure 3.2).

Making Security Intelligence Networks Work

There are many issues raised by the rapid development of security networks, both formal and informal: the final section of this chapter concentrates on their management. Within state hierarchies, management is essentially by means of implementing rules and procedures appropriate to the level of responsibility. While this has never been entirely adequate to explain policing and security organizations where discretion is a highly significant feature of the work, networks are even more fluid – that is precisely their strength. Kickert and Koppenjaan suggest that network management has two main

Source: Gill, 'Not just joining the dots', p. 35

Figure 3.2 *Borders and voids*

features: 'game management' and 'network structuring'.[103] Game management includes:

- activating networks in order to address a particular problem and arranging for the interaction of those actors who can help (activation);
- bringing together otherwise disparate actors, problems and solutions (brokerage); and
- creating the conditions for favourable developments (facilitation).

We can identify a number of recent developments in security intelligence that illustrate these activities – all of them present to some degree before 9/11, but accelerated thereafter. Although the budgets and personnel of state agencies have been significantly increased since 9/11, a combination of neoliberal governance and perception of a range of asymmetrical threats across a wide variety of locations has brought into play increased public–private–community co-operation.

However, barriers to information sharing and operational co-operation are an inevitable by-product of specialization within state hierarchies and are aggravated in intelligence work by the high premium placed on source protection and a general reluctance to pool 'sensitive' information.[104] For example, Eliza Manningham-Buller, MI5 Director General, speaking after the July 2005 bombings in London, said:

> we have a very strong interest in international co-operation, in all similar services having both the full legal powers to collect intelligence and the skill and experience to handle it carefully but if we splash it around carelessly we shall soon have none of it. So I could never agree to a compulsory exchange of intelligence as that would risk compromising valuable sources of intelligence. There would soon be little to exchange.[105]

Thus it is no surprise that European and US officials all complain of the reluctance of the other to share,[106] though we should note that the UK has always considered itself to be more of a transatlantic intelligence partner than a European one.

The main form of 'brokerage' to be found in the intelligence community – before and since 9/11 – has been 'fusion centres' or 'task forces'. Representatives from several agencies are brought together, such as JTAC and NCTC, each with access to their home agency's database, so that they can combine the analytical resources of otherwise separate agencies on a targeted problem or person by overcoming the incompatibility of different databases or privacy restrictions on the sharing of information. The Belgian intelligence oversight committee conducted a survey of EU countries in 2009 which indicated that only about half had a fusion centre, although most had some weekly JIC-like 'co-ordinating committee' for intelligence assessments.[107] In terms of figure 3.2, these centres and liaison officers act as 'bridges' across voids and may provide partial solutions.[108]

Apart from breaking down the borders between agencies,[109] post-9/11 attempts at facilitating networks have addressed technological and political issues regarding access to and combining information in both public and private sectors.[110] Not only have extra powers for technical collection been sought but also, throughout the US and Europe, agencies are seeking improved access to electronic data collected by others. However, access to specific databases is one thing; bringing together multiple databases is another. The 'big idea' since 9/11 is the 'mining' of 'data warehouses' constructed by linking public and private databases. This has been made technically possible by XML (Extended Markup Language) software that enables previously separate databases to be 'merged' via a universal language, and mining 'involves the use of sophisticated data analysis tools to discover previously unknown, valid patterns and relationships in large data sets'.[111]

Some of the examples being considered in the security field are truly awesome: inspired by the conclusion that in the period before 9/11 there was a failure within the US intelligence and law enforcement communities to 'join the dots' between items of information already in the system, major efforts are under way to seek solutions. For example, in a report commended by the 9/11 Commission, the Markle Foundation proposes a Systemwide Homeland Analysis and Resource Exchange (SHARE) Network that will enable information sharing by federal, state, local government and private sector users.[112] Subsequently, the DHS funded a study carried out by the US National Research Council which noted the undoubted success of automated data mining in commercial settings, such as in detecting fraud, but concluded that it was neither feasible nor desirable for the identification of terrorists. The study also argued that behavioural observation and physiological monitoring should only be used to identify individuals for follow-up checks because of the risk of false positives and vulnerability to countermeasures.[113]

A number of factors condition the ability to manage networks: first, diversity – the higher this is the more likely that management will only be possible at a distance (and the diversity of the US intelligence network is extremely high). Second, intelligence networks are self-referential systems. As a consequence of secrecy, the networks are harder to manage except to the extent that their self-regulatory capacity can be utilized. Self-regulation is a characteristic of 'professions' and, as controversies around intelligence assessments of Iraqi WMD show, professionalism among analysts is much needed as an essential (but not necessarily successful) counterweight to 'politicization'. But such 'self-regulation' can also operate negatively; for example, it might sustain 'groupthink' (see discussion in chapter 5). Third, how extensive are the conflicts or convergence of interest? Beyond the simplistic rhetoric of 'all being on the same side', different agencies have varied legal mandates and, given their extensive discretion to identify priorities, may well have even more varied short- to medium-term organizational goals.

Fourth, what is the political and social context within which the network operates and is there the political will and skill to manage in the desired direction? A high profile for the 'problem' in politics and the media will increase the pressure on organizations to commit the resources required for collaboration and, where different legal frameworks are in existence, action might be taken by the agency operating within the most permissive legal context. Fifth, management is facilitated if previous contacts have produced a desire to reciprocate. Eliza Manningham-Buller's comments above show why people do not like passing on information obtained possibly at high cost because of the unpredictable consequences of losing control over it, or they may just fear someone else getting the credit for an operation. Security concerns may be real or exaggerated but they will increase the more extensive the network over which the information will be dispersed. Recalling the discussion of the relationship between knowledge and power in chapter 2, sharing knowledge may be perceived as relinquishing power. Sixth, given broad mandates and limited budgets, the costs of an operation (whether aimed at 'intelligence' or an investigation) will be a prime consideration. The more specific and credible information is, the more likely it is to lead to commitment of additional resources. The greater the complexity of a case in terms of jurisdictions and agencies involved, the more likely it is that a formal agreement will need to be negotiated between the contributing agencies, identifying who will do what.

If problems cannot be 'managed' within existing organizational frameworks then it may be necessary to restructure networks, and we have already discussed some examples of that. The 'misfit' between the structure of the US intelligence network and the task of preventing terrorist attack was clear to many well before 9/11.[114] The Bush Administration perceived that some institutional restructuring was required, and the DHS is one result. Even at the time it was hard to see how this would succeed beyond the level of symbolic politics because, for example, the constituent agencies' varying mandates would prevent them from becoming simply the counterterrorist intelligence clearinghouse that some desired. The enterprise appears driven by a belief in the possibilities for hierarchical co-ordination rather than the creative possibilities of networks. But even this restructuring affects only the national level;

by comparison the regional and local law enforcement community is positively atomistic. Quite how are the approximately 18,000 law enforcement agencies at federal, state, local and tribal levels to get their act together?[115] The task is immense: bearing in mind that a significant number of these agencies are one- or two-person strong, it defies comprehension.

Network structuring also takes place transnationally: in Europe, for example, the Berne Group was formed in 1971 by six European internal security agencies and now includes seventeen, the newest member being Greece. Following 9/11 the Berne Group created a new organization called the Counterterrorist Group (CTG) with a wider membership of EU intelligence and security services plus the US, Switzerland and Norway. CTG is mainly concerned with threat assessments regarding Islamic terrorism and since the Madrid bombings of 2004 has been playing a major role in implementing intelligence-related aspects of the European Council's Declaration on Combating Terrorism. In 1994 the Middle Europe Conference was set up at the suggestion of the Dutch and assisted the preparation for accession to the EU of ten new countries in 2004.[116] Part of the reason for the rapid growth of the corporate sector is that large PSCs are themselves transnational networks and thus provide a degree of flexibility unavailable to state agencies still operating within the confines of national sovereignty.[117]

Conclusion

We have shown that there is a wide range of 'actors' now involved in the intelligence business and that not all of these are in the state sector that has been the traditional focus of IS, as we discussed in chapter 1. However, although state agencies remain very important, a combination of the neo-liberal desire of US and UK governments to control the size of the public sector and the post-9/11 security panic have provided much space that is being occupied readily by PSCs. Citizens too have been mobilized. Security intelligence networks develop partly organically, as security officials and agents make relationships with people who can help them with information, and partly by design, as states, in particular, acknowledge their information-dependence on others. In both cases, however, key issues of oversight and accountability arise: just as, since the late 1980s, we have started to tackle the problem of controlling state intelligence agencies, the explosion of security networks poses us the even more difficult problem of controlling networks – not unlike nailing jelly to the wall. We return to this in chapter 8.

CHAPTER FOUR

How Do They Gather Information?

Introduction

In this chapter we look at the different methods agencies use to acquire the information that forms the basis of intelligence, and at the issues that arise from developing the knowledge component of surveillance. This stage – collection – is by far the most expensive of the intelligence cycle. As former CIA Deputy Director of Intelligence Ray Cline argued in 1976:

> There is no way to be on top of intelligence problems unless you collect much more extensively than any cost-accounting approach would justify . . . You might think you could do without most of what is collected; but in intelligence, in fact, as in ore-mining, there is no way to get at the nuggets without taking the whole ore-bearing compound.[1]

This challenges the notion of the 'cycle' since it seems to exclude the first stage of targeting, and the technologies available in the 1970s would have been less able to collect 'everything' than technologies are now. Nevertheless, this does hint at the sheer scale of collection; the persistent fear that something vital might be missed haunts intelligence, though the inability to analyse all that is collected probably accounts for more failures, as we shall see in chapter 7.

The methods used to acquire information can be placed in four broad categories. (The main methods are depicted in figure 4.1.) First, agencies mine open source or publicly available material (OSINT) such as speeches, official documents, and information published in newspapers, magazines and on the Internet. A second category straddles the open–secret divide. For many years security and intelligence agencies have sought access to citizens' personal records as a means of establishing identities or whereabouts. This would often occur unofficially with the astute intelligence officer having trusted contacts in the relevant department.[2] However, the ICT revolution and e-government have transformed the potential for constructing a virtual picture of someone's life from the masses of electronic data in both the state and corporate sectors – what David Omand has christened PROTINT (protected information).[3]

The other two categories use covert collection methods for information that targets seek to keep secret. HUMINT is obtained by the use of agents or informers, kidnapping and interrogation. TECHINT is simply an umbrella term covering all the technical means of gathering information that are commonly grouped under various disciplines, including SIGINT, that is, information derived from

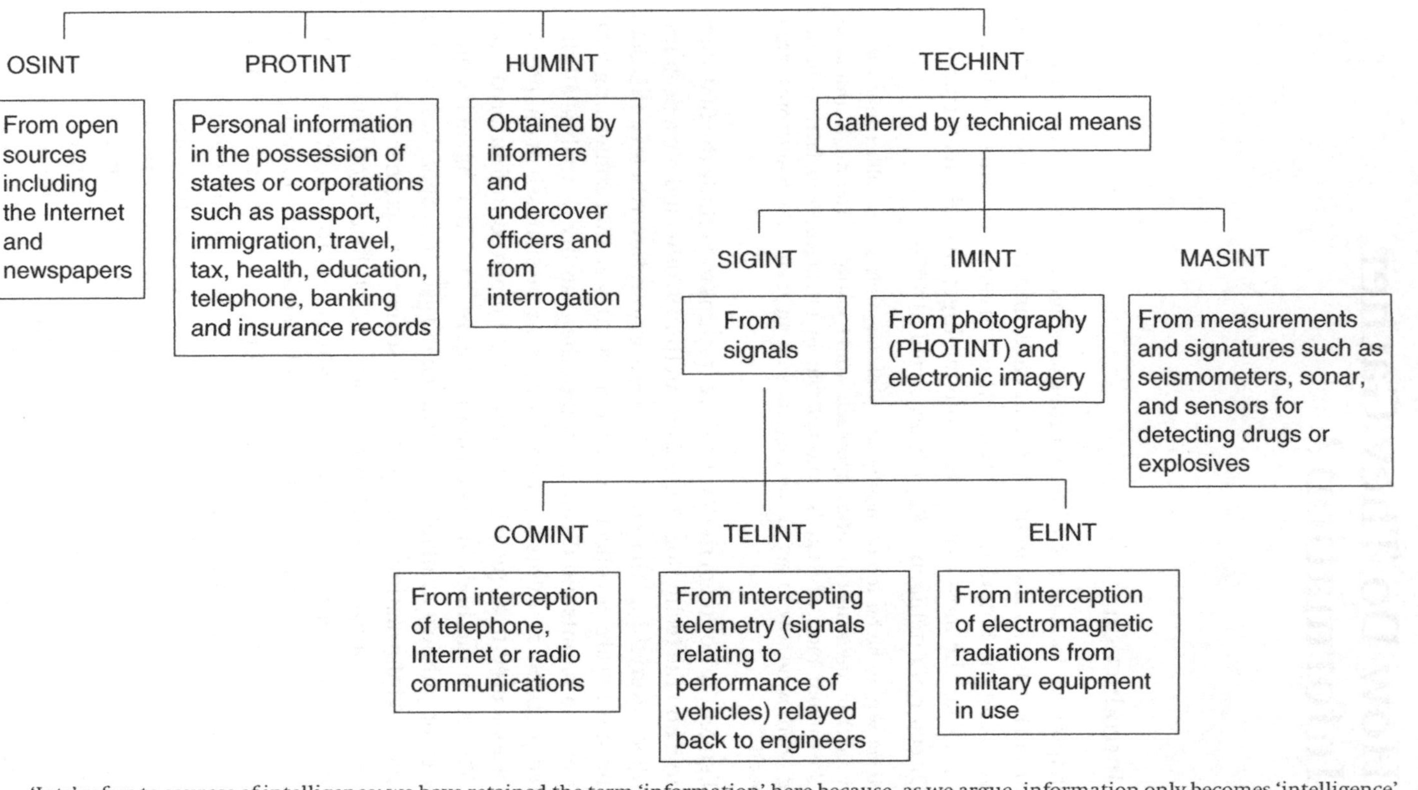

'Ints' refers to sources of intelligence; we have retained the term 'information' here because, as we argue, information only becomes 'intelligence' after analysis.

Figure 4.1 *Sources of information (the 'ints')*

intercepting communications and other electronic signals; IMINT (imagery intelligence), including satellite photography; and MASINT (measurements and signatures intelligence), which derives from sensing devices.

Priorities, Planning and Direction

In figures 1.1 and 1.2 we identified the first stage of the intelligence process as 'planning and direction', sometimes referred to as targeting. Whatever the precise terminology used in different countries and agencies, the point is the same: while there are unimaginable quantities of information potentially available about all manner of threats to the wellbeing of states, corporations and communities, only limited resources are available to intelligence agencies. Therefore, despite Ray Cline's observation, some organizational process is required to allocate priorities for information gathering and analysis. In the UK, for example, the JIC determines the intelligence 'requirements' that define the priorities for MI6 and GCHQ while MI5 has determined its own domestic security priorities. Thus, in general, priorities for targeting may be determined by the agencies themselves or be provided for them by governments. Historically, many agencies would determine their own targets in part because ministers preferred not to know what they were doing, though often there were close informal relationships between agencies and governments. It is now acknowledged that this posed several dangers, for example, that agencies might become 'states within a state' or act as 'rogue elephants'. In response, the new wave of democratization has seen a general shift towards greater ministerial control.[4] Of course, this also involves dangers, specifically that ministers may try to use agencies for the surveillance of political opponents rather than genuine security threats. Hence, in Canada, for example, the 1984 reforms that established the civilian CSIS provided for ministerial directions to the Service, but also provided for independent oversight of those directions to safeguard against political abuse.

Targeting can be seen to take place at different levels: ministers and government committees may lay down broad requirements, but the details of intelligence operations are determined at agency level or, in the case of networks, by some joint mechanism. For example, in Northern Ireland from the late 1970s onwards greater efforts were made to co-ordinate the activities of military, police and MI5 operations in an environment that had earlier been characterized as an 'intelligence war' between different agencies. Tasking and Co-ordinating Groups (TCGs) were established, a practice that has subsequently spread into mainstream police intelligence in the UK.[5]

OSINT: Open Source Intelligence

Traditionally, a large proportion of intelligence material has derived from open sources. Writing in 1970, Harry Howe Ransom estimated that '80 per cent or more of intelligence material in peacetime is overtly collected from nonsecret sources such as newspapers, libraries, radio broadcasts, business and industrial reports, or from accredited foreign service officers.'[6] In the post-Cold War period, this figure may well have risen to over 90 per cent.[7] It is worth noting that the Flood Report into Australia's intelligence agencies emphasized the role played by open source material in the Australian intelligence process, advising that:

> Information from open and diplomatic sources is significantly less expensive to collect than is covert intelligence. Public sources also contain much of the key information required by government analysts. For reasons of principle and practicality, open and diplomatic sources should be exploited fully before information is sought from secret intelligence. Intelligence agencies are therefore the information collectors of last resort. But some information cannot be obtained from open sources or diplomatic reporting.[8]

However, volume should not necessarily be equated with significance. With regard to the US, while, 'overt collection provides the bulk of information gathered by the CIA, covert HUMINT and technical collection often unearth the most important knowledge for decision making'.[9] Nevertheless, as the concept of 'all-source intelligence' suggests, it would be wrong to see the debate over the relative significance of open vs. secret sources as being based on some kind of zero-sum equation. The reality is that both sources can be combined to produce the most effective analyses, as the example in box 4.1 indicates.

Domestic security intelligence also makes extensive use of open source

Box 4.1 Open vs. secret sources: the case of Burundi

During its investigation into US intelligence activities in 1995, the Aspin-Brown Commission explored the relative value of open and clandestine reporting by looking at both sources with respect to events unfolding in Burundi. The Commission asked the firm Open Source Solutions to explore the open side, drawing on the resources of such private information companies as Jane's Information Group, Lexis-Nexis, and Oxford Analytica. The open sources performed well, providing a brief, accurate history of the tribal conflict between the Hutu and Tutsi factions, and detailed order-of-battle statistics and descriptions of weapons in the Burundian inventory. However, contrary to some reports, the US intelligence community shined as well. The CIA generated up-to-date information on the growing political polarization in the country and the high likelihood that violence would soon erupt. The CIA also presented comprehensive data on regional ethnic population patterns, illustrated with impressive four-color maps, along with facts on Burundi's acquisition of arms in the international marketplace. The information provided by Jane's Information Group on the characteristics of weapons in Burundi proved richer than the CIA's profiles, but the CIA offered better insights into the evolving humanitarian crisis in Burundi, the attitudes of leaders in surrounding nations, and the need for the United States to begin preparing for the evacuation of US and European nationals. The open and clandestine sources each revealed pieces of the Burundian jigsaw puzzle; when joined together, the picture became much clearer.

Source: Loch K. Johnson, 'Spies', *Foreign Policy*, Sept.–Oct. (2000), pp. 22–3

materials, for example, monitoring newspapers and websites produced by target groups and attending their public meetings. The importance of the Internet in cases of post-9/11 radicalization, and the fact that it can facilitate rapid radicalization, have been recognized by intelligence agencies.[10] Hence, the Internet has become a particular target for both extremists and intelligence agencies. Moving beyond monitoring target groups to infiltrating them involves moving beyond simple surveillance and engaging in action – a transition that we explain in chapter 6 in terms of the intensification of surveillance.

PROTINT: Protected Information

Information about all of us exists in passport, immigration, travel, tax, health, education, telephone, banking and insurance records held by states and corporations, and will be accessed early in the collection process because it is cheaper and more readily available than information gathered by covert methods. One technique commonly deployed, for example, is using telephone 'metering' records of calls to and from any number in order to construct networks of contacts based on the frequency and duration of calls. The advantage for agencies is that accessing these does not require the warrant that would be required actually to intercept the conversations, but, on the other hand, no information is collected as to the precise nature of the conversation. However, the analytical power of such techniques is leveraged greatly when individual databases are combined into data 'warehouses' so that phone records can be linked with, for example, travel, banking and accommodation. The construction of these warehouses is a primary example of public–private networking and raises questions in relation to data protection and individual privacy as well as whether they provide for effective analysis – an issue we consider further below and in chapter 5. One contemporary development which is already having a somewhat curious but significant impact for police and security agencies seeking to establish people's whereabouts is the popularity of social networking. If people want to tell the world about themselves on Facebook then it seems that concerns with personal privacy are not as great as they once were!

HUMINT: Human Intelligence

HUMINT comes in a variety of forms. First, at the state and corporate level, it comes from the employees of an organization. The 2010 WikiLeaks release of US diplomatic cables revealed a State Department cable on US reporting and collection needs with regard to the UN which told of how: 'The intelligence community relies on State reporting officers for much of the biographical information collected worldwide. Informal biographic reporting via email and other means is vital to the community's collection efforts.' It went on to advise that:

> Reporting officers should include as much of the following information as possible when they have information relating to persons linked to: office and organizational titles; names, position titles and other information on business cards; numbers of telephones, cell phones, pagers and faxes; compendia of contact information, such as telephone directories (in compact disc or electronic format if available) and e-mail listings; internet and intranet 'handles', internet e-mail addresses, web site identification-URLs; credit card account numbers; frequent flyer account numbers; work schedules, and other relevant biographical information.[11]

Defectors and 'walk-ins' provided some of the most important sources of intelligence during the Cold War contest, and their stories and contributions are well documented.[12] Recruiting members from and undercover infiltration of target groups have been a staple of domestic surveillance operations. Political opponents and exiles are another source of information, although a significant degree of risk attaches to these sources because of their vested interests and questionable motivation. A range of agents can be co-opted or bought. For example, businesspeople who frequently travel to target countries and/or work in fields of particular interest, such as the arms trade, can be recruited to provide what are termed 'holiday snaps'. Michael Herman has suggested  a hierarchy of intelligence value by HUMINT source, beginning with casual travellers and experts and ascending through refugees, business contacts, occasional secret informants, political opponents and exiles, defectors and agents/informers in place. However, this does not take full account of the possible political agenda of defectors, or of cases where, because of the limitations on other types of intelligence, businesspeople may provide a highly valuable entrée, as with Iraq in the 1980s.[13]

Where recruiting agents involves an initial approach from an overseas intelligence agency, patriotism is less likely to be a factor, although ethnic or religious identity can play a strong role, as with Israel's Mossad.[14] During the Cold War, of course, ideology played a significant role, although agent-runners tended to dislike working with ideologically motivated agents and preferred those, like Aldrich Ames, who were motivated by money and a sense that they 'didn't see any harm' in what they were doing.[15] Such relationships are inherently corrupt and corrupting because they are based on a combination of deception and financial inducement. Former CIA officer Miles Copeland offered the following advice in relation to agent-running:

> 1. Buy the man, not his information.
> 2. It's the regularity and dependability of the pay that matters, not the amount.
> 3. Supplement the agent's income from regular sources enough to ease his financial worries, but not enough to cause him to make basic alterations in his life-style.
> 4. Pay no bonuses in connection with specific acts. Give the agent only rewards that will make him think in terms of consistent performance rather than individual 'coups'.[16]

As a former CIA station chief in Jordan put it:

> You have to understand what makes a guy tick and how to manipulate him . . . What are his problems – his wife, girlfriend, boss, money? You become the friend he doesn't have.

> You feed his ego. You agree that his boss is unfair. Then you plant a seed. Perhaps he needs money for private school for his kids. You say, 'I can help.' The process of recruitment can take years. It's not overly complicated. It's all about manipulating people, gaining their trust, finding out what makes them tick, and using them to get the information we want.[17]

A different approach was that most associated with the East German Stasi, of utilizing a 'Romeo' network to exploit vulnerable women, usually secretaries, in a position to pass on useful information. 'Romeo' agents would research their target thoroughly before making contact, identifying the area of vulnerability:

> Perhaps she had been left by her boyfriend, or her mother had recently died, or she didn't have many friends. When the Romeo approached her, he already knew everything about her – her likes and dislikes, her history. One woman told me that the agent who approached her knew that she was interested in the environment, and after two days he was calling her his 'little herb witch'. So they got to the point pretty quickly.[18]

When working overseas, intelligence officers adopt 'cover' to conceal their true identity and allow them to penetrate an organization or use it as an entrée into target groups. This kind of cover is termed 'non-official cover' (NOC); for example, working within multinational companies that allow for routine travel and a range of opportunities to recruit agents or gather information.[19] Another form of cover is 'official cover', where intelligence officers act as diplomats attached to an overseas embassy. A third kind is 'notional cover', which can involve the establishment of false identities, cover stories, front companies etc. that are mission-specific and unlikely to withstand sustained scrutiny.[20]

The case of the United Nations Special Commission (UNSCOM) weapons inspection teams in Iraq during the 1990s represents a classic example of intelligence infiltration. Given the problems associated with generating reliable intelligence about Iraq after the 1991 war, this should come as no surprise. Former MI6 officer Richard Tomlinson has recounted how he was offered 'an undercover slot with the UN weapon inspection teams in Iraq' while working for MI6.[21] US intelligence agents spied on Iraq under UNSCOM cover for three years.[22] The context in which they did so was one of divergent agendas – UNSCOM's focused on disarming Iraq, the CIA seeing disarmament as part of a wider strategy of removing Saddam. As UNSCOM inspector Rod Godfrey recalled: 'It did become clear to me throughout 1997 and 1998 that there were people associated with the mission who had functions which were not explained to the rest of us . . . People would travel in with us and travel out with us but nobody ever explained quite what they were doing with the mission.'[23] According to Scott Ritter, US intelligence did not share all of the information collected under the cover of, and ostensibly to aid, UNSCOM:

> In the end the United States took over the whole programme, UNSCOM wasn't in control of anything. We didn't know what was being collected, we didn't know how much was

Box 4.2 Illegals

Upon completion of their training, Russian illegal agents are generally provided with new – false – identities; an illegal's false identity is referred to as his 'legend'. The cornerstones of an illegal's 'legend' are false documents. These false documents concern, among other things, the identity and citizenship of the illegal. Through the use of these fraudulent documents, illegals assume identities as citizens or legal residents of the countries to which they are deployed, including the United States. Illegals will sometimes pursue degrees at target-country universities, obtain employment, and join relevant professional associations; these activities deepen an illegal's 'legend'. Illegals often operate in pairs – being placed together by Moscow Center while in Russia, so that they can live together and work together in a host country, under the guise of a married couple. Illegals who are placed together and co-habit in the country to which they are assigned will often have children together; this further deepens an illegal's 'legend'.

Source: Maria L. Ricci, FBI Special Agent, in *United States of America v. Christopher R. Metsos, Richard Murphy, Cynthia Murphy, Donald Howard Heathfield, Tracey Lee Ann Foley, Michael Zottoli, Patricia Mills, Juan Lazaro and Vicky Pelaez*, Southern District of New York, 25 June 2010, p. 5, www.justice.gov/opa/documents/062810complaint2.pdf, accessed 19 December 2011

> being collected, when it was being collected. We had no control over the process. That shows the corruption of the operation. It became a United States operation, not a United Nations operation.[24]

As one aide put it, Kofi Annan had 'become aware of the fact that UNSCOM directly facilitated the creation of an intelligence collection system for the United States in violation of its mandate. The United Nations cannot be party to an operation to overthrow one of its member states.'[25] Iraqi diplomats, who in private had admitted that they had little or no evidence to justify their repeated claims that UNSCOM was a front for US spying, were reportedly delighted at this public relations disaster for UNSCOM.[26]

Evidence that state efforts to penetrate target states via the use of 'deep cover' agents – so-called 'illegals'[27] – had not completely died out with the end of the Cold War came in June 2010, with the arrest of an eleven-strong Russian spy ring in the US (see box 4.2).

Their purpose was spelt out in a 2009 message sent to Richard and Cynthia Murphy (in reality, Vladimir and Lidiya Guryev) from Moscow Center: 'You were sent to the USA for long-term service trip. Your education, bank accounts, car, house etc. – all these serve one goal: fulfill your main mission, i.e. to search and develop ties in policymaking circles in US and send intels.'[28] The methods by which they sought to communicate this information with Moscow combined the modern – steganography and the use of radiograms – with the more traditional – the use of the 'brush-pass' to hand over data and meetings where the identification of fellow illegals would be confirmed by the use of a planned exchange of conversation ('Excuse me, did we meet in Bangkok in April last year? Reply: I don't know about April, but I was in Thailand in May of that year'[29]). How successful this operation was seems very much open to question. The FBI had identified at least some of the ring by as early as 2001, and placed them under surveillance. Tellingly, the eleven were not charged with espionage, but with lesser offences of failing to register as agents of a foreign government and conspiracy to commit money laundering. The amount of time the ring was left in place after discovery suggests that, in place, they were of greater use to US intelligence than to Russian intelligence. Nevertheless, all were regarded as heroes on their return to Russia, where one – Anna Chapman – achieved a degree of celebrity with her own television series, *Mysteries of the World with Anna Chapman*.

The volume and quality of HUMINT on any given target can be limited by a number of factors. Where there is limited bilateral contact with the target state, the cover provided for collecting intelligence via or under cover of government contacts, diplomatic missions, cultural and educational exchange programmes etc. is also limited. During the Cold War and in the context of the post-9/11 security environment, the most highly prioritized targets have also been the ones that have presented the greatest problems of physical access, meaning that the CIA 'traditionally performed poorly in human operations against the United States's most ardent adversaries'.[30] For relatively isolated target states whose nationals were not as free to travel overseas, sporting exchanges have offered important opportunities. Whenever East German football teams, usually containing a significant number of Stasi informants, played games elsewhere in Europe, it offered an opportunity to gather information.[31] Olympic Games could provide cover for a range of espionage activities.[32]

Where the target state is a relatively closed society and internal travel opportunities are limited, even if defectors appear, their useful knowledge may be severely limited. As noted above, where defectors appear to have knowledge in areas of particular interest, the intelligence they provide may be inaccurate and motivated by a desire to further a particular agenda, by the prospect of financial gain, or both. Unfamiliarity with the language(s) of the target state can represent a further barrier, as with post-2003 Iraq. In March 2005, the *Economist* claimed that: 'About half of all the CIA's case-officers are in Baghdad. But with only a handful of them fluent in Arabic, they are mostly confined to the green zone, condemned to interview Iraqi interpreters and watch endless episodes of *Sex and the City* on DVD.'[33] (However, reversing a language deficit by rapid recruitment heightens a risk of infiltration.[34]) A history of mutual antipathy between the states in question may serve to hamper recruitment of local informants, while the ethnic composition of target groups may create barriers to infiltration. As a former CIA operative explained with regard to infiltrating Islamic fundamentalist groups:

> The CIA probably doesn't have a single truly qualified Arabic-speaking officer of Middle Eastern background who can play a believable Muslim fundamentalist who would volunteer to spend years of his life with shitty food and no women in the mountains of Afghanistan. For Christ's sake, most case officers live in the suburbs of Virginia. We don't do that kind of thing.[35]

In situations where HUMINT is either sparse or unobtainable there could also be a heightened dependence on intelligence shared through the kind of network discussed in the previous chapter. In some cases these are based on a high degree of trust between long-term allies but under the pressure of events such as 9/11 the home agency may only have limited confidence in the partner, or may have a high degree of confidence which proves to have been misplaced.[36] In addition, co-operation with geographically important states may result in the imposition of restrictions on the scope of operations, as with the US experience of seeking approval to fly the Predator surveillance drone over Pakistani airspace in the hunt for the al-Qaeda leadership.[37] This search has also thrown up the problem of intelligence operatives working undetected in a friendly country, 'a country that we're not at war with, if you will, a country that maybe has ungoverned spaces, or a country that is tacitly allowing some kind of threatening activity to go on'.[38] This problem was well illustrated by the case of Raymond Davis, who, in Lahore in January 2011, shot dead two Pakistani men who were following the car he was travelling in. Davis, a former member of the US Army Special Forces and Blackwater employee, was part of a covert CIA operation undertaking surveillance of militant groups such as Lashkar-e-Taiba, widely considered to have links to Pakistan's ISI intelligence service. As one senior ISI official complained in the aftermath: 'We need to be treated with trust, equality and respect as the allies that we are, and not satellites. We have asked that [the CIA] work with us and not behind us, and yes, we have asked that we be informed of who else is there [for the CIA] and doing what.'[39] From the perspective of the CIA, however, Pakistan was not an ally to be trusted with intelligence or operational plans, a point reinforced by the circumstances surrounding the killing of Osama bin Laden just weeks later.

The use of informants within a target organization or community or the undercover infiltration of a target organization or community are also commonly associated with domestic surveillance. In the wake of the 7/7 London bombings the dearth of information coming from Asian communities in the UK made its development a police and MI5 priority, although this seems to have represented a difficult challenge. This may in part be a consequence of the methods employed – for example, the practice of using stop and search powers to detain people before attempting to persuade them to act as informers (see box 4.3).

Even prior to the events of 9/11 and 7/7, both during and after the Cold War, the definition of subversion used in the UK and enshrined in the 1989 Security Services Act (actions 'intended to overthrow or undermine parliamentary democracy by political, industrial or violent means') meant that the domestic surveillance net was cast wide, encompassing far left and far right groups, trade unions, civil liberties groups and student leaders. Growing concern about the potential for disorder from left-wing groups in the wake of the 1968 anti-Vietnam War demonstrations in London led Special Branch to set up the Special Demonstration Squad. Otherwise known as the 'hairies', this

Box 4.3 Recruiting informers from UK Muslim communities

Just after landing at Edinburgh airport on 11 April 2010 Asif Ashmed was met by plainclothes officers and taken away from his wife . . . He was taken to a room by two officers who told him they were from special branch, a police department that deals in intelligence and security matters. Ahmed, 28, was told he was being questioned under schedule 7 of the Terrorism Act 2000. When he asked why, an officer replied: 'No reason, it is just a random stop.' Ahmed told them that they had stopped the only two people on the flight who looked like Muslims. They said they did not know he was Muslim, which he did not believe . . . [O]ne of the officers asked if he would become a spy: 'They asked if I would like to work with special branch, to keep an eye on the Muslim community in Edinburgh . . . They asked me three times. They said do it covertly.' He refused.

Source: Vikram Dodd, 'They asked me to be a spy, to keep an eye on the Muslim community in Edinburgh', *Guardian*, 24 May 2011

was a group of officers who would grow long hair and beards, cut themselves off from family and close friends, assume new identities in the manner of the *Day of the Jackal* graveyard search, study and master the necessary Marxist (or other appropriate) language and positions on key issues, infiltrate left-wing groups on behalf of the state, and report back to Special Branch or MI5.[40] As with the above examples, such infiltration was based on a deception deemed necessary and therefore legitimated by the state, leaving former colleagues feeling betrayed when the true identity of the informer was exposed. As one of those involved, Special Branch Officer Tony Robinson, reflected: 'I suppose the whole business of being a Special Branch Officer in many instances is based on lies, on deception or you can't do your job.'[41] The business of infiltration also took a toll on the agents involved. Former MI5 officer David Shayler recalls a debriefing with a Special Branch officer who had infiltrated the anarchist group Class War:

> When I met M2589 in February 1992, at a safe house in London, it was quite obvious that this peculiar arrangement had affected the agent psychologically. After around four years of pretending to be an anarchist, he had clearly become one. To use the service jargon, he had gone native. He drank about six cans of Special Brew during the debrief, and regaled us with stories about beating up uniformed officers as part of his 'cover'. Partly as a result, he was 'terminated' after the 1992 General Election.[42]

The question of agent-running was brought powerfully to the fore in the context of Irish Republican terrorism with the 2003 unmasking of the long-rumoured British agent at the heart of the PIRA, codenamed Stakeknife, run by military intelligence's Force Research Unit (FRU). Following just one month after the death of Brian Nelson, himself a FRU agent who operated within the Protestant paramilitary Ulster Defence Association (UDA),[43] the identification of the deputy head of PIRA internal security (the 'nutting squad'), Alfredo Scappaticci, as a British agent raised a number of ethical questions. As one of the PIRA's chief 'mole-hunters', his recruitment was similar to, but more significant than, the Soviet recruitment of Aldrich Ames, and was even likened to a situation where British intelligence had been able to run Reinhard Heydrich during his time as head of the Reich security service.[44] Nevertheless, Stakeknife's PIRA role involved the regular torture and disposal of suspected informers. The dilemma, as outlined by former FRU handler Martin Ingram, was that 'Stakeknife produced high-grade intelligence, much of it read at the highest levels of the political and security establishments. He was, without doubt, the jewel in the crown. The problem was, Stakeknife could only shine if he immersed himself in the activities of those he was reporting upon, including murder and other illegal acts.'[45] Could any of these lives have been saved? How many of these were actually informers – that is, agents operating for other British intelligence agencies? Did the FRU let these other intelligence agencies know of Scappaticci's recruitment? How many were innocent? These questions themselves raised even more fundamental ones. How much is intelligence worth? What price should the state pay to secure it? This ethical dilemma is heightened by the suspicion that, according to Ingram, Scappaticci may have killed another FRU agent in his internal security role,[46] and that Brian Nelson was tasked by the FRU to identify an innocent man – Francis Notarantonio – to be murdered by the UDA in 1987 in order to divert loyalist attention from Scappaticci as a possible 'double agent', thereby protecting the FRU's informer at the innocent man's expense. In ethical terms, it is difficult to see any justification, and certainly the principle of double-effect – used to govern the morality of endangering or killing non-combatants in times of war – does not apply here.[47]

One by-product of the unmasking of Scappaticci was to create a mood of uncertainty and mutual suspicion within and around the PIRA.[48] Indeed, with reports of a number of further, unmasked, agents still within its ranks,[49] the situation being described seemed at times not too far removed from that of the Central Anarchist Council in G. K. Chesterton's *The Man Who Was Thursday*. In this, Scappaticci's exposure had an effect that former MI6 officer Baroness Daphne Parks had talked of as being an MI5 tactic, 'to set people very discreetly against one another. They destroy each other. You don't destroy them.'[50] Nevertheless, the Scappaticci affair also contributed to a move away from the use of informers in the aftermath of the 1998 Good Friday Agreement on Northern Ireland when this raised ethical issues. This, in turn, contributed to an intelligence gap in relation to dissident Republican groups – those that rejected the Good Friday Agreement – illustrated by a series of terrorist incidents that the Police Service of Northern Ireland (PSNI) failed to prevent. Privately, some officers complained that, without informers, the PSNI was 'intelligence blind'.[51]

Extraordinary rendition and torture

While some HUMINT will be provided voluntarily, often its collection will be as the result of inducements or coercion and raises clear ethical issues.

The torture, inhuman or degrading treatment of detainees in the name of 'gathering intelligence' has been used throughout history and, more recently, was a characteristic of military regimes in Latin America during the 1970s and 1980s. It was also used in Northern Ireland during the 1970s, but its use has been so extensive since 9/11 that it requires separate consideration. Extraordinary rendition is the practice of seizing terrorist suspects from foreign countries and removing them to third country destinations for interrogation outside of any legal process; in effect it was used to facilitate the use of torture in an attempt to extract information from individuals suspected of having links to al-Qaeda.[52] Hence, extraordinary rendition and torture are umbilically linked. There is by now a substantial literature on extraordinary rendition and torture.[53] The destinations of those rendered have included Egypt, Jordan, Morocco, Afghanistan, Uzbekistan and Syria, with UK airports emerging as key transit points alongside airports in Spain, Portugal, Norway, Sweden, Denmark and Iceland.[54] One example cited by Amnesty International involved two Egyptians seized in Sweden by CIA officers and flown to Egypt, where they were subsequently tortured. The report noted how:

> The two Egyptians were seized by Swedish security police in Stockholm on 18 December 2001, handed to CIA agents at Bromma airport and flown to Egypt on board a US-registered Gulfstream jet. According to a Swedish police officer who was present at the deportations, 'the Americans they were running the whole situation'. The detainees had their clothes cut from them by the masked US agents, were reportedly drugged, made to wear diapers and overalls, and were handcuffed, shackled, hooded, and strapped to mattresses on the plane. The alleged torture they subsequently faced in Egypt included electric shocks.[55]

In the summer of 2005 relations between the US and Italy were affected by a case involving the kidnapping by CIA officers of an Egyptian cleric, Hassan Osama Nasr, in Milan, of which the Berlusconi government denied any knowledge. He was taken by Learjet from a joint US airbase at Aviano to the US airbase at Ramstein in Germany, and then via a chartered Gulfstream jet to Cairo, where the Egyptian claimed he almost died under torture.[56] In June a judge in Milan issued arrest warrants for thirteen US intelligence agents on kidnapping charges after identifying names via mobile phone contracts signed while they were in Italy. One of the phones was being used from Egypt at the same time that Nasr claimed to have been tortured there.[57] By the end of September 2005 warrants for the arrest of twenty-two people had been issued by the Italian authorities.[58]

By this time the scale of the operation was becoming more apparent, alongside reports of captives being held in Soviet-era compounds, so-called 'black sites', in Poland and Romania, as well as claims that detainees were held in Lithuania, Kosovo, Bosnia and north-eastern Thailand.[59] Against mounting international criticism, President Bush admitted the existence of these 'black sites', explaining that: 'This programme has helped us to take potential mass murderers off the streets before they have a chance to kill', whilst also insisting that 'The US does not torture. I have not authorised it and I will not.'[60]

This was a dubious claim, as Bush's memoirs, published in 2010, made clear. In these he recounted his 2002 dilemma over the questioning of the captured senior al-Qaeda figure Abu Zubaydah, implicated in the millennium attempt to detonate a bomb at Los Angeles International Airport. CIA Director George Tenet was convinced that Zubaydah had important information that he was not sharing with his FBI interrogators. As Bush recalled:

> One option was for the CIA to take over Zubaydah's questioning and move him to a secure location in another country where the Agency could have total control over his environment. CIA experts drew up a list of interrogation techniques that differed from those Zubaydah had successfully resisted. George [Tenet] assured me all interrogations would be performed by experienced intelligence professionals who had undergone extensive training. Medical personnel would be on-site to guarantee that the detainee was not physically or mentally harmed.
>
> At my direction, Department of Justice and CIA lawyers conducted a careful legal review. They concluded that the enhanced interrogation program complied with the Constitution and all applicable laws, including those that ban torture.
>
> I took a look at the list of techniques. There were two that I felt went too far, even if they were legal. I directed the CIA not to use them. Another technique was waterboarding, a process of simulated drowning. No doubt the procedure was tough, but medical experts assured the CIA that it did no lasting harm.[61]

As this suggests, the supporting role played by professionals – lawyers and doctors[62] – was essential to the facilitation of torture (as George Tenet put it in his memoirs: 'Despite what Hollywood might have you believe, in situations like this you don't call in the tough guys; you call in the lawyers'[63]). Although this case, and the subsequent waterboarding of Khalid Sheikh Mohammed, involved scenarios far removed from the 'ticking bomb' one that came to dominate discussion of the permissibility of torture, Bush Administration officials, and Bush himself, insisted that they produced valuable intelligence. Bush claimed that:

> Of the thousands of terrorists we captured in the years after 9/11, about a hundred were placed into the CIA program. About a third of those were questioned using enhanced techniques. Three were waterboarded. The information the detainees in the CIA program revealed constituted more than half of what the CIA knew about al Qaeda. Their interrogations helped break up plots to attack American military and diplomatic facilities abroad, Heathrow Airport and Canary Wharf in London, and multiple targets in the United States. Experts in the intelligence community told me that without the CIA program, there would have been another attack on the United States.[64]

However, doubt has been cast on these claims.[65] Similar claims regarding the efficacy of torture would be made by former members of the Bush Administration in the wake of the killing of Osama bin Laden.[66] In December 2007 the CIA admitted destroying videotapes of CIA 'enhanced' interrogations of suspects in November 2005, supposedly because the existence of the tapes represented a security risk for the CIA interrogators shown at work on them. In 2009, President Obama signed an executive order limiting the CIA to the nineteen interrogation methods outlined in the United States Army Field Manual, and ordering that: 'The CIA shall close as expeditiously as possible any detention facilities that it currently operates and shall not operate any such detention facility in the future.'[67] Nevertheless, in July 2011 the Administration did admit to detaining and interrogating a Somali terrorist suspect for two months aboard a US naval vessel.[68]

By this time, allegations of complicity in extraordinary rendition and torture had become political issues that impacted on public confidence in intelligence services in a number of countries allied to the US in the 'War on Terror', none more so than the UK (see the discussion of the Binyam Mohamed case in chapter 8). Here, the heads of the respective agencies moved to restore public confidence. In October 2009 MI5 Director Jonathan Evans stated that: 'I can say quite clearly that the security service does not torture people, nor do we collude in torture or solicit others to torture people on our behalf. That is a very clear and long established principle.'[69] In October 2010, in the first ever public speech by a serving head of MI6, Sir John Sawers explained that torture 'is illegal and abhorrent under any circumstances, and we have nothing whatsoever to do with it. If we know or believe action by us will lead to torture taking place, we're required by UK and international law to avoid that action.'[70] However, this was not quite the full picture. This was hinted at elsewhere in his speech, when he conceded that: 'We can't do our job if we work only with friendly democracies. Dangerous threats usually come from dangerous people in dangerous places. We have to deal with the world as it is. Suppose we receive credible intelligence that might save lives. We have a professional and moral duty to act on it.' In saying this, Sawers reflected the secret guidance that MI5 and MI6 officers were first issued in 2002 to enable them to question prisoners captured in Afghanistan who they knew to have been abused by the US military. Entitled *Agency Policy on Liaison with Overseas Security and Intelligence Services in Relation to Detainees Who May Be Subject to Mistreatment*,[71] this too made clear that the 'Agencies do not participate in, solicit, encourage or condone the use of torture or inhuman or degrading treatment', but went on to advise officers to seek authorization from senior managers in contexts where mistreatment by 'War on Terror' allies was suspected. Such cases would be governed by a straightforward utilitarian calculation:

> They will balance the risk of mistreatment and the risk that the officer's actions could be judged to be unlawful against the need for the proposed action. All of the relevant circumstances will be taken into account. These will include the operational imperative for the proposed action, such as if the action involves passing or obtaining life-saving intelligence, the level of mistreatment anticipated and how likely those consequences are to happen.[72]

In a sense, that the advice was of this nature should not have represented a surprise. The Foreign Office's 2008 annual report on human rights (a publication designed to showcase the UK's promotion of human rights norms) had explained that:

> All intelligence received, whatever its source, is carefully evaluated, particularly where it is clear that it has been obtained from individuals in detention. The use of intelligence possibly derived through torture presents a very real dilemma, given our unreserved condemnation of torture and our efforts to eradicate it. Where there is intelligence that bears on threats to life, we cannot reject it out of hand.[73]

However, in the view of Martin Scheinin, the UN Special Rapporteur on the promotion and protection of human rights while countering terrorism, states 'that receive information obtained through torture or inhuman or degrading treatment are complicit in the commission of the internationally wrongful acts'.[74] In short, while ministers and intelligence professionals clearly recognized the tension between 'War on Terror' intelligence collection and human rights obligations, they had failed to resolve it satisfactorily. As we discuss in chapter 8, this situation resulted in the creation of a commission of inquiry in a bid to restore confidence in MI5 and MI6. In announcing it, Prime Minister David Cameron explained:

> For the past few years, the reputation of our security services has been overshadowed by allegations about their involvement in the treatment of detainees held by other countries. Some of those detainees allege that they were mistreated by those countries. Other allegations have also been made about the UK's involvement in the rendition of detainees in the aftermath of 9/11. Those allegations are not proven, but today we face a totally unacceptable situation. Our services are paralysed by paperwork as they try to defend themselves in lengthy court cases with uncertain rules.[75]

SIGINT: Signals Intelligence

The role of SIGINT in twentieth-century history is increasingly coming to be recognized as one of the biggest remaining gaps in our historical understanding.[76] Figure 4.1 above identifies three forms of SIGINT: TELINT and ELINT concern mainly military intelligence and we do not discuss them in detail here; we concentrate on COMINT, or information derived from the interception of communications. We refer primarily to the US experience with SIGINT as a means of illustrating its potential and limitations, but it is important to bear in mind that a wide range of countries maintain SIGINT capabilities, including Russia, France, the UK, Germany, Canada, China, Israel, India and Pakistan, and a number of other Asian and Middle Eastern states. In recent times it has been the richer cousin of HUMINT, eating up a far higher proportion of national intelligence budgets as new technologies are developed, launched, maintained and perfected. It has also been the principal source of intelligence, in the UK, for example, accounting for around 80 per cent of incoming information.[77] As outlined in chapter 3, within the US intelligence community, the NSA is responsible for SIGINT, derived from a combination

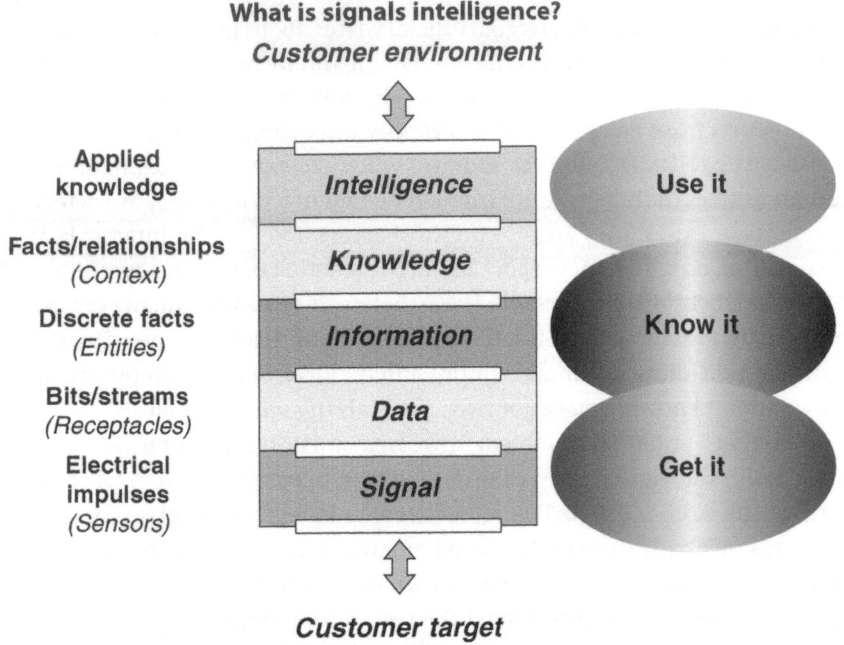

Source: www.nsa.gov/sigint/index.cfm, accessed 1 December 2005

Figure 4.2 *The SIGINT process*

of SIGINT satellites; listening posts, including some covertly operated from within US embassies abroad; and airborne, ship- and submarine-based listening platforms. In a variation of the idea of the intelligence cycle, the NSA represents the SIGINT process as shown in figure 4.2.

While there is a perennial debate over the relative merit (and appropriate relative funding) of HUMINT and SIGINT, except in the aftermath of serious intelligence failures (for example, the fall of the Shah, 9/11 and the failure over Iraqi WMD), SIGINT has been viewed as an essentially superior source, as discussed below.[78] SIGINT has represented the fastest source of current intelligence, as reflected in the view that the NSA gives decision-makers the present, while the CIA and other intelligence bodies provide contextualizing history. SIGINT also claims a flexibility that is absent from HUMINT, connected to the ability to retarget SIGINT as long as the platforms and operating expertise are available. In contrast, the capacity of HUMINT to redirect its focus rapidly and effectively is hampered by the fact that sudden shifts in emphasis could require the time-consuming infiltration of new structures and creation of new networks of informers, although cross-national intelligence co-operation can provide help in such situations.

HUMINT has simply not enjoyed the same reputation for reliability. It is true that SIGINT can provide decision-makers with a sense of reliability that HUMINT cannot always match. As former DCI Stansfield Turner put it;

'electronic intercepts may be even more useful [than agents] in discerning intentions. For instance, if a foreign official writes about plans in a message and the United States intercepts it, if he discusses it and we record it with a listening device, those verbatim intercepts are likely to be more reliable than second-hand reports from an agent.'[79] It is certainly important to apply the appropriate caveats to HUMINT, to bear in mind when considering information from human sources that they are not intelligence agents. Where they are defectors, dissidents or exiles, they are also political actors and have an interest both in the situation on which they report and in the reaction of the agency with which they share their (dis)information. Nevertheless, it would be equally erroneous for agencies to assume that SIGINT could not also mislead, if for no other reason than the 'two idiots' dilemma. Simply stated: 'Electronic intercepts are great, but you don't know if you've got two idiots talking on the phone.'[80]

A further potential problem involves misinterpretation of SIGINT. Potentially, the most costly example of this occurred in November 1983, during 'Able Archer 83', NATO's secret exercise to test release plans for nuclear warheads involving the simulation of launch orders. As part of the exercise, US SIGINT monitored the Warsaw Pact's own monitoring of the test, only to discover that they had misinterpreted the test as representing preparation for a genuine pre-emptive strike: 'Instead of the normal monitoring to be expected from across the Iron Curtain, a sharp increase was registered in both volume and urgency of the Eastern Bloc traffic. The incredible seemed to be happening, namely that the Warsaw Pact suspected it might really be facing nuclear attack at any moment.'[81] Perhaps ironically, it was a HUMINT source, KGB officer Oleg Gordievsky, who first confirmed the extent of Soviet fears of a pre-emptive strike during Able Archer.[82] However, SIGINT was immediately able to inform decision-makers that 'Soviet air units in East Germany and Poland were placed on alert and routine training flights suddenly stopped; Soviet nuclear-capable fighter bombers were placed on runway alert on airfields in East Germany; and the Soviets suddenly ceased broadcasting weather reports throughout the Soviet Union and Eastern Europe.'[83]

A final problem is that the volume of information generated by SIGINT can create an information glut, whereby a significant volume of information is never analysed. Indeed, one of the 'seven sins of strategic intelligence' identified by Loch Johnson was indiscriminate collection of intelligence, resulting in information being warehoused until resources allowed for its processing.[84] However, the rapid expansion of communications technologies in recent years (a greater range of modes of communications, both faster and more affordable, together with access to commercial encryption systems) has vastly complicated the task of SIGINT in two respects. One is the technical question of collection being made more difficult by encryption and other denial techniques. The second is a consequence of the increased volume of traffic, meaning that more sifting is required to find targeted information concealed within the ever-expanding mass, a problem to which Echelon – a global system for the interception of private and commercial communications, co-ordinated by the US and operating as part of the UKUSA Agreement – was one response.[85] While the NSA responded to these developments by investing the majority of its budget in improved collection systems with dazzling capacities,[86] analytical capacities lagged some way behind as there was no equivalent investment in analytical staff. As a result, the NSA was collecting more information, but producing less intelligence. The debate about where to invest within the SIGINT community – systems or personnel – anticipated the wider debate about the relative merits of SIGINT and HUMINT that would erupt post-9/11.

Bugging represented the basic level of electronic surveillance during the Cold War. The CIA employed hundreds of engineers and craftsmen to secrete bugs in a wide range of items, 'from kitchen cutting boards to felt-tip pens. Oil filters, videotape cassettes, tool boxes, toy trains, batteries, cigarette lighters, basket covers, teddy bears, chess sets, paintings, wallets, statues, hot plates, and toilet kits' were all utilized.[87] At one point experiments were even carried out to implant a bugging device in a cat's ear and train it to listen to target conversations.[88] Targets were equally broad; as Ronald Kessler recounts, bugging was routine with regard to:

> Ambassadors' offices, the homes of foreign intelligence officers, the hotel rooms of treaty negotiators and United Nations delegates, the meeting room where OPEC held its deliberations, and the cars of possible terrorists. Trade meetings were usually bugged as well. When foreign countries built new embassies overseas, the CIA obtained the plans and planted bugs in the offices most likely to be used by top officials.[89]

Ethical questions around bugging resurfaced in the run-up to war with Iraq in 2003 and the controversy over the need for a second UN Security Council resolution explicitly authorizing the use of force. GCHQ translator Katharine Gun leaked a memo from the NSA's Defence Chief of Staff (Regional Targets), Frank Koza, asking for UK help in bugging six target delegates to the UN Security Council (Angola, Cameroon, Chile, Bulgaria, Guinea and Pakistan) in order to gather 'the whole gamut of information that could give US policymakers an edge in obtaining results favourable to US goals or to head off surprises'.[90] Gun was prosecuted under Section 1 of the Official Secrets Act. When, in February 2004, the charges were dropped, former Cabinet Minister Clare Short publicly revealed that the UK had also spied on the office of the Secretary-General of the UN, Kofi Annan:

> This had been going on since we came into government and probably before. It may well have been a hangover from the Cold War. It had seemed odd, but basically harmless during the time that we were working closely and very supportively with him; but it became positively insidious when we were engaged with the US in manoeuvring and bullying to try to get Security Council approval for war at a pre-ordained date. I knew the transcripts of phone conversations were closely monitored because a senior intelligence official once came to see me and asked if we could speak alone. He pointed out that after I talked to Kofi from Kigali I had referred to something I could only know because I had

> read previous transcripts of calls to the Secretary-General . . . This meant of course that my calls, like all others, had been carefully monitored and analysed.[91]

Various technical methods for gathering information are used by police and security agencies. These can be summarized as electronic surveillance ('bugging') and interception of communications ('tapping') and the ability to enter private property in order to place bugs or steal records, or for some other purpose (officially referred to in the UK as 'interference with property'). We can get some sense of the extent of these practices from the annual reports of the various commissioners set up to oversee the agencies (see further in chapter 8). For example, it is reported that for the year 2010–11 UK law enforcement agencies received 2,701 property interference authorizations and 398 intrusive surveillance authorizations.[92] The latter is defined so as to include people or devices *in* private dwellings or cars or the use of devices to access what is happening therein.[93] These figures do not change significantly from year to year. Equivalent figures for the three security intelligence agencies, MI5, MI6 and GCHQ, are not published. Unlike bugging, where agencies can normally authorize themselves subject to subsequent judicial check, telephone and mail intercepts require a ministerial warrant, and in 2010, 1,682 new warrants were issued by ministers in England and Wales and 183 by the Scottish government. Figures for warrants issued by Foreign Office and Northern Ireland ministers remain secret.[94]

The problem of accessing electronic communications via e-mail and the Internet has, in recent years, added to the challenge facing security officials. In 2006 *USA Today* revealed that shortly after 9/11 the NSA began to develop a database of the calling patterns of US citizens by collecting the records of tens of millions of phone calls as part of a massive social network analysis programme. The aim was to identify possible terrorist activity by trawling through as close to all telephone activity in the US as possible. As one person interviewed by *USA Today* said: 'It's the largest database ever assembled in the world.' The NSA's aim, they explained, was 'to create a database of every call ever made' within the US.[95] By 2008, proposals existed for a similar data mining approach in the UK, via the anodyne-sounding Intercept Modernization Programme, described by Richard Aldrich as comprising a 'surveillance concept so vast that it was beyond the bounds of the imagination'.[96] Then Home Secretary Jacqui Smith explained:

> Our ability to intercept communications and obtain communications data is vital to fighting terrorism and combating serious crime, including child sex abuse, murder and drugs trafficking. Communications data – that is, data about calls, such as the location and identity of the caller, not the content of the calls themselves – is used as important evidence in 95% of serious crime cases and in almost all security service operations since 2004.[97]

Although in the run-up to the 2010 General Election the Conservative Party criticized the Labour government for the rise of the 'surveillance state',[98] in office the principle underpinning the Intercept Modernization Programme was retained as an element of the new government's Strategic Defence and Security Review.

While engaging in the cyber-monitoring of their own populations, states have also had to address the threat posed by cyber-spying from beyond the state, aimed at government entities, banks and commercial enterprises. It is possible to distinguish between levels of cyber-threat, from cybercrime to industrial espionage and so-called cyber-warfare.[99] At the level of state involvement, China was widely regarded as the most regular offender. In February 2011 British Foreign Secretary William Hague revealed that the Foreign Office had repelled an attack from 'a hostile state intelligence agency' – widely regarded as a reference to China.[100] An August 2011 report by computer security company McAfee identified at least seventy-two governments and organizations – ranging from the UN to the International Olympic Committee, with forty-nine targets in the US and targets in countries such as Taiwan, Vietnam, Singapore and South Korea – that had been attacked by the same spying malware. While it did not name China, the clear message of the report was that China was responsible. The scale of the practice was reflected in the comment of McAfee's head of threat research, Dmitri Alperovitch, who called it 'a problem of massive scale that affects nearly every industry and sector of the economies of numerous countries, and the only organizations that are exempt from this threat are those that don't have anything valuable or worth stealing'. In this environment, he warned, large corporations fell into one of two categories: 'Those that know they've been compromised and those that don't yet know.'[101]

The Internet is one of the fundamental emblems of globalization. With regard to intelligence and security, though, we can identify contradictory trends. On the one hand technological advances mean that methods and resources that were previously the preserve of states are now available to individual hackers, leading to what has been termed the 'democratization of espionage'. Of particular relevance here are botnets, 'agglomerations of remotely controlled, hacked computers that are used for a variety of criminal purposes, from spam, to high-powered, distributed online attacks against virtual targets'.[102] As one IT security consultant explained:

> Whether or not you're a nation state, botnets allow you to mount an operation of this type for almost no cost, and there is pretty much no physical risk. In the spy world they talk about 'black bag ops', where the spy tries to break into the corporate campus or government building to steal information. But with these attacks, there is no risk, and they can just keep trying and trying until they succeed.[103]

And yet, at the same time, in the case of cyber-security the security logic that is held to flow from globalization is reversed. The most significant threats here are posed by states, not by terrorist groups. Low-level criminality exists here as it does in the 'real' world, but it is corporate, financial and military espionage that is the cause of greatest concern. As cyberspace replicates the anarchic 'real' world, the same logic should apply to it. Hence, it would be naïve to imagine that only China and a few other states that seek to use cyberspace to improve their real-world security – Russia, France, Israel and Taiwan have also been mentioned in this regard – engage in cyber-attacks. For example, the US reportedly has its own hackers based within the NSA. These 'attackers' seek to penetrate cyber-defences of states, while at the same time 'defenders' seek to prevent external attacks on US targets.[104] Given that learning from attack may well constitute one of the best guarantees of being able to sustain an effective defence, the intelligence contest in cyberspace looks set to be extensive, expensive, anarchic and largely unacknowledged.

IMINT: Imagery Intelligence

The use of photographic surveillance to monitor targets became public knowledge in the wake of the Soviet downing of a US U-2 spy plane in May 1960, the same year that the CIA's CORONA satellite made its first successful flight, three years after the Soviet Sputnik had become the world's first. At this time, photointerpretation was undertaken in the CIA's National Photographic Interpretation Center by photointerpreters using stereoscopic magnifying instruments. Its founder recalled the process: 'You look at a place and then what it was like last year or yesterday. It's like looking at a movie. The frames are farther apart, but you can infer much more of the intentions by seeing the changes on the ground than by doing it one frame at a time.'[105] By the mid-1990s KH-11 satellites were routinely supplying high-level imagery across a range of sensitive targets, including the sites of a massacre in Bosnia, a North Korean missile test, Chinese military deployments and a Libyan chemical weapons facility.[106] Nevertheless, reliance on satellite imagery was not without its drawbacks.

For instance, employing satellite reconnaissance to compensate for an absence or lack of HUMINT can induce a false sense of confidence. There is a limit to what satellite reconnaissance can reveal, particularly in the field of intent.[107] Indeed, since the events of 9/11 there has been a widespread acceptance that excessive faith in the promise of technical collection methods left the US exposed. One leading proponent of this view, former CIA field officer Robert Baer, writes that: 'Like the rest of Washington, the CIA had fallen in love with technology. The theory was that satellites, the Internet, electronic intercepts, even academic publications would tell us all we needed to know about what went on beyond our borders.'[108] But as former DCI Richard Helms put it:

> This idea that photographic satellites, satellites that pick up electronic emissions, satellites that provide communications, and all the rest of it – all those technical things – they're Jim-dandy when it comes to photographing missile installations, listening to missile firings, checking on telemetry, looking at the number of tanks being produced in certain factories – in other words, bean-counting mostly. Great. But once you eliminate the issue of bean-counting, what good do those pictures do you?[109]

Second, effective concealment from satellites is far from impossible, due largely to the orbital predictability of satellites in their current form. While technological advances in satellites are likely to allow the US to lessen this predictability at least, there does not appear to be any insurmountable barrier to concealment technologies keeping pace with these. States involved in non-conventional weapons proliferation learnt the lesson of the 1981 Israeli attack on Iraq's Osirak reactor, and have developed production, storage and possibly even delivery capabilities underground (e.g., India, Pakistan and North Korea – the Iranian nuclear programme has to date also followed this pattern). The use of readily available tunnelling equipment in place of reliance on blasting with explosives has made these complexes very difficult to detect whilst under construction.[110]

US and coalition forces relied heavily on SIGINT and satellite imagery during the 1991 Gulf War via a combination of high- and low-altitude systems.[111] Indeed, satellite surveillance had played a vital role in capturing the build-up of Iraqi forces on the Kuwaiti border prior to the 1990 invasion, but did not offer a definitive guide as to how to interpret these troop movements. Crucially, the satellite photos did not show *intent* – only HUMINT could provide hard information on this. On their own, the satellite photos created uncertainty about Iraqi intent. As Bob Woodward recorded: '[Colin] Powell realized . . . that in a totalitarian regime, the only way to be sure of intent was to know what was in the leader's mind, and neither the CIA nor DIA had good human sources in the Iraqi government.'[112] Neither was Powell alone in not knowing what Saddam would do next:

> Giving a status report on the location of the 100,000 Iraqi forces, [Norman Schwarzkopf] said they were positioned in a way to give Saddam lots of options – not just an attack. He did not predict an invasion or border crossing.
>
> [Dick] Cheney agreed that everything Saddam had to do to prepare for an invasion was exactly what he also had to do if his intention was simply to scare the Kuwaitis. There was no way to distinguish between the two. The bluff was only credible if Saddam did all the things he had done . . . No one, certainly not Powell, could say for sure what Saddam was going to do. Absent any indication, it seemed there was no immediate response for the US military to take.[113]

Having failed to provide a solid basis from which to predict and possibly prevent the invasion, by October 1990 a number of SIGINT sources, including airborne warning and control systems (AWACS), intelligence ships and ground stations, were monitoring Iraqi military communications, but with limited success as the Iraqis used secure underground cables to communicate between Baghdad and Kuwait, a step taken years previously after a US newspaper disclosed details of an electronic eavesdropping operation aimed at Iraq. Nevertheless, intelligence systems were able to provide information on Iraqi troop deployments in Iraq and Kuwait, assess the degree of damage inflicted by attacks and provide warning of Iraqi Scud missile launches, although here again with limited success as Iraq adopted countermeasures such as electronically shielding communications from eavesdropping, broadcasting false messages, and maintaining silence on prime military channels. As one former NSA official put it, the Iraqis were 'quite sophisticated in matters of electronic deception . . . what Iraq learned from us is having consequences for both SIGINT and imagery'.[114]

Indeed, there was some irony in that less than a decade before, the US was sharing SIGINT and satellite intelligence with Iraq to help it stave off defeat in the Iran–Iraq War. As early as June 1982 the US had offered Iraq satellite intelligence of its vulnerabilities, and even dispatched an intelligence officer to Baghdad to ensure that the images were fully understood. This had been the prelude to President Reagan's 1984 signing of a National Security Directive that formally authorized a 'limited intelligence-sharing program with Iraq'. The information the US supplied thereafter included satellite reconnaissance photographs of strategic Iranian sites for targeting bombing raids, data on Iranian air force and troop positions gathered from US-manned AWACS based in Saudi Arabia, and communications intercepts. Journalist John Simpson was one observer who felt that Iraq's new-found success at the front in early 1988 was facilitated by US Intelligence:

> On 17 April 1988, having spent most of the war on the defensive and refusing to attack even when the opportunity arose, the Iraqi army stormed the Faw Peninsula which two years previously had been captured by Iran. The Iranian positions were thinly manned by old men and reservists; it seemed remarkable at the time that the Iraqis, whose intelligence had never been very good, should have chosen their moment so well. In May the Iraqis recaptured land around Basra which had cost Iran 70,000 casualties during three weeks' bitter fighting the previous year. Again the Iraqis chose their moment with extraordinary perception and the battle lasted only seven hours.[115]

Even in the area of satellite surveillance, a spread of technology has taken away what was previously a state monopoly. There are now several commercial satellite companies, providing images for a market largely comprised of multinational companies in the oil, gas, mining and insurance fields. Reportedly, the images of President Barack Obama's January 2009 inauguration ceremony captured by the GeoEye-1 commercial satellite some 425 miles above the earth were of such high quality that 'you could nearly make out Aretha Franklin's hat'.[116] The 'democratization of espionage' has been facilitated here too by Google Earth, although its pictures are relatively low resolution and always somewhat dated. Nevertheless, they clearly have a utility and were reportedly used in the planning of the Mumbai terrorist attacks of November 2008.[117]

MASINT: Measurement and Signatures Intelligence

There is an increasing array of 'sensing' technologies which are gathered under this general heading. Some were developed for specific military use, such as sonar detection of submerged submarines, while others were developed for peaceful purposes, as with the seismology and earthquake detection which was used to detect underground testing of nuclear weapons. Overground tests are monitored by assessing the increase in radioactivity in the atmosphere. The corporate security bonanza that has followed 9/11 has produced ever more sophisticated ways of monitoring populations at a distance and without intercepting their communications, which may well require some form of legal authorization. These include standard techniques for detecting drugs or explosives in luggage or in people's possession which have proven validity, while some more experimental methods are, to say the least, unproven. One example known to us is located at a major airport in the Middle East and uses subliminal images on advertisements to trigger subconscious responses in people with bad intentions, which are, in turn, picked up by CCTV and enable the authorities to detain these people for extra security checks.[118]

Conclusion: From Collection to Action

As we argued in chapter 1, there has always been a close relationship between intelligence collection and action. In this book we characterize the interface between the two as lying in the intensification of surveillance. The action dimension of intelligence has been a particular feature of 'War on Terror'-era intelligence. The argument that US intelligence needed to move beyond collection and engage in intelligence action in combating al-Qaeda was one clearly articulated by former CIA officer Charles Cogan. For Cogan, post-9/11 intelligence had come to be characterized by an 'offensive hunt' strategy, as a result of which intelligence operatives became 'hunters' as well as (Cogan prefers 'rather than') 'gatherers'.[119]

The shift from gathering to gathering and hunting can be traced back to President Ronald Reagan's January 1986 presidential finding that allowed the CIA to identify terrorists suspected of committing crimes against US citizens abroad and participate in their capture, a provision extended to killing them by President George W. Bush in the aftermath of the events of 9/11. Reagan's finding led to the creation of the CIA's Counterterrorism Center (CTC). Former CIA Director Robert Gates felt that its creation 'represented a huge cultural change . . . Before, we issued analyses to policymakers about terrorist organizations. Now we were operational.'[120]

The post-9/11 situation represented a qualitative advance on this position. As outlined by Cogan, in this environment intelligence operatives 'will not simply sit back and gather information that comes in, analyse it and then decide what to do about it. Rather they will have to go and hunt out intelligence that will enable them to track down or kill terrorists.'[121] In part this was a reaction to the 1990s' insistence on the inherent superiority of SIGINT and IMINT, one which encouraged an undervaluing of the importance of HUMINT and, assisted by the renewed caution and disdain arising from various revelations during the decade, led to its relative neglect. The view, expounded by Robert Baer and others,[122] that this neglect was a contributory factor in the events of 9/11 found a receptive audience in Washington, and led to a renewed emphasis on the operational aspects of HUMINT. However, the pendulum swung rapidly and too far; the practices HUMINT embodies are corrosive of the very norms it purports to protect. In particular, the post-9/11 practice of extraordinary rendition was constructed so as to side-step the need for accountability and conformity with human rights norms. However, while kidnapping and torture must now be considered as central to any review of how, in the post-9/11 world, intelligence agencies have collected information, there could be no certainty that the information thus yielded was either useful or reliable.[123] This brings us to the subject of the next chapter: how is 'information' analysed and turned into 'intelligence' and to whom is it disseminated?

CHAPTER FIVE

How Is Information Turned into Intelligence?

Introduction

We have already made the distinction between 'information' and 'intelligence', identifying the former with material (documents, maps, photos, taped conversations, computer files) that may be donated, found or collected and the latter with what is produced after analysis – the process of evaluation of the information. While attempting to ascribe meaning to or interpret information is something we all do in everyday life, being a social science student is similar to being an analyst, and in state and corporate organizations the position of analyst is increasingly specialized. Sometimes referred to as assessment, this process is one of the two main foci of this chapter.

The second focus is dissemination: what, if anything, is done with the intelligence that is produced? Is it passed on to other people or agencies? Is it passed to executives for some action to be taken? Much of the information gathered by agencies – whether analysed or not – goes no further than the files, or 'store' of information in the organization itself. If intelligence is disseminated it may take various forms – oral briefings, short or longer papers addressing immediate or longer-term issues. Whatever the form or substance of the intelligence, analysts frequently complain that they find it difficult to make their executives listen. In the short term one of the main problems is the dissemination of 'warnings': how certain does an agency want to be before it will tell its 'customer' of a threat of attack? Executives are people of action; they crave certainty whereas analysts occupy a world of uncertainties – very rarely will analysts be able to provide warnings with the degree of certainty that executives demand. There is a danger that, if analysts find they are not heeded, they may exaggerate the certainty of their judgement. If they get it wrong, then it is going to be even harder to convince the executive of the accuracy of their analysis in future, like the boy who 'cried wolf'. On the other hand, if an analyst errs on the side of caution and there is an attack without warning then executives will demand explanations and possibly resignations. Fear of this may lead to an inbuilt tendency to adopt worst-case scenarios, with the consequent distortion of the policy process.

Although much military and security policy is based to a greater or lesser extent on intelligence, public policy pronouncements do not normally state this explicitly. Yet in the controversial case of Iraqi WMD, intelligence was used explicitly as part of an attempt by governments to justify and gain support for their policies. During 2003 in those countries of the 'coalition of the willing' that invaded Iraq, unprecedented public controversies regarding intelligence and policy developed because of the failure to find the WMD that had been the primary justification for the invasion. The deeper sources of the controversy lay in the redefinition of the circumstances under which 'defensive' war might be waged; specifically, a doctrine of *prevention* was embraced on the grounds that nations could, after 9/11, no longer risk catastrophic attack from states or non-state groups, possibly by non-conventional means of chemical, biological, radiological or nuclear attack (CBRN).

As we have discussed, intelligence has always been central to states' efforts to protect themselves, but the new doctrine embraced by both Bush and Blair Administrations gave it, crucially, more public significance. Governments of states finding themselves under military attack from outside do not need intelligence to tell them (if they have no forewarning then they would certainly regard this as a catastrophic intelligence 'failure', but that is another issue), and their publics would need no persuasion that defence was required. However, intelligence is much more crucial if states are to prevent anticipated attacks. It is central to the process by which the seriousness of the threat is assessed, and it will have to provide the basis for some process of convincing sceptical publics that preventive war is required. In the case of Iraq, this has caused enormous controversy, as we discuss in chapter 7.

Analysis

As we saw in chapter 4, large sums of money have been poured into the development of ever more sophisticated technical systems for the collection of information. By comparison the funds expended on analysis are minuscule. However, failures of intelligence are as likely to result from incorrect or inadequate analysis as from a failure to gather, access and process information. For example, the 9/11 Commission reported that:

> the FBI's information systems were woefully inadequate. The FBI lacked the ability to know what it knew: there was no effective mechanism for capturing or sharing its institutional knowledge. FBI agents did create records of interviews and other investigative efforts, but there were no reports officers to condense the information into meaningful intelligence that could be retrieved and disseminated.[1]

The modern transformation of intelligence by the application of highly sophisticated surveillance and information technology has overshadowed the fact that, at its core, it remains an intellectual process. Technology can contribute to analysis – for example, since 9/11 there has been great emphasis on developing relational software to provide links between disparate data sets in order to develop 'data warehouses'[2] – but the 'attribution of meaning' to items of information or linked networks of items requires the application of thought and judgement. However many 'facts' are compiled or integrated, they still do *not* 'speak for themselves', and analysis requires the testing out of different possible explanations against the evidence – what we called 'abduction' in chapter 2.

Intelligence analysts seek knowledge with a degree of certainty sufficient to satisfy and inform those who wish to act upon it. As Reginald Hibbert put it: 'Assessment is the search for truth. How do you arrange it so that you have the maximum chance of coming near to that elusive ideal, and how do you ensure that if you come near to it you are listened to?'[3] Hibbert's ideal is certainly elusive, even in principle. The objects of intelligence are often divided into mysteries and secrets – the latter being those things that are, with sufficient access, knowable while the former are those things, such as the intentions of a foreign leader, that may be unknown even to the leader herself or himself. In practice, examining the realities of the intelligence process demonstrates just how far short of 'the truth' its product may be.

The processing of information never takes place in a vacuum – there is always a personal or organizational context[4] – but there are factors intrinsic to information processing that may be problematic whatever the context. Fundamental are the problems of overload and complexity. In order to deal with the former, all systems must *select* information as being relevant to the purpose for which it is required, but if the methodology for selection is misguided or outdated then relevant information may be missed. The less an agency or analyst knows about a problem, the greater the danger of overload; on the other hand, experts in their fields may be the most likely to cling to long-standing interpretations in the face of anomalous information – the 'paradox of expertise'.[5] One way of reducing complexity is to narrow the focus of analysis. However, the more this is done the more there is a risk of error as a result of over-simplification. A frequent reaction to the difficulties of analysing other societies and cultures is 'mirror-imaging': assuming, simplistically, that they operate much like one's own.[6]

The very sophistication of the modern information gathering systems discussed in chapter 4 produces the problem of overload. Intelligence systems may demand ever more data in the empirical illusion that more data will solve the mysteries and secrets – rather, they are likely to suffer the fate of the thirsty individual who tries to drink from a fire hose.[7] As the 9/11 Report noted: 'one can see how hard it is for the intelligence community to assemble enough of the puzzle pieces gathered by different agencies to make some sense of them . . . Accomplishing all this is especially difficult in a transnational case. We sympathize with the working-level officers, drowning in information and trying to decide what is important.'[8] Overload manifests itself also in the concept of 'noise', wherein the glut of extraneous material inhibits the analyst from focusing on the information that is central to the analytical problem or even prevents the analyst from spotting it.[9] Despite the problems of overload, of course, it may well be that the information system just does not contain the information that it needs in order to develop the required 'intelligence'.

Broadly speaking, analysts are deployed to produce two main types of analysis: tactical (short-term or limited in area) and strategic (long-term or more extensive in area). Ideally, agencies will achieve some balance of effort towards both but, in the security field, there is enormous pressure dragging the agencies towards the tactical at the expense of the strategic. Certainly law enforcement is dominated by tactical intelligence with respect both to investigations of past offences and to disrupting ongoing illegal markets, and pressure from investigators and managers tends to ensure that little strategic intelligence is carried out. Since 9/11 similarly, most intelligence effort has been put into the investigation and prevention of terrorist attacks. Many analytical techniques deploy sophisticated software facilitating the analysis of relational data. However, the cleverness of the software cannot provide a 'technological fix': analysis remains at heart an intellectual exercise based on reasoning.

One basic technique is risk assessment, deployed in the corporate world for many purposes in addition to security, but at heart involving 'the estimation of the likelihood of an adverse event balanced against the possible harm caused by the event'.[10] Other examples of techniques used extensively in both crime and security intelligence include networks analysis, used to 'map' networks of target individuals, organizations and locations. This is relatively easy to do in terms of measuring quantities of contacts between 'nodes' in the network, for example by the metering of telephone calls, but is much harder and more expensive if it is to examine the quality or nature of those contacts. Here, techniques derived from social network analysis will be used, but this is time-consuming and expensive.[11] Another analytical technique based on the large data warehouses now under construction (see chapter 3) is profiling – in essence, the examination of large data sets for unusual or suspicious patterns of behaviour that are used as the basis for targeting decisions for stops, searches and additional checks at airports.

Agencies may tend to recruit people from similar backgrounds and then to indoctrinate them thoroughly into the traditions and ways of the agency. This may well produce (more or less) subtle pressures towards conformity of thinking that is not receptive to contrary ideas.[12] This is assuming, of course, that agencies do actually recruit people with appropriate education, experience and skills. The 9/11 Commission shows that this was not always the case in the CIA:

> Security concerns also increased the difficulty of recruiting officers qualified for counterterrorism. Very few American colleges or universities offered programs in Middle Eastern languages or Islamic studies . . . Many who had travelled much outside the United States could expect a very long wait for initial clearance. Anyone who was foreign-born or had numerous relatives abroad was well-advised not even to apply.[13]

Within organizations there are numerous possible obstacles to the 'search for truth'; some result from formal, others from informal aspects of organizations. Specialization is a key feature of the Weberian bureaucracy and serves many useful purposes, but maximizing the efficiency of information flows and encouraging imagination are not prominent among them. In intelligence bureaucracies there are additional hurdles that, again, may be soundly based, but further hinder the flow, notably secrecy and compartmentalization of information.[14] This may occur within and between organizations: because they are perceived not to 'need to know' aspects of specific operations, analysts may be in complete ignorance of information that would be important for their work, such as the degree of confidence in sources. This may be compounded by the existence of different databases; if they cannot be linked, the information is effectively hidden from analysts.[15] The 9/11 Commission showed how, given the poor state of the FBI's information systems, analysts' ability to access information depended largely on whether they had a personal relationship with anyone in the squad where the information resided. These problems were further aggravated in the Bureau when procedures intended to manage carefully the flow of information from investigators to *prosecutors* became misunderstood as inhibiting sharing of information between different groups of investigators. Over time these procedures became known as 'the wall' and, in the eyes of many officials, became a serious constraint on intelligence sharing.[16]

Organizational mandates vary and officials may well judge the priorities of another organization to be less important than their own. Of course, good management, training and supervision can alleviate these factors but they cannot be eliminated entirely. Research into how organizations work and what they actually produce indicates the great importance of organizational or bureaucratic subcultures. In part because they are made up of people with varying attitudes and beliefs and in part because bureaucratic formality creates obstacles to 'getting the job done', the way in which information processes actually work (or not) may depart significantly from the images presented by organization charts and mission statements. Within agencies, typical differences exist between the 'doers' and the 'thinkers': in the CIA this difference is institutionalized in the split between the Directorate of Operations and the Directorate of Intelligence; in UK police forces there is evidence of the divide between detectives (usually sworn, male police) and analysts (usually younger, civilian, better-educated and often female).[17] The low status of analysts may mean that they are reduced to not much more than inputting endless streams of information[18] or are diverted to immediate investigative tasks rather than actually doing analysis.

Linguistic barriers may limit the number of analysts not susceptible to basic mistakes of translation or interpretation. The more difficult accurate, first-hand understanding of the target becomes, the easier it becomes for politicians to apply their own ideologically informed explanations to specific behaviour and see these explanations carry the day. There will simply be few qualified dissenting voices. Elsewhere, in certain contexts, members of the analytical community may consciously or subconsciously engage in groupthink that acts as a barrier to the application of intuition and to taking imaginative approaches to the study of problems.[19]

Mandel has argued that bureaucratic obstacles to information processing are at their greatest when co-ordination is required within and between many organizational units, and personal obstacles can be seen at their worst when rapidly changing political circumstances expose the rigidity fostered by groupthink and cognitive consistency.[20] Mandel identified crisis, the failure of past policies and the need for quick decisions as the conditions most likely to provoke serious problems. These may accumulate: 'From the vantage point of national security, many of the circumstances when there is the greatest need for sound intelligence are precisely those when these distortions are worst.'[21] As we shall see in chapter 7, the period after 9/11, including the decision to invade Iraq, illustrate the accuracy of Mandel's argument. We can see how a combination of 'groupthink' *within* agencies or sections, and turf wars over access and sharing information *between* agencies, have the potential to produce a cocktail of dysfunctions that will be fatal to states' efforts to develop security intelligence.

The 9/11 Commission concluded that failure of imagination was one of the main factors causing that intelligence failure, and in its report it considered the enormous (if not entirely contradictory) task of building imagination into the national security bureaucracy. It pointed out that, with respect to terrorism, the agencies simply had not developed the sort of warning indicators and had not performed the kind of competitive analysis that was done with respect to more traditional forms of military attack.[22] In the UK the Butler Review made a number of recommendations aimed at improving analysis and JIC assessments and the government responded by increasing the size of the assessments staff, appointing a Professional Head of Intelligence Analysis (PHIA) to advise on careers structures, common training and methodologies.[23]

It seems as though the analytical communities within intelligence, especially those in the US and UK, have suffered something of a collective nervous breakdown as a result of first 9/11 and then Iraq. They were comprehensively blamed for not 'joining the dots' and missing vital pieces of information in the first case and of serious misinterpretation of the evidence (or lack of it) in the second case. Leaving to one side for a moment the question of whether pillorying analysts is fair given the evidence of political inaction prior to 9/11 and the abuse of intelligence prior to the invasion of Iraq (see chapter 7), it is clear that there were errors in analysis, and much has been written in recent years contemplating how such errors might be prevented in future.[24]

Some proposals are conventionally organizational and concentrate on how, in the US, the ODNI must take responsibility for ensuring more coherent community-wide co-ordination, analytic training and methodologies; in the UK the new PHIA is charged similarly. A Rand study for the ODNI in 2008 found not only that the US agencies had separate research priorities and products (which is not entirely surprising given their different mandates) but also that each knew little of what the others did, let alone worked with them to develop and validate analytic techniques.[25] But, recalling our discussion in chapter 1 as to the utility of the intelligence cycle, others argue that analysis can no longer be the Cinderella of intelligence and simply follow collection but must actively guide it.[26] Modern equivalents of the relatively static and predictable targets of the Cold War have not disappeared entirely, but the much larger number of mobile and unpredictable targets in the context of the information revolution mean that 'knowledge management' of the entire 'cycle' must replace the rather simplistic idea of analysis as sifting through collected data.[27]

Analysts may well be taught techniques involving the 'analysis of competing hypotheses[28] (a process similar to that of abduction discussed in chapter 2). Analysts should set the evidence against several alternative hypotheses in the search for some 'best fit'. As Bruce points out, even if such an approach had not brought an entirely different result on Iraq, it would certainly not have delivered the same wrong conclusions with such high levels of confidence. Noting that much of the problem with pre-invasion intelligence on Iraq stemmed from the unwitting adoption of induction as a methodology, James Bruce argues for the greater application of 'scientific method' to analysis. However, intelligence rarely has time for this and certain key elements – the possibility of replicating research, open sharing of information etc. – are just not available.[29]

For others, still more radical innovations are required. While intelligence may benefit from greater use of 'scientific method', Wilhelm Agrell argues that this has been the equivalent of Thomas Kuhn's 'normal science', slowly accumulating fresh information and incorporating it into existing frames of reference ('Iraq is a deceptive regime concealing its possession of WMD . . .'), and rejecting information which does not fit until the conventional paradigm collapses. This is followed by a period of uncertainty and contestation until, eventually, a new 'normal' is established.[30] The question is whether the intelligence failures of the early twenty-first century will lead to a new paradigm or whether the conventional wisdom will reassert itself. For some the problem is not just that the intelligence cycle is a simplification but that it is 'also a model for intellectual activity that limits and perhaps even renders impossible precisely the type of imaginative analysis that appears as the only feasible way out of the current intelligence crisis'.[31] Similarly, Carmen Medina argues that what is most wrong with analysis is its 'essential design', which has failed to adapt to new threats, new understandings of human and social dynamics and, probably most important, new technologies.[32] Elsewhere, Medina and Rebecca Fisher, in considering the lessons of the 2008 economic crisis for intelligence, note the underlying reality that the 'complexity of the modern world has outpaced the capabilities of our current intellectual and informational models' and that therefore 'sense-making' might be a better term to describe the challenge for analysis.[33] This would certainly be consistent with how organizations in general have for some time thought about risk and threats[34] and suggests that analysis may have as much to learn from art as from science.[35]

New technologies represent, as we have seen, a major challenge to traditional intelligence techniques but, for some, they also represent at least part of the answer. Some of the most interesting innovations in this respect involve the use of web-based information-sharing technologies. Intelink grew out of military dissatisfaction with the many disparate intelligence systems they were asked to operate during the first Gulf War in 1991,[36] and in 1994 it was declared to be the overall strategy within the US for the sharing of secure and classified information between agencies. Intelink now has a number of components:

- *Intelink-U* (or *-SBU* for 'sensitive but unclassified'), formerly known as the Open Source Information System, enables sharing between federal, state, tribal and local officials.
- *Intelink-S* operates on SIPRNet at the 'secret' level mainly in the departments of Defense, State and Justice and has perhaps as many as three million users.
- *Intelink-TS* (or *Intelink-SCI* – 'sensitive compartmented information') operates at the highest classification level using the Joint Worldwide Intelligence Communications System (JWICS), the Defense Department's private equivalent of the Internet. SIPRNet and JWICS were the systems to which US Army private Bradley Manning had access and from which he allegedly downloaded the vast trawl of documents then sent to WikiLeaks in 2010.
- *Intelink-P* is now more commonly known as CapNet and provides White House and congressional consumers with access to CIASource, which the Agency uses for the dissemination of its analytical products.
- *Intelink-C* (for Commonwealth) is a top secret network run by the DIA that facilitates sharing between the US, UK, Australia and Canada. This is more commonly referred to now as Stone Ghost.[37]

These were essentially different systems requiring separate hardware, which made for a cluttered desk for those cleared for access to multiple systems, and to compound the problem there are additional stand-alone departmental systems run by the federal agencies. So, however much Intelink may have facilitated increased communication within specifically defined spaces, it was still geared for the preparation of products for consumers by hierarchically organized agencies. By the turn of the century, of course, Google was transforming search and research through the application of link analysis to sites and documents on a common subject, and thinking shifted to how the intelligence community could make use of Web 2.0 tools such as blogs and wikis.[38]

One of the more successful innovations has been Intellipedia, developed by CIA analysts and deploying the same software as Wikipedia, which by 2009 contained 900,000 pages, had 100,000 user accounts and received 5,000 page edits a day.[39] Working on the principle of putting information out to the broadest audience possible while respecting three levels of classification – unclassified, secret (hosted on SIPRNet) and top secret (on JWICS) – wikis clearly increase the possibility of the bottom-up collaboration and sharing that were missing prior to 9/11, and provide an audit trail of who added what. More recently still comes A-Space, which enables analysts to create workspaces on specific topics on which they can share information and collaborate on projects. This has been described as 'essentially a mashup of Facebook, LinkedIn and GoogleDocs'[40] and has expanded significantly the information available to analysts and their awareness thereof. It started in September 2008; a year later it was reported that 150 new people were signing up to A-Space each day.[41] As well as its potential as a social networking tool, it incorporates access for all analysts to the Library of National Intelligence, which is intended to create a repository of summaries of all the intelligence community's disseminated intelligence, regardless of the original classification of the document.[42]

One can see the potential for such technologies for intelligence analysts, just as for any other group of researchers, but whether or not the potential is fulfilled depends on many factors. For example, the conundrum for intelligence is how to maximize the use of networking tools in the interest of more effective working while maintaining security. There are not only vertical levels of classification but also horizontal barriers to accessing information one does not 'need to know'. These will always slow down and inhibit collaborative working to a greater or lesser extent, as will the extensive bureaucratic fragmentation of US intelligence, which may be ameliorated but will not be eliminated by technological links. On the other hand, the more these barriers are surmounted, the greater is the danger of even worse 'overload'. The new technologies will gain acceptance not just because analysts find them useful but because managers and customers believe them to be productive. What they cannot do is solve the essentially human intellectual challenge of understanding social complexity. Nor, finally, can they ensure that customers will even be aware of, let alone pay attention to, the 'product'.

'No Good Will Come of This':[43] Problems with Dissemination

Dissemination is the crux of the intelligence process – the link between knowledge and power; between intelligence and policy. The adequacy or otherwise of agencies' performance will be judged on the utility and timeliness of what they produce.[44] If intelligence is to amount to more than a self-serving cycle of endlessly collecting and storing information and actually to inform ministers, governments and executives, then it must be communicated to them but, in fact, dissemination 'tends to be intelligence's Achilles' heel'.[45] The central questions to be asked about this process are 'what, how much, when, how and to whom?' The fact that these questions so closely mirror Harold Lasswell's definition of politics – who gets what, when and how[46] – serves to remind us of the fact that this is an inherently political process.

What is produced and when

Sherman Kent's work on US intelligence is generally regarded as providing the basis for much subsequent intelligence scholarship, even though he concentrated on strategic foreign intelligence and was not concerned with police, security, counterintelligence or tactical intelligence. Kent argued that there were three main forms in which strategic intelligence was produced: basic descriptive, current reportorial and speculative-evaluative.[47] Taking this classification as a starting point, the basic intelligence report will be a standard product of any state or corporate intelligence system, in which analysts will provide an overall assessment of the state of play in some other government, military, market or company, usually based on open sources but including available secret information to 'add value'. Current intelligence seeks to provide executives with the latest information on current events: in the US the best-known examples of this kind of product are the President's Daily Brief (PDB) and the more widely circulated Senior Executive Intelligence Brief (SEIB). During the 1990s the growth of continuous news channels reinforced the pressure on analysts to disseminate their reports at an ever faster pace. These are not intended simply to repeat what has been dominating the 24-hour news but to analyse it within a broader context and with the benefit of secret information. However, they are not always successful. Daily briefings may amount to no more – or in some cases even less – than journalism, thus failing to add any value to what ministers may have seen on TV.[48]

Taking a broader view of intelligence than Kent's and moving from the immediate past to the immediate future, another form of current intelligence that is particularly important for policing and security intelligence is warnings. In the broadest sense, all intelligence provides warnings, but states and corporations alike view warnings of nasty surprises as the central intelligence function. During the Cold War sophisticated systems were developed for the surveillance of indicators that an attack might be pending; for example, during 1950–75 the US had a Watch Committee and National Indications Center, and Soviet military intelligence (GRU) and the KGB maintained similar systems for indications of western attacks.[49] Now that the fear of attacks from non-state actors has replaced these, the process of providing appropriate indicators is much more difficult and the judgements to be made in issuing warnings are acute. The 9/11 Commission noted that, with the exception of the analysis of al-Qaeda attempts to obtain WMD, the US intelligence community failed to apply warning methodologies to the potential threat of terrorist attack on the US.[50]

Generalized warnings to the public are highly unsatisfactory since they may just increase a general level of anxiety without enabling anyone actually to do anything to minimize their vulnerability. Over time such warnings may fall foul of the 'cry wolf' problem, while if an attack takes place without a warning there will be much negative evaluation of the agencies (see box 5.1). The

Box 5.1 The problem of warning

Most of the intelligence community recognized in the summer of 2001 that the number and severity of threat reports were unprecedented. Many officials told us that they knew something terrible was planned, and they were desperate to stop it. Despite their large number, the threats received contained few specifics regarding time, place, method, or target. Most suggested that attacks were planned against targets overseas; others indicated threats against unspecified 'U.S. interests'. We cannot say for certain whether these reports, as dramatic as they were, related to the 9/11 attacks.

Source: 9/11 Commission Report, pp. 262–3

'paradox of warning' is that if an attack is covertly prevented or called off as a result of a warning, then agencies may be criticized for exaggerating threats (because nothing happened), having done their job successfully. In the UK, JTAC determines the threat level, using a five-step ladder from low (attack is unlikely) to critical (attack is expected imminently), while in the US, the DHS had a similar five-step 'traffic-light' system that was widely criticized for being useless since it did not distinguish between the intentions and capabilities of groups or the likelihood and consequences of an attack.[51] In April 2011 a new National Terrorism Advisory System (NTAS) was introduced in the US. It starts from the notion of a 'heightened risk of terrorist attack' and will only issue time-limited alerts of an 'elevated' or 'imminent' threat plus recommended actions.[52]

The third main form of intelligence attempts to 'estimate' or 'assess' possible futures; in other words, to provide the forewarning that we included in our definition in chapter 1. These are the most ambitious and problematic of intelligence products. In the US the NIC builds on the work of analysts throughout the intelligence community to produce NIEs. These may be self-generated from within the community or requested from elsewhere in government, including Congress. More urgent requirements may be met by special NIEs (or SNIEs).[53] A NIE was distributed in July 1995 predicting future terrorist attacks against and in the US; it specified particularly vulnerable symbolic targets such as the White House, the Capitol building and civil aviation, and was described by the 9/11 Commission as 'an excellent summary of the emerging danger, based on what was then known'. Thereafter, there was an updated NIE on terrorism in 1997 and a series of 'very good analytical papers' on specific topics, but no further NIE prior to 9/11.[54]

To whom is it disseminated and how?

There is nothing automatic about the process of delivering intelligence to customers – as with all communications, as much attention needs to be paid to how it will be received as to how it is sent. The language of the market-place (if not all its practices) has crept into the vocabulary of intelligence:

policymakers are 'consumers' or 'customers' for intelligence and so, for the agencies, 'Salesmanship is part of the game.'[55] So the means of disseminating intelligence has shifted in line with the general advance of ICT, but for customers outside the community, the emphasis may well be upon brevity and snappy presentation, electronic or otherwise, including 'death by PowerPoint', as agencies compete for the scarce time of policymakers. Briefings will often be distilled to one or two pages for no other reason than that the recipient will not read anything longer. Indeed, it is reported that, being aware of Ronald Reagan's dislike of reading and love of movies, Bill Casey, then CIA Director, encouraged colleagues to present intelligence pictorially so that the President could watch it on a cinema screen.[56]

Traditional hierarchical organization of state intelligence production is not conducive to the free flow of information but is especially inimical to the rapid production of intelligence about fast-moving events in non-traditional threat areas. Michael Herman noted that 'security reinforces formal organization against loose structures and easy information flows'.[57] As we saw in chapter 3, 'fusion centres' are designed specifically to eliminate organizational barriers to sharing. More radical proposals have been made to 'marketize' intelligence on the grounds that the greater flexibility of markets will serve customers better and prevent the politicization of intelligence.[58] Essentially, this applies to intelligence arguments based on new public management (NPM) as it has been introduced throughout the public sector in many western states since the 1980s. But a number of its claims cannot be sustained. For example, the proposal that requests for intelligence could be posted on the Internet (like the FBI's 'ten most wanted') might certainly attract more information from a myriad of open sources and expertises beyond the capacity of any agency, but ignores the fact that the information generated would then need to be evaluated – police appeals for public information can be very helpful but also generate enormous amounts of work to sort the wheat from the chaff. It may well be that a decentralized network of analysts will make it easier for dissenting views to survive but markets are not apolitical; indeed, they provide the fora within which the most affluent and powerful interests prosper. While there may well be a need for intelligence to provide more 'customized' products for their policymakers, the more control the customers have over what analysts produce the more likely it is that the product will represent what the customers *want*; this, however, may be far from what they *need* in terms of 'truth'. The market model may simply increase the propensity for analysts to tell policymakers what they want to hear.

How intelligence is presented will depend on to whom it is addressed. Some reports prepared within agencies may simply stay within the agency, entering the 'store' of knowledge. It is by no means certain that intelligence will be shared even within an agency. This may be the result of short-sightedness; for example, analysts need to know the credibility of the sources of the information with which they are dealing but handlers may be reluctant to admit their own doubts or, as we saw above, fail to share because of misunderstandings about the rules. Obstacles to sharing information with other agencies are even more extensive: this may reflect the choice of the agency not to share the information outside or simply a lack of awareness that anyone outside would be interested. Much criticism since 9/11 in the US has concentrated on the failure of intelligence agencies to share information with others. In some cases this rightly aimed at failures to share based on nothing more than ignorance, poor understandings and so on, but there are also understandable and defensible reasons that may apply. For example, all agencies jealously guard their sources and methods not just because they are short-sighted but also because they fear their compromise if information they provide is used unwisely. Recipients outside the community may not appreciate that the publication of an item of intelligence can enable a target to identify and eliminate its source – in some cases a person. Nevertheless, the 9/11 Commission recommends that the Cold War assumption that intelligence can only be shared with those who 'need to know' must be replaced by a 'need-to-share' culture of integration.[59]

Whether or not an agency will share with another will depend partly on the nature and location of that agency, its mandate and the framework of rules. On the face of it, agencies will be most willing to share with those within their own national community, but this cannot be assumed; to the extent that different national agencies believe they are competing for resources, they may use their intelligence to maintain their 'comparative advantage' over others. For example, there is anecdotal evidence that agencies operating with similar techniques – say SIGINT – but in different countries would be more willing to share with each other than with their national agencies involved in a different intelligence discipline – say counterintelligence. Indeed, the whole point of the transnational intelligence networks identified earlier is that they provide a vehicle for intelligence sharing and co-operation across borders.[60] Yet the 9/11 Commission described clearly the failures of sharing information between national agencies prior to the attacks.[61]

As we have seen, great efforts were made in the US after 9/11 to institute procedures to prevent another attack. It is officially asserted that these have improved information sharing such as to prevent 'countless' ongoing plots,[62] but these attracted little if any publicity, whereas the potentially catastrophic failure to prevent Umar Farouk Abdulmutallab from boarding a flight from Amsterdam to Detroit on Christmas Day 2009, armed with explosive sufficient to bring the plane down, certainly did. The preliminary White House review found that there was no failure of collection or sharing – the US government had sufficient information to have prevented Abdulmutallab from boarding, but there was a failure of both analysis and the watchlisting system. Noting that both the NCTC and the CIA have responsibility for all-source analysis, the review maintained that this 'intentional redundancy' was designed to provide an extra layer of protection, but did not seem to connect this with the fact that 'no single component of the [counterterrorism] community assumed responsibility for the threat reporting'.[63] Thus, clearly anxious not to endorse yet further reorganization of intelligence, the analysis falls back on the same failure 'to connect the dots' that the 9/11 Commission identified. Collection had increased so dramatically after 9/11 that the number of potential 'dots' was now exponentially larger and, as Mark Lowenthal has pointed out, the minuscule proportion of them that would have been relevant were not numbered. So, as an explanation of failure, this is an unhelpful analogy.[64]

The NCTC's Terrorist Identities Datamart Environment (TIDE) increased its name records fivefold from 150,000 in 2004 to 724,000 in 2007, but had reduced these to 550,000 by 2009. The NCTC or FBI would then decide whether someone would move on to the Terrorist Screening Database (TSDB) maintained by the FBI-led Terrorist Screening Center (TSC). Abdulmutallab had been entered onto TIDE in November 2009 but had not made it into the TSDB's list of 14,000 people identified for extra screening at airports and borders or the 4,000-name 'no-fly' list.[65] The Review criticized NCTC and CIA personnel who had not searched all available databases to uncover the additional material relating to Abdulmutallab that would have seen him included on the TSDB. But this prompts the question of why they would have selected him (from among thousands of others) for that targeted search. Although the review notes that analysts had identified the strategic threat from al-Qaeda in the Arabian Peninsula (AQAP), some combination of human error, inadequate technologies and procedures is blamed for this 'tactical' failure.[66] We would confidently predict the same findings in any future review of a subsequent intelligence 'failure'!

Dissemination within the community is an important factor in the quality of final products but it is dissemination outside of the community that establishes the credibility and utility of intelligence. The primary consumers of intelligence are the 'doers' – political or corporate. The way intelligence conclusions are presented is important: specifically, how are degrees of uncertainty presented? The use of language is crucial; indeed, it is determinative of what, in the end, is considered to be the 'knowledge' upon which policy may be based or by which it is rationalized. Intelligence seeks to improve knowledge by reducing uncertainty but, by widely varying degrees in different conditions, is only ever partially successful. The way in which different national systems seek to convey this uncertainty varies. For example, US NIEs incorporate footnotes recording the dissents of particular agencies from the main conclusions and the CIA provides percentage probabilities of success in possible future operations.[67] An excellent example of the significance of language is provided by the 9/11 Commission in its account of the discussions in the Clinton administration as to how to respond to the attack on the *USS Cole* in August 1998 (see box 5.2).

In the UK the JIC eschewed dissenting footnotes and the Butler Report described how the JIC accommodated uncertainty as of 2004. When the intelligence was unclear or inadequate the JIC reported alternative interpretations as long as the membership agreed they were viable,[68] but alternative or

Box 5.2 Language, certainty and knowledge

President Clinton told us that before he could launch further attacks on al Qaeda in Afghanistan, to deliver an ultimatum to the Taliban threatening strikes if they did not immediately expel Bin Ladin, the CIA or the FBI had to be sure enough that they would 'be willing to stand up in public and say, we believe that he did this'. He said he was very frustrated that he could not get a definitive enough answer to do something about the Cole attack . . .

. . . on December 21 [2000], the CIA made another presentation to the Small Group of principals on the investigative team's findings. The CIA's briefing slides said that their 'preliminary judgment' was that Bin Ladin's al Qaeda group 'supported the attack' on the Cole, based on strong circumstantial evidence tying key perpetrators of the attack to al Qaeda . . .

. . . A CIA official told us that the CIA's analysts chose the term 'preliminary judgment' because of their notion of how an intelligence standard of proof differed from a legal standard. Because the attack was the subject of a criminal investigation, they told us, the term preliminary was used to avoid locking the government in with statements that might later be obtained by defense lawyers in a future court case.

Source: 9/11 9/11 Commission Report, pp. 193, 195 and 196

minority hypotheses were not produced. So it normally attempted to reach a consensus in the assessment, and the section of 'Key Judgements' would often include warnings as to any thinness of the evidence. Inevitably this search for consensus 'may result in nuanced language. Subtleties such as "the intelligence indicates" rather than "the intelligence shows" may escape the untutored or busy reader. We also came across instances where Key Judgements unhelpfully omitted qualifications about the limitations of the intelligence which were elsewhere in the text.' [69] But if language was nuanced in order to satisfy those who were producing it, the subtleties of what they meant might well escape those who received it. If, as Butler noted, not even the producers were clear as to the significance of the language:

> We have been told that some readers believe that important distinctions are intended between such phrases as 'intelligence indicates . . .', 'intelligence demonstrates . . .' and 'intelligence shows . . .', or between 'we assess that . . .', 'we judge that . . .' and 'we believe that . . .'. We have also been told that there is in reality no established glossary, and that drafters and JIC members actually employ their natural language.[70]

then what hope was there for the reader? Butler did not suggest any particular way of trying to deal with this problem – it is indeed inherent in any process involving language – but did recommend that the intelligence community review their conventions.[71] The government's response was that the guidance to staff on use of language had been reviewed and reissued (we might also hope that politicians are inducted into it!) and that JIC minutes were now to include 'alternative and minority hypotheses or uncertainties'.[72]

Even if intelligence is disseminated, it may not be 'heard': ministers and other executives may not receive it, they may not believe it, they may pay attention only to those parts that tell them what they want to hear, they may lack the resources to do anything with it or they may simply not know what to do with it. The 9/11 Commission examined the response of US security agencies to the increased threat information during the summer of 2001:

> In sum, the domestic agencies never mobilized in response to the threat. They did not have the direction, and did not have a plan to institute. The borders were not hardened. Transportation systems were not fortified. Electronic surveillance was not targeted against a domestic threat. State and local law enforcement were not marshaled to augment the FBI's efforts. The public was not warned.[73]

The other main consumer of intelligence, albeit rather more sporadically, is the media and, through them, the public. Until relatively recently all intelligence agencies made efforts to minimize their contact with media (and some still do) apart from planting stories with friendly journalists.[74] It is now more likely that agencies will have press liaison officers with whom journalists will make contact; some, such as the CIA, will themselves deal openly with the media through press statements, while others will still deal at one remove through their sponsoring departments; for example, the UK Home Office deals with the press on behalf of MI5. There has always been an unofficial and symbiotic aspect to relationships between the media and intelligence agencies: all agencies have tended to cultivate those working in the media both as potential outlets for information that the agency wants to see in the public domain and as potential sources. Journalists, for example, have often acted (with or without payment) as sources for agencies (after all, the job of a journalist is indistinguishable from that of other information collectors). This relationship has sometimes given rise to great controversy and danger. For instance, in the wake of revelations about the CIA's use of journalists, the agency was forbidden from recruiting them. On other occasions, the suspicion that journalists were working for a foreign intelligence agency – whether correct or not – have led to their murder, as in the case of Farzad Bazoft in Iraq in 1990.[75]

Also, a less noted aspect of the row between the British government and the BBC in 2003 regarding the accuracy of the government's Iraq dossier was that the fateful meeting between BBC journalist Andrew Gilligan and weapons inspector David Kelly on 22 May was their second; the first was when Gilligan had sought Kelly's advice on what to look out for on an upcoming trip to Iraq earlier in 2003. So, for Kelly, the object of the 22 May meeting was mainly to find out what Gilligan had seen.[76] Also, agencies may well use the media as outlets for information as exercises in disinformation. For example, giving evidence to the ISC, David Kelly explained in answer to a question from the chair, Ann Taylor, that within the DIS he liaised with the 'Rockingham cell' which serviced the UNSCOM weapons inspectors in Iraq.[77] This DIS group had the role, according to former weapons inspector Scott Ritter, of using intelligence from the UNSCOM inspectors in order to sustain in public the claims that Iraq was not in compliance with UN resolutions while ignoring ambiguous or contrary findings.[78] The Butler Report gave a more anodyne account of Rockingham as the means by which UK intelligence assessments were provided *to* UNSCOM,[79] but did not address the issue of what was done with the material received *from* UNSCOM via post-inspection briefings, and therefore did not deal with the question of whether or to what extent Rockingham was part of a propaganda operation.

Agencies may now make some of their analyses directly available to the public; by definition these will be unclassified and they are only likely to be in the category of basic intelligence, but they are a welcome element of the more general democratization of intelligence in recent decades. Many agencies now have their own websites on which reports are available. Typically they include descriptions of the agency mission, information about applying for jobs with the agency, lists of previous publications (in some cases, such as the Australian Security Intelligence Organization (ASIO) and CSIS, these include corporate-style annual reports) and, especially since 9/11, special reports and assessments of terrorist threats and invitations to contact the agency with information. Some include an archive of press releases; SOCA publishes a non-classified version of its annual threat assessment for serious and organized crime in the UK; and CSIS publishes *Commentary*, providing single-issue reports, some by CSIS personnel and others written by outsiders.[80]

Conclusion

In this chapter we have discussed the processes by which information gathered by intelligence agencies is translated into what we call 'intelligence', how it is passed on to others and how it informs police or government action. As a result of the controversies around the (ab)use of information and intelligence with respect to the decision to invade Iraq, we now have access to a good deal more information about these processes than previously. Although there is a growing array of highly sophisticated software that increases the possibilities of analysing the relationships between data, analysis remains at heart an intellectual exercise in which analysts struggle to ascribe meaning to information. But this is a process carried out within organizational contexts, and therefore to the cognitive problems that may afflict individuals there have to be added organizational problems that can range from an excess of conformity (groupthink) to political battles over turf and interpretations. Increasingly, intelligence communities are exploiting Web 2.0 technologies to facilitate information sharing, but how far that can actually improve the quality of analysis in the face of exponential increases in information accessed and gathered is difficult to assess.

In the same way that much of what is gathered may not actually be analysed beyond an initial assessment of credibility, so much of what an agency produces by way of intelligence may not be disseminated. This is not necessarily because of short-sightedness or incompetence. A reluctance to share information may indicate a concern to protect sources or simply result from a lack of appreciation that some other body would be interested. (One problem with a market model of intelligence in which producers simply give consumers what they ask for is the assumption that consumers understand what they need.) How dissemination takes place (verbal? visual? written? how long? including examples of raw data?) will be only one factor in determining how it is received, but the policy interests of the consumer will also affect what they hear. This factor is reinforced by the nuanced way in which intelligence is written – analysts deal with uncertainty, and this gives consumers more 'space' within which to hear what they want to hear. What, if anything, they do with this intelligence is the subject of the next chapter.

CHAPTER SIX

What Do They Do with Intelligence?

Introduction

In chapter 1 we discussed the issue of whether covert action should be considered a part of 'intelligence', and went on to discuss the limitations of the concept of the intelligence cycle. One of these was that it did not accommodate or account for the 'action' role of intelligence agencies, regardless of whether this action was overt or covert. In this chapter we develop this 'action' theme, and begin by offering a framework that helps us understand the point at which intelligence becomes action. This we term the intensification of surveillance.

Where Intelligence Becomes Action: The Intensification of Surveillance

Recalling our definition of 'surveillance', which includes both the monitoring of behaviour and attempts to 'discipline' it (or, the development of knowledge in order to deploy power), then we must acknowledge that, in practice, the two may be indistinguishable. For example, while the use of informers may be intended primarily to acquire information about their target, they may also (knowingly or unknowingly) have some impact on the activities of the target. Technical surveillance may be used overtly so that it simultaneously gathers information and acts as a 'scarecrow' to deviant behaviours. As Fry and Hochstein have noted, intelligence is not simply an objective 'eye' seeing and describing reality but one which, for a range of reasons, may introduce distortions, with the consequence that intelligence 'participates in the creation and reproduction of international political reality' and therefore 'does not merely describe the world in which the state operates, but in fact actively "creates" that world for each state'.[1] For his part, Michael Warner has written of how: 'Intelligence should be seen by students not as a set of organizations and processes, but instead studied more like astronomers view the solar system, as a set of entities in motion that constantly influence one another. Those entities, moreover, are intentional actors – very complex ones at that.'[2]

There is a time element to this: with strategic intelligence, time may not be so crucial and it will be easier to observe how intelligence affects policy, whether the latter is pursued overtly or covertly, or, as we shall see in the next chapter, how policy affects intelligence. But where time is of the essence the distinction may disappear: counterinsurgency doctrine talks of F3EA, 'Find, Fix, Finish, Exploit, Analyse', in which Finish is not only aimed at the kill or capture of a 'target' but also at seizing documents and computers ('collection'), as special forces seek to establish a continuous 'battle-rhythm' for the 'intelligence/operations cycle'.[3] Thus 'intelligence is operations'.[4]

Figures 6.1 and 6.2 seek to summarize and classify the major forms of action that might be deployed as a result of intelligence. This needs to be grounded at the most general level in the literature on power. We saw in chapter 2 that there are two broad theoretical streams with respect to power: the constant-sum or 'sovereign' view that power is exercised *over* people and a second, variable-sum view of power as 'facilitative'. Using ideas from these two streams of power, Scott argues that two complementary modes of power can be identified: corrective influence and persuasive influence. The former operates through two main sub-types of force and manipulation. Force is the use of *physical* sanctions to compel or prevent some action on the part of others, while manipulation involves the use of positive or negative *material* sanctions such as money, credit and food. Persuasive influence operates by offering reasons for acting in some way, and the success or otherwise of the offer depends on factors such as the reputation or expertise of the offerer and the extent to which there are shared values and commitments between the two sides. We might summarize these resources as *symbolic*. Actual patterns of power may, of course, combine these different forms in varying combinations.[5]

In figures 6.1 and 6.2 symbolic, material and physical sanctions are deployed along a spectrum but, do note, this is for analytical purposes. Moving from left to right along the spectrum, we can see an escalation in the deployment of power such as would be familiar to students of IR,[6] but, perhaps more usefully, it is the varying combinations of the three resources deployed in any situation that indicate the seriousness with which the issue is viewed by the power-holder or their thinking on the costs and benefits of different forms of action.[7] This is another way of looking at 'soft power' and 'hard power'.[8] In the second row of figure 6.1 there are some examples of 'above-the-line' policies that might be deployed. These are overt in the sense that resources are deployed openly: ambassadors and ministers urging particular forms of behaviour on other states or non-state actors make public speeches. They may also lobby in private, but the point is that the people they are trying to influence know exactly where the effort is coming from. More materially, loans or 'most favoured nation' trade status is offered as an inducement, while economic sanctions may be applied unilaterally or multilaterally through UN procedures. Examples include South Africa during the later years of apartheid, Iraq following the 1991 Gulf War and the Taliban in Afghanistan from December 2000. Physical resources will normally be military forces available for an invasion or a naval blockade, such as President Kennedy's blockade of Cuba to prevent Soviet ships delivering missiles there in 1962. Sometimes states may openly support the use of force by proxies or provide support for

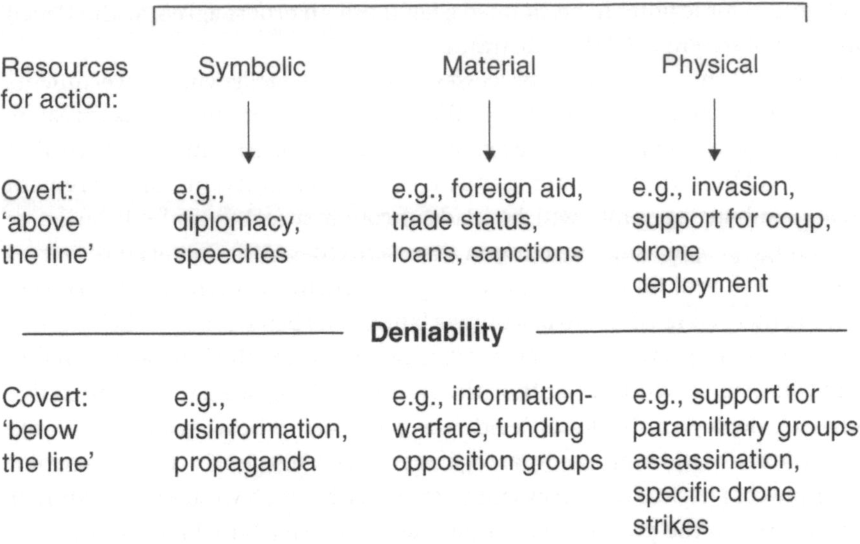

Figure 6.1 *The intensification of surveillance: external*

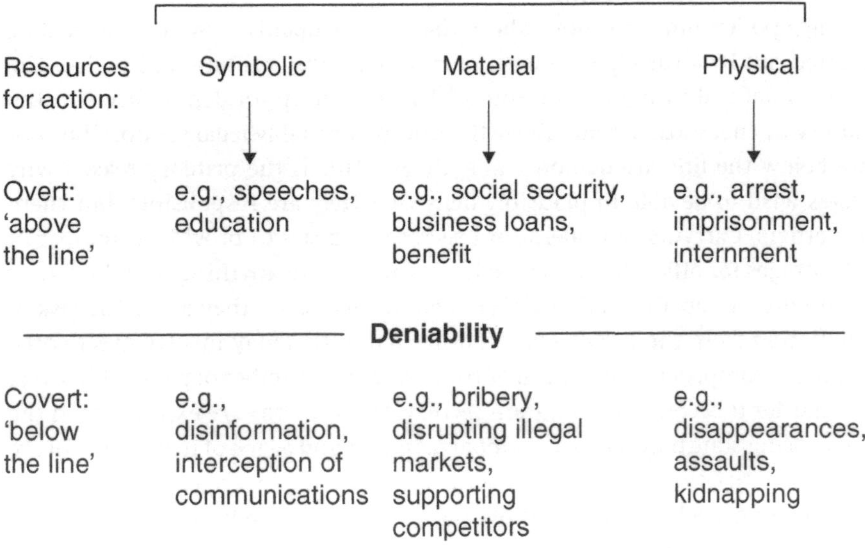

Figure 6.2 *The intensification of surveillance: internal*

domestic opponents of a regime to take power. NATO bombing of Libya in 2011 was clearly intended to have the same effect although officially it was simply in support of UN Resolution 1973 to prevent attacks by the government on civilians. Note that referring to these measures as 'above the line' indicates that responsibility for them can be seen clearly; it does not necessarily mean that they are legal. Usually they will be, since states prefer not to take actions generally acknowledged as illegal,[9] but international law is often sufficiently ambiguous for legality to be claimed even if not all others agree, as the US-led invasion of Iraq in 2003 demonstrates.

Figure 6.2 shows the same processes at work *internally* when governments seek to translate information into policy. Activities that are seen as threatening to the social, political and economic fabric of societies may be defined as breaches of the criminal law or as infringements of regulations, or will remain legal. Symbolic attempts will be made through speeches and education to discourage people from engaging in these activities. Also, material resources may be deployed; for example, the UK government in recent years has been making increasing efforts to discourage 'anti-social behaviour' – officially, this is a level of disorderly behaviour remaining just below the line of criminality – and has supported local authorities in establishing special administrative units to deploy professional 'evidence gatherers' whose evidence is used to support eviction proceedings against those engaged in the behaviour. Examples of physical resources will be those with which we are more familiar – police retain the power to arrest and detain those whose behaviour is 'reasonably suspected' of being criminal and a small minority of these cases will proceed through the criminal justice system and result in a conviction that may result in imprisonment.

Since policy and operations above the line are openly avowed, they will be carried out by a variety of state agencies including military and police. The 'line' is defined in figures 6.1 and 6.2 by the concept of deniability – in the same way that most actions above the line are arguably legal so most (but not all) below the line are demonstrably illegal. This is the primary reason why states wish to be able to plausibly deny that they are responsible, but there are others. Carrying out operations secretly appears to provide a number of advantages for officials: they avoid having to explain anything in public, they retain greater operational flexibility and, if successful, they avoid the risk of retaliation from the target. On the other hand, this may involve great costs: the more complex the operation or the greater the number of people involved, the harder it becomes to maintain secrecy. If operations are exposed then the sponsoring state may face great embarrassment and a lack of trust in its future actions. A variation on this theme is the use of intelligence agencies as a means of providing 'back channels' to adversaries; these are useful precisely because, for example, governments cannot admit publicly that they are 'talking with terrorists'. So, in Northern Ireland, while police, security and military agencies sought to defeat the PIRA during the 1970s and 1980s, some MI6 officials maintained lines of contact with a view to developing a peaceful political process.[10] It is as likely that this reflected different attitudes and organizational mandates as any sophisticated grand strategy.

The question of trust raises the ethical issue of whether states that claim to be democratic should be involved at all in deniable actions against others. It would not make sense for states to deny themselves the possibility of clandestine diplomacy to achieve peaceful solutions to intractable problems. Hence some argue that where covert action can provide states with cheaper, more convenient means of protecting themselves, they would be foolish not to take advantage of it.[11] But others argue that such actions violate acceptable norms of international behaviour in ways for which officials will not be held accountable. There will be others who do not take either of these absolutist positions but argue that the so-called 'quiet option' is rarely as effective as some claim.[12]

In terms of their formal mandate not all security agencies will be empowered to take action at all. CSIS, for example, is instructed to collect, analyse and retain information regarding activities threatening Canadian security 'and report to and advise the Government'.[13] In the UK, by comparison, MI5's function is defined more broadly as 'the protection of the national security',[14] thus incorporating a mandate to take action as well as gather information. The 1994 ISA, which provided MI6 and GCHQ with a statutory mandate for the first time, also included a section seeking to indemnify officers who took actions abroad for which they would be criminally liable if the acts were committed in the UK[15] – a clear acknowledgement that covert operations are conducted. Police also have a broader mandate: since the introduction of the 'new police' in London in 1829 a central function has been the 'prevention' of crime, which, similarly, involves both the collection of information and some form of action.[16]

Figures 6.1 and 6.2 give examples of some of the most frequently deployed covert techniques: symbolic resources are most often used as part of disinformation or propaganda campaigns. The information disseminated by radio, pamphlet or website may or may not be accurate, but what these techniques have in common is they are 'below the line' in that the true origin of the information is disguised. The history of deception in intelligence can be traced back to at least Leonidas and Themistocles in the Persian Wars.[17] Michael Herman tells us that intelligence: works closely with deception. Military deception is an operational activity; strictly speaking it is not intelligence. But intelligence should be the expert on the foreign intelligence organizations to be deceived, and if it controls a double agent it provides the deception channel.'[18] Deception can be used to manipulate perceptions of a state's capabilities or of its intentions. Ironically, arguably the most effective deception of recent years – arising from Saddam Hussein's interest in leading elements of the international community to suspect that he may have retained some WMD capability – proved a complete disaster for the deceiver. Considered by western intelligence analysts – particularly in the US – to be a master of deception, his deception was understood to lie in claiming that he had no WMD when he did, whereas in reality his deception was to hint that he did when he didn't. Screening out attempts to plant deceptive or misinformation is a key function of counterintelligence.

States may seek to provide material support to opposition or dissident groups in another country,[19] may bribe officials and may disrupt their raising of funds. There is a long history of national intelligence services funnelling

Box 6.1 The 'chilling' of covert action

After the Watergate era, Congress established oversight committees to ensure that the CIA did not undertake covert action contrary to basic American law. Case officers in the CIA's Clandestine Service interpreted legislation, such as the Hughes-Ryan Amendment requiring that the president approve and report to Congress any covert action, as sending a message to them that covert action often leads to trouble and can severely damage one's career. Controversies surrounding Central American covert action programs in the mid-1980s led to the indictment of several senior officers of the Clandestine Service. During the 1990s, tension sometimes arose, as it did in the effort against al Qaeda, between policymakers who wanted the CIA to undertake more aggressive covert action and wary CIA leaders who counselled prudence and making sure that the legal basis and presidential authorization for their actions were undeniably clear.

Source: 9/11 Commission Report, p. 90

arms to groups contesting power in other countries – in the 1980s in the US this practice was formalized as the Reagan Doctrine and lay at the heart of the Iran–Contra affair.[20] Such dealings may just reflect state corruption and the involvement of national intelligence agencies in this corruption rather than the pursuit of political ends. The WikiLeaks release of US diplomatic cables revealed an example of the latter in a January 2010 briefing for US officials by Spanish prosecutor José González, in which he claimed that Russian intelligence officials organized shipments of weapons to Kurdish groups to destabilize Turkey and had also attempted to organize weapons deliveries to Iran. As an example of the former, he claimed that the FSB had two ways to eliminate 'OC [organized crime] leaders who do not do what the security services want them to do': either kill them or jail them so as to 'eliminate them as a competitor for influence'.[21] One of González's informants had been Alexander Litvinenko, the former KGB and FSB officer, who told him that Russia's intelligence and security agencies – the FSB, Foreign Intelligence Service (SVR) and GRU – controlled the country's organized crime network.[22]

Military force may be applied covertly in different ways (see box 6.1). This is not really an option available to many nations but major countries tend to have some 'special operations' units for covert work: the US now has a Special Operations Command (SOCOM) and the UK deploys the Special Air and Special Boat Services (SAS and SBS).

Another technique is to offer support to indigenous paramilitary groups, such as the Northern Alliance in Afghanistan,[23] to carry out the action, or, increasingly in these days of 'outsourcing', to subcontract the operation to a PMC as we discussed in chapter 3. For example, Sandline International was contracted to help re-install the elected President of Sierra Leone, Ahmed Kabbah, who was ousted in a coup in 1997. Sandline's involvement was underwritten by the financier Rakesh Saxena, memorably described by Foreign Secretary Robin Cook as 'an Indian businessman, travelling on the passport of a dead Serb, awaiting extradition from Canada for alleged embezzlement from a bank in Thailand',[24] in return for diamond concessions in Sierra Leone. In March 1998 the company assisted a Nigerian-led force to retake the capital. However, Sandline's shipment of arms was held to be a violation of a UN embargo and HM Customs raided the firm's London offices in pursuit of their investigation. In an echo of the 'arms to Iraq' affair a few years earlier, Sandline responded that their operation had been undertaken with the full knowledge of the Foreign Office.[25] This was originally denied but later shown to be true and exposed contradictions in the 'ethical foreign policy' that Cook claimed to be following.[26]

Related to this, working to facilitate the overthrow of governments lies at the high end of the covert physical spectrum. During the Cold War era, intelligence agencies on both sides sought to install friendly governments in the Third World. Although now little more than a footnote in history,[27] one of the more infamous examples is that of the CIA's role in the 1973 overthrow of the (elected) Allende government in Chile. In 2000 the CIA released 16,000 documents covering the Pinochet era and the agency's role in the coup that ushered it in.[28] These revealed, *inter alia*, that US President Nixon personally ordered the CIA intervention in Chile as soon as Allende was elected and before he had assumed office. DCI Richard Helms' handwritten note of a September 1970 White House meeting outlined the framework dictated by Nixon:

- 1 in 10 chance perhaps, but save Chile!
- Worth spending
- Not concerned risks involved
- No involvement of embassy
- $10,000,000 available, more if necessary
- full-time job – best men we have
- game plan
- make economy scream
- 48 hours for plan of action[29]

After the US Ambassador to Chile pointed out that the constitutionalist commander-in-chief of the Chilean armed forces, General René Schneider, represented an obstacle to plans either to prevent Allende assuming office or thereafter to remove him by means of a coup, the CIA became involved in a plan to kidnap Schneider. During the kidnap attempt Schneider was killed. The following day a telegram from the director of the CIA Chile Task Force in Langley congratulated those involved: 'The Station has done excellent job of guiding Chileans to point today where a military solution is at least an option for them. COS [and others involved] are commended for accomplishing this under extremely difficult and delicate circumstances.'[30] The destabilization programme was antithetical to notions of democracy[31] and culminated in the 11 September 1973 coup in which Allende died.[32]

'Covert action' is not limited to foreign targets. Famously, under J. Edgar Hoover from the 1950s onwards the FBI developed a range of covert programmes that were deployed against the Ku Klux Klan, the Communist Party

USA (CPUSA), and the black power, civil rights and anti-Vietnam War movements. Counter Intelligence Programs (COINTELPRO) incorporated a range of techniques including false documents aimed at fomenting splits within political groups, inciting violence and spreading false rumours about activists' personal lives.[33] The controversies when these techniques were revealed, Hoover's death in 1972, the Watergate investigations of 1972–4 and legal actions against the Bureau all contributed to a significant shift in its targets and internal procedures so that, by the later 1970s, it was concerned more with white-collar and organized crime than political and security targets.[34] However, as we saw in chapter 3, the widespread criticism of the FBI for its contribution to the intelligence failure of 9/11 has led to a rapid reappraisal of the Bureau's role, including attempts to reorient it towards counterterrorism involving the resurrection of COINTELPRO tactics of the 1960s.[35]

Police may also deploy 'covert action' towards crime, though that is not what it will be called. In the UK during the 1990s police increasingly made use of 'disruption' as a way of countering the activities of professional or organized criminals. This might involve passing information or disinformation regarding the presence of informers within a group, or more physical measures such as overt surveillance at the site of an anticipated crime. Drugs might be confiscated even if no arrests or charges followed because of evidential difficulties, or people might be arrested not with a view to prosecution but in order to obtain information or disrupt a planned crime. The advantage of these tactics to police is that they can avoid the costs and uncertain outcomes of the full criminal justice process. The idea of targeting criminals and then disrupting their activities is the essence of the 'intelligence-led' model of policing.[36]

It is a small step from infiltrating target groups, as discussed in chapter 4, to seeking to alter their behaviour from the inside; that is, from surveillance to action. This was certainly the case with regard to Mark Kennedy, an undercover police officer in the Special Demonstration Squad (SDS) who infiltrated the environmental protest community from 2003 until 2010 both within the UK and internationally (he took part in protests in a range of countries, including Germany, Spain, Ireland, the Netherlands and Iceland). One tactic to gain the trust of the target group was for the undercover officer to form a sexual relationship with group members. One former SDS officer defended this practice on the grounds that 'being with women in very, very, very promiscuous groups such as the eco-wing, environmental movement, leftwing, or the Animal Liberation Front – it's an extremely promiscuous lifestyle and you cannot not be promiscuous in there'.[37] Having thus gained the confidence of the target group, the undercover officer could manipulate its agenda. In the case of Kennedy, protest group member Emily Apple recalled:

> The last time I saw him was at the Earth First gathering in August [2010] when he came to a meeting about how to best oppose the English Defence League (EDL) in Bradford.

> He was vocal but, in retrospect, very keen on diverting the discussion away from mass mobilization in the city centre and concentrating on targeting the coaches the EDL would be using.
>
> It has already been pointed out that this is provocation. Kennedy was openly and actively promoting illegal activity – suggesting people either damage or obstruct vehicles. However, I believe his motives went beyond provocation. The police were most afraid of a major public order incident in Bradford. By suggesting the coaches, Kennedy had an ideal way of not losing face in terms of action, at the same time as trying to keep people away from the city centre.

As Apple pointed out, 'subtle manipulation ensures that an action is implemented in a way that suits the policing agenda'.[38] However, in July 2011, three Appeal Court judges took a different view in quashing the convictions of twenty environmental activists whose group Kennedy had infiltrated. They judged that Kennedy's deployment amounted to entrapment and that he had acted as an *agent provocateur*.[39]

Northern Ireland provides many examples of the dangers of uncontrolled covert action in counterterrorism. After many years of official denials, inquiries by a Canadian judge and a senior British police officer indicate that state agencies 'colluded' with loyalist paramilitaries in the killing of lawyers and others alleged to be Republicans. 'Colluded' is a slightly euphemistic term to describe the subcontracting of murder to paramilitary groups in such a way as to conceal state involvement. Judge Cory's report into the 1989 murder of Patrick Finucane, a Catholic lawyer, concluded 'that there is strong evidence that collusive acts were committed by the Army (Force Research Unit), the Royal Ulster Constabulary Special Branch and the Security Service'.[40] Sir John Stevens, Commissioner of the London Metropolitan Police, concluded his Third Report into the Finucane and other murders: 'there was collusion in both murders and the circumstances surrounding them. Collusion is evidenced in many ways. This ranges from the failure to keep records, the absence of accountability, the withholding of intelligence and evidence, through to the extreme of agents being involved in murder.'[41]

The first to report of the three Northern Ireland inquiries established as a result of Cory's findings examined the shooting dead of Billy Wright, a leading Loyalist paramilitary figure, by Republican prisoners inside the Maze prison in December 1997. It confirmed Cory's findings that a series of wrongful acts and omissions by various state authorities had directly or indirectly facilitated Wright's murder but, adopting a much narrower definition of collusion than had Cory or Stevens, was not persuaded there was evidence of any agreement or arrangement 'to achieve an unlawful or improper purpose'.[42] In May 2011 the report was published into the murder of Rosemary Nelson (like Finucane, a Catholic lawyer) by a car bomb in March 1999. Again, the inquiry found no evidence of any *acts* by state agencies facilitating her murder but did find a series of *omissions*, including a failure to analyse intelligence and a corporate failure to warn Nelson of her vulnerability.[43]

An abiding dilemma for security agencies is whether, having identified and located targets, to maintain surveillance in the interests of developing intelligence (and/or evidence) while risking the perpetration of an attack or to intervene earlier to disrupt, arrest or interrogate and risk cutting off the information flow. This balance has clearly been shifted towards the latter by 9/11 because of the heightened fears of WMD attacks (however fanciful some of these may be). Contemporary plots usually have transnational dimensions and involve more than one state's intelligence and security agencies, raising the possibility of disagreement over the optimal timing of arrests. As discussed in chapter 1, a good example of this can be found in the case of Operation Overt, which thwarted a plot to explode transatlantic aircraft departing from the UK. The ringleaders of this terrorist cell, Abdullah Ahmed Ali Khan and Tanvir Hussein, were from east London. In 2003 Ahmed Ali travelled to Pakistan to assist refugees from the post-9/11 war in Afghanistan. There he met a further conspirator. On their return, they were placed under surveillance, their flat was covertly entered and a live-feed video camera and listening device were secretly installed. This allowed the surveillance team to monitor the production of hydrogen peroxide bombs concealed in drinks bottles and the recording of suicide videos. Ahmed Ali was observed downloading airline timetables, and the conspirators were recorded discussing the favourite US destinations of British tourists. The decision to move to arrest the conspirators was taken because of the August 2006 arrest in Pakistan of Rashid Rauf, the link between the plot and al-Qaeda in Pakistan, and the risk that they would suspect they had been compromised, destroy the evidence and/or change their plans. It has been suggested that the US orchestrated Rauf's arrest to force the hand of the British authorities for fear that continuing to monitor the plot rather than intervene to arrest the conspirators could result in the attacks going ahead. However, it did mean that the evidentiary base was not sufficient to gain convictions at the conspirators' initial trial.[44]

As discussed in chapter 4, cyber-espionage represents a growing form of covert action. A related development involves the covert manipulation of social media by the development of false personas. In the 'War on Terror', for example, the US has used this as a tool to spread pro-American propaganda and contest the claims made by jihadists and would-be jihadists online via Operation Earnest Voice (OEV). Here, a single person could manage up to ten false identities and so dominate chat-room conversations and channel them in the desired direction. Under US law none of the interventions from these so-called 'sock puppets' could be in English. Languages to be used were said to include Arabic, Farsi, Urdu and Pashto. In the words of US General James Mattis, OEV 'supports all activities associated with degrading the enemy narrative, including web engagement and web-based product distribution capabilities'.[45] Initially, the US will be entering a virtual vacuum in terms of state attempts to manipulate thinking via social media, but given that nature and intelligence both abhor a (virtual) vacuum it seems unlikely that this dominance will be unchallenged for long. Hence, one future for intelligence personnel in rival states may well involve them wasting each other's time as they attempt to mould the thinking of seemingly genuine people who are in reality their military or intelligence counterparts in rival states assuming similarly false cyber-identities (another contemporary echo of G. K. Chesterton's *The Man Who Was Thursday* scenario). Beyond seeking to manipulate the way people think via a covert online presence, intelligence can seek simply to close down target websites. For example, Dana Priest and William Arkin have reported on how the US JSOC 'has its own cyberwarriors, who, on Sept. 11, 2008, shut down every jihadist Web site they knew'.[46]

For all the emphasis on Chinese and Russian use of cyber-espionage, the most effective cyber-attack to date may well be that conducted by Israel and the US on Iran's nuclear programme via the Stuxnet computer worm. This malware has been described as including 'one component designed to send Iran's centrifuges spinning out of control and another to record normal operations at the nuclear plant and then play them back so that everything would appear normal while the centrifuges were tearing themselves apart'.[47] The worm seems to have contributed to a decline in the number of centrifuges enriching uranium at Iran's Natanz plant, recorded by an IAEA inspection team as falling from a peak of 4,920 machines in May 2009 to 3,772 in August 2010.[48] At the beginning of 2011, the head of Mossad, Meir Dagan, estimated that Iran's nuclear programme had been put back by at least one year.

Another contributory factor could well have been the high mortality rate amongst Iranian nuclear scientists. In January 2010 Iranian physicist Masoud Ali Mohammadi was killed by a remotely detonated bomb attached to his motorcycle. In November 2010 two leading Iranian nuclear scientists, Majid Shahriari and Fereydoon Abbasi, were victims of bomb attacks in Tehran. In both cases attackers on motorcycles attached a bomb to the cars and sped away before detonating the bombs from distance. Shahriari was killed in the attack.[49] Where diplomacy was deemed to have failed, states had turned to high-end covert intelligence action.

Indeed, intelligence-based assassination seems to be on the rise, especially if the use of CIA-operated drones to undertake targeted assassinations is factored in, placing the established norm against assassination under significant strain.[50] It has arguably become legitimized, if not rendered legal, in counterterrorism contexts. For a number of years Israel's intelligence services have targeted Palestinian militants, including the assassination of Khalil al-Wazir (aka Abu Jihad), a founder of Fatah, in Tunis in 1988; of Yahya Abdel-Tif Ayyash of Hamas in Gaza in 1996; and the attempted assassination by poisoning of Hamas' Khaled Mashal in Jordan in 1997 (a public relations disaster for Mossad and Israel).[51] At the same time, post-9/11 Russia admitted killing Chechen leaders, as in the assassinations of Zelimkhan Yandarbiyev in Doha in 2004 and Shamil Basayev in 2006.[52] More infamously, also in 2006, former KGB and FSB officer Alexander Litvinenko was poisoned in London, in what was widely regarded to be a state assassination.[53] In July 2006, the upper chamber of the Russian parliament had approved a law that had the effect of domestically legalizing state-sanctioned execution against individuals deemed 'extremists'. Russia claimed to be merely following US and Israeli practice.[54] In 2010 Mossad was implicated in a further assassination, that of Hamas official Mahmoud al-Mabhouh, in a Dubai hotel. The eleven-strong assassination team entered Dubai using forged passports, several of them British, precipitating a diplomatic crisis between the UK and Israel, and leading to the expulsion of the senior Mossad officer in London. Foreign Secretary David Miliband explained:

> Given that this was a very sophisticated operation, in which high-quality forgeries were made, the Government judges it is highly likely that the forgeries were made by a state intelligence service. Taking this together with other inquiries, and the link with Israel established by SOCA, we have concluded that there are compelling reasons to believe that Israel was responsible for the misuse of the British passports. This Government takes this matter extremely seriously. Such misuse of British passports is intolerable.[55]

On one reading, this case indicates the potential pitfalls of covert actions that become very public and cause embarrassment to the initiator and its allies. On another, the initiator, in this case Israel, not only kills an enemy but also reinforces its reputation for taking ruthless actions *pour encourager les autres*.

Notwithstanding these cases, it is, however, with the rise of the armed drone that the norm against assassination has been most acutely challenged.

Drone Wars: The Intensification of Surveillance Exemplified

The rise of the 'unmanned aerial vehicle' (UAV) or drone epitomizes the relationship between surveillance and action. The origins of the UAV can be traced back to experiments conducted by the CIA and the Pentagon in the early 1980s. What became the Predator developed out of an earlier drone named Amber, designed by the former chief designer for the Israeli air force, Abraham Karem, who had emigrated to the US in the late 1970s and set up an aircraft company in California. Under the Clinton Administration, CIA Director James Woolsey bought Predators from Karem (an intermediate version was called the Gnat), although the early version had the disadvantage of sounding like 'a lawnmower in the sky',[56] and as such was the antithesis of stealth technology.

The early Predator was first deployed over Bosnia in 1995. While it offered clear surveillance opportunities – it could fly for up to 24 hours as far as 500 miles from its base – it had clear limitations:

- Take-off and landing had to be managed by radio signal. Once the Predator had taken off, communications were managed by military satellites. However, take-off and landing required the remote control pilots to be positioned near the runway of the base out of which the drones ope This involved a rather conspicuous combination of unmarked var rounded by satellite dishes and generators. This limited the use that c be made of drones – they could only take off from 'friendly countries'. G that the target was unlikely to be a 'friendly' country, it required the acquiescence of allies bordering the target; for example, for Bosnia the Predator was flown out of Hungary and Albania.

- Early video images were not in real time and pilots had difficulty in controlling the drone from the time-delayed video images.
- The early Predator was slow, struggling to make progress in strong headwinds (it was even known to go backwards in these situations), and so vulnerable to anti-aircraft fire.

Post-Bosnia, a debate developed between those who saw the Predator as having solely an intelligence collection function and those who believed that to meet its full potential it should be armed (a technological challenge at the time), or equipped with laser target finders which would lock on to a target and guide a missile launched from, for example, a submarine. Experiments with this latter technology were conducted over Kosovo during the 1999 war, although without firing any missiles.

The debate about the benefits of arming the Predator became particularly intense in the context of the Clinton Administration's attempts to capture or kill Osama bin Laden, then based in Afghanistan. This operation also led to a further development in Predator technology. Given the problems with attempting to launch and operate the Predator from contiguous countries, amongst which the US had few if any unqualified allies, experiments were conducted in operating the drones from CIA headquarters in Langley, Virginia, with the entire flight being controlled from there via satellite.

The Clinton Administration approved using the unarmed Predator over Afghanistan in the search for bin Laden in the autumn of 2000. There, while flying over Tarnak Farm near Kandahar, it relayed pictures of a man thought to be bin Laden, adding to a body of intelligence that suggested that bin Laden was based there. However, at this point a more legalistic approach to the question of targeted killing prevailed, and President Clinton decided against launching a missile strike on the target for fear of killing nearby civilians.[57] Nevertheless, the quality of the images that the Predator had provided meant that it had proved its worth. The implication was clear: where a missile strike was likely to result in civilian casualties in the surrounding area, an armed Predator might reduce these. However, further reflecting the legalistic approach that prevailed, the question of arming the Predator had become subject to debate as to whether this might contravene the Intermediate Nuclear Forces Treaty under which the US was not permitted to acquire new long-range cruise missiles – was an armed Predator a cruise missile?

As we saw in chapter 5, one reason for Clinton's cautious approach was the

CIA's hesitancy in ascribing the *USS Cole* attack to al-Qaeda. Another was the fact that Clinton believed he only had a '40 per cent chance' of killing bin Laden.[58] Post-9/11 this caution was supplanted by Vice President Dick Cheney's 'one percent doctrine' – that if there was a 1 per cent chance of an event deemed detrimental to the security of the US (what was termed a 'low probability, high impact' event), then the US should act pre-emptively to prevent it from occurring.[59]

But even before 9/11, throughout the first half of 2001, tests were being conducted involving firing Hellcat missiles from Predator drones. Although it was not the first lethal attack involving a Predator (this occurred in Afghanistan in February 2002), the November 2002 killing of Qaed Senyan al-Harthi, the man thought to be responsible for the attack on the *USS Cole*, and several others, catapulted the Predator into the international spotlight.

Since then, in the absence of a more pronounced international reaction, a *de facto* US policy of remote-controlled targeted assassination has become normalized. The drone programme has been quietly expanded by the Obama Administration. In the same year in which Obama was awarded the Nobel Peace Prize, 2009, there were, according to the BBC, a total of 473 deaths from US drone strikes.[60]

The drone programme has implications for our understanding of intelligence, and in particular represents a further challenge to the concept of the intelligence cycle. Within the drone programme, and within a broad remit, intelligence officers are taking decisions on action arising out of intelligence, and the time-frame within which this occurs is highly compressed. In the case of the Predator, individuals are *targeted* and information is *collected* by the officers remotely piloting the drone and watching the real-time footage it relays; the *analysis* is undertaken immediately by the same people involved in collection; and the *response* (action) follows immediately from the analysis (to launch or not to launch a Hellcat missile with the intention to kill). There is no need for any wider *dissemination*. Analysis and action are so closely linked in this case as to be inseparable. Hence, this development presents another reason why 'action' now needs to be considered as a stage of the intelligence cycle.

The extensive use of drones raises a number of key ethical and legal issues. The first relates to the secrecy which attaches to the CIA's drone campaign, which makes arriving at reliable data problematic. The US government does not publicize attacks or release figures on the number of attacks or number of casualties. In fact, its formal position is 'neither [to] confirm nor deny the existence or nonexistence' of such records.[61] The BBC figure, cited above, is based on data compiled by the BBC Urdu Service from BBC correspondents in North Pakistan and the tribal areas (the vast majority of the attacks to date have occurred in the North and South Waziristan regions). Another thorough guide is that maintained by Peter Bergen and Katherine Tiedmann at the New America Foundation (see tables 6.1–6.3). This data is based on reports from

Table 6.1 Estimated total deaths from US drone strikes in Pakistan, 2004–11

Year	Deaths (low)	Deaths (high)
2011a	378	536
2010	607	993
2009	369	725
2008	274	314
2004–7	89	112
Total	*1,717*	*2,680*

Source: Data from Peter Bergen and Katherine Tiedemann's drones database at the New America Foundation, http://counterterrorism.newamerica.net/drones

Table 6.2 Estimated militant deaths from US drone strikes in Pakistan, 2004–11

Year	Deaths (low)	Deaths (high)
2011a	362	500
2010	581	939
2009	266	502
2008	134	165
2004–7	81	103
Total	*1,424*	*2,209*

Source: Data from Peter Bergen and Katherine Tiedemann's drones database at the New America Foundation, http://counterterrorism.newamerica.net/drones

a wider range of news agencies, including the BBC, CNN, Reuters, AP and a range of local news media. However, not all of these media report each strike or death, raising the possibility that some strikes are missed entirely or that the estimate of deaths resulting from a strike may, in some cases, be based on incomplete information. This database attempts to distinguish between the killing of militant leaders, militants and others (i.e., civilians) in strikes. This could facilitate a utilitarian calculation of proportionality. However, in many cases the number of 'others' killed is unknown, presumably because news reports at times focus on the headline killing arising from a strike. Reflecting the degree of uncertainty that arises from the compilation of this data, Bergen and Tiedmann's database records both a high-end estimate of deaths and a low-end figure. However, these figures can vary widely (for example, by almost 60 per cent in 2009 and January–September 2010). Hence, one reason why the Obama Administration has 'got away with it' – that is, succeeded to a significant degree in 'normalizing' the use of drones for targeted assassination – is that it is impossible to know for certain how many people have been

Table 6.3 Estimated militant leader deaths from US drone strikes in Pakistan, 2004–11

Year	Deaths (low)
2011a	6
2010	12
2009	7
2008	11
2004–7	3
Total	*39*

These figures are included in estimated militant deaths and estimated total deaths, tables 6.1 and 6.2.

Source: Data from Peter Bergen and Katherine Tiedemann's drones database at the New America Foundation, http://counterterrorism.newamerica.net/drones

killed or injured in drone strikes, or what proportion of these have been civilians. However, this fact became a less significant obstacle to opposition as the number of strikes and deaths mounted.

A more significant reason behind the US success in normalizing targeted remote-controlled assassination lies in its construction of a legal defence for the use of armed drones. This is rooted in the argument that the US is in a state of war with al-Qaeda. A form of it was first articulated in the wake of the strike that brought the use of armed drones to international attention in November 2002 – that which killed al-Harthi and several others near the Yemeni capital of Sana'a. However, this argument has been consistently contested. In the case of al-Harthi, for example, Swedish Foreign Minister Anna Lindh termed his killing 'a summary execution that violates human rights'.[62] Similarly, Amnesty International argued that:

> Under international human rights standards, lethal force should have been used only as a last resort. If the US authorities deliberately decided to kill, rather than attempt to arrest Haitham al-Yemeni, his killing would amount to an extrajudicial execution. Under international standards, extrajudicial executions are always unlawful, and 'a state of war or threat of war, internal political instability or any public emergency may not be invoked as a justification of such executions'.[63]

At the same time a number of legal experts have questioned whether the core premise necessary to arguing the legality of the strikes – that the US can be said to be in a state of war with al-Qaeda – can be sustained, and argue that such a claim misrepresents the nature of war or armed conflict. For example, the Protocols to the Geneva Convention define an 'armed conflict' in part in reference to concepts of *intensity* and *organized fighting* that are absent from the 'War on Terror' given its sporadic and isolated nature.[64]

Beyond this debate, there are clearly ethical problems with a policy of targeted assassination.[65] As Jane Mayer has observed:

> You've got a civilian agency [the CIA] involved in targeted killing behind a black curtain, where the rules of the game are unclear, to the rest of the world and also to us. We don't know, for instance, who is on the target list. How do you get on the list? Can you get off the list? Who makes the list? What are the criteria? Where is the battlefield? Where does the battlefield end?[66]

This also represents a legal problem, and was the basis of an ACLU (American Civil Liberties Union)/Center for Constitutional Rights (CCR) lawsuit filed in August 2010 challenging the Obama Administration's authority to carry out targeted killings. As Vince Warren, Executive Director of CCR, put it:

> The law prohibits the government from killing without trial or conviction other than in the face of an imminent threat that leaves no time for deliberation or due process. That the government adds people to kill lists after a bureaucratic process and leaves them on the lists for months at a time flies in the face of the Constitution and international law.[67]

To take another case that illustrates the ethical problems raised by the use of the Predator in this way: on 5 August 2009 Baitullah Mehsud, a leading figure in the Taliban in Pakistan, was killed by two Hellfire missiles fired from a Predator drone controlled by the CIA from Langley, Virginia. But so too were eleven others, including his wife, father-in-law, mother-in-law and several bodyguards.[68] Was Mehsud a legitimate target? Who determined that the possibility of this level of 'collateral damage' was justified in killing Mehsud? (Given the nature of the strike it would have been clear that Mehsud was not alone and that others would be killed.) Even on a utilitarian basis, were the attacks counterproductive in generating greater opposition than they (physically) eliminated? As the drone campaign expanded inside Pakistan's borders, was it likely to do more damage than good to the US national interest by fatally undermining the government of Pakistan? Was the attack counterproductive in terms of the potential damage done to normative assumptions against assassination? As former CIA general counsel Jeffrey Smith has noted, the use of armed drones in targeted assassinations could 'suggest that it's acceptable behaviour to assassinate people . . . Assassination as a norm of international conduct exposes American leaders and Americans overseas.'[69] This became more than an academic observation with the 30 December 2009 suicide bombing at a CIA base in the eastern Afghan province of Khost, from where Predator strikes along the Afghanistan–Pakistan border area were co-ordinated, which resulted in the deaths of seven CIA officers, including the station chief, and serious wounding of six others. It was the largest loss of life in a single attack suffered by the CIA since the Beirut US embassy bombing in 1983 and was regarded as having been carried out in revenge for the killing of Mehsud.[70]

In this respect it is interesting to note that the increased use of the Predator by the CIA occurred against a background in which the US Army was reflecting on the counterinsurgency lessons of the debacle in Iraq and, during 2006 under David Petraeus, was working on a revised version of the Army and Marine Corps counterinsurgency manual. The lessons it drew and the actions of the CIA in expanding its use of the Predator were almost diametrically opposed. For example, the Petraeus manual warned that: 'An operation that kills five insurgents is counter-productive if collateral damage leads to the recruitment of fifty more insurgents.' In terms of ethics, it warned that: 'At no time can soldiers and marines detain family members or close associates to compel suspected insurgents to surrender or provide information.' In seeking to be politically useful, and overcome the legacy of mutual mistrust between agencies and policymakers that was a product of Iraq, the CIA and, as we saw in chapter 3, the JSOC were engaging in a type of behaviour that the Army was moving away from.

A key point concerning the 'war defence' in the use of armed drones is that there is a link between legality and institutionalization of practice, that is, of a practice gaining wider social acceptability.[71] Being able to demonstrate (or, at least, argue with a degree of plausibility) that something is legal, or at least not clearly illegal, impacts (immediately and more so over time) on how people come to view a particular practice. In the UK, for example, it might be suggested that the legalization of abortion had both an immediate and even greater long-term impact on perceptions of the social acceptability of abortion.

In this respect it is significant that in March 2010 the Legal Advisor to the State Department, Harold Koh, set out – against a background of increased use of armed drones, rising civilian casualties, growing anger within Pakistan and what even supporters admitted was a legal 'grey area' – a full and explicit legal defence of the use of armed drones, part of what he termed the 'Law of 9/11', rooted in the arguments noted above and invoking principles of Just War by way of further legitimization. Koh began by framing the use of armed drones in terms of the US's right to self-defence as enshrined in Article 51 of the UN Charter, arguing that:

> al-Qaeda has not abandoned its intent to attack the United States, and indeed continues to attack us. Thus, in this ongoing armed conflict, the United States has the authority under international law, and the responsibility to its citizens, to use force, including lethal force, to defend itself, including by targeting persons such as high-level al-Qaeda leaders who are planning attacks. As you know, this is a conflict with an organized terrorist enemy that does not have conventional forces, but that plans and executes its attacks against us and our allies while hiding among civilian populations. That behavior simultaneously makes the application of international law more difficult and more critical for the protection of innocent civilians . . . In particular, this Administration has carefully reviewed the rules governing targeting operations to ensure that these operations are conducted consistently with law of war principles, including:
>
> - First, the principle of *distinction*, which requires that attacks be limited to military objectives and that civilians or civilian objects shall not be the object of the attack; and
> - Second, the principle of *proportionality*, which prohibits attacks that may be expected to cause incidental loss of civilian life, injury to civilians, damage to civilian objects, or

> a combination thereof, that would be excessive in relation to the concrete and direct military advantage anticipated.
>
> In US operations against al-Qaeda and its associated forces – including lethal operations conducted with the use of unmanned aerial vehicles – great care is taken to adhere to these principles in both planning and execution, to ensure that only legitimate objectives are targeted and that collateral damage is kept to a minimum.[72]

It is the insistence that a state of war exists between the US and al-Qaeda that forms the basis of Koh's legal case for the permissibility of using armed drones. Establishing this basis opens the way for him to invoke Just War theory to further legitimize their use, by way of the principle of *distinction* – but only in so far as civilians should not be the *object* of attack rather than that attacks should be abandoned if there is a clear risk of civilian casualties – and then by the additional application of the principle of *proportionality*, which immediately undermines the *distinction* principle by conceding the legitimacy of civilian deaths. Such reasoning does damage to Just War theory, highlighting its own utilitarian dimension; that is, despite the appearance of an objective standard, it is necessarily applied and understood in relation to specific national contexts. Who makes the judgement that the likelihood of a given number of civilian deaths is proportionate to the gains to be made from eliminating a named individual? How is this judgement made? Is there a ranking of targets and sliding scale of acceptable civilian deaths alongside it?

Even if US allies have been largely silent about the drone wars issue, there has been an increasing chorus of UN and NGO disapproval of the Obama Administration's reliance on remote-controlled targeted assassination. The clearest expression of this was contained in a May 2010 report by Philip Alston, the UN Special Rapporteur on extrajudicial, summary or arbitrary executions. Alston regarded Koh's defence as inadequate, and recommended that states should be much more transparent about the rationale for targeted assassination in each case it was used and publicly identify the basis for such action in international law. He warned that the rise in targeted killings posed a challenge to the international rule of law, and called for the UN High Commissioner for Human Rights to convene a meeting of states and international law experts to arrive at an agreed definition of what constitutes 'direct participation in hostilities' – a prerequisite for targeting an individual under international law.[73]

There has been little or no international reaction to Alston's conclusions and recommendations, which is significant. Defenders of the use of armed drones cite the absence of protest from other countries as meaning that the use of drones is in effect regarded as acceptable in terms of customary international law. Similarly, arguments as to the legality of drones, and hence their acceptability, are affected by whether the host state over whose territory the drones are operated and the strikes take place supports the strikes – in this case for the most part, it is Pakistan. Here, supporters ignore the power dynamic of US–Pakistan relations to claim total Pakistani government support, premised on the fact that the drones take off and land inside Pakistan and the apparent absence of formal protest from Pakistan to the US about drone strikes. However, this is to ignore wilfully or downplay the extent of Pakistani displeasure and the limited options its politicians and military feel they have in this context.

Furthermore, the absence of protest from other countries needs to be seen in the context of the desirability of armed drone technology. More than forty countries possess drone technology and a number are pursuing the development of armed variants. These include Iran, raising the fear that non-state actors such as Hizbullah may receive the technology from states in a context in which widespread US use of drones for the purpose of targeted assassination has weakened, if not eliminated, normative barriers to their use in this way. This is especially significant for those states that have secret or explicit policies of targeted assassination, such as Israel and Russia, as, by extension, the use of armed drones legitimates their practice – an irony, given earlier opposition to it by both the US and several of its 'War on Terror' allies, all of whom are silent on the question of killing by drone. Nothing better illustrates the fact of Alston's assertion that US practice will undermine the international 'rules designed to protect the right to life and prevent extrajudicial executions'.[74]

Killing bin Laden

In this chapter we have discussed the relationship between intelligence and action. As well as intelligence providing the knowledge-base for governments' publicly acknowledged foreign diplomatic policies and domestic security policies, it also provides the basis for secret policies conducted to counter or disrupt social, economic, military or political threats. Such policies can be very attractive to officials because they *seem* to offer relatively 'quick fixes' to complex problems, but they can be highly problematic if examined in a broader light and over a longer term. President Clinton recalled once remarking to his Chairman of the Joint Chiefs of Staff, 'You know, it would scare the shit out of al-Qaeda if suddenly a bunch of black ninjas rappelled out of helicopters into the middle of their camp.'[75] In effect, this is precisely how the decade-long hunt for Osama bin Laden ended, an exemplary illustration of the relationship between intelligence and action – as incoming Director of the CIA David Petraeus made clear in his pre-hearing before the US Senate Select Committee on Intelligence (SSCI; see box 6.2).

Conclusion

Nevertheless, even in the extreme case of bin Laden – the mastermind and financier behind the 9/11 and other attacks on US targets – some argued that his killing via a covert intelligence-based operation amounted to an assassination and that he should, instead, have been captured and placed on trial.[76]

Box 6.2 David Petraeus on the lessons learned by the CIA in hunting Osama bin Laden

- First and foremost, identifying and locating Bin Ladin's primary facilitator was the key to finding him. Analysts and targeters spent years whittling down the list of Bin Ladin's trusted aides until they were finally able to zero-in on Abu Ahmad al-Kuwaiti, who was Bin Ladin's caretaker and courier in Abbottabad.
- We were again reminded that history matters and that whoever was protecting Bin Ladin probably had known him for years. This key assumption compelled the Agency to systematically and repeatedly review historical intelligence reporting to develop new leads.
- We must not forget that our foes are adaptable. We could not be wedded to old stereotypes of Bin Ladin hiding in caves and moving frequently under the protection of large Arab security details. As it turned out, Bin Ladin had located in an affluent neighborhood where his profile was almost nonexistent.
- Finally, it is clear that once a trail goes cold – as it did following Bin Ladin's escape from the mountains of Tora Bora, Afghanistan in December 2001 – it is very difficult to reacquire. Difficult, however, must never be seen as impossible. The success in finding Bin Ladin showed that tenacity and ingenuity should never be underrated.

CIA also learned several important lessons in planning the raid that resulted in Bin Ladin's death, and these lessons will be instructive when considering other high-risk intelligence-based operations:

- It is essential to devote sufficient resources to effectively exploit opportunities that arise during the pursuit of high-value targets.
- We must always strive to be clear and explicit in differentiating facts from analysis, identifying intelligence gaps, and articulating risks associated with potential courses of action.
- CIA's Counter Terrorism Center seamlessly integrated different streams of collection to offer policymakers the most complete intelligence picture available in this operation, highlighting the benefits of close teamwork across CIA and with other agencies.
- Finally, CIA's close work with military partners in planning the raid was vital; the Agency provided tactical and strategic intelligence and analysis to help ensure mission success.

Source: United States SSCI, 'Responses to additional prehearing questions for General David H. Petraeus upon his selection to be the Director of the Central Intelligence Agency', 23 June 2011, pp. 7–8.

There is a sense in which covert action is a kind of institutionalized hypocrisy in which ethics and the rule of law are subjugated to the achievement of short-term political gains, when the costs are borne by some national or ethnic or political 'other'. If there is a sense of this in some quarters in relation to the extreme case of bin Laden, then it is even more so in lesser cases, such as of those targeted for assassination in the US drone wars. In the longer term, of course, such policies may come back to haunt the perpetrators as, for example, did the presence within al-Qaeda of *mujahideen* trained and equipped initially by the US to fight the Soviet Union in Afghanistan.[77] Such policies tend to be justified, implicitly or explicitly (as in Harold Koh's defence of the use of drones to kill suspects), on purely utilitarian grounds. Yet even on these grounds, they may carry potentially high costs. As the foregoing indicates, the international norm against assassination has been challenged in the post-9/11 environment. Ultimately, the success or failure of all policies, whether overt or covert, depends at least in part on the reaction to them from those they are intended to affect; specifically, in the security field, the amount of resistance. Even if policy is developed in a relatively open process, predicting its outcomes – intended and unintended – is notoriously difficult; in the closed world of intelligence where covert actions may be planned by a small group, the danger of wishful thinking is paramount.

CHAPTER SEVEN

Why Does Intelligence Fail?

Introduction

This chapter discusses the limits of intelligence. In doing so it draws almost exclusively on examples of US intelligence failure, for the good reason that such failures are debated more openly in the US than in any other political system, hence evidence on which to base analysis is more readily available. This allows us to understand better the nature of intelligence failure by locating its primary source at a given point in the intelligence cycle. However, this should not lead us to the enticing conclusion that intelligence failure can always be so easily pigeon-holed. As the case of intelligence on Iraqi WMD makes clear, intelligence failure is not necessarily mono-causal or confined to just one point of the cycle. Moreover, failure can be a consequence of *structures* as much as *processes*, something that is not well captured by thinking solely in terms of the intelligence cycle. Nevertheless, the concept of the intelligence cycle does act as a useful mechanism for locating the causes of intelligence failure and considering reforms aimed at reducing the risk of its recurrence.[1]

The Limits of Intelligence

In 2002 US Defense Secretary Donald Rumsfeld was widely derided when he sought to explain how: 'Reports that say that something hasn't happened are always interesting to me, because, as we know, there are known knowns; there are things we know we know. We also know there are known unknowns; that is to say we know there are some things we do not know. But there are also unknown unknowns – the ones we don't know we don't know.'[2] In fact, Rumsfeld did capture one central and inescapable fact: in a highly complex world uncertainties and insecurities abound and intelligence, however well funded and organized, cannot be omniscient.

Some of the 'limits' of intelligence are more apparent than real, however, and arise as a consequence of the fact that intelligence is poorly understood. At times, its advocates have made unjustifiable claims for what it can achieve; at others, decision-makers, especially those with limited experience of intelligence, have had unrealistic expectations of what it can deliver. Failures of power are at least as frequent as failures of 'knowledge'. 'Intelligence' is not the holy grail; it cannot, and should not claim to, offer a crystal ball for seeing the future clearly. As we saw in chapter 5, the process by which it is developed is fraught with potential distortions and problems that can derail the production of accurate intelligence. Some of these relate to the inherent shortcomings and cognitive limits of personnel, others are to a greater or lesser extent inherent in the process. These include the intrinsic difficulties of identifying targets and the tendency to concentrate, for practical or ideological reasons, on the 'usual suspects'; internal bureaucratic obstacles (intelligence agencies are prone to 'turf wars'); and failures to share information that derive, in part, from the very concern with 'secrecy' that is seen as the *sine qua non* for effective intelligence. Finally, as we have seen, those states, organizations, groups or people who are the targets of intelligence operations are unlikely to remain passive. They have their own objectives and deploy their own techniques to counter attempts to discover their secrets. These may just be defensive (secrecy) but may also attempt to mislead deliberately and thus disrupt an opponent's operations.

In the wake of 9/11, Iraq and 7/7, it is clearly essential to identify and understand the nature of intelligence failure and where it occurs so as to be able to improve systems and processes and thereby minimize the risk of future failures, even if it is true that such modifications can only bring about marginal improvements in the efficacy of intelligence agencies. This is essentially the argument put forward some years ago by Richard Betts:

> In the best-known cases of intelligence failure, the most crucial mistakes have seldom been made by collectors of raw information, occasionally by professionals who produce finished analyses, but most often by the decision makers who consume the products of intelligence services. Policy premises constrict perception, and administrative workloads constrain reflection. Intelligence failure is political and psychological more often than organizational.[3]

Diagrammatically, we might represent this argument as in figure 7.1.

Betts went on to argue that:

> Observers who see notorious intelligence failures as egregious often infer that disasters can be avoided by perfecting norms and procedures for analysis and argumentation. This belief is illusory. Intelligence can be improved marginally, but not radically, by altering the analytic system. The illusion is also dangerous if it abets overconfidence that systemic reforms will increase the predictability of threats.[4]

Hence, the limits of intelligence dictate that intelligence failure is inevitable. Partly this is a consequence of the impossibility of perfect predictive success; partly it is a consequence of decision-makers' natural tendency to err on the side of caution by subscribing to worst-case scenarios, or simply to ignore intelligence that does not fit their own preferences. The extent to which they do this is related to a strategic environment and past history, but given that their core function is the security of the state and its citizens, they all share essentially the same commitment to ensuring that vulnerabilities are not exposed, and that they themselves are not exposed as a consequence of unpreparedness or failure to act on what is subsequently demonstrated to have been

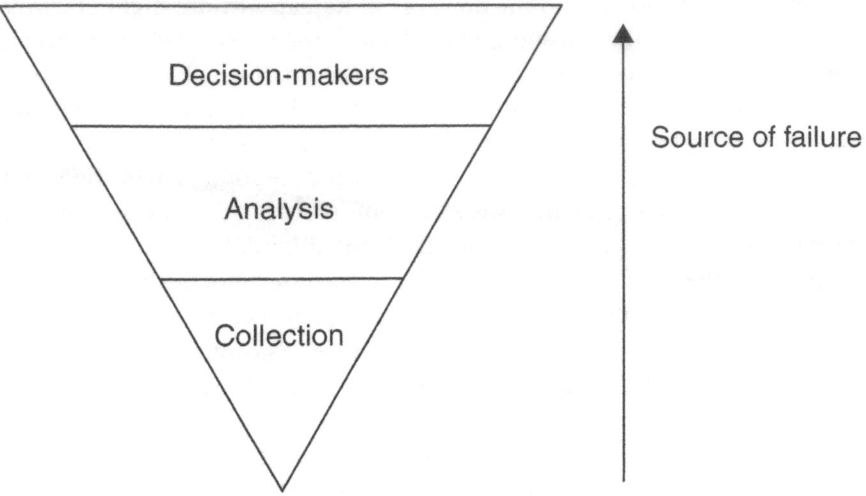

Figure 7.1 *Betts' sources of intelligence failure*

actionable intelligence. This tendency is heightened in the aftermath of an attack or failure to prevent some other form of strategic surprise.[5]

Betts' analysis of failure, however, is directly challenged by Amy Zegart, who identifies the reasons for the 9/11 failure as lying in

> 1) cultural pathologies that led intelligence agencies to resist new technologies, ideas, and tasks; 2) perverse promotion incentives that rewarded intelligence officials for all the wrong things; and 3) structural weaknesses dating back decades that hindered the operation of the CIA and FBI and prevented the US Intelligence Community from working as a coherent whole.[6]

Hence, 'structural fragmentation'[7] imposed limits on communication. On this reading, it follows that the key to minimizing the risk of future failure lies in organizational reform, management style and willingness to encourage an environment where competing hypotheses can be explored.

The 'dominant assumption' within agencies, handed down as a given in training programmes, must also be challenged. For example, Frank Snepp, principal analyst for the CIA on North Vietnam for a time from the late 1960s, has recalled how:

> When I was training in the Agency to go to Vietnam, I was hit over the head with the Domino theory. I was told that it was what would define the future of South Vietnam. The ideology that propelled us into the war obscured history, and it was obviously a terrible oversight because in embracing the domino theory we perpetuated our presence there, we justified staying in.[8]

Dominant assumptions similarly constrained responses to developments in the US relationship with the Soviet Union. In 1983 a series of factors, including the heightened confrontational rhetoric of President Reagan's references to the Soviet Union, reaction to the downing of Korean Airlines flight 007 over Soviet airspace and the unveiling of the 'Star Wars' missile defence concept, convinced the Soviet leadership that the US was preparing to launch an attack. When Soviet defector Oleg Gordievsky visited Washington in 1986 he found that analysts had completely misread this state of Soviet paranoia, recalling that 'one important analyst told me it was a huge deception plan by the Soviet leadership to deceive us. So they were so deeply rooted in their own dogmas of the previous time, when they received fresh and different information which clashed with their dogmas, they didn't like it. They were not flexible enough.'[9]

As noted above, 'failure' can also be a consequence of unrealistic expectations. Predictions drawn from analysis as to future behaviour will never be 100 per cent accurate. In this, intelligence work has something in common with meteorology, the science of weather forecasting. The latter, resting on a firmer scientific basis, can predict general trends with a high degree of confidence, but it cannot always predict accurately, nor can it always be relied on to predict the *impact* of poor or freak weather reliably, especially where this differs markedly from past experience. For example, the US government appeared completely unprepared for the inundation of New Orleans after Hurricane Katrina in September 2005 despite a warning from the Federal Emergency Management Agency (FEMA) in early 2001 that it was one of the three most likely disasters to happen – the other two being a terrorist attack on New York and a Californian earthquake.[10]

Intelligence services are not only expected to be able to assess trends and anticipate deviations from trends, they are also expected to be able to gauge the *impact* of these. In this, there is a risk that too much is being expected. For example, there were clear failings of US intelligence in relation to its analysis of the immediate post-war situation that would face US forces in Iraq, so much so that:

> Intelligence officials were convinced that American soldiers would be greeted warmly when they pushed into southern Iraq [hence] a CIA operative suggested sneaking hundreds of small American flags into the country for grateful Iraqis to wave at their liberators. The agency would capture the spectacle on film and beam it throughout the Arab world. It would be the ultimate information operation.[11]

This erroneous macro analysis bears responsibility for numerous micro failures, including the failure to anticipate the resistance role of paramilitary forces in southern Iraq during the US advance towards Baghdad; the failure to identify and secure arms caches across the country, subsequently raided by or on behalf of resistance forces; and underestimation of both the devastation brought about by a combination of sanctions and war to Iraq's infrastructure, and hence the extent of reconstruction required.[12] Echoing one of the explanations for intelligence failures over Vietnam some thirty years earlier (and discussed below), former CIA Deputy Director Richard J. Kerr explained that: 'The intelligence accurately forecast the reactions of the ethnic and tribal factions in Iraq', but nevertheless, 'collection was poor. Too much emphasis was placed on current intelligence and there was too little research on important social, political and cultural issues.'[13] The Butler Report made a similar point in relation to gaps in pre-war UK intelligence.[14]

The limits to intelligence are easily demonstrated by reference to several defining events of the last century that US intelligence failed to anticipate. The list includes the Soviet testing of its first atomic bomb, the North Korean invasion of South Korea, the construction of the Berlin Wall, an apparent string of failures over Vietnam, the Soviet invasions of Czechoslovakia in 1968 and of Afghanistan in 1979, the Iranian revolution of 1979, the Polish crisis of 1980–1[15] and – more centrally given that US intelligence's primary focus for over forty years was the USSR – the end of the Cold War. We discuss Vietnam and Iran in more detail below. With regard to the Soviet atomic bomb, just five days before it was exploded the CIA produced a report echoing earlier analyses that mid-1953 was the most probable date for Soviet acquisition.[16] Although U-2 spy planes identified Soviet missile sites under construction in Cuba, US intelligence had failed to anticipate their siting there. With regard to the North Korean invasion of South Korea, the CIA reported as early as March 1950 that an invasion *could* occur in June and subsequently sent over 1,000 reports covering the North Korean military build-up, only for these to be overridden by the military because they conflicted with the prevailing strategic consensus of the day, that North Korea would not risk such an adventure.[17] As the British Ambassador to Japan told the Foreign Office at the time:

> While the actual attack itself came as a complete surprise to everybody both here and in Korea, my Military Adviser tells me that Military Intelligence had learnt in April last that preparations were being made for such an attack. The Americans therefore should have been ready for it at least to the point of making up their minds exactly what should be done, in the technical way, when the storm broke.[18]

The failure to anticipate the Soviet invasion of Afghanistan represents another analytical failure, based on a persistent belief that the USSR would not introduce large numbers of conventional forces into the neighbouring country. As a March 1979 CIA assessment concluded:

> The Soviets would be most reluctant to introduce large numbers of ground forces into Afghanistan to keep in power an Afghan government that had lost the support of virtually all segments of the population. Not only would the Soviets find themselves in an awkward morass in Afghanistan, but their actions could seriously damage their relations with India, and – to a lesser degree – with Pakistan. As a more likely option, the Soviets probably could seek to reestablish ties with those members of the Afghan opposition with whom Moscow had dealt profitably in the past.[19]

Hence the invasion caught the intelligence community off guard. The failure was not a consequence of an absence of information that could be held to point in the direction of an imminent Soviet invasion. Rather, it was a consequence of a mindset that did not consider an invasion to be a rational choice and so discounted it, and which sought to fit subsequent, potentially contradictory, evidence into this mindset rather than assess how far the evidence undermined the validity of the prevailing assumption. Hence, this case illustrates a problem highlighted by Jack Davis: 'Whatever the analyst's level of expertise, the "hard-wiring" of the mind tends to make confirming information seem more vivid and authoritative than information that would call an established bottom line judgment into question.' Compounding this problem is the fact that 'general recognition of cognitive vulnerability does not remove risk of unmotivated bias in evaluating information'.[20]

In 1983 the case of Afghanistan was included in a report commissioned to examine the quality of intelligence relating to 'significant historical failures over the last twenty years or so'.[21] This situated the core analytical error as being a misunderstanding of Soviet intentions rooted in an accurate assessment of the costs, but one to which US analysts then attached an inappropriate cost–benefit measure. 'In hindsight', the report concluded:

> the intelligence community accurately estimated the advantages and disadvantages of intervention. The community held to a premise that the disadvantages of intervention outweighed the advantages and concluded therefore that the Soviets would act rationally in accordance with our perception of Soviet self-interest. As real as the penalties to the Soviets have proved to be, we failed to comprehend the imperatives of Soviet policy as they perceived them. We had a clear understanding of their capabilities, but we misjudged their intentions.[22]

The extent of the apparent failure to predict the end of the Cold War is contested. Douglas J. MacEachin has contended that from the mid-1970s the Soviet Union was correctly described by CIA analysts as being 'plagued by a deteriorating economy and intensifying societal problems'.[23] Nevertheless, others have argued that the CIA's overestimation of Soviet economic growth shows that they were wide of the mark. On Soviet military strength, it has been claimed that the CIA was misled by double agents who exaggerated the preparedness and strength of the Soviet military, feeding into CIA reports that helped persuade Congress to grant funding for projects such as the F-22 fighter aircraft.[24] MacEachin refers to a CIA assessment produced in autumn 1989 pointing to turbulent times ahead for the USSR which it was 'doubtful at best' that Gorbachev would be able to control. However, this concern over the domestic impact of Gorbachev's reforms is not the same as predicting his acquiescence in the downfall of communism in East Germany or role in dismantling the Warsaw Pact as a unified military alliance. MacEachin is correct to note that the CIA identified trends that could lead in a given direction with the assistance of the appropriate agency, which arrived in the shape of Gorbachev,[25] but it could not predict when this would happen, or its scale or impact – as noted above, much like the meteorologists who struggle to translate weather indicators into precise predictions.

The post-Cold War world has also featured significant failures at the levels of collection and analysis. In May 1998, Clinton Administration officials found out about India's nuclear tests from media coverage of the Indian government's official announcement. Senate Intelligence Committee chairman

Richard C. Shelby called it a 'colossal failure'. Echoing the failure to foresee the Soviet invasion of Afghanistan, the subsequent Jeremiah Report pointed to mirror-imaging (the assumption that a target would behave in the same way as the customer of the intelligence would in similar circumstances) as a key cause of the failure, along with limited co-operation within the fragmented US intelligence community. In addition, an almost complete absence of HUMINT inside India had left the US dependent on satellite imagery.[26] The utility of this had been hampered by a meeting in 1995 when the US Ambassador to India had shown Indian officials spy satellite photographs showing test preparations, allowing the Indians to improve concealment techniques. In fact, US satellites had picked up evidence of test preparation during the night before the detonation, but CIA satellite intelligence analysts slept through it, not having been put on alert.[27] As George Tenet told the SSCI: 'There is no getting around the fact that we did not predict these particular Indian nuclear tests . . . We did not get it right, period.'[28] More recently, President Obama was reportedly critical of US intelligence over its performance in predicting the course of unrest and revolt in the 2011 'Arab Spring', particularly around its failure to anticipate the rapidity with which President Zine el-Abidine Ben Ali would fall in Tunisia.[29]

In all of the above cases, what intelligence failed to do was to anticipate strategic shifts in behaviour, leaving its customer vulnerable to strategic surprise. However, the anticipation of strategic shifts is problematic. It is far easier for analysts to predict on the basis of the continuation of identified trends. Deviation from these trends by an intelligence target can only be anticipated with certainty via information from sources close to decision-makers – the 'what do they think?' dilemma.

The Policymaker–Intelligence Interface as a Site of Intelligence Failure

It is at the policymaker–intelligence nexus – that is, dissemination – that, if Betts' model is to hold good, we would expect to find the most serious sources of potential failure. Loch Johnson characterized 'disregard of objective intelligence' by policymakers as one of what he termed the 'seven sins of strategic intelligence'.[30] As with Stalin's refusal to believe intelligence that the Nazis were preparing to invade the Soviet Union in 1941, 'no shortcoming of strategic intelligence is more often cited than the self-delusion of policymakers who brush aside – or bend – facts that fail to conform to their *Weltanschauung*'.[31] This kind of 'intelligence failure' is essentially political in that the failure is not primarily that of the intelligence community, beyond failing to convince the policymaker of the validity of its analyses, and is closely related to the politicization of intelligence – that is, the manipulation of evidence to fit preferred and pre-existing explanations, or the selection of evidence (involving omission as well as inclusion) so as to fit a known desired outcome.

Vietnam

Where intelligence does not fit policy preferences, it can be ignored by policymakers. This was the case with large numbers of pessimistic CIA analyses during the 1960s (and before) on the situation in Vietnam. One illustrative example concerns an evaluation of a new Vietnam initiative drafted by Director for Intelligence R. Jack Smith, who has recalled how:

> If one based one's decision on the conclusions of our study, the result was obvious: the gain was not worth the cost. Nevertheless, the President announced the next day that he intended to go ahead. Distinctly annoyed that an admirable piece of analysis, done under forced draft at White House request, was being ignored, I stomped into Helms's office. 'How in the hell can the President make that decision in the face of our findings?' I asked.
>
> Dick fixed me with a sulphurous look. 'How do I know how he made up his mind? How does any president make decisions? Maybe Lynda Bird was in favor of it. Maybe one of his old friends urged him. Maybe it was something he read. Don't ask me to explain the workings of a president's mind.'[32]

For his part, Chester Cooper, a former NSC staff officer, noted how Lyndon Johnson's memoirs,

> which are replete with references to and long quotations from documents which influenced his thinking and decisions on Vietnam, contain not a single reference to a National Intelligence Estimate or, indeed, to any other intelligence analysis. Except for Secretary McNamara, who became a frequent requester and an avid reader of Estimates dealing with Soviet military capabilities and with the Vietnam situation, and McGeorge Bundy, ONE [Office of National Estimates] had a thin audience during the Johnson administration.[33]

It would be wrong to present CIA thinking on the Vietnam War as constituting a unified vision. There was a considerable gap between the views of officers involved in the operational side of the war and those involved in producing analysis, and even within these two groups there were divisions.[34] While operationally, the CIA was centrally and enthusiastically involved in the Phoenix programme[35] – a (supposedly) intelligence-led operation aimed at physically neutralizing the Vietcong leadership which gave rise to serial allegations of torture and extrajudicial execution – analysts tended to offer policymakers consistently pessimistic assessments. However, analysts were susceptible to pressure. Harold Ford concedes that, 'at times some CIA analysts overreacted to certain assertive personalities from other offices who happened to be arguing wholly unsupportable optimism', and that in a 'handful' of cases, 'analytic officers caved in to pressures from above and produced mistakenly rosy judgments'. One source of pressure was from DCIs themselves, some of whom 'brought pressure on Agency officers to make their Vietnam analyses more palatable to policymakers'.[36]

One of these was John McCone. Ford gives an example from early 1963, weeks before the riots in Hue that led to a deterioration in the situation in South Vietnam which culminated in the self-immolation of Buddhist monks and the assassination of South Vietnamese president Diem. At this time McCone, the Joint Chiefs of Staff, the US Embassy in Saigon and other policymakers objected to a draft NIE which concluded that Vietnam suffered from a catalogue of debilitating woes, including an absence of 'aggressive and firm leadership at all levels of command, poor morale among the troops, lack of trust between peasant and soldier, poor tactical use of available forces, a very inadequate intelligence system, and obvious Communist penetration of the South Vietnamese military organization'. As Ford recounts:

> Those criticisms by Community analysts raised a firestorm of protest among the policymaking officers. They brought such pressure on DCI McCone and ONE that the latter caved in and agreed to a rewritten, decidedly more rosy NIE, in which the earlier criticisms of the ARVN [Army of the Republic of Vietnam] were muted and the tone of the Estimate changed: the first sentence of the revised NIE now read, 'We believe that Communist progress has been blunted [in South Vietnam] and that the situation is improving.' This was not one of the CIA's proudest moments.[37]

This was not an isolated incident. For example, while intelligence community analyses were sceptical of the validity of the 'domino effect', McCone sided with the military in their belief in it and, as the individual charged with 'telling it like it is' to policymakers, failed to challenge this belief by pointing out his Agency's own scepticism.[38] McCone was not alone in failing to represent and defend analysis, however unpalatable to policymakers. The CIA's Special Assistant for Vietnam Affairs, George Carver, regularly gave policymakers more upbeat assessments of the situation in Vietnam than the analyses supported.

All of which points to the biggest hurdle facing analysts seeking to get their message across to policymakers, 'the fact that the decisions on what to do in Vietnam were not taking place in a vacuum but in a highly charged political arena'.[39] In such an atmosphere, policymakers were unlikely to be receptive to intelligence unless it supported the positions they were already defending. It also presented McCone with a conundrum as DCI. Challenging core policymaker assumptions would affect his credibility and perhaps even his access. Yet while not challenging these assumptions his access was ineffective. After he did diverge from Johnson on the best way forward, his access was duly affected. McCone was frozen out and resigned in April 1965. The lessons of his experience cannot have been lost on subsequent DCIs, including George Tenet. The credibility/access conundrum remains for DCIs, and it may well be that Tenet's 'slam dunk' reassurance on Iraqi WMD in December 2002 is just a relatively recent expression of it.[40]

Iran

Similar problems around 'telling it like it is' contributed to the failure to predict the coming of revolution in Iran, so much so that in just a year before the Shah fell, President Carter during a visit to Tehran publicly praised him as 'an island of stability in one of the more troubled areas of the world'.[41] In a classic example of confusing intelligence with policy, Carter's DCI, Admiral Stansfield Turner, subsequently offered the view that:

> For us in the intelligence world to have gone to the President and said, 'We think Iran is about to crumble,' would have been a major change in US policy. It's hard for anybody to go that much against the opinion that has built up in this country as to what the relationship with Iran should be . . . to come to the conclusion that this was the truth would have been very difficult because it would have been running so contrary to the tide of opinion about what our relationship with Iran was.[42]

The failure over Iran, however, went beyond a failure at the level of the intelligence community–policymaker interface. It stands out because of the scale of the US stake in the stability of the Shah's rule. Others have criticized the short-term character of analyses on Iran, focused on individual disturbances or riots at the expense of attention to the wider trend and, linked to this, the role the US could play in attempting to persuade the Shah to moderate or change his approach to governance.[43] Analyses were based on a dominant assumption that the Shah would survive the crisis. It may well be that this insistence on the solidity of the Shah's rule was based on the fact that, as Gary Sick, a former NSC staffer with responsibility for Iran, has observed, 'the CIA were not a neutral observer and they had something at stake. And the stake was their relationship with the Shah and his regime that was extremely important to them. They were simply not prepared to sit back and look at it objectively.'[44] Crucially, their focus was not on Iranian domestic politics, but on the Cold War advantage that close alliance with the Shah offered and in backing his rule in order to aid its continuation:

> The Shah was prepared to co-operate very actively with regard to intelligence on the Soviet Union – we had several big sites located in Iran, secret sites that tracked missile development in the Soviet Union – and to keep track of regional affairs, the co-operation between the Shah and the station chief in Iran was very, very close. So the station chief basically had an appointment to see the Shah on a regular basis, like once a week. And they had a long, detailed discussion and an exchange of information in which the CIA found this to be just an extraordinarily useful relationship. And, as a result, they were probably the last who were willing to admit that something terrible was going on here when the Shah started to fall. They were far, far behind the game.[45]

Similarly, Robert Jervis, in a post-mortem analysis prepared for the CIA, drew attention to the extent to which policymakers and analysts shared the same assumptions about the Shah. The policy environment impacted on judgements about the Shah's position and the existence of any alternatives:

> Looking over the range of beliefs held by people in and out of government it is clear that, as a generalization, those people who thought that the Shah's regime was on balance good for the citizens of Iran and thought that supporting him was in the American interest also thought that his government was quite strong. Those who thought he was evil also believed that it was bad for the United States to aid him and saw his regime as relatively vulnerable.[46]

At the same time, as Michael Donovan has emphasized, even though the US–Iranian relationship was very close, Iran remained a 'hard target' for US intelligence, and the eventual outcome was so hard to predict that, as Donovan writes, 'in 1976–77, to have concluded that the Shah of Iran would fall to millions of Iranians rallied by an aging cleric in exile, one would have needed the Oracle of Delphi'.[47] Yet there were fundamental failures. As a 1979 House of Representatives inquiry into the debacle concluded: 'In the case of Iran, long-standing US attitudes toward the Shah inhibited intelligence collection, dampened policy-makers' appetite for analysis of the Shah's position, and deafened policy makers to the warning implicit in available intelligence.'[48]

Politicization of Intelligence

This, then, leads us into the realm of politicization of intelligence. Gregory Treverton has usefully outlined five different forms that politicization can take, ranging from what may be considered 'hard' to 'soft' forms.[49] At the 'hard' end of the scale lies *direct pressure* from senior figures in government to arrive at a desired conclusion in line with an existing policy preference. A second form is the *house line*, whereby a dominant assumption emerges, any challenge to which is regarded as heresy. A third form is *cherry-picking*, whereby senior policymakers select the intelligence that best supports their policy preference from a wider picture presented by overall assessments. Treverton also notes that with regard to US intelligence on Iraq's WMD, policymakers were not content simply to engage in cherry-picking, but went so far as to 'grow their own'. A fourth form is *question asking*, wherein the form in which a question is asked suggests the desired answer, or analysis that is not consistent with a policy preference is subjected to repeated questioning in a bid to shift it more towards that policy preference. Finally, at the 'softer' end of the scale comes *shared mindset*, wherein strong presumptions are shared by both policymakers and the intelligence community – as, for example, in the case of Iran discussed above.

Thus, politicization can be an almost intangible process. As Paul Pillar, the former US National Intelligence Officer for the Near East and South Asia from 2000 to 2005, remarked with regard to US inquiries into intelligence on Iraq's WMD:

> Unfortunately, this issue [i.e., politicization] has been reduced in some post-mortem inquiries to a question of whether policy-makers twisted analysts' arms. That question is insufficient. Such blatant attempts at politicization are relatively rare, and when they do occur are almost never successful. It is more important to ask about the overall *environment* in which intelligence analysts worked. It is one thing to work in an environment in which policy-makers are known to want the most objective analysis, wherever the evidence may lead. It is quite another thing to work in an environment in which the policy-maker has already set his course, is using intelligence to publicly justify the course, will welcome analysis that supports the policy, and will spurn analysis that does not support it. The latter environment was what prevailed on Iraq in the year before the war.[50]

Moreover, policymakers naturally form their own policy preferences – a product of a combination of their own backgrounds, experiences, interests and world-view – in advance of receiving intelligence analysis on an issue. Martin Petersen has suggested four reasons why politicians might resist intelligence:

- Policymakers consider themselves highly competent political analysts: 'What money is to New York and celebrity is to Los Angeles, politics and the knowledge of politics is to Washington. Policymakers know they are politically savvy – that is why they are in the positions they are in – and they have tremendous and justified confidence in their own political judgment.'[51]
- Policymakers are essentially 'people people' who 'think in terms of people, not history or trends. They see politics as people making deals, people maneuvering for advantage, people acting. Historical precedents and larger political, military, economic, or social forces register less than individuals. From a policymaker's perspective, France, China, Russia, etc. do not act; their counterparts in these countries act. History is made by powerful people like themselves.'[52]
- Policymakers have met the people intelligence analysts write about.
- Policymakers believe they read all people equally well.

As in the case of Iraq, they might then seek supporting evidence for these preferences from the intelligence and can be resistant to any intelligence that points to a different policy direction. For example, in relation to the 1973 Arab–Israeli war, Avi Shlaim identified the omnipresent risk that

> Individuals who work for an organization that displays a strong commitment to a policy or outlook will be tempted to send back news which shows that they are on the right side, and to ignore or underplay uncomfortable facts so as not to risk unpopularity with their colleagues and superiors. In these circumstances, it is not always possible to distinguish between what is seen and what is regarded as expedient to see . . . If the intelligence is dominated by a group of powerful decision makers, it will become the prisoner of these decision makers' images, dogmas, and preconceptions. Instead of challenging these dogmas and correcting these images when they clash with its objective findings, the intelligence service will be no more than a rubber stamp of these preconceptions.[53]

Complicating matters somewhat, there is also the view that analysts' training has placed too great an emphasis on 'straight line, single outcome' analysis, a view that finds perfect harmony with policymakers' natural belief in their own ability to divine outcomes. As articulated by US Defense Secretary Donald Rumsfeld, this can be taken to mean that: 'If you think about it, what comes out of intelligence is not fixed, firm conclusions. What comes out are a speculation, an analysis, probabilities, possibilities, estimates. Best Guesses.'[54] In this context it can be argued, as Jack Davis does, that: 'Policy officials have the licence to . . . ask that assumptions and evidence be examined more thoroughly, and to request customized follow-on assessments. That is part of their job description, whether they are seeking fresh insights or analytic support for their established views.'[55] However, the idea that analysts offer just one view is dangerous, the thin end of a wedge that raises the unwelcome spectre of an internal market in analysis, and which can lead to policymaker demands for access to raw intelligence and exclusion of analysts from the generation of assessments. This is precisely what John Bolton did as Under-Secretary of State for Arms Control, explaining that: 'I found that there was lots of stuff that I wasn't getting and that the INR analysts weren't including. I didn't want it filtered, I wanted to see everything – to be fully informed. If that puts someone's nose out of joint, sorry about that.'[56] When Bolton's subsequent nomination to be US Ambassador to the UN was held up in Congress, one of the areas of controversy was his attempt to sack the national intelligence officer for Latin America, a career intelligence official, who would not agree with Bolton's assertion that Cuba had biological weapons.[57]

But if policymakers do not get what they want, bodies can be created to produce it – in Treverton's terms, they can 'grow their own' – as with the Paul Wolfowitz-inspired Pentagon Office of Special Plans (OSP) in the run-up to the 2003 invasion of Iraq. By mid-2002 intelligence was being 'stovepiped' from the Pentagon, via the Vice President's office, to the White House without any professional intelligence filtering. Seymour Hersh felt that Wolfowitz, along with Donald Rumsfeld,

> came into office openly suspicious of the intelligence community and the bureaucracy. They thought they were too soft on Iraq, not tough enough with Saddam, not able to make the decisive choices. So what you have is a bunch of people who weren't lying; they simply had fixed the system so it couldn't give them information they did not want to hear.[58]

As one disaffected former intelligence official told Hersh: 'One of the reasons I left was my sense that they were using the intelligence from the CIA and other agencies only when it fit their agenda. They didn't like the intelligence they were getting, and so they brought in people to write the stuff . . . If it doesn't fit their theory, they don't want to accept it.'[59] In this context, devil's advocacy was unwelcome whereas worst-case assessments on Iraqi WMD issues were regularly requested by the Vice President's office. Ironically, in his pro-war manifesto *The Threatening Storm*, Kenneth Pollack highlighted Saddam's unwillingness to accept intelligence except what he wanted to hear and the consequent tendency of those in government and military circles to furnish him with just that, and argued that this was one of the sources of the threat posed by Saddam.[60] Politicization, then, remains a constant danger, seemingly transcending regime type.

There is, however, a legitimate question – with no clear answer – concerning the appropriate distance and independence that intelligence should have from policymaking. Michael Herman has written that: 'Intelligence is part of the government system, and has to have empathy and credibility with the policy-makers it serves. It cannot adopt an Olympian objectivity, or detach itself completely from government's policies and preconceptions. It has to sell its product, and has to be sensitive to its audience to do so.' But the recurrent problem facing US professionals, Herman continues, has been 'getting sufficiently close to policy to be heard at all, amid all the size, diffusiveness and clamour of Washington. Alternative interpretations are always available to help policymakers pick and choose what suits them. Cherry-picking leaders can have a ball, at least in the short term.'[61]

It is clear from the cases cited in this chapter that strong pressure from policymakers can have a corrupting effect on the production of analysis, although it is worth noting at this point that intelligence is not the only area where governments have pressured experts to produce findings in line with their policy preferences – the tendency is more widespread.[62] In the terms of chapter 2, knowledge does not necessarily inform the exercise of power, but power may determine what is to be defined as knowledge.

The *9/11 Commission Report*: Explaining Intelligence Failure?

There was never any doubt that the events of 9/11 represented the kind of surprise attack that the CIA had been formed to secure against, and hence a catastrophic intelligence failure. The task of the 9/11 Commission was essentially to identify the nature of the failure, in so doing locate its source, and make recommendations to prevent further catastrophe. A close reading of the report shows clearly where failures occurred, although the evidence that policymakers failed to act on intelligence warnings was not translated into criticism of the principals in the Bush Administration. Perhaps fearing criticism for failure to heed intelligence warnings, the Administration was initially reluctant to establish the Commission, and once it had done so was hardly enthusiastic in its co-operation. It attempted to prevent National Security Advisor (NSA) Condoleezza Rice from testifying, and insisted that the president himself would only testify if he could be accompanied by Vice President Dick Cheney and not be required to testify on oath. As with the later Butler Inquiry in the UK, a compromise agreement kept any 'individual blame' out of the report.[63]

In terms of timely intelligence warnings and the political failure to act on them, chapter 8 of the report, 'The System Was "Blinking Red"', is key, with its headings ('The drumbeat begins', 'High probability of near-term "spectacular" attacks', 'The calm before the storm' and 'Government response to the threats') effectively conveying the same story that former Clinton and Bush Administration terrorism co-ordinator Richard Clarke had already told of serial warnings but no policy response.[64] In part this reflected the dominant assumptions among the foreign policy experts relied upon by the new president. These assumptions were still shaped by the experience of the Cold War, and their view of threats as being essentially state-centric meant they were insufficiently flexible to make the cognitive adjustments required in order to recognize the warnings. The key document that should have alerted the

Box 7.1 6 August 2001 PDB: 'Bin Laden determined to strike US'

Clandestine, foreign government, and media reports indicate bin Laden since 1997 has wanted to conduct terrorist attacks in the U.S. Bin Laden implied in U.S. television interviews in 1997 and 1998 that his followers would follow the example of World Trade Center bomber Ramzi Yousef and 'bring the fighting to America'.

After U.S. missile strikes on his base in Afghanistan in 1998, bin Laden told followers he wanted to retaliate in Washington, according to a – – service.

An Egyptian Islamic Jihad (EIJ) operative told – – service at the same time that bin Laden was planning to exploit the operative's access to the U.S. to mount a terrorist strike.

The millennium plotting in Canada in 1999 may have been part of bin Laden's first serious attempt to implement a terrorist strike in the U.S.

Convicted plotter Ahmed Ressam has told the FBI that he conceived the idea to attack Los Angeles International Airport himself, but that in – –, Laden lieutenant Abu Zubaydah encouraged him and helped facilitate the operation. Ressam also said that in 1998 Abu Zubaydah was planning his own U.S. attack.

Ressam says bin Laden was aware of the Los Angeles operation. Although Bin Laden has not succeeded, his attacks against the U.S. Embassies in Kenya and Tanzania in 1998 demonstrate that he prepares operations years in advance and is not deterred by setbacks. Bin Laden associates surveyed our embassies in Nairobi and Dar es Salaam as early as 1993, and some members of the Nairobi cell planning the bombings were arrested and deported in 1997.

Al Qaeda members – including some who are U.S. citizens – have resided in or traveled to the U.S. for years, and the group apparently maintains a support structure that could aid attacks.

Two al-Qaeda members found guilty in the conspiracy to bomb our embassies in East Africa were U.S. citizens, and a senior EIJ member lived in California in the mid-1990s.

A clandestine source said in 1998 that a bin Laden cell in New York was recruiting Muslim-American youth for attacks.

We have not been able to corroborate some of the more sensational threat reporting, such as that from a – – service in 1998 saying that Bin Laden wanted to hijack a U.S. aircraft to gain the release of 'Blind Sheikh' Omar Abdel Rahman and other U.S.-held extremists.

Nevertheless, FBI information since that time indicates patterns of suspicious activity in this country consistent with preparations for hijackings or other types of attacks, including recent surveillance of federal buildings in New York.

The FBI is conducting approximately 70 full-field investigations throughout the U.S. that it considers bin Laden-related. CIA and the FBI are investigating a call to our embassy in the UAE [United Arab Emirates] in May saying that a group of bin Laden supporters was in the U.S. planning attacks with explosives.

Source: 9/11 Commission Report, pp. 261–2. Redactions are indicated by – –.

Administration was a 6 August 2001 PDB, containing an item headed 'Bin Laden determined to strike US' (see box 7.1.). It was the thirty-sixth time in 2001 that bin Laden or al-Qaeda had figured in a PDB. The analysts who produced the item were responding to an inquiry by the president about whether any threats to the US existed, and, to them, 'represented an opportunity to communicate their view that the threat of a Bin Laden attack in the United

States remained both current and serious'. The president told the inquiry that the report 'was historical in nature' and that 'if his advisers had told him there was a cell in the United States, they would have moved to take care of it'. However, the PDB contained a number of potential warnings, including the fact that FBI information, 'indicates patterns of suspicious activity in this country consistent with preparations for hijackings or other types of attacks, including recent surveillance of federal buildings in New York'.[65]

At the same time, analysts' fears about the possibility of an attack on the US were not reaching the right people. The Commission reported that: 'Most of the intelligence community recognized in the summer of 2001 that the number and severity of threat reports were unprecedented.' However, despite the *number* of fragments, there were too few specifics to point to a named target. Moreover, the 9/11 planning fell into 'the void between foreign and domestic threats', which made it harder to make sense of the fragments:

> The foreign intelligence agencies were watching overseas, alert to foreign threats to US interests there. The domestic agencies were waiting for evidence of a domestic threat from sleeper cells within the United States. No one was looking for a foreign threat to domestic targets. The threat that was coming was not from sleeper cells. It was foreign – but from foreigners who had infiltrated into the United States.[66]

The President's style of governance, and indeed level of engagement with the material, can themselves be interpreted as a contributory factor in the 9/11 failure. No NSC meetings were called to discuss the threat outlined in the 6 August briefing, and the Commission could find 'no indication of any further discussion before September 11 among the President and his top advisers of the possibility of a threat of an al Qaeda attack in the United States'. One reason for this is that the President retired to his Texas ranch for the summer. DCI Tenet visited him there on 17 August but 'did not recall any discussions with the President of the domestic threat during this period'. The report saw 'little evidence that the progress of the plot was disturbed by government action. The US government was unable to capitalize on mistakes made by al Qaeda. Time ran out.'[67]

Part of the reason for this was political – the Bush Administration had other policy priorities that conflicted with what would be required to reduce or eliminate a terrorist threat. As Stephen Marrin has argued:

> In the end, it appears that the influence that intelligence analysis has on decision-making depends on the decision-makers, the resources available to them, the policy options they consider, and the political context that shapes the process. To understand the failure of decision-makers to respond effectively to early warning from intelligence agencies about the threat from Al Qaeda, one must start with the policy environment at the time rather than the adequacy or sufficiency of the intelligence that they were provided with. One cannot understand the influence, or lack of influence, of intelligence analysis on policy by studying intelligence. Instead, one must study policy.[68]

There are analyses that seek to explain the post-9/11 limits of intelligence without reference to politicization, but they are the weaker for it.[69]

The Iraq WMD Failure

The question of how far failure was the responsibility of policymakers and how far it was that of the intelligence community ran through national inquiries into intelligence on Iraq WMD and the decision to go to war in Iraq. There were several of these; two SSCI inquiries and an inquiry by a presidential commission (Silberman-Robb) in the US, five inquiries that dealt with pre-war intelligence on Iraq in the UK (in chronological order, by the House of Commons Foreign Affairs Committee, by the ISC, the Hutton Inquiry, the Butler Inquiry and the Chilcot Inquiry) and a parliamentary inquiry followed by a review of the intelligence agencies in Australia. All were themselves highly political processes, from the drafting of their terms of reference to the writing of their reports.[70] The extent to which they could or should cross the line dividing intelligence performance from the political context in which it occurred was an issue that all had to address. All did so to differing extents and with differing degrees of willingness. Ultimately, though, the evidence that these inquiries uncovered, in what became the single most heavily investigated question in intelligence history, enabled the construction of a nuanced understanding of the nature of the failure which sees it as lying at multiple points in the intelligence cycle and also involving failure at the policymaker level.

US inquiries

The SSCI's investigation into 'the US intelligence community's pre-war intelligence assessments' on Iraq focused on the production and content of one document – the October 2002 NIE *Iraq's Continuing Programs for Weapons of Mass Destruction*. According to the CIA, the NIE process is designed to provide the 'best, unvarnished, and unbiased information – regardless of whether analytic judgments conform to US policy'.[71] This focus allowed the Committee to consider how close the CIA came in the case of Iraq to achieving its Directorate of Intelligence's goals of producing analysis that is rigorous, is well-reasoned and has appropriate caveats. Its answer was 'nowhere near'. 'Most of the major key judgments' contained in the NIE, it concluded, 'either overstated, or were not supported by, the underlying intelligence reporting. A series of failures, particularly in analytic trade craft, led to the mischaracterization of the intelligence.' The failure, then, was firmly located as one of analysis, with some failures in collection, all compounded by poor management and an environment that seemed to militate against information sharing.[72] In short, the report assigns responsibility for the failure first to analysts, second to managers and bureaucratic structures, and third to failures in collection. This would appear to call into question the validity of Betts' model, which would suggest that the major responsibility for failure would lie with policymakers, with the additional possibility of some analytical errors, and even of some failings in collection.

One factor that the SSCI decided was not contributory was the timescale for production of NIEs. The 1994 drafting guidelines contain three broad timescales for drafting: a 2–3-week 'fast track'; a 4–8-week 'normal track'; and a 2-month or more 'long track'.[73] In a mid-1970s essay on the matter, Sherman Kent observed that up to that point NIEs had historically taken 6–8 months to produce, although in the case of the 1956 Suez crisis a draft NIE, bypassing key stages, was produced in a record 30 minutes.[74] The timescale for the Iraqi WMD NIE was 'fast track'. The process began on 12 September (concurrent with the production in the UK of the Downing Street dossier); a draft was prepared by 23 September and discussed at an all-day co-ordination meeting on 25 September; and a second draft was sent out the following day.

While the 1994 drafting guidelines indicate that at this point the draft should have been submitted to intelligence community peers and a panel of intelligence community experts for review, and that a summary of the outside experts' views should have been included in the NIE, the Iraq NIE bypassed these stages. The NIC Vice Chairman explained to the SSCI that: 'I think all you could have called in is an amen chorus on this thing, because there was nobody out there with different views.' The NIE was approved and printed on 1 October 2002. Despite this abbreviated route to publication, the SSCI concluded that the 'fundamental analytical flaws' it contained were not a consequence of this limited time-frame.[75]

There certainly were failures of collection and analysis. The SSCI criticized the heavy reliance during the 1991–8 period on UNSCOM inspectors and the fact that the intelligence community did not use the period of the inspections to establish HUMINT sources that could replace the inspectors in the event of their departure. Incredibly, in the light of the certainty of the conclusions contained in the October 2002 NIE, after 1998 the intelligence community did not have any HUMINT source of its own reporting on Iraqi WMD. With hindsight, this is not surprising – after all, there were no Iraqi WMD. A CIA official told the SSCI that 'despite an intense, vigorous recruitment campaign against Iraq WMD targets . . . we were never able to gain direct access to Iraq's WMD programs',[76] but this difficulty apparently failed to generate any competing hypotheses within the intelligence community as to why this was the case.

Patchy collection left significant gaps in knowledge which heightened the risk of analytical error. For example, the SSCI found that the assessment that Iraq 'is reconstituting its nuclear program' was supported by intelligence that showed that dual-use equipment was being purchased, but failed to show that it was destined for an Iraqi nuclear programme.[77] As with the British government's dossier of the previous month, judgements that Iraq 'has chemical and biological weapons' overstated conclusions that could be safely reached on the basis of the available intelligence.[78] On chemical and biological weapons (CBW), suspicions based on Iraq's past technological capabilities in this area, deception practised against UNSCOM, and past failure to account satisfactorily for all CBW holdings and precursors could have supported a conclusion that Iraq *may have had* such weapons, but the leap to asserting that it *actually had* them was not justified by the raw intelligence. Hence, the claim in the NIE that 'Baghdad has biological weapons' went beyond what could be concluded on the basis of existing information.[79] Similarly, the claim that 'all key aspects – R&D [research and development], production, and weaponization – of Iraq's offensive BW [biological warfare] program are active and that elements are larger and more advanced than they were before the [1991] Gulf War' was not supported by the intelligence.[80] Claims regarding a possible Iraqi mobile biological weapons programme (which could 'exceed the production rates Iraq had prior to the Gulf war'[81]) came mainly from a single HUMINT source subsequently exposed as unreliable and, in any case, 'overstated what the intelligence reporting suggested'. Claims that 'Baghdad has . . . chemical weapons' similarly overstated existing knowledge. Several assessments on Iraq's chemical weapons programme contained within the NIE, for example that 'Saddam probably has stocked at least 100 metric tons and possibly as much as 500 metric tons of chemical weapons agents – much of it added in the last year', were not based directly on intelligence reporting, but were analytical judgements which built on earlier, with hindsight erroneous, analyses – that is, they were a consequence of 'layering'.[82]

Furthermore, the SSCI found that the language used throughout the NIE 'did not accurately portray the uncertainty of the information', and instead 'portrayed what intelligence analysts thought and assessed as what they knew and failed to explain the large gaps in the information on which the assessments were based'.[83] Policymakers were denied the context that open acknowledgement of the gaps in the intelligence picture would have provided. Moreover, where uncertainty was expressed (as was also the case in the UK and Australia), it was used to suggest that Iraq's WMD were even more extensive than indicated, but that clever Iraqi denial and deception techniques, refined throughout the period since 1991, had effectively concealed the scale.[84]

For example, the October 2002 NIE referred to the Amiriyah Serum and Vaccine Institute as 'a fixed dual-use BW agent production' facility. When, in November 2002, UN weapons inspectors under Dr Hans Blix found no evidence to support this claim, the CIA response was to discount the findings 'as a result of the inspectors' relative inexperience in the face of Iraqi denial and deception'. In fact, most of the intelligence on this site had been provided by a HUMINT source, codenamed CURVEBALL, subsequently deemed to be a fabricator (see below). In another example, the assessment in the NIE that Iraq's development of UAVs was 'probably intended to deliver biological warfare agents' not only overstated existing knowledge, but was reached despite Air Force dissent and other agencies' belief that the UAVs' purpose was reconnaissance.[85]

While HUMINT sources were sparse,[86] those that offered what, with hindsight, turned out to be the most accurate information were the ones most readily dismissed as merely rehearsing official propaganda. The report discusses how:

> A former manager in the CIA's Iraq WMD Task Force also told Committee staff that, in retrospect, he believes that the CIA tended to discount HUMINT sources that denied the existence of Iraqi WMD programs as just repeating the Iraqi party line. In fact, numerous interviews with intelligence analysts and documents provided to the Committee indicate that analysts and collectors assumed that sources who denied the existence or continuation of WMD programs and stocks were either lying or not knowledgeable about Iraq's program, while those sources who reported ongoing WMD activities were seen as having provided valuable information.[87]

One important factor in the tendency of analysts to err on the side of worst-case scenarios was the nature of the issue under consideration – WMD – and hence the potentially catastrophic consequences of being wrong. In this, the intelligence community's then-recent failure to 'join the dots' and prevent the 9/11 attacks, and the criticism this had generated, were an important factor in understanding the pessimistic nature of the analysis concerning Iraq – that is, either consciously or subconsciously intelligence analysis was compensating for past failure. A further factor conditioning the response was that a decade earlier the community had failed to identify the active nuclear weapons programme that did exist in Iraq and that was discovered and destroyed after 1991.[88] The Iraq failure itself may well have contributed to the 'key judgments' of the November 2007 NIE, 'Iran: nuclear intentions and capabilities', which opened with the statement: 'We judge with high confidence that in fall 2003, Tehran halted its nuclear weapons program.'[89] Having overestimated in the case of Iraq, now there was a danger of over-compensating and underestimating over Iran. The Bush Administration disowned the NIE and, rather than policymakers being accused of interfering in intelligence, in this case the intelligence community was accused of interfering in policy.[90]

As in the UK case, excessive compartmentalization of HUMINT regarded as sensitive was identified as a factor inhibiting the production of the most effective analysis. The Committee concluded that the process by which the intelligence community 'calculates the benefits and risks of sharing sensitive human intelligence is skewed too heavily toward withholding information'. However, the Committee found that the problem of information sharing went further, and that there was a tendency for the CIA to deny information to more specialist agencies that could have allowed for input that challenged existing presumptions. Known dissenting views from other parts of the intelligence community were not always included in assessments where they would have challenged the dominant assumption – as, for example, over the debate concerning the purpose of aluminium tubes. In some cases assessments that conformed to the dominant assumption bypassed specialist agencies that were in a position to challenge them.[91]

Elsewhere, concerns about the credibility of sources were not reflected in assessments or otherwise disseminated to policymakers. One such case concerned an Iraqi mobile biological weapons production programme cited by Secretary of State Colin Powell in his February 2003 speech to the UN. The intelligence on this was based on four sources. Of these, one was an Iraqi asylum seeker, and another an Iraqi major who had defected, was brought to the attention of the DIA by the Iraqi National Congress, and became the subject of a May 2002 fabrication notice.[92] The most important source on this question was CURVEBALL, described as a project engineer involved in biological production facilities, whose debriefings produced 112 reports[93] that were shared with the SSCI, and who, as noted above, was subsequently deemed to be another fabricator. Such was his importance that an INR BW specialist told the SSCI that without his evidence, 'you probably could only say that Iraq would be motivated to have a mobile BW program and that it was attempting to procure components that would support that'.[94]

Shortly before Powell's UN speech, a DoD employee contacted the CIA to share concerns about the reliability of CURVEBALL. He had the distinction of having met CURVEBALL in May 2000, and as such was the only US intelligence official to do so prior to the 2003 invasion of Iraq. He warned that at the time of his contact, he and his agency: 'were having major handling issues with him and were attempting to determine, if in fact, CURVEBALL was who he said he was. These issues, in my opinion, warrant further inquiry, before we use the information as the backbone of one of our major findings of the existence of a continuing Iraqi BW program!' In response, the Deputy Chief of the CIA's Iraqi Task Force emailed him:

> Greetings. Come on over (or I'll come over there) and we can hash this out. As I said last night, let's keep in mind the fact that this war's going to happen regardless of what Curve Ball said or didn't say, and that the Powers That Be probably aren't terribly interested in whether Curve Ball knows what he's talking about. However, in the interest of Truth, we owe somebody a sentence or two of warning, if you honestly have reservations.[95]

Failures at the most senior level of management – that of the DCI – were also identified. Damningly, the report concluded that while George Tenet was 'supposed to function as both the head of the CIA and the head of the Intelligence Community, in many instances he only acted as head of the CIA'.[96] By his own account he was unaware of dissenting opinions within the intelligence community on the possible use of the aluminium tubes at the centre of speculation relating to Iraq's nuclear programme. The fact that he did not, as DCI, expect to be made aware of dissenting opinions until the end of the analytic process meant that 'contentious debate about significant national security issues can go on at the analytic level for months, or years, without the DCI or senior policymakers being informed of any opinions other than those of CIA analysts'. As a result, the DCI was unable to fully perform his role as 'the President's principal intelligence advisor'.[97]

Hence, the explanation for the failure seemed to lie firmly within the intelligence community. However, to return to the earlier point about the highly political nature of commission processes, in February 2004 it had been announced that the SSCI's investigation would be conducted and published in two phases, the second of which would only appear after the 2004 presidential election. This was intended to cover the more politically contentious issues, such as 'whether public statements, reports and testimony regarding Iraq by US Government officials made between the Gulf War period and the commencement of Operation Iraqi Freedom were substantiated by intelligence information'; pre-war intelligence assessments on post-war Iraq; 'any intelligence activities relating to Iraq conducted by the Policy Counterterrorism Evaluation Group (PCTEG) and the Office of Special Plans within the Office of the Under Secretary of Defense for Policy'; and the use of information provided by the exile-based Iraqi National Congress.[98] The phase 2 report was published in several parts, despite considerable Republican resistance, beginning with two parts in September 2006.[99]

Following the 2006 mid-term elections, which saw the Democrats gain a majority in the Senate and hence the chairmanship of the SSCI, a further part, *Prewar Intelligence Assessments About Postwar Iraq*, was published in May 2007, followed by a final part, *Whether Public Statements Regarding Iraq by US Government Officials were Substantiated by Intelligence Information*, in June 2008. This presented a catalogue of unsubstantiated statements by Bush Administration principals. To coincide with this final publication, Chairman Jay Rockefeller released a statement saying that:

> Before taking the country to war, this Administration owed it to the American people to give them a 100 percent accurate picture of the threat we faced. Unfortunately, our Committee has concluded that the Administration made significant claims that were not supported by the intelligence. In making the case for war, the Administration repeatedly presented intelligence as fact when in reality it was unsubstantiated, contradicted, or even non-existent. As a result, the American people were led to believe that the threat from Iraq was much greater than actually existed.
>
> It is my belief that the Bush Administration was fixated on Iraq, and used the 9/11 attacks by al Qa'ida as justification for overthrowing Saddam Hussein. To accomplish this, top Administration officials made repeated statements that falsely linked Iraq and al Qa'ida as a single threat and insinuated that Iraq played a role in 9/11. Sadly, the Bush Administration led the nation into war under false pretenses.
>
> There is no question we all relied on flawed intelligence. But, there is a fundamental difference between relying on incorrect intelligence and deliberately painting a picture to the American people that you know is not fully accurate.[100]

Nevertheless, the relative importance of what we might term 'genuine analytic failure' and that which was a consequence of political pressure remains a contested issue. Robert Jervis has suggested that the Iraq case is one of 'politicization late in the day', from late 2002 onwards – that is, 'once people came to see that the United States and United Kingdom were committed to overthrowing Saddam, they understood that reevaluations would be unacceptable and stopped examining the evidence with much care'. Jervis argues that those who suggest that politicization occurred draw their evidence from this late period but then erroneously apply it to all pre-war intelligence. After all, if earlier intelligence on Iraq 'had bent to the administration's will, then there would have been no need to cherry-pick or distort, since an accurate portrayal of what intelligence was saying would have served the administration's purposes. It is only when intelligence does not yield that policy-makers may have to misreport what it is saying.'[101] However, this has been contested by Fulton Armstrong, then a member of the NIC, whose account suggests that political pressure existed throughout the process, and that CIA analysts strove to generate analyses that supported the Administration line once it was clear what that was.[102] Rather than politicization 'late in the day' this was politicization from at least breakfast time. The debate about the relationship between analytical failure and political pressure continues. Bearing in mind Paul Pillar's emphasis on the importance of 'the overall *environment* in which intelligence analysts worked' (see p. 153), and the absence of a scale by which to measure *environment*, it is a debate which is unlikely to invite a definitive scientific conclusion.

UK inquiries

British inquiries also noted patchy collection and inaccurate analysis. Just as the focus of the US inquiries was the October 2002 NIE, so in the UK case the focus was the Blair government's September 2002 dossier, *Iraq's Weapons of Mass Destruction: The Assessment of the British Government*, and the JIC assessments that fed into it, given that the dossier contained the imprimatur of the JIC. The first inquiry to have access to these assessments was the Butler Inquiry. The picture that emerges from the Butler Report is one of sparse intelligence on Iraqi weapons production, one consistent with the picture that emerges from the US and Australian inquiries, and no surprise given that they were pooling and dealing in essentially the same material. In particular, primary HUMINT sources were thin on the ground. (It is worth noting that the report is silent on SIGINT.) The 2002 push to secure intelligence of the quality required to feed into the September 2002 dossier did produce HUMINT. However, the political imperative meant that insufficient discrimination was applied to the different kinds of information the limited number of sources supplied.[103] In sum, the quality of intelligence gathered from human sources proved to be highly dubious, but at the time it contributed to the capacity to produce intelligence in line with governmental requirements, and so was gratefully accepted. The report's scathing conclusion on these sources of intelligence is that:

- One main SIS source was passing on what was sometimes authoritative reporting but at other times essentially gossip.
- Reports to a further main source of SIS intelligence from a sub-source that were 'important to JIC assessments on Iraqi possession of chemical and biological weapons must be open to doubt'.
- Reports from a third source were withdrawn because they were unreliable.
- Reports from a liaison service on biological agent production were so

flawed that 'JIC assessments drawing on those reports that Iraq had recently produced stocks of biological agent no longer exist'.
- Finally, two main sources produced intelligence regarded as reliable at the time of writing the Butler Report. However, their intelligence was downplayed because it was less alarmist in nature.[104]

This is a dismal picture and one that the Butler Report explains via references to the length of reporting chains, the scarcity of sources leading to more credence being given to untried agents than was the norm, and hitherto reliable agents being quizzed on issues outside their areas of usual reporting. Despite the collection problems, as in the US case the explanation for the failure is identified as existing at analytical and managerial levels. There is no doubt that each of these contributed to the intelligence failure but, as in the US, they cannot of themselves constitute the entire explanation. Underpinning all of these was the political requirement and the timescale surrounding it. This produced political pressure to find information that pointed in a given direction. This pressure corrupted the intelligence process. That the assessment process (at the level of the JIC) was either not alert to this possibility, especially as latterly more alarmist evidence was being unearthed on demand where previously it had been absent, or not sufficiently robust to resist it, represents a further intelligence failure – one of intelligence management.

In this respect, the Butler Report is critical of both the Prime Minister, Tony Blair, and the JIC Chairman, John Scarlett. It criticizes Blair for his language in presenting the dossier to Parliament, which served to reinforce an impression that the actual intelligence struggled to support. Moreover, the report concluded that

> the publication of such a document in the name and with the authority of the JIC had the result that more weight was placed on the intelligence than it could bear. The consequence was to put the JIC and its Chairman into an area of public controversy and arrangements must be made for the future which avoid putting the JIC and its Chairman in a similar position.[105]

Tellingly, the report suggested that there was 'a strong case for the post of Chairman of the JIC being held by someone with experience of dealing with Ministers in a very senior role, and who is demonstrably beyond influence, and thus probably in his last post'.[106] The report also noted that: 'The assessment process must be informed by an understanding of policy-makers' requirements for information, but must avoid being so captured by policy objectives that it reports the world as policy-makers would wish it to be rather than as it is.'[107] In a similar vein, former JIC chair Roderic Braithwaite felt that in this case, the JIC had 'stepped outside its traditional role. It entered the Prime Minister's magic circle. It was engulfed in the atmosphere of excitement which surrounds decision-making in a crisis. Whether they realized it or not, its members went beyond assessment to become part of the process of making and advocating policy. That inevitably undermined their objectivity.'[108]

The 7 July 2005 London Bombings: An Intel Failure?

Did the 7 July 2005 London suicide bombings represent an ure? Not in the strategic sense, as ever since 9/11 security an had warned of the risk. However, there were certainly inst opportunities. Moreover, in the immediate aftermath of the intelligence services and police seemed to have little idea of potential problem. As one newspaper reported:

> Knowledge about the overall strength and structure of al-Qa'ida and its associates in Britain is, at best, patchy and blurred. Scotland Yard has said about 200 British citizens and foreign nationals have travelled to al-Qa'ida training camps and returned to the UK. But the intelligence officers believe the true figure could be up to 3,000.[109]

In other words, there was little concrete idea of the scale of the potential problem, or of whether the bombers were foreign nationals or radicalized British Muslims. Indeed, for the first week after the bombings, in off-the-record briefings police and intelligence officials indicated that they believed the bombers had escaped – they did not think they were looking at a case of suicide bombing.[110]

One possible explanation for this uncertainty related to a historic focus on Irish terrorism, now viewed to have been at the expense of other forms.[111] As table 3.1 above shows, a year after 9/11 and four years after the Good Friday agreement in Northern Ireland, MI5 was still devoting almost as much of its budget (31.5 per cent) to Irish as to international terrorism (37.1 per cent). Yet by the mid-1990s the UK's intelligence agencies and police knew that London was increasingly being used as a base for political violence in the Balkans and Middle East. In particular, a number of young British Muslims fought in Bosnia in the mid-to-late 1990s. One report estimated that up to 200 British Muslims trained in camps in Pakistan before going on to fight in Bosnia.[112] However, these individuals were not considered a threat to UK national security and so there was no attempt to intervene and prevent their activities. In the immediate aftermath of 9/11, £54 million was pumped into MI5, MI6 and GCHQ and 'directed towards more collection (including surveillance, interception and agent-running), investigation, and dissemination of intelligence'.[113] Annual budgets have increased year on year since then.[114] The proportion of MI6 and GCHQ resources devoted to counterterrorism is classified, but we know that MI5 is now essentially a counterterrorist agency devoting almost 80 per cent of its resources to international terrorism (see table 3.1 above).

From 2003 a steady flow of young British Muslims travelled to Iraq to join the insurgency/resistance there. Whereas in the case of Bosnia in the 1990s such individuals were not thought likely to pose a significant threat to the UK if they returned, in this case the potential threat was recognized, but the clear expectation was that a proportion would die in Iraq, some as a result of suicide bombings, others killed by US, UK or Iraqi forces. As one intelligence source put it: 'We have monitored some of them leaving, sometimes via France, but we haven't yet seen them returning. Some of them have multiple identities, which makes them difficult to track.'[115] The month before the 7/7 suicide bombings JTAC reduced the level of threat from al-Qaeda from 'severe-general' to 'substantial', reflecting their belief that 'at present there is not a group with both the current intent and the capability to attack the UK'.[116] Clearly, this did represent an intelligence failure in that analysis was moving in the wrong direction, raising fundamental questions about how intelligence is collected and analysed.[117]

So too did a further revelation. Two of the 7/7 bombers, Mohammad Sidique Khan and Shazad Tanweer, had come to the attention of MI5 in 2004 on the fringes of the CREVICE bomb plot, but had not been investigated and identified because MI5 did not consider them to be involved in planning an attack. The issue as to whether MI5 could have done more to identify Khan, Tanweer and thus the other 7/7 plotters in time to prevent their attack was the central issue at the coroner's inquest into the 7/7 deaths. In its second 7/7 report the ISC was told that MI5 had not diverted resources away from known plots since they believed Khan to be a minor criminal.[118] The Coroner's report indicated some surprise at this: 'I am concerned about the fact that the Security Service's other commitments prevented a more intense investigation of a possible terrorist, who made long and suspicious journeys to meet known terrorists at a time when they were obviously planning an attack.'[119] Other more specific criticisms were made of the confusion caused by MI5 showing very inferior photographs to potential witnesses while trying to identify potential plotters, and misleading the ISC as to the basis on which it prioritized targets. Perhaps most remarkably in a security and *intelligence* organization, MI5 faced considerable problems in discovering what they actually knew. The Director General's chief of staff gave evidence, as witness G, to the effect 'that it "can be very difficult" to "dig into" the files and computer systems at the Security Service to try to find out if a particular person has previously come to their attention'.[120] As we shall see in chapter 8, the problem of MI5 not knowing what it knows (or, at least, choosing not to reveal it to oversight bodies) is apparently quite widespread. This suggests that Amy Zegart's focus on cultural pathologies as an explanation for failure may well have an application beyond the US.

But do the suicide bombings of 7/7, taken overall, represent an intelligence failure? Clearly, to an extent, they do, although here it is important to emphasize again that popular notions that intelligence can provide a failsafe mechanism have created false expectations as to just what intelligence can deliver.[121] In the case of the London bombings, efforts to guard against such an attack could have been complicated by the inability of politicians to admit publicly the link between radicalization of British Muslim youth and the war in Iraq, leading to fuzzy characterizations of terrorist motivation and the nature of al-Qaeda. Finally, neither the ISC nor the coroner challenged the judgements made by MI5 and the police at the time in terms of their priorities.[122] This case raises again the question of whether the attacks represent more of a policy failure than an intelligence failure, and whether in this case government policy created a potential threat of a scope well beyond that which the intelligence services could reliably guard against in their current form and scale and in the context of existing liberal-democratic norms.

Conclusion

As this chapter makes clear, locating the source of intelligence failure is a complex task. The concept of the intelligence cycle, implying sequential processes rather than concurrent activity at various levels, can encourage commentators to seek to locate intelligence failure at one particular stage of the cycle. However, the distinction between the stages is not always as clear cut in practice as the model might suggest. As the 9/11, Iraqi WMD and 7/7 cases suggest, intelligence failure can be multi- rather than mono-causal. With regard to Iraq's WMD, for example, the failure can be located at various, sometimes overlapping, points – in collection, analysis, dissemination and intelligence management.

Understanding failure only in terms of the intelligence cycle or process, however, is limiting in that it tends to shift the emphasis away from structural or organizational factors of the kind emphasized by Zegart. It also fails to account for the political environment in which intelligence is collected, analysed and disseminated and the beliefs and preferences of policymakers. It rests on the assumption that policymakers always want 'objective' intelligence regardless of whether it fits with policy preferences or personal belief systems. The concept of the intelligence cycle implies that they do, and that they await this analysis before acting – that policy is a blank canvas awaiting analytical colour and contours. As the Iraq case shows, this is a flawed assumption. In both the US and UK, policy ran ahead of intelligence and required that intelligence be shaped to fit it, rather than vice versa. The relationship between policy and intelligence was more complex than the notion of the intelligence cycle allows. From this perspective, political pressure or politicization does not simply represent an occasional episode in intelligence history, but is a fundamental part of the intelligence landscape. Our overall argument emphasizes that the search for causes of failure must pay attention both to process and to structure: in conditions of complexity and uncertainty, organizational 'fixes', as Betts demonstrates, cannot prevent failures, but might help to reduce their occurrence. Finally, the question is whether agencies 'learn' from failures, or, rather, what they learn. If pathologies of cognition, process and organization are addressed, then agency effectiveness will increase, and that is more likely the more vigilance is exercised by oversight bodies, to which we turn our attention in the next chapter.

CHAPTER EIGHT

Can Intelligence Be Democratic?

Introduction

Arguably, the idea of 'democratic intelligence' is as oxymoronic as 'military music'. While the central tenets of democratic governance are transparent decision-making and the acceptance of responsibility by those doing it, the secrecy that pervades security intelligence means that taking responsibility for intelligence failure can frequently be avoided. Since there is no immediate prospect of the abolition of the agencies, we need to consider the conditions under which secret agencies might be better controlled in the interests of democracy so as to reduce any tendencies towards illegal activities, increase the efficiency with which they warn and protect against genuine security threats and reduce the likelihood of intelligence being politically abused, as in the case of Iraq during 2002–3.

As the previous chapters have shown, this task raises major challenges that have only become greater in the wake of the post-9/11 security panic.[1] To use this phrase is not to deny that there are real security threats but to note that they may become exaggerated. States vary widely in the extent of the commitments they make to their populations. Some promise very little – indeed authoritarian regimes are more parasitic on than servants of their populations – while others understand that they are expected to provide widespread economic, social and political security. Yet, according to social contract theory, the core task of the state is to provide a basic element of personal and collective security against threats to life and wellbeing. Governments view 'security intelligence' as a key element in the fulfilment of that task and therefore guard jealously their ability to carry it out, necessarily involving some degree of secrecy. The greater the *perception* of threats, the more intensely this view will be held. This is not necessarily a problem for democratic governance if governments are trusted not to abuse the rights of citizens and others in their pursuit of information and conduct of security policy. But the historical record suggests that officials should not be allowed to work away in complete secrecy, not because they are necessarily dishonest or corrupt (though they may be both), but because it is wrong in principle and, as the historical record shows, a combination of security fetishism and secrecy can quickly lead even the most upright of officials to abuse the rights of others.

'Who guards the guardians?' is the question to be answered.[2] Just as intelligence agencies engage in surveillance to carry out their security and safety tasks, overseers must carry out surveillance in order to ensure that the agencies do not themselves threaten the security and safety of citizens. So what is needed is some structure for oversight or surveillance of secret state officials. As recently as the 1970s the very idea would have been rejected as naïve and dangerous even within countries with otherwise liberal democratic systems.[3] But then a series of scandals, often involving the abuse of human rights by security intelligence agencies, gave rise to governmental inquiries that resulted in various innovative oversight structures. Further, the democratization of governments in Latin America since the late 1970s and of Eastern European countries since 1989 has been accompanied by serious efforts to get to grips with the challenges of overseeing intelligence. The precise arrangements adopted have varied in line with different political histories and cultures, and some have brought about more genuine change than others, but all these efforts have sought to deal with a common set of challenges.[4]

The character of these challenges can be gauged from previous chapters. First, we recall that surveillance is central to contemporary governance. Our concern with security intelligence – the generation of knowledge and application of power in secret – places a very high premium on oversight to counter the risks. Second, there are a number of organizational issues. Political executives have normally established state security intelligence agencies without seeking parliamentary approval and therefore the precise mix of agencies has reflected what executives wanted at the time. These structures have not always been especially efficient or may have been entirely inimical to a democratic culture, and therefore a task for oversight bodies everywhere is to consider the appropriate mix and number of agencies. Overseeing state agencies can be challenge enough but, as long as they operate in the normal manner of bureaucracies, at least we understand the basic principles on which oversight can proceed: clear lines of authority and responsibility, auditing and inspection. A contemporary challenge for oversight is the development of security networks as examined in chapter 3. These do not just cross jurisdictional boundaries within nations but may also involve foreign agencies and organizations from the private and NGO sectors. How can the resulting complexity be overseen?

Third, there are issues in relation to the gathering of information and the ability of agencies to turn this into intelligence via a process of analysis. The former covers issues of both efficacy and propriety: do agencies have adequate resources to gather the information they require and, in doing so, do they pay proper heed to the rights of those from whom information is sought? By definition, some of the covert techniques used by agencies go beyond those normally deployed by states for the purposes of governance. Indeed, many of these techniques would normally be illegal, so any oversight regime presupposes some legal regime for the authorization of such techniques; otherwise there is the danger of 'plausible deniability', in which agencies and their political masters simply deny their use of illegal techniques and there is no real check on possible abuses at all. The need for oversight has been further reinforced with the post-9/11 shift in doctrine towards collectors as active 'hunters' rather than passive 'gatherers' of information, as we discussed at the end of chapter 4. In this context overseers must consider carefully how to do their job: whether to wait for issues to erupt and then deal with them (a reactive or fire-fighting approach) or to adopt a more proactive, 'police patrol' approach.[5]

The concern with covert techniques normally concentrates on technical forms of gathering information – telephone tapping, bugging and so on. The threat they pose to privacy is aggravated by, for example, the large 'data warehouses' being constructed from multiple public and private sources that apparently overthrow principles of data protection. But events since 9/11 have returned the relatively neglected area of human sources or informers to the centre of controversy. Technical means certainly raise issues of rights in connection with the invasion of privacy but the ethical issues are relatively straightforward compared with those raised by the search for human sources. To take one example, the recruitment of informers can involve blackmail and their motivations can compromise entirely the value of information they provide. To take another, interrogation techniques amounting to torture have been used against those captured or kidnapped as terrorist suspects since 9/11. In a number of cases detainees have died as a result. Although some soldiers have been tried, the ability to check systematic abuses has been seriously hindered by the unilateral declaration by the US that it is not bound by various conventions on the treatment of prisoners.[6]

Fourth, as we saw in chapter 5, issues arise concerning what agencies do with the information gathered. How successful are they in interpreting the meaning of the information correctly, or how is the *absence* of information interpreted? How efficient or otherwise are they in sharing intelligence with others who are in a position to act on it? When it comes to action being taken, are there adequate arrangements in place for ensuring that this is in accordance with law? If secret actions are to be taken against those perceived to constitute threats, what checks exist to ensure that the actions are proportionate? Finally, how can we inhibit the politicization of intelligence? We use the term *inhibit* rather than *prevent* since intelligence is so central to government and state activities that it is idle to suppose that it can be completely insulated from the political process. Indeed, in democratic regimes it should *not* be completely insulated, because a corps of Platonic Security Guardians would themselves constitute a security threat; this is the central paradox of security.[7] There is no neat solution to the oversight problem – there will always be tensions within democratic states between security professionals and their overseers. If there are no tensions then the oversight system is simply not working.

Defining Control, Review and Oversight

Some of these tensions are reflected in debates as to the terminology used to describe the functions of overseers. These are not semantic debates but reflect the contest for access to information about and influence over security intelligence agencies. The clearest and least controversial distinction is between 'control' and 'oversight'. It is generally acknowledged that the head of an agency requires adequate powers to manage and direct its operations – this is what we shall call 'control'. Oversight,[8] by comparison, refers to a process of superintendence of the agencies that is concerned not with day-to-day management but with ensuring that the overall policies and methods of the agency are consistent with its legal mandate. The key political debates involve the nature and extent of this 'superintendence'.

Should oversight cover current operations or, in the interests of security, be restricted to *post hoc* review? On the principle that stable doors should be shut before horses can bolt, we would argue that the former is required so as to prevent agencies doing things that are illegal, improper or just stupid, but there are risks for overseers. The US congressional committees provide the clearest manifestation of this arrangement, so that, for example, presidents wishing to authorize covert actions have to notify congressional overseers in advance. While this maximizes the opportunity for overseers to exert influence, it also raises the danger of attempts to 'micro manage' the agencies from afar. This will not always make sense in terms of effectiveness and insiders will always fear leaks, but prior knowledge may also compromise the ability of overseers to criticize if and when things go wrong. But before we examine the mechanics of control and oversight, we need to consider the more fundamental question of what we mean by intelligence 'democratization'.

Democratizing Intelligence

In authoritarian regimes the primary, if not sole, objective of security and intelligence agencies is the preservation of the regime and suppression of opposition.[9] As such, agencies may be controlled by the ruling party, be part of a military command structure or function as an autonomous 'state within a state', but what they all enjoy is the absence of any independent oversight. In democracies, monitoring 'enemies of the state' remains the job of security intelligence but the key distinction is that the regime incorporates political freedoms and competition. A further distinction is that intelligence activities should be subject to control and oversight in the interests of effectiveness, efficiency, legality and propriety.

Without suggesting some required sequence for democracy to come about, it seems to us useful to distinguish three periods: the legacy, the change and where the country is now. Most of the literature to date has concentrated on authoritarianism as the legacy for democratizing countries. This has had two main manifestations – in Europe, Soviet-style communism or 'state socialism', and in Latin America, military dictatorships or the national security state. Of course, these broad classifications concealed variations; for example, the security and intelligence services of the Warsaw Pact were not just modelled on the Soviet KGB but were largely subservient to it in what amounted to a denial of national sovereignty. Other East European states, notably Romania and Yugoslavia, retained greater national independence even if their security services could be just as unpleasant. There were also differences in Latin American military regimes: Estevez distinguishes the relatively 'progressive' militaries of Peru and Ecuador from the 'neo-liberal' Argentina.[10] However, what these countries shared was an effective merging of internal and external security in a single doctrine of regime protection by means of widespread surveillance of society and the repression of dissent by 'political police'. Authoritarianism will not be the only legacy – in some countries there will have been a previous period of colonial rule or even a short period of democracy. These earlier legacies may be very significant; for example, it is impossible to understand developments in the Western Balkans without taking into account the historical relationships of its several national and ethnic groups prior to the period of communist rule instituted at the end of the Second World War.

Democratization is a process rather than an event and therefore may stop or go into reverse;[11] however defined, change may well take a 'long and winding road'. As we discussed in chapter 2, the social sciences examine change through the prisms of agency and structure. Using the former term when discussing intelligence can be confusing since we are concerned with intelligence 'agencies'. Hence, we use the term 'actors' and these can be significant in an area of state policy that, under authoritarian regimes, is so clearly linked to the fate of specific rulers. Ministers in fledgling democracies may well view agencies as a key instrument for the surveillance of opposition politicians in the context of competitive elections that are a new experience for all concerned. The ubiquity of secrecy in intelligence governance constrains debate in many ways; insiders can manipulate it to reduce the numbers of people involved in debates and to set the parameters of what is possible, and so the closed nature of intelligence systems can minimize the impact even of scandals. Another aspect of structure is the international context within which national intelligence architectures develop. Potential entry to NATO and the EU has provided a distinctive set of sticks and carrots for former communist countries in Central and south-eastern Europe, though intelligence governance has not received the same degree of attention there as police and military reform. There are no real Latin American equivalents to these multi- and supra-national organizations in relation to democratization, but there has been a clear change in the position of the regional hegemon. For the duration of the Cold War, the United States' main priority was that governments in its Central and South American 'backyard' were anti-communist, and this was a significant factor in the installation and/or maintenance of military regimes.

Since the early 1990s, however, the US has found it easier to embrace democratizing tendencies in the region, even if these have been rather narrowly defined in terms of free-market liberalism.

Before we consider where states are now, there are preliminary questions as to whether a 'state' actually exists and, if so, what kind of 'state' it is. As our introductory review of the IS literature demonstrated, it is dominated by studies of modern Anglo-American Westphalian states. This is understandable and has been highly productive in generating more general ideas of how intelligence and its governance 'work' or, ideally, 'should work'. But we must be aware that these ideas cannot be simply transplanted world-wide, and more recent and current developments suggest strongly that we may be reaching the limits of what can be learned from ever more detailed studies of western state intelligence architectures. For example, note the implications of debates about ethnicity or nationality, sometimes connected with border issues. In Bosnia and Herzegovina and Kosovo, these amount to serious contestation of the 'state'. Further, we should not assume that current attempts to reform intelligence in, say, Egypt and Indonesia [12] will result in recognizably western structures any time soon.

The Legal and Ethical Bases for Democratic Control and Oversight

One of the ever-present dangers inherent in the shift towards the democratization of intelligence since the early 1980s has been that legal reform might be more symbolic than real; that behind new governmental architectures of legality and accountability, largely unreconstructed subcultures of political policing and denial of human rights would survive. Written reports can be constructed in such a way that agency operations appear to be compliant with whatever minimal legal standards have been adopted. Lawyers are, after all, 'hired guns'. Within the Bush Administration, for example, much legal energy was put into the task of finding ways in which techniques commonly assumed to be torture might be 'legalized'.[13] Thus, a legal framework for security intelligence is a necessary but not sufficient condition for democratic oversight. Therefore, the standards to be established for oversight must include not just the legality but also the broader issue of propriety involving consideration of ethical and human rights issues.

Although executives may consider they have very good reason for minimizing external oversight of intelligence agencies, they understand that it may make their life easier if there is some legal framework. For example, they are less likely to fall foul of human rights conventions and, in Europe, having a legal framework will help them to negotiate access to favoured organizations such as NATO and the EU. Starting in Europe but now extending to Asia and Africa, much work has gone into advice and discussion with newly democratized regimes as to how intelligence services might best be controlled. This has resulted in the publication of a handbook of best legal practice that provides an excellent summary of current thinking.[14]

Broadly speaking there are two main senses in which special powers may restrict rights. First, the ECHR allows restrictions on privacy, freedom of thought, expression and association (Articles 8–11) if they are 'prescribed by law' and 'necessary in a democratic society' and are proportionate to the protection of national security, the protection of morals, the rights of others and public safety. Second, derogation from most rights can be made 'in time of war or other public emergency threatening the life of the nation' (Article 15[1]), though there can be no derogation from the Article 3 prohibition on torture or inhuman or degrading treatment. This is especially significant in the light of the use of torture in post-9/11 interrogations that was discussed in chapter 4. Of course, precisely what constitutes a 'threat to the life of the nation' is debatable, but it should be imminent and exceptional.[15]

The basic intelligence statute needs to identify clearly the specific threats to national security that the agency is to address, and what powers it will have. For example, is the agency a 'passive' gatherer and analyst of information or is it empowered to act, for instance, by way of disruption or arrest powers? How is the Director to be appointed, including safeguards against improper pressure from ministers? What special powers for information gathering does the agency possess and who may authorize their use? Hans Born and Ian Leigh deploy the principles generated in 1980 by the McDonald Commission in Canada in its investigation of abuses by the RCMP:[16] that the rule of law should be strictly observed; that investigative techniques should be deployed in proportion to the security threat and weighed against the possible damage to rights; that less intrusive alternatives should be used if possible; and that the greater the invasion of privacy involved, the higher the necessary level of authorization.[17] Rules must be established limiting the purposes for which information may be gathered, retained and disseminated, and any exemption of the agency from normal freedom of information and access legislation should extend only so far as is necessary in relation to the national security mandate. Finally, agency employees must be trained to appropriate ethical standards and, as the first line of defence against abuse of agency powers, be protected if they feel obliged to 'blow the whistle'.

A legal framework is required for the relationship between ministers and agencies. This requires a delicate system for checking since different problems result if there is either too much or too little ministerial control of intelligence agencies, especially those with internal security mandates. If there is too much, then the problem may be just one of inefficiency as security professionals are directed by an enthusiastic but ignorant minister, but, more likely, ministers may fall into the temptation of deploying security agencies for their own partisan ends; for example, spying on and disrupting opposition parties or dissenters. Alternatively, if ministers adopt the position that they would prefer not to know what agencies are doing since it may be messy and illegal, then the problem will be that of agencies as 'rogue elephants', acting primarily on the political and ideological preferences of their own employees. Imbued as they may well be with a strong belief in their own understanding of national security requirements, the chances that they ride roughshod over the rights and freedoms of others are indeed high. So, while elected ministers clearly have to be responsible for establishing the main targets and operational guidelines for agencies, they must not have direct managerial responsibility. The issue of covert action, discussed in chapter 6, represents the very sharpest end of the issue of executive knowledge and/or authorization, especially if states wish to maintain 'deniability'. Since the actions envisaged will be, by definition, illegal in the state in which they take place, it is highly tempting for ministers to find a way of 'plausibly denying' knowledge of them should they become public. However, this is to invite serious abuses.

Security intelligence is 'low-visibility' work and there is extensive scope for discretion. This is particularly the case for those operating 'in the field', handling informers and deploying other information-gathering techniques. Therefore, before we go on to examine external oversight by parliamentary and other bodies, we discuss the ethical issues that provide the important counterweight to legal standards. If the question posed in this chapter – can intelligence be democratic? – struck some readers as odd, even more may laugh at the idea of discussing intelligence and ethics. Since intelligence cannot be disinvented, however, we should seek to develop it in progressive ways so it becomes a servant of the collective good, as in supporting public safety and peacekeeping, rather than treating it as a necessary evil until we can work out a way of doing away with it, like WMD.[18]

Toni Erskine provides an illuminating summary of how three main approaches – realist, consequentialist and deontological – might be applied to intelligence activities, and these were evident in our discussion of torture in chapter 4 and drones in chapter 6.[19] She discusses Hobbesian realism, which rests on the moral duty of the sovereign to protect her or his subjects. The resulting argument that intelligence activities are justified if they serve the wellbeing of the state and nation lends legitimacy to intelligence collection as currently practised. The second approach is utilitarian and judges actions by the value of their consequences and, compared with realism, may extend consideration to the interests of those outside the immediate national political community. Here, intelligence activities will be acceptable if they maximize the good through balancing the benefits of increased knowledge against the costs of how it might have been acquired, in a way similar to that in which the principle of 'double-effect' operates in the field of Just War theory.[20] There is no place for calculations of costs and benefits with the deontological approach, based on the work of Kant, where some actions are simply prohibited. The key principles guiding one's action are that it might become universally adopted by all other agents and that other people are treated as ends in themselves, not as tools. Clearly, many intelligence methods fail to meet such standards, including any deployment of deception and coercion.[21]

There are clear implications here for oversight: not only are individual security officials 'moral agents', but so are the agencies and governments of which they are part,[22] so statutes, guidelines and codes of practice must all be drawn up within the context of ethical agreements. But, again, final resolutions of ethical dilemmas will not be found in statutes or even declarations of human rights. As we saw above, the latter deploy a deontological prohibition of activities such as murder and torture but are utilitarian in other respects; for example, permitting the breach of rights in order to safeguard the nation in times of emergency. Since current intelligence practice is dominated by realist ethics, perhaps the most we can strive for is harm minimization: we need to regulate the 'second oldest profession'[23] in such a way as to minimize the harm it does to producers, consumers and citizens.

One way in which this can be done is to resist the frequently used but essentially inappropriate metaphor of *balancing* security and rights.[24] Intelligence scandals have often been followed by inquiries and increases in oversight, sometimes accompanied by restrictions on agency powers. Perceived intelligence failures such as 9/11 have been followed by increases in agencies' legal powers, thus establishing a pendulum swinging between the poles of, first, rights and then security. Yet the idea of balance is misplaced since, finally, rights and security cannot simply be traded off against each other. There is actually little evidence that increased security can be achieved by reducing the legality and propriety with which security intelligence is conducted.

Rather, there are two broad justifications for placing human rights and freedoms at the centre of security intelligence: it is right *in principle*, as enshrined in the UN Charter and ECHR. Also, it is right on a *pragmatic* level: states cannot achieve long-term democratic legitimacy unless they respect human rights and freedoms. Of course, in the short term, this raises difficulties for police and security officials who might feel overwhelmed by the extent of, for example, organized trafficking of arms, drugs and people. There *is* tension between security and rights: in the short run, the ability to conduct surveillance of an individual or group may be reduced by the requirement to follow procedures that seek to protect privacy, but, in the longer term, such procedures are required if a state is to gain democratic legitimacy from its citizens. Procedures should be designed in order that, even in the short term, the invasion of rights is *proportionate* to the alleged threat, but also to prevent surveillance being directed at the wrong person or conducted in such a way as to amount to intimidation. Thus legal rules and ethical codes themselves will contribute to the effectiveness of security as much as to propriety.[25]

Equally, the very denial of rights may trigger insecurity and political violence, as happened in Northern Ireland in the late 1960s. This may well be recognized by those drawing up guidelines and codes of practice; for example, those developed for UK agency employees in the mid-2000s for dealing with liaison services where torture was suspected are explicit about the danger. Deploying a utilitarian argument, officials are asked to weigh up the costs and benefits of sharing information:

> 9. . . . if the possibility exists that information will be or has been obtained through the mistreatment of detainees. The negative consequences may include any adverse effects on national security if the fact of the Agency seeking or accepting information in those circumstances were to be publicly revealed. For instance, it is possible that in some circumstances such a revelation could result in further radicalization, leading to an increase in the threat from terrorism, or could result in damage to the reputation of the Agencies, leading to a reduction in the Agencies' ability to discharge their functions effectively.[26]

However, to what extent such guidelines would actually dictate officials' practice when under pressure to 'get results' is another matter. And, as we have seen, in the US other guidelines were being drawn up which paid no attention to the risks of torture but rested on the false presumption that more coercion would produce more information.

Organizing External Oversight

Four 'levels' of control and oversight are required. We have already discussed aspects of the first two: the agency and the executive. So, for example, the immediate 'control' of an agency is conducted by its director but within the parameters of ministerial directions that are, in turn, required by the relevant statute passed by the legislature. The statute will, in its turn, reflect the preferences of the governing party or coalition and, possibly, the contribution of NGOs or other groups. Similarly, oversight should begin within the agency, but this must be reinforced by officials in the executive branch, a parliamentary committee and, whenever appropriate, judges. Finally, the media, citizens and NGOs will also provide oversight, albeit sporadically.

This overall framework is represented in figure 8.1. This inevitably oversimplifies what can be quite complex institutional arrangements within particular nation-states but shows the basic relationship between control and oversight. The forms of control that we have already discussed – statutes, codes etc. – are drawn up by the institution at the appropriate 'level' – agency director, minister, Parliament. Historically, if there was any 'oversight' of intelligence agencies, it was carried out by the same offices: for example, parliamentary systems rely on a general notion of ministerial responsibility to Parliament for the actions of their departments, so, theoretically, if it emerged that an intelligence agency had acted illegally or improperly the minister with overall responsibility for the agency would be held to account. Of course, there were several problems with this: ministers preferred not to know about most agency operations, there was no independent mechanism by which ministers could find out about agency operations if they wanted to, and their normal response to parliamentary questions would be to refuse comment on matters of national security. Assemblies were similarly ill equipped to oversee

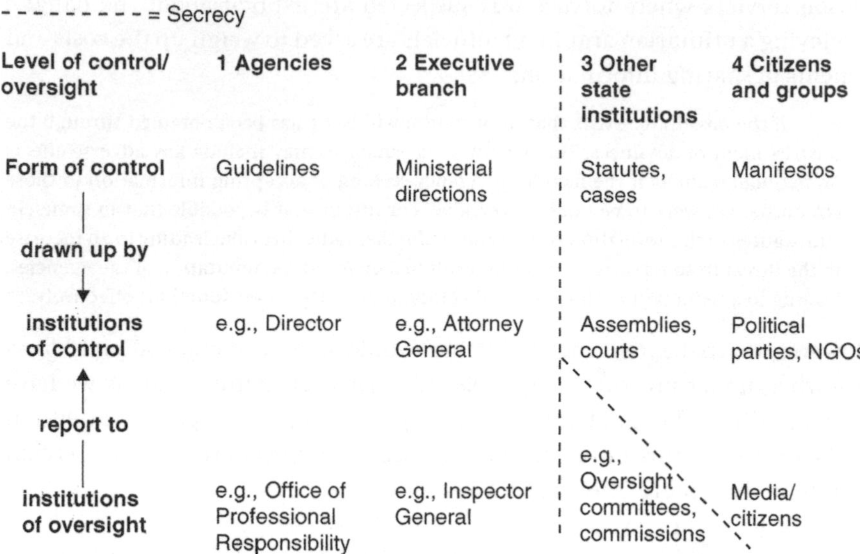

Source: Adapted from Peter Gill, *Policing Politics: Security Intelligence and the Liberal Democratic State* (London: Frank Cass, 1994), p. 252

Figure 8.1 *Control and oversight of security intelligence agencies*

intelligence agencies; even in presidential systems where their powers did not depend entirely on the executive, they often chose not to exercise the powers they did have.

There are a number of different ways in which secrecy breaks up the flow of security intelligence information – both between and within the levels depicted in figure 8.1. The ostensible motive for this is to retain the security of operations so they are not exposed in ways that would destroy their effectiveness and, possibly, endanger sources. For example, even those within agencies may not have access to information regarding operations into which they have not been indoctrinated and therefore have no 'need to know' about. But the most significant in terms of oversight is the barrier of secrecy between those who have received security clearance in order to do their agency or ministerial jobs[27] and those who have not – the public at large, parliamentarians, judges etc. Clearly, if those with oversight responsibilities are to be able to do their job they must have access to information in the possession of the agencies and, therefore, must be inside the 'ring' of secrecy. Their problem is that, having been granted this privileged access, they are then compromised by their inability to speak publicly about what they have seen. This is a problem especially for parliamentarians, whose *raison d'être* is that of representing the public. There is some variation in the extent to which parliamentarians are or are not granted full access to agency information – this ambiguity is reflected in figure 8.1 by the barrier of secrecy marking them off from both the executive and the public.

Having identified the need for legal and ethical codes to be promulgated, the responsibility for ensuring that these are incorporated into agency training and working practices rests primarily with agency directors. Legal and ethical standards have to be taken seriously if they are to become part of the organizational culture rather than just window dressing. Changing the culture within intelligence agencies is a more difficult task than providing them with a more democratic legal charter.[28] If pressure for cultural change comes only from external oversight bodies there is a danger that it will be viewed by officials and insiders as meddling, and mainly about public relations. Therefore, there is increasing recognition of the need for some internal oversight mechanism to reinforce changes made to operational guidelines and training. The work of such offices, often with titles such as Office of Professional Responsibility, treads a fine line: on the one hand, there is a danger that they too might be seen as carrying out a tokenistic role for the sake of appearances; on the other, if they are too enthusiastic they may face criticism from insiders that they are hamstringing operators and leading to a culture of fear and low morale. Arguably, the people most likely to become aware of inefficiency or impropriety by security agents are those most familiar with agency operations and *modus operandi*, that is, those within the agency.

Their work must also be linked into the next, ministerial, level. It is very likely that ministers will have more responsibilities than just those for the security intelligence agency or agencies, and it will be useful for ministers to have some assistance in ensuring that agencies act in accord not only with established legal standards but also with ministerial directions. Yet it will also be desirable to provide some insulation from ministers in order to avoid political misuse of the agency. One mechanism that has been developed to perform this role is the office of Inspector General. Around a dozen Inspectors General can be found in the US intelligence community and others in Canada, Australia, South Africa and Bosnia-Herzegovina. Their roles and reporting relationships vary – some also report to Parliament – but their primary function is to strengthen executive oversight.[29]

When we consider oversight from outside the executive a range of new issues arise. Should external overseers be located in Parliament or in some other body? What should be their mandate, or, over what precisely should they have oversight? How are they to be chosen and by whom? Must they be vetted? What powers will they have to obtain access to intelligence personnel and files? To whom do they report? World-wide we are now faced with a variety of institutional structures that have been developed as different countries have confronted these questions, but it is possible to detect some patterns. For example, the idea of Parliament itself providing the core of oversight structures, if not the only one, is more or less universal.[30] As the first steps were made towards external oversight, there were fears that parliaments would not be appropriate, for example because of their tendency to partisanship and to leak information for political advantage. However, committees are now to be found in the parliaments of almost all European states, while South

Africa and several Latin American states established committees in the 1990s. Many countries have also created external review bodies outside Parliament, sometimes in addition to, sometimes instead of parliamentary committees: an Inspector General in Australia (1986), a Standing Intelligence Agencies Review Committee (Committee I) in Belgium (1991), the Security Intelligence Review Committee (SIRC) in Canada (1984), the Review Committee on the Intelligence and Security Services in Netherlands (2002) and a combination of Commissioner and Tribunal in the UK (1985 and 1989).

One historical source of legislative assertions of power over executives is the 'power of the purse', that is, budgetary control. Historically, intelligence budgets have been regarded as closely kept secrets on the argument that, by adding to the 'jigsaw' of information available, knowing the size of the budget makes it easier for target states to work out the extent of intelligence operations against them. This would clearly be true of line-by-line budgets but is highly unlikely if single-line intelligence budgets are published, and this is becoming the norm. For example, the Single Intelligence Account (SIA) for MI5, MI6 and GCHQ for 2010–11 was £1,920m, having risen from £863m in 2000–1. In real terms, the budget almost doubled in the decade following 9/11 but was planned to remain at that level until 2014–15 because of general government austerity.[31] The total US intelligence budget for October 2009–September 2010 was US$80.1 billion.[32] Even these figures do not take account of intelligence work within police, border and revenue agencies or expenditure at state/provincial and local levels. This is especially significant in the US.

In the US Congress the intelligence committees wield potentially great influence over intelligence policies and programme, but the impact of oversight is much reduced because separate appropriations committees retain their power over budgets. This was one of a number of dysfunctions with congressional oversight identified by the 9/11 Commission but which has remained unchanged.[33] Parliamentary intelligence committees tend to oversee and report on the adequacy, efficiency and efficacy with which budgets set by the executive are spent. For example, the mandate for the UK ISC is the 'expenditure, administration and policy' of the agencies. The other potential area of parliamentary oversight will concern the legality, propriety and rights implications of agency activities. Given the general tension between issues of 'security efficiency' and 'propriety', it can be difficult for committees to pay adequate attention to both. It may be the case that parliamentary committees are drawn too much into management issues and forget their important role in checking for rights abuses.

At the heart of the issue of whether oversight is to be real and effective rather than tokenistic is the issue of access to information. Clearly, parliamentarians require a degree of access that enables them to fulfil their mandate, but the extent of their formal powers is only part of the answer. Parliamentary committees may be privileged in many ways, but at root they face the same problems of negotiating gatekeepers as do all researchers into powerful organizations. Even where legislation formally enables untrammelled access, committees will still need to deploy skill in negotiating with informal gatekeepers in ministries and agencies, and there are likely to be disputes. Legislation in Australia and the UK deploys the term 'sensitive' to describe information that ministers may prevent committees from accessing. In the US, agency heads have a legal obligation to keep the committees 'fully and currently informed' of covert actions, though 'to the extent consistent with due regard for the protection from unauthorised disclosure of classified information relating to sensitive intelligence sources and methods'.[34]

Since 1980 US legislation has given the executive authority to limit advance notification of especially sensitive covert actions to a 'Gang of Eight' members of Congress – the majority and minority leaders of both houses and of the intelligence committees. Alongside this, practice, but not legislation, has developed whereby the 'Gang of Four' leaders on the committees rather than the full membership will be informed of sensitive intelligence activities that are not 'covert action', such as details of intelligence collection.[35] Controversy lasted throughout the Bush presidency as to what precisely members of the committees were or were not told by the CIA about the new 'coercive interrogation' methods in 2002, but the system for advance notification of the Gang of Eight as agreed with the Obama administration in the Intelligence Authorization Act 2010 was changed only in minor details. For example, all members of the committees must receive the notification six months after the leadership. Thus there is provision for some formal oversight of sensitive operations in that congressional committees must be informed, but the problem remains that they are unable to prevent what they believe to be wrongful actions and may, subsequently, appear as stooges for the executive if controversial activities become public.

The secrecy of intelligence work means that it is relatively easy for insiders to mislead external visitors, especially if their visits are sporadic, predictable and limited to interviews with selected officials and files. Security and intelligence personnel are skilled at answering precisely the question that is asked and no more. Therefore the first task for any committee is to discover what the right questions are. This, in turn, depends on the expertise and experience available to members and staff that they have. For example, the extent of the legislative inquiries into 9/11 was largely but not entirely determined by the availability of staff. The US Congressional Joint Inquiry team had twenty-four researchers divided into five investigative teams that interviewed officials, reviewed documents and submitted questionnaires not only at the FBI, CIA and NSA but also other departments.[36] Staff reviewed almost 500,000 pages of documents, conducted 300 interviews and participated in briefings and panel discussions involving 600 officials from the intelligence agencies and elsewhere.[37] Most parliamentarians can only gawp in envy at the staff resources available to members of the US Congress, yet the effectiveness of oversight is never determined by resources alone. The UK effort, by comparison, was hampered from the start by the fact that half of the nine-person ISC (including the chair) were newly appointed after the 2001 election. The members themselves 'took evidence' over the year from thirty-seven witnesses (ministers, heads of services and other officials) and made 'visits' to the agencies. The conclusions drawn by the ISC appear to have been based entirely on briefings from agency heads; at least, there is nothing in the report to lead one to suppose otherwise. Similarly, when the ISC first investigated the 7/7 London bombings they 'just listened'[38] to what they were told by senior agency officials, having neither the will nor the resources to do anything else. Only when the shortcomings of their May 2006 report[39] emerged in 2007 and the ISC returned to the case did they carry out a more thorough investigation: 'We have gone even further into the detail, looking at the raw evidence – reviewing operational documents, surveillance photographs, transcripts of conversations, police action logs and covert recordings.'[40] Certainly the 2009 report provides much operational material of interest to students of counterterrorist intelligence, as does the subsequent material produced by the inquest into the deaths that occurred on 7/7.[41]

The final factor for parliamentarians is their reporting relationship with their parent assembly. The privileged position inside the 'ring of secrecy' requires that there be some mechanism for ensuring that their public reports do not include compromising material but, again, the precise procedures vary. Ideally, the committee itself will make this decision after consultation with the agencies has produced agreement as to what if anything should be omitted, but in some cases the executive retains a firmer grip. For example the UK ISC reports to the Prime Minister, who then presents the report to Parliament and public. Even though security and intelligence issues have had a much higher profile since 9/11, they are still not ones on which members of parliaments are likely to gain great popularity. These issues always pose the risk for politicians that they become seen as some kind of political risk if they are seen as connected with the spooks or, if they are critical, they may find themselves portrayed as 'irresponsible' or 'unpatriotic'. On the other hand, agencies may well succeed in co-opting critics.[42] So, to be effective, parliamentarians require a strong commitment of time, given all the other demands on it, and of energy, given the relatively difficult areas into which they are inquiring; and, at the end of the day, they should not expect too many thanks.

Extra-Parliamentary Oversight

There are various other external oversight institutions that we need to consider, some permanent, others set up on an *ad hoc* basis. As we noted above, in the early days of increasing oversight there was some suspicion of parliaments from both agencies and ministers. For example, in Canada the McDonald Commission recommended an oversight structure for the new CSIS that would culminate in a parliamentary committee, but the government in 1984 instead established SIRC, to which between three and five people would be appointed with the tasks of reviewing CSIS policies and investigating public complaints; for example, against refusals of security clearance. SIRC would report at least annually to the minister, who would lay the reports before Parliament. Parliament itself was not entirely happy with having only this indirect role in oversight and established a national security subcommittee in the 1990s, but it always struggled, without government blessing, since it could not access the information such committees require if they are to do a serious job. SIRC also raised parliamentary ire by being less forthcoming on its work than parliamentarians thought was their due; for their part SIRC members took the view that they could not say anything publicly to members that had not been authorized by the minister to go to Parliament. It is fair to say that, in its early days, SIRC produced informative reports, established that it was serious about oversight and accelerated the transition from the old RCMP Security Service to the civilianized CSIS. During the 1990s a less activist leadership and smaller membership that resulted in part from the electoral upheaval in 1993, when the previous governing party was virtually wiped out in the Commons, reduced the legitimacy and impact of the Committee.[43] In 1996 the government responded to (or took advantage of) publicity concerning Canada's SIGINT agency, the Communications Security Establishment (CSE), by appointing a commissioner with similar powers to SIRC to review CSE activities to ensure compliance with law, to respond to public complaints and to report at least annually to the Minister of National Defence, who tables the report in Parliament.

The general shift towards legislative oversight of intelligence has not, paradoxically, reduced the establishment of *ad hoc* commissions of inquiry by governments in the face of scandal or controversy. Between them, 9/11, Iraq and the involvement of intelligence officials in torture have given rise to many *ad hoc* inquiries since the early 2000s. All such inquiries raise substantial issues of procedure that will determine whether they are effective in getting answers that will achieve widespread acceptability. What is the objective: to get the government out of a tricky situation, to calm an outraged public, to enable victims to ascertain the 'truth', to improve governance or some mixture of these? Will an inquiry be private or public? The former will probably be quicker and cheaper but may be less likely to achieve public legitimacy. Are the terms of reference designed to enable a commission to examine all potentially relevant matters or to keep the investigation more narrowly focused and away from 'sensitive' areas? How independent are the members (often judges are chosen to chair inquiries because of their perceived independence from government) and are the rules on access to information drawn in such a way that they can overcome the great reluctance of intelligence agencies to give up their documents? How and to whom do inquiries report? It makes a great deal of difference to inquiries if they are to apportion blame or identify more general 'lessons learnt' and make policy recommendations. If their objective is to ascribe responsibility, then procedures are bound to be much more costly and slow given the needs, in the interests of due process, to permit people to defend themselves.[44]

In the US, the frustration of senior members of the joint congressional inquiry into 9/11 at inadequate co-operation from the executive branch led the members to endorse the establishment of a separate commission of inquiry.[45] This idea had been growing in strength for some months and was supported by the families of victims of 9/11. Although the White House initially insisted that this would distract the agencies from their primary tasks, it subsequently changed its mind.[46] However, it was only after further wrangling between White House and Congress that agreement was reached in the last session before Congress adjourned in 2002 and the 9/11 Commission was created.[47] Like the congressional inquiry, the Commission struggled against persistent obstruction from the executive failing to provide access to documents and key personnel for testimony.[48] When it did hold public hearings, however, with *inter alia* Attorney General John Ashcroft, former FBI Director Louis Freeh, CIA Director George Tenet and NSA Condoleezza Rice in mid-April 2004, they were questioned vigorously on the basis of the Commission's initial findings itemizing the lack of preparedness throughout the US counterterrorism architecture.[49]

The problems of inquiring into intelligence matters are well illustrated by recent investigations in the UK into alleged collusion in the murder of paramilitaries by security forces.[50] As part of the peace process, initial investigations into a number of 'disputed killings' were conducted by Peter Cory, a Canadian judge, and in five of the six cases he found sufficient evidence of collusion to warrant a full public inquiry. Although three were set up in 2004, by 2011 only two had reported, reflecting not just the problems of 'legalization' but serial problems of obtaining information. To take one case: Billy Wright was a dissident Loyalist who was shot and killed by Republican paramilitaries inside the Maze prison in December 1997. In effect the inquiry was delayed for two to three years while it struggled to obtain relevant documentation from the Northern Ireland Prison Service (NIPS) and police. The final report of Lord Maclean's inquiry set out the problems: the wholesale destruction of documents by NIPS, partly in relation to the intervening closure of the Maze but also because of officials' ignorance of procedures and their 'scandalous' destruction of security files after it was known there would be a public inquiry into Wright's murder. The inquiry team produced a specific paper detailing the problems of obtaining police documents – being bombarded with irrelevant material, failure of Special Branch to tell the inquiry of its separate word-processing and e-mail system – leading it to the conclusion that this could have amounted to deliberate malpractice.[51]

Other inquiries in Northern Ireland struggled similarly; for example, the Police Ombudsman investigated a complaint in relation to the police's failure to investigate a murder, and uncovered a string of murders committed by a special branch informant in the 1990s. The Ombudsman's report detailed a range of malpractices, including the regularity with which Special Branch officers misled colleagues, prosecutors and courts as well as destroying or losing forensic exhibits.[52] In one of the cases where Cory recommended a public inquiry – the murder of the Catholic lawyer Pat Finucane – by 2011 it had not even been established. Apparently spooked by not only the costs of yet another inquiry but also what might be revealed, the government ensured the passage of a new Inquiries Act in 2005. This increased the potential for ministerial control over inquiries: ministers can suspend inquiries before they are finished, and can restrict who can attend and what evidence the inquiry can publish. This was so controversial that a number of judges made clear they would not chair inquiries under such rules, and the Finucane family's refusal to accept such an inquiry has led to an impasse.[53] As we shall see below, the inquiry set up to investigate allegations of collusion by security officials in torture is afflicted by the same problem of achieving legitimacy. Given the tenuous relationship between intelligence practices and the law, and government's underlying concern to control what becomes public, it is difficult to escape the conclusion that inquiries into intelligence will probably never establish 'truth'.

Media, NGOs and Citizens

Space permits only a few examples of oversight taking place at level four. First, there have been challenges to the detention of terrorist suspects without trial and to other provisions of the new counterterrorist legislation, such as the USA PATRIOT Act and the UK Anti-Terrorism, Crime and Security Act (ATCSA) 2001, undertaken by civil liberties groups such as the ACLU and Liberty in the UK. Second, there have been efforts at more wide-ranging critiques of executive initiatives: for example, the Electronic Privacy Information Center (EPIC) and Privacy International produced a joint report regarding the impact of current and proposed laws in fifty countries since 9/11. It identifies four main trends: swift erosion of pro-privacy laws; greater data sharing between corporations, police and security agencies (see chapter 3); greater eavesdropping (see chapter 4); and, sharply increased interest in people-tracking technologies.[54] In the UK, Statewatch provides a running critical commentary on the impact of new counterterrorist laws, especially within Europe, including a 'scoreboard' on the extent to which EU measures taken since the Madrid bombing in March 2004 relate specifically to terrorism or more generally to crime and disorder issues.

The media in general remain a significant, if inconsistent contributor to oversight.[55] Certainly, the heightened public concern with security in the wake of 9/11 has increased greatly the media attention to intelligence matters, and the media have played an important role in alerting the public to concerns among intelligence professionals at the politicization of their product.[56] However, bitter battles over information control have resulted, and their long-term impact on the relationship between democratic governments, intelligence agencies and the public could be problematic. For example, journalist Andrew Gilligan's report in May 2003 that the British government had included in its 2002 dossier the claim that Iraq could launch WMD in 45 minutes knowing that it was wrong led to a bare-knuckle fight between Downing Street and the BBC. On the other hand, the following case study indicates just what an indispensable role the media can play in oversight.

Torture, Intelligence Networks and Oversight: The Cases of Binyam Mohamed and Rangzieb Ahmed

The necessity for a range of actors – parliaments, courts, civil society organizations – to be involved in intelligence oversight is nowhere better illustrated than by two of the UK extraordinary rendition cases. Binyam Mohamed, an Ethiopian, sought political asylum in the UK in 1994 and was given indefinite leave to remain while his application was considered. It was refused in May 2000 and in June 2001 he travelled to Pakistan, planning to return in April 2002. In April 2002 he was arrested at Karachi airport, having left Afghanistan, where he was alleged to have been fighting with the Taliban. He was held in Pakistan for a few months during which time he was interviewed by a member of the Security Service and then, in July 2002, he was rendered to Morocco. He was tortured there over a two-year period before being rendered to Kabul in January 2004. In September 2004 he was transferred to Guantánamo, where he was held until released back to the UK in February 2009. By then, however, his case had become a very high-profile embarrassment to both US and UK authorities.

While Mohamed was in Guantánamo the US announced that he would be tried before a military commission; accordingly his lawyer sought disclosure of documents relating to his treatment. Since the UK government, as a third party, refused to provide Mohamed with documents on grounds of national security, a case was brought in the UK High Court in May 2008. The UK government provided documents to the court, but only in confidence, because to disclose the forty-two documents provided by the CIA publicly or to the defendant would breach the 'control' or 'third party' principle, by which an intelligence agency never discloses intelligence received from another without its permission. The judges were highly critical of this refusal because of the seriousness of the allegations.[57] The strength of the evidence that Mohamed had been tortured, and statements in private court hearings by the Security Service officer (known in court as 'witness B') who flew to Karachi to interview Mohamed in May 2002, led the UK Attorney General to refer the case for investigation to the Metropolitan Police in March 2009. In November 2011 the Director of Public Prosecutions (DPP) announced his conclusion that there was insufficient evidence on which to prosecute the officer.[58]

But a long legal battle continued between the executive and the judiciary as to the status of the 'control' principle. The series of hearings and appeals culminated in one of the most senior British judges, the Master of the Rolls,

Box 8.1 Binyam Mohamed and the Secretary of State for Foreign and Commonwealth Affairs, 10 February 2010

168. Fourthly, it is also germane that the Security Services had made it clear in March 2005, through a report from the Intelligence and Security Committee, that 'they operated a culture that respected human rights and that coercive interrogation techniques were alien to the Services' general ethics, methodology and training', indeed they 'denied that [they] knew of any ill-treatment of detainees interviewed by them whilst detained by or on behalf of the [US] Government'. Yet, in this case, that does not seem to have been true: as the evidence showed, some Security Services officials appear to have a dubious record relating to actual involvement, and frankness about any such involvement, with the mistreatment of Mr. Mohamed when he was held at the behest of US officials. I have in mind in particular witness B, but the evidence in this case suggests it is likely that there were others. The good faith of the Foreign Secretary is not in question, but he prepared the certificates partly, possibly largely, on the basis of information and advice provided by Security Services personnel. Regrettably, but inevitably, this must raise the question whether any statement in the [Public Interest Immunity; PII] certificates on an issue concerning the treatment of Mr. Mohamed can be relied on, especially when the issue is whether contemporaneous communications to the Security Services about such treatment should be revealed publicly. Not only is there some reason for distrusting such a statement, given that it is based on Security Service's advice and information, because of previous, albeit general assurances in 2005, but also the Security Services have an interest in the suppression of such information.

Source: EWCA Civ 65 Case No. T1/2009/2331, www.judiciary.gov.uk/media/judgments/2010/ binyam-mohamed-judgments, accessed 6 March 2012

finding that the Security Service had not only failed to respect human rights but deliberately misled Parliament and suppressed information such that their assurances could not be trusted. Jonathan Evans, director of MI5, maintained that the only reason for the long challenge to the specific publication of the seven-paragraph summary of the forty-two CIA documents was to safeguard the 'control' principle.[59] However, despite repeated assertions by US and UK governments that the control principle was inviolable, that publication of the documents would damage the national security of both countries and that the US would reduce intelligence sharing with the UK, the courts pointed out that the paragraphs did not contain information that, if released, would damage national security, even if it would embarrass the agencies. The control principle might be very important but could not be beyond the law. Therefore, the judges took the view that the paragraphs should be published in order to uphold the rule of law.[60] When the judges first circulated their draft judgement to the parties to the case, the government made a further effort to suppress what they saw as a particularly damning paragraph 168, but after further legal argument and some amendment, this was published two weeks later (see box 8.1).

Following the February 2010 decision to disclose the documents, Mohamed plus others brought a civil action against Her Majesty's Government (HMG), accusing MI5 and MI6 of aiding and abetting their unlawful imprisonment and extraordinary rendition. The case was brought to an end by government agreement in November 2010 to pay compensation (of an undisclosed amount) to a total of sixteen claimants, but the legal question of whether civil, as opposed to criminal, cases could be determined if intelligence material was not disclosed to the claimants continued. The compensation was primarily intended by the government to bring to an end the potential publication of masses of intelligence documents. At the time of the deal fewer than a thousand of an estimated quarter million intelligence documents had been disclosed to the claimants, and these had already shown the extent to which British ministers were involved in decision-making that led to suspects being rendered to Guantánamo.[61] In July 2011 the UK Supreme Court found that, subject to established exceptions such as the issue by a minister of a Public Interest Immunity (PII) certificate, principles of open justice defeated the government's claim that there was a general common law power for courts to keep such material closed to claimants.[62] However, the government had already announced they would prepare a Green Paper designed to prevent the courts from releasing intelligence information in future and this was published in October 2011.[63]

This case clearly had significant implications for the ISC. Well before the February 2010 court ruling, it was obvious that its earlier reports were inadequate. The documents showed that MI5 was aware that Mohamed was being subjected to torture, contrary to what they told the ISC as noted in their report on handling of detainees in March 2005.[64] Prompted by the court's criticism of the Security Service in the first Mohamed hearing in 2008, the ISC re-investigated the case, and thirteen further documents which should have been disclosed to the court were discovered. The ISC reported to the Prime Minister, Gordon Brown, on 17 March 2009,[65] the day before he announced that new guidance to intelligence officers on detention and 'interviewing' would be published.[66] The committee maintained that the 'mislaid' documents in the Mohamed case, and others during their 7/7 investigation as revealed by the inquest, represented more administrative failures by the agencies to maintain adequate records than deliberate deception, but Michael Mates, the committee's then longest-serving member, noted that MI5 had treated the committee's requests for documents with less rigour than when legal disclosure was required.[67] There was much criticism that the inadequacies of the ISC had been exposed by its failure to determine earlier the role of the UK agencies in rendition, and the committee itself acknowledged the damage caused to its reputation by the agencies' regular failure to provide accurate information.[68]

Any process of oversight in relation to interrogation practices and treatment of detainees would need to know what the guidelines were for intelligence officers. The draft of the new guidance was passed to the ISC for comment in November 2009, and they carried out interviews with the heads of agencies and relevant departments before responding in March 2010. But the new *Consolidated Guidance to Intelligence Officers and Service Personnel on the Detention and Interviewing of Detainees Overseas, and on the Passing and Receipt of*

Intelligence Relating to Detainees was not actually published by the new coalition government until July 2010. We do not know the precise status of the pre-existing guidance, but when concerns were first expressed by an SIS officer in Afghanistan in January 2002, instructions were copied to both MI5 and MI6 officers there that included a reminder of their legal status under the Human Rights Act:

> It appears from your description that (detainees) may not be being treated in accordance with the appropriate standards. Given that they are not within our custody or control, the law does not require you to intervene to prevent this . . . In no case should they be coerced during or in conjunction with an SIS interview of them. If circumstance allow, you should consider drawing this to the attention of a suitable senior official locally.[69]

Arguably, the point about non-intervention was inaccurate given the obligations of signatories of the Convention against Torture not only to criminalize torture but also to work proactively for its eradication.[70] By March 2002 both agencies were giving oral advice to staff before interviewing detainees at Guantánamo 'that interviews must be free from pressure or coercion, must not include inhumane or degrading treatment, and that staff should withdraw if they considered the interview regime to be unacceptably harsh or unreasonable'.[71] In June 2003 the ISC raised concerns about detainees during a meeting with Prime Minister Blair and followed this up with a letter seven months later asking for an explanation of the 'basis and authorities for the agencies' involvement in questioning detainees'. Blair's response in January 2004, as cited by the ISC, referred only to the objective of questioning – to obtain information relevant to the protection of national security – but made no reference to any guidelines, formal or otherwise.[72]

This changed rapidly after the photographs of detainee abuse at Abu Ghraib appeared and Blair wrote again to the ISC in May 2004, asserting that intelligence personnel were required to report any evidence of inhuman or degrading treatment, although, as we saw above, the January 2002 instructions only required them to think about drawing it to the attention to local US officials. Between June and August 2004 several sets of formal guidance were provided to agency personnel.[73] However, the Labour government refused to publish this guidance because, in the words of David Miliband while Foreign Secretary, to do so would 'give succour' to the UK's enemies.[74]

In July 2010 Prime Minister David Cameron announced an inquiry, to be headed by Sir Peter Gibson, a former appeal court judge and Intelligence Services Commissioner, to examine whether the UK was implicated in the improper treatment or rendition of detainees by other countries after 9/11. The inquiry was not to start until the completion of police investigations of 'witness B' in the Binyam Mohamed case and a parallel police investigation of MI6 officers involved in interrogations at Bagram airbase in Afghanistan in January 2002. The inquiry announced its procedures in July 2011: it would not request information from any foreign agencies, and victims of torture would not be able to ask questions of MI5 or MI6 officers. Should there be disagreements between the inquiry and the government as to what information it might publish, these would be resolved in the last instance by the Cabinet Secretary. A number of NGOs including Amnesty International and Liberty declined to co-operate because the inquiry's procedures lacked the necessary transparency and would not fulfil ECHR requirements to investigate allegations of torture. Victims' lawyers said that their clients would play no part.[75]

In January 2012 the inquiry was abandoned, at least temporarily, when another police investigation was announced into two renditions to Libya carried out by MI6 in 2004 in co-operation with Muammar Gaddafi's intelligence services. These renditions were revealed by chance when an investigator from Human Rights Watch discovered documents in a Libyan office building abandoned during the revolution.[76]

The inquiry's 'primary focus' would have been Guantánamo, but there are many serious allegations of UK complicity in torture elsewhere that do not involve the US policy of extraordinary rendition. Many of these involve, rather, the co-operation between UK police and intelligence officials with their counterparts, especially in Pakistan. The ISI is the most significant intelligence agency in Pakistan, with responsibility for foreign intelligence, counterintelligence and counterterrorism. Formally within the structure of the Ministry of Defence, it actually operates with a great deal of autonomy, was credited with a significant role in the support for the *mujahideen* in Afghanistan to fight against the Soviet Union and has, to put it mildly, been seen as playing an ambiguous role in the post-9/11 Afghan war against al-Qaeda and the Taliban. However, there is no doubt that ISI methods of interrogating suspects, especially those suspected of terrorism, include routine use of torture. So it is not surprising that many allegations regarding UK complicity in torture have arisen from the interviewing by UK officials of people in ISI custody. One case involves Rangzieb Ahmed, a British citizen, who was deported from Pakistan in September 2007, arrested on arrival in the UK, convicted in December 2008 at Manchester Crown Court of directing terrorism and sentenced to life imprisonment.

Yet many aspects of this case were so shocking that David Davis MP, a former Conservative Shadow Home Secretary, took advantage of parliamentary privilege to set out the details of the case.[77] Ahmed was suspected of terrorism by the Greater Manchester Police (GMP) and was under surveillance for a year following the 7/7 London bombings, including during a trip to Dubai. His conviction in 2008 was based on evidence gathered during this period. Yet he was allowed to fly to Pakistan, where he was arrested on 20 August 2006 by the ISI on the suggestion of the UK authorities. GMP and MI5 together compiled a list of questions for Ahmed that were passed to the ISI and put to him while he was subjected to beatings with wooden staves, whipping with a three-foot length of rubber nailed to a wooden handle and, over a period of days, having three fingernails pulled out with pliers. A few days later he was visited by an officer from each of MI5 and MI6 and Ahmed says he told them he was being tortured; after which they did not return although he was questioned further by Americans. After two months, Ahmed became ill and, after twice collapsing, he was subjected to no more torture until, after just over a year of being held without charge, he was deported back to the UK.

This case has been very well documented – for example, an independent pathologist employed by the Crown Prosecution Service (CPS) confirmed that Ahmed's fingernails had been extracted during the period when he was in custody in Pakistan – and it raises some very serious issues around the possibilities of control and oversight of such abuse. First, even the then unpublished guidelines issued to intelligence officers after the Abu Ghraib revelations indicate that requesting an agency known to use torture to detain someone, to provide questions to that agency to be put to the detainee, and sending officers to interview someone who will almost certainly have been tortured would all amount to a criminal offence.[78] Second, continuing controversies around the emerging details of the US extraordinary rendition policy led the ISC to investigate the extent of UK agencies' knowledge and/or involvement in these cases and the general policies in relation to intelligence liaison. The ISC reported in July 2007 and included detailed consideration of several cases, including that of Binyam Mohamed. Now, Rangzieb Ahmed was not subjected to rendition since he flew voluntarily to Pakistan, but his arrest there was at the behest of the UK agencies and therefore his case comes within the guidance on agencies working with liaison services. According to the ISC Report:

> At the outset the guidance makes it clear that, whilst it is necessary for the UK agencies to work with foreign liaison services to counter terrorism, the UK agencies will not condone the use of torture or mistreatment. When a risk of mistreatment is foreseen, then caveats and assurance are used to minimize the risks. Finally, where, despite the use of caveat and assurances, there is still considered to be a risk of mistreatment, senior managerial or Ministerial approval is required.[79]

So, given what happened to Ahmed, presumably senior managerial or ministerial approval was obtained, but the ISC has not returned to consider this.

Third, since Ahmed was brought to trial it might be assumed that the legal process would provide some check, but the jurors heard neither about MI5 and police preparing questions for the ISI to put to Ahmed, nor about the removal of his fingernails. Before the trial began, the judge rejected an application by his lawyers that the case should be dismissed because of his mistreatment, and MI5's response to allegations of their collusion in torture were heard *in camera* after the exclusion of press and public.[80] In other words, this case could be argued to demonstrate the failure of executive guidelines as well as parliamentary and judicial oversight.

The Challenge of Controlling and Overseeing Intelligence Networks

At a time when governments seek greater integration between national security operations, it is crucial that review mechanisms develop similarly lest the democratic deficit grows ever wider. We can identify two clear dimensions to the current problem: first, *within* each nation, oversight may be compartmentalized so that the crucial intelligence and operations sharing between agencies in different sectors escapes effective review. Second, there has been an equally exponential growth in co-operation *between* nations since 9/11 as threats and responses have become increasingly globalized. Meanwhile accountability structures remain formally rooted within national territories.[81] So how can individual and organizational actors working within these networks, or 'network of networks', as Hayez describes the multiple liaisons, meetings and electronic communications of current international collaboration,[82] be overseen so that they are effective and conducted properly (not just legally)?

It is easier to list the problems inherent in the project of overseeing intelligence networks, given the flexibility, informality and secrecy within which they operate, than it is to identify solutions. There is an absence of any legal standard on intelligence sharing that can be used as a benchmark by reviewers. It would help if national reviewers could establish minimum legal standards for information exchange, say, on the lines of UN and Council of Europe codes of practice for police[83] and ask that intelligence-sharing agreements be made by governments in writing and be subject to inspection, but, as we know, the major strength of intelligence networks from the point of view of practitioners is their very informality.

Exchange of information between people who know and trust each other is the lifeblood of transnational intelligence co-operation. Under pressure, formal policies may simply be disregarded, as Maher Arar and others discovered to their cost. The control principle or ORCON (originator control) remains at the heart of the accountability problem, and as intelligence sharing increases so does the proportion of intelligence that is 'contaminated' with foreign information and thus 'undisclosable'.[84] Wright's review of extraordinary rendition inquiries showed how, in the Canadian and German cases, governments tended to 'overclaim' confidentiality and thus cause delays in the process,[85] and the litigation in the Mohamed case showed the same (see above).

The secrecy regarding sources, methods and third party information that is required for reasons of security can cloak illegal and improper behaviour. Overseers face the reality that 'national security' can be used by government to 'trump' any other form of investigation, including criminal investigations: in the UK, then Prime Minister Tony Blair and his Attorney General, Lord Goldsmith, forced the Serious Fraud Office to stop their investigation of allegations of bribery and corruption between BAE Systems and Saudi Arabia over deals involving the selling of fighter aircraft. Court action challenging the legality of Blair's intervention has made it clear that he felt the UK government had no choice given that the Saudis had threatened to halt intelligence collaboration regarding terrorism.[86]

Oversight of intelligence, whoever carries it out, is inescapably political.

Overseers must remember that they are engaged in contests of power in which the stakes are high. They must avoid paranoia as they traverse the wilderness of mirrors but must remain alert to the possibility of being misled. There is a long history of agencies misleading reviewers in order to conceal malfeasance; in his inquiry into rendition, Dick Marty noted that the CIA had specifically sought to avoid the possibility of accountability by enlisting the co-operation of those agencies least subject to review.[87] In 2002 the CIA videotaped hundreds of hours of interrogations, including waterboarding of 'high value detainees', but when the tapes' existence became known and a trial judge ordered them produced, the Bush Administration denied the fact and shortly thereafter the head of CIA clandestine operations ordered subordinates to destroy the tapes.[88] Some mixture of 'plausible deniability', long-time allies misleading each other or just plain incompetence is alive and well in the field of international intelligence co-operation: allegations that the US had used the base on Diego Garcia were repeatedly denied by ministers,[89] until the Foreign Secretary was forced to apologize to Parliament on 21 February 2008 after the US government told the UK that, in fact, two flights had stopped there in 2002.[90]

John Stevens, a former Commissioner of the Metropolitan Police, carried out three separate inquiries in Northern Ireland into the allegations of 'collusion' between security agencies and Loyalist paramilitaries referred to earlier. The only part of his reports to have been published is a summary version of the third, in which he recounts the attempts to obstruct his inquiries from the outset: the army giving him written statements that documents he requested did not exist but which he later obtained; an army intelligence unit training their informer in counter-interrogation techniques in case he was arrested by the Stevens team; and the destruction of his inquiry's office by a fire that Stevens concluded was arson.[91] Not many efforts at resisting oversight will be as dramatic as this, but it makes clear that, apart from legal powers and investigative resources, overseers also need a great deal of 'political will'. This may weaken, since overseers may tend towards self-denial when they appreciate their dependency for co-operation on the agencies, which insist that their discretion vis-à-vis co-operating agencies is crucial to their operational effectiveness.[92]

It is worth consulting recent Canadian experience in this respect. Justice O'Connor's inquiry into the rendition in 2002 of Maher Arar by the US to Syria, where he was detained and subject to torture over a period of twelve months, found that RCMP officers passed a whole investigative file over to the US without the information being screened for relevance, reliability or personal information; it included information that was 'inaccurate and imprecise', overstating any involvement Arar might have had in terrorist activity.[93] The commission was also charged with recommending how review of the RCMP's activities might be better conducted. After considering Canadian and foreign experience, it proposed a structure that would have the separate agency review bodies co-operating in cases where the agencies themselves co-operated operationally and shared information. The review bodies would deploy 'statutory pathways' that would enable them to exchange information as necessary to carry out their duties, and an Integrated National Security Review Coordinating Committee, comprised of the chairs of the individual review bodies and an independent chair, would have the mandate to ensure that the gateways worked, to avoid duplicative reviews, to provide a single mechanism for the receipt of public complaints and to report on the impact of national security practices on rights and freedoms.[94]

Acknowledging that no country can simply 'import' reforms from another, the principles developed by O'Connor require serious attention. 'Statutory pathways' already exist in the UK, for example, between the Independent Police Complaints Commission and the parliamentary ombudsman. The ISC has grasped this nettle in some respects by extending its review beyond the three central agencies to include the DIS and SOCA. For some years the ISC has met annually for 'informal discussions' with the Interception of Communications and Intelligence Services Commissioners as to their respective roles and, in 2011, for the first time met similarly with the Investigatory Powers Tribunal, but there is no indication that they actually collaborate on oversight.[95]

In many countries parliamentary committees are at the centre of oversight structures – and they are required for symbolic reasons – but parliamentarians just do not have the time, resources or expertise to carry out systematic monitoring and review of intelligence activities. Often there will be different parliamentary committees touching on intelligence matters, and members must try to avoid the 'turf wars' between committees so they can take a holistic view of intelligence. For example, if one looks at instances of detainee abuse by UK personnel in Iraq and Afghanistan, most would appear to have taken place at the hands of military rather than intelligence personnel, although some, certainly, were connected with the 'softening up' of prisoners prior to interrogation for purposes of intelligence. In the UK there are several inquiries into this, but have the ISC and Defence Select Committee put their heads together about this problem? We do not know.

Further, national overseers must also lift their eyes above the horizon and respond to both national and transnational constituencies.[96] An example of just this kind of thinking can be seen in the recent initiative of the Belgian Standing Intelligence Agencies Review Committee: 'With increased globalization in mind, the Standing Committee I(ntelligence) wishes to meet the expectations of a broader public.'[97] Accordingly, it translated its Activity Reports for 2006 and 2007 into English and took the initiative of gathering together information on the spread of fusion centres throughout Europe.[98] Since 2010 it has been seeking to establish a Review Agencies Knowledge Centre for the exchange of information and best practice, and the Dutch review committee has taken similar initiatives.[99] Members of national review agencies meet at the biennial International Intelligence Review Agencies Conferences.[100] These are (more or less) closed – they may well be of value for participants but they should consider having an additional day to which NGOs, researchers, media etc. would be invited for exchanges of ideas and to establish a review network.

Unlike the well-staffed congressional intelligence committees in the US Congress, most parliamentary committees have few if any research or investigative staff. Therefore, if they are to provide an overview of governments' intelligence and security policies and expenditure as well as practices, they need the help of some other investigative and monitoring body such as an Inspector General to make oversight more effective.[101] They must also maximize the use of findings by academics, scholars, journalists, NGOs and activists who can produce highly relevant knowledge even in the unpromising context of highly secret intelligence collaboration. For example, the work of Amnesty International, investigative journalist Stephen Grey, and the All-Parliamentary Group on Extraordinary Rendition was significant in mapping rendition.[102] A similar example can be found in the exposure of the US-operated ECHELON system for the interception of global communications, involving journalists, activists and eventually the European Parliament,[103] and Aldrich notes that the press got further in uncovering the Niger 'yellow cake' saga than did official inquiries.[104]

Extraordinary rendition has provoked both transnational inquiries by the European Parliament (EP) and the Council of Europe (CoE) and special national inquiries. Of the latter, Andrea Wright has compared the impact of O'Connor on the Arar rendition, and the Bundestag's special committee into the rendition of German citizen el-Masri in Macedonia, as well as the ISC's rendition inquiry.[105] These three differed in details of aim and process but all suffered from the refusal of foreign officials to co-operate, and none of them enabled victims to hear the secret evidence that had caused their ordeals. Even if compensation was obtained for victims in some cases, Wright wonders whether the protracted hearings, disputes with government over access to documents, and extent of the 'unknown unknowns' they faced meant that the inquiries actually undermined their own *raison d'être* by giving a false impression that accountability was possible. Wright suggests that such inquiries can help by adding to an overall picture but need to display procedural flexibility and make use of 'evidence' that has been credibly ascertained abroad. Clearly, there is a tendency for inquiries to become 'legalized', leading to long delays and the search for a level of 'evidence' that is simply not going to become available in the secret world of intelligence. It might be argued that inquiries would benefit from a broader deployment of social science methodologies, so that inquiries could draw more useful conclusions about 'lessons learnt' from an examination of organizational processes than the search for individuals to blame.[106]

Extensive transnational inquiries were conducted for the CoE by Senator Dick Marty, who provided a graphic account of the rendition process,[107] and by the European Parliament. Both were triggered by Dana Priest's November

2005 article about CIA secret prisons[108] and aimed to apply pressure to national parliaments to institute their own inquiries. Marty had greater freedom to define his own mandate and methodology and eventually produced two detailed and focused reports. The EP temporary committee had forty-six members and, unsurprisingly, found itself more bogged down in political disputes and attempts by some members at obstruction. Both did add to public knowledge of extraordinary rendition and its transnational implications, but their lack of powers to investigate or compel any co-operation from national governments meant that the reports had little real impact on those.[109] Transnational intelligence networking has also received much more scholarly attention in the wake of the rendition scandal.[110] What is certain is that, as this scandal has demonstrated, intelligence collaboration is a multidimensional mix of politics, law and morality.[111]

Thorsten Benner and colleagues identify a number of mechanisms with potential for network accountability within governance generally;[112] and we should consider to what extent, if any, these can be applied to intelligence.[113] First, there is professional/peer evaluation; for example, via codes of conduct. Of course, professionalism is also important in establishing networks in the first place, as in the case of transnational policing.[114] Informality remains the main stumbling block: in the words of Fred Hitz, former CIA Inspector General, 'formal intelligence liaison relationships between cooperating services are seldom reduced to writing, even between long term allies. The less said the better is the norm.'[115] But whether formal or not, the main code is that of ORCON, and networks for sharing intelligence and participating in joint operations are formed only when partners trust each other. The only way by which trust is gained and kept is by having a reputation for keeping secrets – especially each other's – and respecting the caveats attached to intelligence received.

Second, Benner et al. identify 'public reputational' mechanisms, such as naming and shaming (but they note this will not work with rogue actors, of which intelligence has a few!). Also, even legitimate intelligence actors will be very hesitant to denounce others because it may involve breaching secrecy and will threaten the possibility of future co-operation ('you never know today on whom you may depend in future . . .'). Further reducing the likelihood of this, it has been suggested that agencies may actually acquire a 'badge of honour' by failing to co-operate with their oversight bodies.[116]

Third, the need to account for funds in contractual relationships has some potential. Control of budgets and spending has been central to the historical development of democratic oversight of executives by parliaments, and so it is with intelligence. For example, a key problem facing attempts to control intelligence in countries such as Egypt or Indonesia is that the agencies retain a capacity to generate their own income from running businesses. But, again, the prospects for democratic control are reduced to the extent that intelligence organizations use 'grey' financial channels as part of covert operations.

Fourth, there is the law, although Benner et al. note this is relatively little used in networks. This was especially true of intelligence that operated outside the law, but the role of law is more significant than it used to be. For example, establishing legal mandates, standards and controls has been a major aspect of the widespread democratization of intelligence in former authoritarian regimes,[117] and Aldrich shows how law has had more impact since 9/11 than 'toothless' political mechanisms.[118] Yet the sorry saga of the corruption of legal control of intelligence through the politicization of the US Justice Department's Office of Legal Counsel – the government's lawyer – on the subject of interrogation and torture is a cautionary tale.[119] Leigh argues that courts have made little headway in challenging international co-operation, through a combination of deference and lacking jurisdiction, but notes also that the Mohamed case is a sign of changing attitudes and less readiness to accept blanket assertions of secrecy.[120]

Yet questions remain as to the effectiveness of law over the generality of intelligence co-operation. Craig Forcese has suggested that 'borderless review' might be achieved by requiring that intelligence-sharing agreements include a provision by which each party acknowledges the rights of the other to exercise oversight.[121] A variation on this would be bilateral agreements between countries in which each would agree to disclose requested information to the other's inquiries.[122] It is not hard to see the problems with these – when agencies regard it as a 'badge of honour' to resist oversight in their own country it is difficult to imagine circumstances under which they would agree to subject themselves to foreign review.[123]

Conclusion

Solutions to the dilemmas of intelligence oversight can only be found if reviewers develop trust with each other across national and sectoral divides; they can help each other by sharing experiences and their alternative sources of information.[124] Of course, co-operation will never be complete or simple because of different legal mandates and institutional positions. This means that there will always be a plurality of mechanisms incorporating official, civil society and media.[125] Co-operation through sharing and reciprocity can, in the long run, only improve the review performance of all those involved. It may not achieve instant results but can raise public awareness and therefore, over time, a greater readiness to challenge illegal and improper intelligence practices. We agree with Bayley and Shearing that, if the 'public interest' is to be safeguarded, then government must retain the functions of regulation, auditing and facilitation of security networks.[126] At a minimum, it can only be tackled at each of the levels of oversight identified here: training in ethical guidelines within agencies, ministerial oversight via an institution such as inspector general, parliamentary oversight and, finally, public vigilance.

CHAPTER NINE

Intelligence for a More Secure World?

We argued at the beginning of this book that the study of intelligence must strive to become more self-consciously analytical and theoretical than hitherto because it is so significant for both domestic and international security. At the domestic level, intelligence may help to save lives; internationally it can provide, or be used to provide, the basis for decisions to go to war and hence cost lives. The events of the past few years – 9/11, Afghanistan, Iraq and, most recently, the Arab uprisings against dictatorial regimes of which repressive security was a core feature – indicate that a systematic analysis of intelligence structures and processes is long overdue. Historically, intelligence has been the exclusive province of insiders, and there is no denying that much intelligence work must take place in secret if it is to be of value. However, it is clear from both the regularity and costs of intelligence failures, including at the ethical level, that intelligence is too important to be left to the spooks.

Citizens have been excluded for too long from any knowledge of intelligence policies and practices but now live in societies in which security fears apparently increase remorselessly. In one sense this is highly ironic, given the lifting of the Cold War fear of mutual annihilation, as none of the current threats is on that scale. But in another sense it is not: the multiplicity of potential security threats, the regularity of serious incidents, the rapid growth in the market for security products and services, and the actions of governments seeking to demonstrate that they are still 'in control' through pronouncement and legislation all combine to create an occasionally febrile atmosphere in which a 'politics of fear' can thrive. One important task for researchers is to make sense of and communicate the extent to which fears are well founded or how far they are imaginary if not actually manufactured. An essential part of this process is to educate people as to the realistic possibilities of what intelligence can deliver – and what it cannot. Some events may be better explained in terms of a political failure or a combination of policy and intelligence failure rather than of failures of intelligence alone. It is important not to lose sight of the dangers inherent in state and corporate intelligence-related activities that can damage both human rights and the broader democratic process, even if initiated with the best of intentions – for example, to intervene on humanitarian grounds. 'Defending democracy' in the post-9/11 world has involved significant erosions of liberal-democratic norms, and IS needs to address the risk outlined by Bernard Porter in 1989, 'that the medicine can, if not administered under the very strictest and widest supervision, have effects which are as damaging as the disease'.[1] Therefore, improving control and oversight of intelligence remains the central challenge for democratic governance.

In the early chapters of this book we discussed core definitional issues and identified the point that, historically, security intelligence has been associated with the operation of states and governments. All maintain intelligence agencies whose function is *surveillance* – the monitoring of populations in order to generate *knowledge* that can inform security policies and thus the exercise of governmental *power*, as well as enhance the relative security of the state in relation to potential adversaries. All states, whether liberal-democratic or authoritarian, maintain agencies whose function is to gather information about internal threats to the regime, and the extent of such surveillance impacts on the quality of democracy in liberal-democratic states – that is, it plays a role in determining where they are situated on a liberal-democratic state continuum. At the same time, some states enjoy so little legitimacy and/or perceive themselves to be so threatened by foreign interests that surveillance for the purposes of state security is almost the only meaningful state activity. Here, the label of 'counterintelligence' or 'national security' state might be applied to reflect the lack of concern with any more general issues of public safety and security. However, change is possible and, therefore, the 'research map' we proposed in chapter 2 can be used by researchers to compare agencies between different types of regime and to chart shifts, whether progressive or regressive, over time.

But states, wherever located on a spectrum between 'national security' and 'liberal-democratic', are not the only players. In chapter 3 we discussed the development of security and intelligence networks involving both the corporate and 'sovereignty' sectors. Since 9/11 states have reasserted their primacy as security actors in a plethora of new counterterrorism laws, new doctrines regarding prevention and pre-emption, and increased resources poured into state intelligence agencies. So was our analysis in chapter 3 premature in emphasizing the diverse nature of contemporary security intelligence? We do not think so; we did not use the globalization concept in order to suggest that states were less significant but, rather, to point to the increasing plurality of security intelligence actors. Corporations and communities have always provided for their own security to some extent, but states have *chosen* to empower them further in order to increase the potential for surveillance via a greater number of eyes and ears while restricting their own expenditures. Yet these other actors are not just incorporated smoothly into state security systems; their own priorities may lead them to act differently on occasion. Thus intelligence networks are not simply a vehicle through which states extend their capacity for security governance; we must analyse carefully the interrelationships of the agencies involved and the security policies and practices they develop.

One central question is how we should characterize the role of the United States within the contemporary global intelligence network. Reg Whitaker described the US as a 'global Leviathan' in the post-9/11 world,[2] raising the intriguing possibility that it had become the first 'transnational security state'. There is nothing new in the US seeing itself as the 'world policeman' – its insistence on its right and duty to act in this way can be traced back to the early nineteenth-century Monroe Doctrine – but the current situation is qualitatively different. After 1991 the US retained a particularly expansive definition of its national security interests but also became the sole superpower – the only state with sufficient economic and military resources to enable independent action almost anywhere on the planet. Beyond this, the possibility of collective international action depended heavily on US willingness to lend political and/or material support – as, for example, in Kosovo, Rwanda, Sudan and Libya. The global 'War on Terror' was declared and defined in Washington and its primary emphases were established by the Bush Administration and changed little under Obama. There has been resistance by some states to some elements of it, but the international community has essentially danced to a tune called by Washington, either willingly or after some cajoling. Shifts in domestic laws aimed at facilitating information gathering and sharing, increased efforts to enhance cross-national intelligence co-operation, and war in Afghanistan and Iraq all reflect this US dominance, and where international law stood in the way, the US sidestepped it. However, the continuing precariousness of 'democracy' in Iraq, the apparent limits to state building in Afghanistan, a general war-weariness in the US, the impact of the 2008 financial crisis, and a revival of isolationist sentiment in the Republican Party may herald a period of relative retreat from overt interventionism. This could, though, merely create a greater space for US intelligence agencies to expand their covert military programmes, which we discussed in chapter 6.

One consequence of the 'War on Terror' decade has been the militarization of US intelligence (note the 2011 appointment of General David Petraeus as CIA Director, straight from the war in Afghanistan), as evidenced by the increased paramilitary activities of both the CIA and US JSOC, sometimes in collaboration, as in the killing of Osama bin Laden, and the expanding drone wars. As Greg Miller and Julie Tate have written: 'In the decade since the Sept. 11, 2001 attacks, the agency has undergone a fundamental transformation. Although the CIA continues to gather intelligence and furnish analysis on a vast array of subjects, its focus and resources are increasingly centred on the cold counterterrorism objective of finding targets to capture or kill.'[3] In legitimating or excusing this, Americans draw on the notion of a 'state of exception',[4] which both implies a future return to a more established norm of conduct and draws on deeply embedded notions of American Exceptionalism. However, this can disguise a worrying trend: while the last couple of decades have seen a definite 'normalization' of intelligence in many parts of the world,[5] the US has witnessed an 'exceptionalization' of intelligence which has challenged established norms and provided an alibi for other states, such as Israel and Russia, that seek to pursue offensive intelligence strategies that can involve targeted assassination.

There is also an issue here for the governance of intelligence agencies that have grown exponentially since 9/11. For example, within the CIA, the CTC, which had 300 employees on 9/11, a decade later had approximately 2,000 – around 10 per cent of the agency's workforce.[6] At what point do they declare their 'War on Terror' to be over, the enemy defeated and the need for their role at an end? Historically, intelligence agencies, as bureaucracies, have been highly reluctant to concede the end of a threat. If the experts insist that the *risk* of future terrorist threat remains – and plots are uncovered regularly enough to sustain the idea of *some* threat – policymakers will remain receptive to the message for fear of being held responsible for another 9/11 or 7/7 should they ignore intelligence warnings. Such a future, of militarized intelligence not as an exceptional state but as a new norm for the US, has clear implications for international relations.

In chapter 7 we discussed the nature of intelligence failure and showed that intelligence failures are inevitable. In discussing failure, it is necessary to distinguish, broadly, between intelligence (or knowledge) failures and policy (or power) failures; that is, two sets of people are involved here – intelligence professionals and policymaking executives. We also made a distinction between *structural* and *procedural* explanations for failure. With regard to the latter, we identified key 'pressure points' where 'knowledge' failures are most likely to occur. For example, targets might be misidentified or the wrong targets chosen; information gathering might fail for many reasons – many states just do not have adequate resources to indulge in sophisticated technical gathering, or targets' counterintelligence may be very effective. But even if relevant information can be gathered on the right targets, analysis might fail. As we saw in the case of Iraq's WMD, for all the information gathered by the sophisticated intelligence apparatus of the world's most powerful nations, supplemented by the work of specialist UN weapons inspectors, the lack of evidence of WMD was continually evaluated as indicating that the regime continued to conceal them effectively rather than as indicating that they had been destroyed. Certainly, regime concealment efforts did continue throughout the 1990s for various political and security reasons – Iraq, after all, existed in a hostile regional environment – but there was a distinct lack of analytical imagination, which was then used by policymakers to help sustain their case. As Tony Blair repeatedly asked, if Saddam Hussein had destroyed his WMD why didn't he just come clean to the inspectors?

Policy or political failure can occur for a variety of reasons, some of them unanticipated. However, it also arises where policy is based on conviction or ideology rather than solely on *knowledge*. The decision to displace the regime of Saddam Hussein was not rooted firmly or solely in intelligence. Intelligence was used to justify a policy decision that was arrived at for different reasons.

Even George Tenet has conceded that the US 'did not go to war in Iraq solely because of WMD . . . I doubt it was even the principal cause. Yet it was the public face that was put on it.'[7] The Butler Inquiry in the UK exposed as false the idea that intelligence in 2002 showed Iraq to represent any greater risk to the countries that went to war than it had in the immediately preceding years. A combination of 'cherry-picking', failures across the intelligence–policymaker fault-line, and policymaker exaggeration meant that power determined 'knowledge'. Indications are that the Chilcot Inquiry will reinforce these conclusions.

Other sources of failure may be found at the stage of dissemination: intelligence may not reach the people who can do something with it, or it may simply be too imprecise for any specific action to be taken. In the last few years, the problem of warning intelligence has vexed agencies and governments. What is the point of issuing vague warnings about a general possibility of future terrorist attack, unspecific as to time or place, since the benefit of some general increase in 'vigilance' might be far outweighed by increased levels of fear and insecurity? Further, the more these occur the higher the risk that security fatigue will set in, bringing with it the consequential risk of the 'boy who cried wolf' syndrome. On the other hand, if governments disseminate exaggerated versions of intelligence to the public in order to bolster support for unpopular policies, as happened in 2002–3, then, again, the failure is far more political than professional.

The costs of failure can be very high, whether it is in the sense that intelligence does not provide adequate forewarning of some 'surprise' attack, as on 9/11 or 7/7; warns us of a 'threat' that does not actually exist, as in the case of Iraq's WMD; or threatens the integrity of the political process. This might be seen at an international level; for example, the use of covert information gathering against members of the UN Security Council, and Secretary of State Powell's February 2003 presentation at the UN of inaccurate material as 'fact' in order to justify the use of force against Iraq, both constituted an abuse of UN processes.

Within nations, also, the abuse of intelligence can be highly damaging to democratic structures and processes. This may lead some to argue that there is a complete incompatibility between democracy and secret intelligence activities. We do not agree with this, since all states exist in an anarchic international environment and all face potential challenges from those who contest the territorial claims they make or the territorial identities they ascribe, and from those who simply contest specific policies. In the face of this, governments have a primary obligation to provide protection against threats – this is precisely the source of the state's claim to legitimacy. Moreover, while intelligence in the first decade of the twenty-first century was dominated by terrorism, arguably much greater political and social harms are caused in most countries by the corrupt relationships between criminal organizations, governments and economic interests. Such relationships are conducted secretly and cannot be exposed without the use of covert intelligence and investigative techniques such as those we discussed in chapter 4. The trick is, of course, to ensure that security intelligence is properly directed at 'genuine threats' to public safety and security rather than at the opponents of the government of the day or some minority who can be scapegoated as a distraction from intractable social problems. The ideological frameworks involved in making these judgements mean there will inevitably be tensions here, as in the case of undercover policeman Mark Kennedy's infiltration of the environmental movement discussed in chapters 4 and 6. However, security intelligence must remain a limited means of governance and not become an end in itself.[8]

Whatever the cause, 'failures' generate demands for reform. We must take care in analysing the causes – political and/or professional – of failure because, if we misdiagnose the problem, the chances of any reforms improving security in the future will be remote indeed. We must also beware the possibility that reforms are more about giving concerned publics (i.e., electorates) the impression of action and change than actually bringing it about. This will be even more the case where governments seek to disguise political failure (a characteristic of liberal democracies) by blaming the professionals – something we saw in the Iraq debacle. To the political pressures we might add economic ones. An important element in the growth of security intelligence networks is the profitability of selling technological 'solutions' to security problems. Each needs to be evaluated on its merits but, in general, we must be aware that technological 'fixes' to otherwise intractable political and social issues rarely exist. Just as, half a century ago, US President Eisenhower warned against the accumulation of unwarranted influence over policymaking by the 'military-industrial complex', so we must beware the accumulation of excessive power by a 'security-intelligence-industrial complex' growing fat on fears of terrorism.

There are many reasons why intelligence reform rarely works. Reassuring publics as to competence on security issues is crucial to state legitimacy, and failure increases politicians' dependence on intelligence officials. Of course, these may be the very people who are either responsible for the failure or *held* responsible for it (a different thing), and their expertise and positions, enhanced by secrecy, may enable them to resist reforms. Security intelligence failures normally produce demands and resources for more of the same. Since surveillance itself tends to be defined narrowly as information gathering rather than in our broader sense of developing knowledge and exercising power, failures can be held to result from inadequate collection. Then the remedy appears to be legislation and budgets for yet more intrusive gathering techniques at home and more resources for technical and human foreign intelligence. Issues of analysis and the translation of intelligence into policy often receive less attention. The consequence of this is ever-increasing information overload so that, as we have seen, agencies may not even know what information they have, let alone be able to process and analyse it. Since analysis is essentially an intellectual task that cannot be carried out entirely by machines, one of several paradoxes of intelligence is that the more collection problems are solved, the worse analytical problems become.[9]

Another typical government response to policy failure is reorganization. A central aspect of democratization in Eastern Europe has been the reform of authoritarian, often military, Soviet-style agencies, whose primary, if not sole, concern was domestic counterintelligence, into civilianized, law-based agencies with a broader range of targets including transnational crime and terrorism. This process has been very uneven; notwithstanding the normalization of intelligence in some states, in others apparent changes disguise essentially unreconstructed practices – for example, with regard to the FSB in Russia.

Less dramatically, we have seen how the US has sought to reorganize its intelligence community in the wake, first, of 9/11 and, second, of the Iraq failure. Clearly, governmental reorganization is inextricably bound up with politics and, just as in former Central and East European countries, intelligence reform was a central symbol of the democratization process so, in the United States, intelligence reform has been symbolic of governmental determination to place security at the heart of US politics. Ironically, even before 9/11, probably more was written on the subject of intelligence reform in the US than in the rest of the world combined. Through the 1990s a series of inquiries and commissions deliberated on the subject of 'fixing' the US intelligence structure, but precious little happened. After 9/11 two main shifts were inaugurated: first, the DHS was constructed from the amalgamation of various domestic departments covering borders, immigration, secret service, coastguard and emergency management. The resulting gargantuan bureaucracy may well provide a potent *symbol* of the new concern with security, but it is far from clear that it has actually enhanced the domestic security of Americans. One major criticism of the lamentable performance of FEMA in the wake of the devastation that Hurricane Katrina inflicted on New Orleans was that its focus and resources had been disproportionately diverted towards counterterrorism.[10] The second main reorganization has been the establishment of the ODNI, with greater authority over the ill-named federal intelligence 'community' than that enjoyed previously by the DCI.[11] On paper, the DNI certainly has greater authority, but whether she or he is actually able to make it stick remains to be seen. The rapid turnover of DNIs since 2004 suggests it may not be a very fulfilling role.

Thinking more generally about the prospects for intelligence reform, however, we should not take the US as a template. Although issues relating to coordination and intelligence sharing affect all national intelligence structures, the relatively small number and scale of intelligence agencies in most states mean that there is some reasonable prospect of alleviating problems. In the US the problems are qualitatively different, deriving from the fragmented federal system of government and, paradoxically, such wealth that agencies proliferate at all levels of government. In July 2010 the *Washington Post* published the results of a major attempt to map 'top secret America' and identified 45 federal government organizations (composed of over 1,200 sub-units), 1,931 private sector companies and over 4,000 federal, state and local organizations working on intelligence and homeland security below the federal level.[12] The result is an intelligence 'community' that is so large and so fragmented that the prudent answer to the question of how it should be reformed for better performance is 'I wouldn't start from here.'

If one were starting afresh then one would begin with strategy and doctrine in the light of the threat environment and only then consider how agencies might be best organized to gather information about and counter those threats. However, the reality of day-to-day government is that these issues are viewed from the perspective of existing agencies, and necessary changes may simply be impossible. As it is, a common reaction to the co-ordination problem is to establish new task forces or agencies that are meant to overcome organizational fragmentation but which, in the longer term, may simply compound it. A related organizational issue is that much greater flexibility is required on the part of agencies as they seek to comprehend the apparent fluidity of extremist networks. Perhaps what is needed is a reversal of 'mirror-imaging': instead of the problem of analysts making culture-bound assumptions about how others organize, what is needed is imitation of the flexibility of target organizations and networks.

Yet intelligence officials and practitioners still face major challenges. Beyond the rapid application of lethal force, which has reduced the length of the traditional intelligence 'cycle' to practically nothing, can they adapt time-honoured organizations, policies and practices to develop useful foreknowledge of a world in which threats appear to be more diverse, fluid and complex? The pressure on them to perform, coming from governments and publics alike in the context of a world of heightened sensitivities that sometimes border on paranoia, alerts us to the clear danger that they may be drawn into illegal, improper and even counterproductive methods. This is by no means inevitable, but we already have enough evidence from the history of counterterrorism policies in, for example, Northern Ireland and the post-9/11 statement by the Bush Administration that it did not consider itself bound by international agreements such as the Geneva conventions on the treatment of detainees. The torture and ill-treatment of detainees in Afghanistan, Iraq, Guantánamo Bay and the various CIA-run 'black sites' make clear the urgent need to reiterate the importance of democratic control of intelligence in order to enhance both effectiveness and propriety. The problem, as we discussed in chapter 8, is that the institutional mechanisms for overseeing transnational and trans-sectoral networks are extremely primitive.

The sorry saga of intelligence agencies' involvement or collusion in extraordinary rendition and torture has exposed the shortcomings of current oversight institutions in all of the countries involved. However tempting short-term security gains might appear, overseers have a democratic duty to look beyond the political welfare of current presidents and prime ministers in order to address the longer-term needs for both public security and public education. Just as surveillance defines what intelligence agencies do in respect of their societies, so publics need robust and reliable surveillance of the agencies that operate in their name. The lesson of the century so far is that it still does not exist.

Notes

INTRODUCTION

1 Wesley K. Wark, 'Introduction: the study of espionage: past present, future?', *Intelligence and National Security*, 8,3 (1993), pp. 1–13.

2 Len Scott, 'Sources and methods in the study of intelligence: a British view', *Intelligence and National Security*, 22,2 (2007), pp. 185–205; David Kahn, 'Intelligence studies on the continent', *Intelligence and National Security*, 23,2 (2008), pp. 249–75; Martin Rudner, 'Intelligence studies in higher education: capacity-building to meet societal demand', *International Journal of Intelligence and Counterintelligence*, 22,1 (2009), pp. 110–30; Eric Denécé and Gérald Arboit, 'Intelligence studies in France', *International Journal of Intelligence and Counterintelligence*, 23,4 (2010), pp. 725–47; Gustavo Díaz Matey, 'The development of intelligence studies in Spain', *International Journal of Intelligence and Counterintelligence*, 23,4 (2010), pp. 748–65.

3 Academic: Christopher Andrew, *Secret Service: The Making of the British Intelligence Community* (London: Heinemann, 1985). Memoirs: Percy Sillitoe, *Cloak without Dagger* (London: Pan Books, 1956). Five volumes of an official history of *British Intelligence in the Second World War*, mainly by F. H. Hinsley, were published: vols. 1–3 concerned the influence of intelligence on strategy and operations; vol. 4, security and counterintelligence; vol. 5, strategic deception. Journalists: Chapman Pincher, *Their Trade Is Treachery* (London: Sidgwick & Jackson, 1981); Nigel West, *A Matter of Trust: MI5 1945–72* (London: Weidenfeld & Nicolson, 1982). Critical: Stephen Dorril, *The Silent Conspiracy: Inside the Intelligence Services in the 1990s* (London: Heinemann, 1993).

4 Stephen Twigge and Graham Macklin, *British Intelligence: Secrets, Spies and Sources* (London: National Archives, 2008).

5 Michael Herman, *Intelligence Power in Peace and War: Intelligence Services in the Information Age* (Cambridge: Cambridge University Press, 1996); Richard J. Aldrich, *The Hidden Hand: Britain, America and Cold War Secret Intelligence* (London: John Murray, 2001) and *GCHQ: The Uncensored Story of Britain's Most Secret Intelligence Agency* (London: HarperPress, 2010); Philip H. J. Davies, *MI6 and the Machinery of Spying* (London: Frank Cass, 2004). Whistleblowers: Annie Machon, *Spies, Lies and Whistleblowers* (Lewes: Book Guild, 2005); Richard Tomlinson, *The Big Breach: From Top Secret to Maximum Security* (Edinburgh: Cutting Edge, 2001).

6 Christopher Andrew, *The Defence of the Realm: The Authorized History of MI5* (London: Allen Lane, 2009); Keith Jeffery, *MI6: The History of the Secret Intelligence Service 1909–1949* (London: Bloomsbury, 2010).

7 As John le Carré wrote: 'When a secret service professes a new openness, we do well to count our silver. When it appoints its own trusted writer and feeds him selected top-secret documents that would land the less favoured in gaol, we have every right to be sceptical, as the recent "official histories" of MI5 and MI6 demonstrate all too clearly' ('Agent Zigzag', *The Times*, 5 March 2011).

8 Christopher Andrew and Vasili Mitrokhin, *The Mitrokhin Archive: The KGB in Europe and the*

West (London: Allen Lane/Penguin, 1999); *The Mitrokhin Archive II: The KGB and the World* (London, Allen Lane/Penguin, 2005).

9 Kahn, 'Intelligence studies on the continent', pp. 249–62.

10 Denécé and Arboit, 'Intelligence studies in France'.

11 Kahn, 'Intelligence studies on the continent', pp. 262–71.

12 www.bstu.bund.de/DE/Home/home_node.html, accessed 18 September 2011.

13 Matey, 'Development of intelligence studies in Spain'.

14 James J. Wirtz, 'The American approach to intelligence studies', in Loch K. Johnson (ed.), *Handbook of Intelligence Studies* (Abingdon: Routledge, 2007), pp. 28–38.

15 Rudner, 'Intelligence studies in higher education', p. 133.

16 Justice McDonald conducted the Commission of Inquiry Concerning Certain Activities of the Royal Canadian Mounted Police. Justice O'Connor conducted the Commission of Inquiry into the Actions of Canadian Officials in Relation to Maher Arar; http://publications.gc.ca. Kealey and Whitaker's multi-volume series was published in the 1990s by the Canadian Committee on Labour History.

17 Main examples are Michael Warner, 'Wanted: a definition of intelligence', *Studies in Intelligence*, 46,3 (2002), www.odci.gov/csi/studies/vol46no3/article02.html, accessed 5 December 2011; Peter Gill, 'Theories of intelligence: where are we, where should we go and how might we proceed?', in Peter Gill, Stephen Marrin and Mark Phythian (eds.), *Intelligence Theory: Key Questions and Debates* (London: Routledge, 2009), pp. 208–26.

18 Wilhelm Agrell, *When Everything Is Intelligence – Nothing Is Intelligence*, Sherman Kent Center for Intelligence Analysis Occasional Papers, 1,4 (2002),, https://www.cia.gov/library/kent-center-occasional-papers/pdf/OPNo4.pdf, accessed 12 December 2011.

19 Wirtz, 'American approach', pp. 31–4.

20 Richard K. Betts, 'Analysis, war and decision: why intelligence failures are inevitable', *World Politics*, 31,1 (1978), pp. 61–89 (reprinted in Gill et al., *Intelligence Theory*, pp. 87–111).

21 Mark Phythian, 'Intelligence theory and theories of international relations: shared world or separate worlds?', in Gill et al., *Intelligence Theory*, pp. 54–72.

22 E.g., Herman, *Intelligence Power*, chs.16–18; Davies, *MI6*; Amy B. Zegart, *Spying Blind: The CIA, the FBI and the Origins of 9/11* (Princeton: Princeton University Press, 2007); Peter Gill, *Policing Politics: Security Intelligence and the Liberal Democratic State* (London: Frank Cass, 1994), pp. 48–55.

23 We give a number of examples in chapter 3, n. 39.

24 Frank J. Donner, *The Age of Surveillance: The Aims and Methods of America's Political Intelligence System* (New York: Vintage Books, 1981); William W. Keller, *The Liberals and J. Edgar Hoover: Rise and Fall of a Domestic Intelligence State* (Princeton: Princeton University Press, 1989).

25 KGB: Andrew and Mitrokhin, *Mitrokhin Archive*. There is now a considerable literature on the Stasi. Key works in English include: Gary Bruce, *The Firm: The Inside Story of the Stasi* (New York: Oxford University Press, 2010); Kristie Macrakis, *Seduced by Secrets: Inside the Stasi's Spy-Tech World* (New York: Cambridge University Press, 2008); Mike Dennis, *The Stasi: Myth and Reality* (Harlow: Longman, 2003); and Anna Funder, *Stasiland: Stories From Behind the Berlin Wall* (London: Granta, 2003).

26 E.g., Toni Erskine, '"As rays of light to the human soul?" Moral agents and intelligence gathering', *Intelligence and National Security*, 19,2 (2004), pp. 359–81; Jan Goldman (ed.), *Ethics of Spying: A Reader for the Intelligence Professional* (Lanham: Scarecrow Press, 2006); Michael Herman, 'Ethics and intelligence after September 2001', *Intelligence and National Security*, 19,2 (2004), pp. 342–58; David Omand, *Securing the State* (London: Hurst, 2010); Michael Quinlan, 'Just intelligence: prolegomena to an ethical theory', *Intelligence and National Security*, 22,1 (2007), pp. 1–13.

27 E.g., Hans Born and Ian Leigh, *Making Intelligence Accountable: Legal Standards and Best*

Practice for Oversight of Intelligence Agencies (Oslo: Parliament of Norway, 2005); Hans Born, Loch K. Johnson and Ian Leigh (eds.), *Who's Watching the Spies? Establishing Intelligence Service Accountability* (Washington, DC: Potomac Books, 2005); Thomas C. Bruneau and Steven Boraz (eds.), *Reforming Intelligence: Obstacles to Democratic Control and Effectiveness* (Austin: University of Texas Press, 2007).

28 Jeffrey T. Richelson and Desmond Ball, *The Ties That Bind*, 2nd edn (Boston: Unwin Hyman, 1990).

29 Hans Born, Ian Leigh and Aidan Wills (eds.), *International Intelligence Cooperation and Accountability* (London: Routledge, 2011).

30 Paul Maddrell, 'Intelligence studies at UK universities: an expanding subject', CIISS, http://users.aber.ac.uk/rbh/iss/uk.htm, accessed 31 August 2011.

31 Rudner, 'Intelligence studies in higher education', pp. 114–15.

32 Michael S. Goodman and David Omand, 'What analysts need to understand: the King's intelligence studies program', *Studies in Intelligence*, 52,4 (2008), https://www.cia.gov/library/center-for-the-study-of-intelligence/csi-publications/csi-studies/studies/vol-52-no-4/teaching-intelligence-analysts-in-the-uk.html, accessed 12 December 2011.

33 With colleagues we have tried to set an example; e.g., Stuart Farson, Peter Gill, Mark Phythian and Shlomo Shpiro (eds.), *PSI Handbook of Global Security and Intelligence: National Approaches*, vol. 1: *The Americas and Asia*; vol. 2: *Europe, the Middle East and South Africa* (Westport: Praeger Security International, 2008); Farson and Phythian (eds.), *Commissions of Inquiry and National Security: Comparative Approaches* (Santa Barbara: Praeger, 2011). See also Peter Gill, '"Knowing the self, knowing the other": the comparative analysis of security intelligence', in Johnson, *Handbook of Intelligence Studies*, pp. 82–90.

34 E.g., Matey, 'Development of intelligence studies in Spain'.

35 Roger Hilsman 'Intelligence and policy-making in foreign affairs', *World Politics*, 5,1 (1952), pp. 1–45.

36 Zegart, *Spying Blind*, p. 91

37 Scott, 'Sources and methods', p. 195.

38 E.g., Amy B. Zegart, 'Cloaks, daggers, and ivory towers: why academics don't study U.S. intelligence', in Loch K. Johnson (ed.) *Strategic Intelligence*, vol. 1: *Understanding the Hidden Side of Government* (Westport: Praeger Security International, 2007), pp. 21–34.

39 www.aaanet.org/issues/policy-advocacy/CEAUSSIC-Releases-Final-Report-on-Army-HTS-Program.cfm, accessed 18 September 2011.

40 William Boyd, 'The truth about spies', *Guardian Review*, 17 September 2011.

CHAPTER 1 WHAT IS INTELLIGENCE?

1 This is one favoured explanatory approach. As James Pavitt, former CIA Deputy Director for Operations, once put it: 'At the end of the day, the human spy business is the way the human spy business was at the battle of Jericho many hundreds of years ago – human beings stealing secrets and giving those secrets to someone for gain, for advantage' (cited in Charles E. Lathrop (ed.), *The Literary Spy* (New Haven: Yale University Press, 2004), p. 138).

2 Robert Kitson and Tim Kelso, 'England hunt rugby spies', *Guardian*, 18 November 2003. In a further incident, in November 2005 two men were caught while covertly filming the All Blacks rugby team during a training session. Robert Kitson, 'All Blacks discover spies in the bushes', *Guardian*, 16 November 2005.

3 Stephen Pritchard, 'Espionage in sport', *Infosecurity*, 7,1 (Jan.–Feb. 2010), pp. 16–18.

4 Throughout the book we use 'MI5' and 'MI6' when referring to the UK Security Service and Secret Intelligence Service (SIS) respectively as a widely recognized shorthand (as, indeed, the agencies themselves do with their website addresses), but recognize the

essentially historical nature of these titles; see www.mi6.gov.uk/output/Page50.html. See also www.mi5.gov.uk/output/Page7.html.

5 CSIS, *Our Priority Areas*, https://www.csis.gc.ca/prrts/index-eng.asp.

6 We use the term 'customer' here in recognition of the fact that the end-users will differ according to the level or context in which intelligence is being sought. At the level of states, policy-makers are the customers.

7 Butler Committee, *Review of Intelligence on Weapons of Mass Destruction: Report of a Committee of Privy Counsellors*, HC898 (London: Stationery Office, July 2004), para. 52, p. 15 (henceforward 'Butler Report').

8 Philip Flood, *Report of the Inquiry into Australian Intelligence Agencies* (Canberra: Australian Government, July 2004), p. 8 (henceforward 'Flood Report').

9 Daniel Patrick Moynihan, *Secrecy* (New Haven: Yale University Press, 1998), p. 202.

10 As Sherman Kent pointed out, 'intelligence' can, in fact, refer to any of three things: a kind of *knowledge*; the type of *organization* that produces the knowledge; or the *activity* pursued by the organization (*Strategic Intelligence for American World Policy* (Princeton: Princeton University Press, 1966; first pub. 1949), p. ix).

11 www.odci.gov/cia/publications/facttell/intelligence_cycle.html, accessed 1 December 2005.

12 Kent, *Strategic Intelligence*, p. 16.

13 The funnel of causality is used as a framework in Charles W. Kegley and Eugene R. Wittkopf, *American Foreign Policy*, 5th edn. (New York: St. Martin's Press, 1996), ch. 2.

14 Arthur S. Hulnick, 'What's wrong with the intelligence cycle', *Intelligence and National Security*, 21,6 (2006), p. 960.

15 See, e.g., Mark Phythian, 'Policing uncertainty: intelligence, security and risk', pp. 187–205; Peter Gill, 'Intelligence, threat, risk and the challenge of oversight', pp. 206–22; David Strachan-Morris, 'Threat and risk: what's the difference and why does it matter?', pp. 172–86; and Michael Warner, 'Fragile and provocative: notes on secrecy and intelligence', pp. 227–40; all in *Intelligence and National Security*, 27,2 (2012).

16 Eliza Manningham-Buller, 'Security', Reith Lecture broadcast on BBC Radio 4, 13 September 2011, www.bbc.co.uk/programmes/b014fcyw, accessed 19 September 2011.

17 See, e.g., Mike Dennis, *The Stasi: Myth and Reality* (Harlow: Longman, 2003), pp. 44–9.

18 See Sally Bowen and Jane Holligan, *The Imperfect Spy: The Many Lives of Vladimiro Montesinos* (Lima: PEISA, 2003).

19 Stephen Marrin, 'Intelligence analysis and decision-making: methodological challenges', in Peter Gill, Stephen Marrin and Mark Phythian (eds.), *Intelligence Theory: Key Questions and Debates* (London: Routledge, 2009), p. 144.

20 David Omand, *Securing the State* (London: Hurst, 2010), p. 119. See also the diagram on the same page.

21 For a thoughtful argument as to why covert actions should not be regarded as part of 'intelligence', see Jennifer Sims, 'Defending adaptive realism: intelligence theory comes of age', in Gill et al., *Intelligence Theory*, pp. 151–65.

22 Intrinsic: Roy Godson, 'Intelligence for the 1990s', in Godson (ed.), *Intelligence Requirements for the 1990s* (Lexington: Lexington Books, 1989), p. 4. Allied: Michael Herman, *Intelligence Power in Peace and War: Intelligence Services in the Information Age* (Cambridge: Cambridge University Press, 1996), pp. 54–6.

23 Michael Herman, 'Ethics and intelligence after September 2001', *Intelligence and National Security*, 19,2 (2004), pp. 342–58 at 342.

24 E.g., in the Pinochet era the extent of recourse to 'high-end' covert actions was a reflection of the nature of the regime and the prevailing security culture. See John Dinges, *The Condor Years: How Pinochet and His Allies Brought Terrorism to Three Continents* (New York:

New Press, 2004), and Hugh O'Shaughnessy, *Pinochet: The Politics of Torture* (London: Latin America Bureau, 2000), chs. III and IV.

25 Loch K. Johnson, 'On drawing a bright line for covert operations', *American Journal of International Law*, 86 (1992), p. 286. We discuss this question further in chapter 8.

26 www.mi5.gov.uk/output/how-we-operate.html, accessed 6 March 2012. Emphases in original.

27 For a recent account of US covert operations in this period, see James Callanan, *Covert Action in the Cold War: US Policy, Intelligence and CIA Operations* (London: Tauris, 2010).

28 Michael Warner, 'Wanted: a definition of intelligence', *Studies in Intelligence*, 46,3 (2002), www.odci.gov/csi/studies/vol46no3/article02.html, accessed 5 December 2011.

29 Ibid.

30 Commission on the Roles and Capabilities of the United States Intelligence Community, *Preparing for the 21st Century*, p. 5, cited in Warner, 'Wanted'.

31 Loch K. Johnson, 'Intelligence', in Bruce W. Jentleson and Thomas G. Paterson (eds.), *Encyclopedia of US Foreign Relations* (New York: Oxford University Press, 1997), pp. 365–73 at 365.

32 Warner, 'Wanted'.

33 Richard Betts has argued that: 'The comparative advantage of the intelligence community over outside analysts is in bringing together secret information with knowledge from open sources. The more far-seeing a project, the less likely secret information is to play a role in the assessment' ('Fixing intelligence', *Foreign Affairs*, 81,1 (2002), pp. 43–59 at 50). This suggests that intelligence services' comparative advantage over bodies using exclusively open source material lies in particular in short-term analysis, and that over medium- and long-term analysis the relative advantage that secret information bestows on intelligence agencies is progressively eroded, increasing the likelihood that the projections of open source analysts will be similarly valid.

34 With regard to Vietnam, e.g., Daniel Ellsberg has written of how: 'I had never questioned the assumption of many students of presidential power that secrecy is vital to preserve a president's range of options. But I now saw how the system of secrecy and lying could give him options he would be better off without' (*Secrets: A Memoir of Vietnam and the Pentagon Papers* (New York: Viking, 2002), p. 205).

35 Jennifer E. Sims, 'A theory of intelligence and international politics', in Gregory F. Treverton and Wilhelm Agrell (eds.), *National Intelligence Systems: Current Research and Future Prospects* (New York: Cambridge University Press, 2009), pp. 58–92 at 62.

36 Ben Macintyre, *Operation Mincemeat: The True Spy Story That Changed the Course of World War II* (London: Bloomsbury, 2010).

37 Michael Warner, 'Intelligence as risk shifting', in Gill et al., *Intelligence Theory*, pp. 16–32 at 19.

38 This adaptation was first used by Peter Gill, 'Theories of intelligence: where are we, where should we go and how might we proceed?', in Gill et al., *Intelligence Theory*, pp. 208–26 at 214.

39 On this, see Mark Phythian, 'Intelligence theory and theories of international relations: shared world or separate worlds?', in Gill et al., *Intelligence Theory*, pp. 54–72.

40 Omand, *Securing the State*, pp. 137 and 136.

41 HM Government, *A Strong Britain in an Age of Uncertainty: The National Security Strategy* (Cm 753 Oct 2010), www.direct.gov.uk/prod_consum_dg/groups/dg_digitalassets/@dg/@en/documents/digitalasset/dg_191639.pdf?CID=PDF&PLA=furl&CRE=nationalsecuritystrategy, accessed 12 December 2011.

42 See, e.g., Walter Laqueur, *Terrorism* (London: Abacus, 1978), pp. 18–20.

43 Thucydides, *The Peloponnesian War* (Harmondsworth: Penguin, 1983), pp. 172–3.

44 See, e.g., ch. XXIV.

45 On the distinction between 'threats' and 'vulnerabilities', see Barry Buzan, *People, States and Fear*, 2nd edn. (Hemel Hempstead: Harvester Wheatsheaf, 1991), ch. 3.
46 See Loch K. Johnson, 'Bricks and mortar for a theory of intelligence', *Comparative Strategy*, 22 (2003), pp. 1–28, esp. 3–4.
47 Robert Hutchinson, *Elizabeth's Spy Master: Francis Walsingham and the Secret War That Saved England* (London: Weidenfeld & Nicolson, 2006).
48 Peter Gill, *Policing Politics: Security Intelligence and the Liberal Democratic State* (London: Frank Cass, 1994), p. 163.
49 Stephen F. Knott, *Secret and Sanctioned: Covert Operations and the American Presidency* (New York: Oxford University Press, 1996), ch. 3.
50 Bernard Porter, *The Origins of the Vigilant State: The London Metropolitan Police Special Branch Before the First World War* (London: Weidenfeld & Nicolson, 1987); Rupert Allason, *The Branch: A History of the Metropolitan Police Special Branch 1883–1983* (London: Secker & Warburg, 1983).
51 See Bernard Porter, *Plots and Paranoia: A History of Political Espionage in Britain 1790–1988* (London: Unwin Hyman, 1989), and more generally Mark Mazower (ed.), *The Policing of Politics in the Twentieth Century: Historical Perspectives* (Oxford: Berghahn Books, 1997). McKinley's assassination: Sidney Fine, 'Anarchism and the assassination of McKinley', *American Historical Review*, 60 (1955), pp. 777–99. Development of a political police in nineteenth-century Czarist Russia: P. S. Squire, *The Third Department: The Political Police in the Russia of Nicholas I* (Cambridge: Cambridge University Press, 1968).
52 Christopher Andrew, *The Defence of the Realm: The Authorized History of MI5* (London: Allen Lane, 2009), esp. pp. 3–52.
53 Keith Jeffery, *MI6: The History of the Secret Intelligence Service 1909–1949* (London: Bloomsbury, 2010), ch. 6. See also Harry Ferguson, *Operation Kronstadt* (London: Hutchinson, 2008).
54 Christopher Andrew and Oleg Gordievsky, *KGB: The Inside Story of its Foreign Operations from Lenin to Gorbachev* (New York, HarperCollins, 1991), ch. 2; Andrew, *Secret Service: The Making of the British Intelligence Community* (London: Heinemann, 1985), ch. 6; Porter, *Plots and Paranoia*, chs. 7–8.
55 See Krivitsky's autobiography, *I Was Stalin's Agent* (London: Hamish Hamilton, 1939). The full record of his MI5 debriefing was released at the National Archives in 2003, at files KV2/802–805. See also Gary Kern, *A Death in Washington: Walter G. Krivitsky and the Stalin Terror* (New York: Enigma Books, 2003); John Callaghan and Mark Phythian, 'State surveillance of the CPGB leadership: 1920s–1950s', *Labour History Review*, 69,1 (2004), pp. 19–33.
56 See, e.g., John J. Dziak, *Chekisty: A History of the KGB* (Lexington: Lexington Books, 1988), p. 21.
57 On these national contexts, see Hal Klepak, 'Cuba', in Stuart Farson, Peter Gill, Mark Phythian and Shlomo Shpiro (eds.), *PSI Handbook of Global Security and Intelligence: National Approaches*, vol. 1: *The Americas and Asia* (Westport: Praeger Security International, 2008), pp. 146–61; Carlyle A. Thayer, 'Vietnam', ibid., pp. 300–17; and Meir Javedanfar, 'Islamic Republic of Iran', in Farson et al., *PSI Handbook of Global Security and Intelligence: National Approaches*, vol. 2: *Europe, the Middle East and South Africa*, pp. 533–50.
58 Andrew, *Secret Service*, pp. 260–1 and 298.
59 Percy Sillitoe, *Cloak without Dagger* (London: Pan Books, 1956), pp. 196–8.
60 For an account of his role in publicizing the existence of the D-Notice system, see Alan Watkins, *A Short Walk Down Fleet Street* (London: Duckworth, 2000), ch. 4.
61 See James Chapman, *Licence to Thrill: A Cultural History of the James Bond Films* (New York: Columbia University Press, 2000).
62 Jeremy Black, 'The geopolitics of James Bond', *Intelligence and National Security*, 19,2 (2004), pp. 290–303 at 302. There are similar examples of fiction feeding reality from US intelligence; e.g., actress Barbara Feldon, Agent 99 in the 1960s television spy spoof *Get Smart*,

has recalled how she was 'invited to visit the CIA for an exhibit they had of gadgets from "Get Smart", "I Spy", "The Man from U.N.C.L.E.", the Bond movies, and so forth. And they said that during those years, the CIA actually did watch those shows and made some of those devices actually work' (cited in Lathrop, *Literary Spy*, p. 153).

63 E. P. Thompson, 'The secret state within the state', *New Statesman*, 10 November 1978, p. 612.

64 Chapman Pincher, *Their Trade Is Treachery* (London: Sidgwick & Jackson, 1981); *Too Secret Too Long* (London: Sidgwick & Jackson, 1984); and *The Spycatcher Affair: A Web of Deception* (London: Sidgwick & Jackson, 1987).

65 The revelations from ex-MI5 officers Miranda Ingram and Cathy Massiter were significant here. See the excerpts in Nigel West (ed.), *The Faber Book of Espionage* (London: Faber & Faber, 1993), ch. XI.

66 See Tony Geraghty, *The Irish War: A Military History of a Domestic Conflict* (London: HarperCollins, 1998); Paul Foot, *Who Framed Colin Wallace?* (London: Macmillan, 1989).

67 See Seamus Milne, *The Enemy Within: MI5, Maxwell and the Scargill Affair* (London: Verso, 1994); Christopher Hitchens, 'Who runs Britain?', *London Review of Books*, 8 December 1994, pp. 3–4.

68 Peter Wright, *Spycatcher: The Candid Autobiography of a Senior Intelligence Officer* (New York: Viking, 1987); see also Stephen Dorril and Robin Ramsay, *Smear! Wilson and the Secret State* (London: Fourth Estate, 1991); David Leigh, *The Wilson Plot* (London: Heinemann, 1988); and Tony Benn, 'The case for dismantling the secret state', *New Left Review*, 190 (1991), pp. 127–30.

69 Mark Hollingsworth and Nick Fielding, *Defending the Realm: MI5 and the Shayler Affair* (London: André Deutsch, 1999); Richard Tomlinson, *The Big Breach: From Top Secret to Maximum Security* (Edinburgh: Cutting Edge, 2001).

70 Porter, *Plots and Paranoia*, p. viii.

71 Richard J. Aldrich, '"Grow your own": Cold War intelligence and history supermarkets', *Intelligence and National Security*, 17,1 (2002), pp. 135–52 at 148.

72 For a typology identifying three types of national security (outward-oriented, national securitism and inward-oriented), see J. A. Tapia-Valdés, 'A typology of national security policies', *Yale Journal of World Public Order*, 9,10 (1982), pp. 10–39. More generally, see Alain Rouquie, *The Military and the State in Latin America* (Berkeley: University of California Press, 1992).

73 The classic exposé, demonstrating the siege mentality of the apartheid state, is Gordon Winter, *Inside BOSS: South Africa's Secret Police* (Harmondsworth: Penguin, 1981).

74 Dziak, *Chekisty*.

75 See Ian Black and Benny Morris, *Israel's Secret Wars: A History of Israel's Intelligence Services* (London: Warner Books, 1992), ch. 9. The available intelligence allegedly included a personal warning from King Hussein of Jordan to Prime Minister Golda Meir; see p. 321. See also Dan Raviv and Yossi Melman, *Every Spy a Prince: The Complete History of Israel's Intelligence Community* (Boston: Houghton Mifflin, 1991), ch. 10.

76 The flavour of the debate can be seen in Theodore Draper, 'Is the CIA necessary?', *New York Review of Books*, 14 August 1997. For the debate in a UK context see Peter Gill, '"Sack the spooks": do we need an internal security apparatus?', in Leo Panitch (ed.), *Are There Alternatives? Socialist Register 1996* (London: Merlin Press, 1996), pp. 189–211.

77 Kathryn S. Olmsted, *Challenging the Secret Government: The Post-Watergate Investigations of the CIA and Watergate* (Chapel Hill: University of North Carolina Press, 1996).

78 See Paul Rogers, *Losing Control: Global Security in the Twenty-First Century* (London: Pluto Press, 2000), ch. 4.

79 Peter Schweizer, 'The growth of economic espionage: America is target number one', *Foreign Affairs*, 75,1 (1996), pp. 11–12.

80 Cited in Loch K. Johnson, 'Spies', *Foreign Policy*, Sept.–Oct. (2000), p. 20.

81 Gregory F. Treverton, 'Intelligence and the "market state"', *Studies in Intelligence*, 10 (2001), https://www.cia.gov/library/center-for-the-study-of-intelligence/kent-csi/vol44no2/html/v44i5a09p.htm, accessed 12 December 2011, p. 73.

82 Ibid., p. 76, n. 5.

83 See chapter 4.

84 See, e.g., Toby Harnden, 'Wikileaks: US diplomats "have been spying on UN leadership"', *Daily Telegraph*, 28 November 2010.

85 Aldrich, 'Grow your own', pp. 136–8.

86 Michael J. Hogan, *Cross of Iron: Harry S. Truman and the Origins of the National Security State 1945–1954* (Cambridge: Cambridge University Press, 1999); Melvyn P. Leffler, *A Preponderance of Power: National Security, the Truman Administration and the Cold War* (Stanford: Stanford University Press, 1992).

87 John Keegan, *Intelligence in War: Knowledge of the Enemy from Napoleon to Al-Qaeda* (London: Hutchinson, 2003), pp. 383–4.

88 Phillip Knightley, *The Second Oldest Profession: The Spy as Patriot, Bureaucrat, Fantasist and Whore* (London: André Deutsch, 1986); Stephen Dorril, *MI6: Fifty Years of Special Operations* (London: Fourth Estate, 2001); and Rhodri Jeffreys-Jones, *Cloak and Dollar: A History of American Secret Intelligence* (New Haven: Yale University Press, 2002).

89 Phillip Knightley, 'The biggest con-trick', *New Statesman*, 19 July 2004, p.14.

90 E.g., as articulated in the introduction by Julius Mader (ed.) to the 1968 East German publication *Who's Who in CIA* (Berlin: Julius Mader): 'We know, it is true, that the extensive intelligence machinery of imperialist USA was not, is not, and never will be, in a position to turn back the wheel of history. The destinies of the nations cannot be fixed in the offices of the CIA' (p. 14).

91 For a sense of the scope of the KGB's overseas operations, see Christopher Andrew and Vasili Mitrokhin, *The Mitrokhin Archive II: The KGB and the World* (London, Allen Lane/Penguin, 2005).

92 Michael Herman, *Intelligence Services in the Information Age* (London: Frank Cass, 2001), pp. ix and 159.

93 Robin W. Winks, *Cloak and Gown: Scholars in the Secret War, 1939–1961*, 2nd edn (New Haven: Yale University Press, 1996), p. 63.

94 John Lewis Gaddis, 'Intelligence, espionage, and Cold War history', *Diplomatic History*, 13,2 (1989), pp. 191–212 at 114.

95 Quoted in Kegley and Wittkopf, *American Foreign Policy*, p. 132.

96 E.g., with regard to the 1956 Suez crisis see W. Scott Lucas and Alistair Morey, 'The hidden "alliance": the CIA and MI6 before and after Suez', *Intelligence and National Security*, 15,2 (2000), pp. 95–120.

97 Aldrich, 'Grow your own', p. 144.

98 Richard K. Betts, 'Analysis, war and decision: why intelligence failures are inevitable', *World Politics*, 31,1 (1978), pp. 61–89 at 62 (reprinted in Gill et al., *Intelligence Theory*, pp. 87–111).

99 Avi Shlaim, 'Failures in national intelligence estimates: the case of the Yom Kippur War', *World Politics*, 28,3 (1976), pp. 348–80 at 378.

100 Ronald Kessler, *The CIA at War* (New York: St. Martin's Press, 2004), p. 261. In a UK context, former MI5 officer Annie Machon offers the example of the reluctance of managers in F Branch, the counter-subversion section, to acknowledge that the threat from groups such as the Militant Tendency had receded (Machon, *Spies, Lies and Whistleblowers* (Lewes: Book Guild, 2005), pp. 37–53).

101 The phrase 'wilderness of mirrors' comes from the 1920 T. S. Eliot poem 'Gerontion' and was used by David A. Martin as the title of his study of US counterintelligence and Cold War paranoia (London: HarperCollins, 1980).

102 See Peter Taylor, *Talking to Terrorists: A Personal Journey from the IRA to Al Qaeda* (London: HarperPress, 2011), ch. 13.

103 Eliza Manningham-Buller, 'Security', Reith Lecture broadcast on BBC Radio 4, 13 September 2011, www.bbc.co.uk/programmes/b014fcyw, accessed 19 September 2011.

104 On this point, see David Kahn, 'An historical theory of intelligence', *Intelligence and National Security*, 16,3 (2001), pp. 79–92 (reprinted in Gill et al., *Intelligence Theory*, pp. 4–15).

105 Douglas MacEachin, 'Predicting the Soviet invasion of Afghanistan: the intelligence community's record', https://www.cia.gov/library/center-for-the-study-of-intelligence/csi-publications/books-and-monographs/predicting-the-soviet-invasion-of-afghanistan-the-intelligence-communitys-record/predicting-the-soviet-invasion-of-afghanistan-the-intelligence-communitys-record.html, accessed 13 December 2011.

106 This is in essence the argument of Richard A. Clarke, former National Co-ordinator for Security, Infrastructure Protection, and Counterterrorism, in *Against All Enemies: Inside America's War on Terror* (London: Simon & Schuster, 2004). See also James Mann, *Rise of the Vulcans: A History of Bush's War Cabinet* (New York: Viking, 2004).

107 Judith Miller and Don van Natta Jr, 'In years of plots and clues, scope of Qaeda eluded US', *New York Times*, 9 June 2002.

108 Carrie Johnson, Karen DeYoung and Anne E. Kornblut, 'Obama vows to repair intelligence gaps behind Detroit airplane incident', *Washington Post*, 30 December 2009.

CHAPTER 2 HOW DO WE UNDERSTAND INTELLIGENCE?

1 Cf. Wilhelm Agrell and Gregory Treverton, 'The science of intelligence: reflections on a field that never was', in Treverton and Agrell (eds.), *National Intelligence Systems: Current Research and Prospects* (Cambridge: Cambridge University Press, 2009), pp. 265–80 at 279–80.

2 Len Scott and Peter Jackson, 'The study of intelligence in theory and practice', *Intelligence and National Security*, 19,2 (2004), p. 147.

3 Christopher Andrew and David Dilks (eds.), *The Missing Dimension: Governments and Intelligence Communities in the Twentieth Century* (London, Macmillan, 1984); Oliver Hoare (ed.), *British Intelligence in the Twentieth Century: A Missing Dimension?*, special issue of *Intelligence and National Security*, 17,1 (2002); Christopher Andrew, 'Intelligence, international relations and "under-theorisation"', *Intelligence and National Security*, 19,2 (2004), pp. 170–84 at 172.

4 Michael G. Fry and Miles Hochstein, 'Epistemic communities: intelligence studies and international relations', *Intelligence and National Security*, 8,3 (1993), pp. 14–28 at 17–18. For a restatement of the neo-realist case and the primacy of security in an anarchic world see John J. Mearsheimer, *The Tragedy of Great Power Politics* (New York: Norton, 2002).

5 E.g., Arthur S. Hulnick, *Fixing the Spy Machine: Preparing American Intelligence for the Twenty-First Century* (London: Praeger, 1999); Mark M. Lowenthal, *Intelligence: From Secrets to Policy*, 2nd edn. (Washington, DC: CQ Press, 2003); William E. Odom, *Fixing Intelligence* (New Haven: Yale University Press, 2003). Notable exceptions include Loch K. Johnson, 'Bricks and mortar for a theory of intelligence', *Comparative Strategy*, 22 (2003), pp. 1–28, and 'Preface to a theory of strategic intelligence', *International Journal of Intelligence and Counterintelligence*, 16 (2003), pp. 638–63.

6 David Kahn, 'An historical theory of intelligence', *Intelligence and National Security*, 16,3 (2001), pp. 79–92 (reprinted in Peter Gill, Stephen Marrin and Mark Phythian (eds.), *Intelligence Theory: Key Questions and Debates* (London: Routledge, 2009), pp. 4–15).

7 Colin Hay, *Political Analysis: A Critical Introduction* (Basingstoke: Palgrave, 2002), pp. 10–13; David Sanders, 'Behaviouralism', in David Marsh and Gerry Stoker (eds.), *Theory and Methods in Political Science*, 2nd edn. (Basingstoke: Palgrave, 2002), pp. 45–64.

8 Cf. David Marsh and Paul Furlong, 'A skin not a sweater: ontology and epistemology in political science', in Marsh and Stoker, *Theory and Methods*, pp. 17–41; Anthony Bottoms, 'The relationship between theory and research in criminology', in R. D. King and E. Wincup (eds.), *Doing Research on Crime and Justice* (Oxford: Oxford University Press, 2000), pp. 15–60.

9 Philip H. J. Davies, 'Theory and intelligence reconsidered', in Gill et al., *Intelligence Theory*, p. 200.

10 E.g., Stephen Marrin, 'Intelligence analysis and decision-making: methodological challenges', in Gill et al., *Intelligence Theory*, pp. 140–4.

11 Sheila Kerr noted that Roger Hilsman's 1958 critique of US strategic intelligence 'found that contemporary US doctrine put too much emphasis on the accumulation of descriptive facts as the essence of knowledge' ('Turning knowledge into wisdom: British and American approaches', paper given to Intelligence Studies Panel, International Studies Association, Portland, OR, March 2003, p. 9). See also Hilsman, 'Intelligence and policy-making in foreign affairs', *World Politics*, 5,1 (1952), pp. 1–45 at 12–15.

12 Graham Allison and Philip Zelikow, *Essence of Decision: Explaining the Cuban Missile Crisis*, 2nd edn. (New York: Longman, 1999), p. 4.

13 Richard Norton-Taylor, *Truth is a Difficult Concept: Inside the Scott Inquiry* (London: Fourth Estate, 1995), p. 86.

14 Terry Terriff, Stuart Croft, Lucy James and Patrick Morgan, *Security Studies Today* (Cambridge: Polity, 1999), pp. 99–114; Raymond A. Morrow with David D. Brown, *Critical Theory and Methodology* (London: Sage, 1994), pp. 62–82; Marsh and Furlong, 'A skin not a sweater', pp. 25–6.

15 E.g., Vicky Randall, 'Feminism', in Marsh and Stoker, *Theory and Methods*, pp. 109–30.

16 An exception is Gillian Youngs, 'Feminist international relations and intelligence in a high-tech age', in Annika Bergman-Rosamond and Mark Phythian (eds.), *War, Ethics and Justice: New Perspectives on a Post-9/11 World* (London: Routledge, 2011), pp. 112–27. See also Cynthia Enloe, *Bananas, Beaches and Bases: Making Feminist Sense of International Politics* (Berkeley: University of California Press, 1990).

17 Jan Jindy Pettman, *Worlding Women: A Feminist International Politics* (London: Routledge, 1996), pp. 4 and 105.

18 James der Derian, *Antidiplomacy: Spies, Terror, Speed, and War* (Oxford: Blackwell, 1992), pp. 27 and 46.

19 Andrew Rathmell, 'Towards postmodern intelligence', *Intelligence and National Security*, 17,3 (2002), pp. 87–104 at 95–6 and 97.

20 Ibid., pp. 97–8. For a specific argument on this fifth factor see John Ferris, 'Netcentric warfare, C4ISR and information operations: towards a revolution in military intelligence?', *Intelligence and National Security*, 19,2 (2003), pp. 203–4.

21 Rathmell, 'Towards postmodern intelligence', p. 101. Cf. also Deborah G. Barger, *Toward a Revolution in Intelligence Affairs* (Santa Monica: RAND, 2005), p. 99. David Lyon puts it more strongly in his discussion of postmodernists 'embracing chaos' (*Postmodernity* (Minneapolis: University of Minnesota Press, 1994), pp. 74–8).

22 'Objectivity' is not possible in social and behavioural sciences, but intersubjectivity is its pragmatic surrogate and ensures that an observation could have been made by any other observer in the same situation. Abraham Kaplan, *The Conduct of Inquiry: Methodology for Behavioral Science* (New York: Transaction, 1998), pp. 127–8. Similarly, Mark Bevir and Rod Rhodes argue that the quality of narratives produced by interpretist work can be evaluated by comparisons of comprehensiveness, consistency and heuristic value ('Interpretive theory', in Marsh and Stoker, *Theory and Methods*, pp. 131–52 at 142).

23 Hence the title of the book by Bruce Berkowitz and Allan Goodman, *Best Truth: Intelligence in the Information Age* (New Haven: Yale University Press, 2000).

24 Richard Eyre, 'Ballot-box blues', *Guardian*, 26 March 2005. See also David Brooks, 'The art of intelligence', *New York Times*, 2 April 2005.
25 Discussing the writing of his 2004 novel, *Absolute Friends*, John le Carré said: 'you have got to write a novel to tell the truth'. *Front Row*, BBC Radio 4, 1 January 2004. More generally, Nigel West, 'Fiction, faction and intelligence', *Intelligence and National Security*, 19,2 (2004), pp. 275–89.
26 Lyon, *Postmodernity*, pp. 48–52.
27 Hamilton Bean, 'Organizational culture and U.S. intelligence affairs', *Intelligence and National Security*, 24,4 (2009), pp. 479–98 at 482.
28 Kjetil Anders Hatlebrekke and M. L. R. Smith, 'Towards a new theory of intelligence failure? The impact of cognitive closure and discourse failure', *Intelligence and National Security*, 25,2 (2010), pp. 147–82 at 148 and 167, emphasis added.
29 Lyon, *Postmodernity*, pp. 6–7; Rathmell, 'Towards postmodern intelligence', p. 93.
30 See, e.g., Michael J. Hogan, *Cross of Iron: Harry S. Truman and the Origins of the National Security State 1945–1954* (Cambridge: Cambridge University Press, 1999).
31 On the role of deception, e.g., see Edward Jay Epstein, *Deception: The Invisible War Between the KGB and the CIA* (London: W. H. Allen, 1989).
32 E.g., David Lyon, *Surveillance after September 11* (Cambridge: Polity, 2003), pp. 40–55.
33 Cf. Richard J. Evans' objections to postmodernism in both *In Defence of History* (London: Granta, 1997) and *Lying About Hitler: History, Holocaust, and the David Irving Trial* (New York: Basic Books, 2001).
34 Hay, *Political Analysis*, p. 47.
35 Berth Danermark, Mats Ekstrom, Liselotte Jackson and Jan Ch. Karlsson, *Explaining Society: An Introduction to Critical Realism in the Social Sciences* (London: Routledge, 2002), pp. 91–3. E.g., Johnson, 'Bricks and mortar', p. 1; Stephen Marrin and Jonathan D. Clemente, 'Improving intelligence analysis by looking to the medical profession', *International Journal of Intelligence and Counterintelligence*, 18,4 (2005–6), pp. 707–29.
36 Fry and Hochstein, 'Epistemic communities', p. 25.
37 Kahn, 'An historical theory of intelligence', p. 79.
38 Bhaskar, *Scientific Realism*, p. 51 (as cited in Morrow, *Critical Theory*, p. 78).
39 Marsh and Furlong, 'A skin not a sweater', pp. 30–1.
40 Dennis H. Wrong, *Power: Its Forms, Bases, and Uses* (Oxford: Blackwell, 1988), ch. 1.
41 Hay, *Political Analysis*, p. 94
42 Ibid., ch. 3, for a summary; see also S. D. McAnulla, 'Structure and agency', in Marsh and Stoker, *Theory and Methods*, pp. 271–91.
43 Allison and Zelikow, *Essence of Decision*.
44 This is elaborated in Peter Gill, 'Theories of intelligence: where are we, where should we go and how might we proceed?', in Gill et al., *Intelligence Theory*, pp. 219–22.
45 Bob Jessop, 'Interpretive sociology and the dialectic of structure and agency', *Theory, Culture and Society*, 13,1 (1996), pp. 119–28. This is an equivalent approach to role theory in foreign policy analysis: Charles W. Kegley and Eugene R. Wittkopf, *American Foreign Policy*, 5th edn. (New York: St. Martin's Press, 1996), pp. 464–5.
46 Hay, *Political Analysis*, pp. 126–34.
47 Stuart Farson, Peter Gill, Mark Phythian and Shlomo Shpiro (eds.), *PSI Handbook of Global Security and Intelligence: National Approaches*, vol. 1: *The Americas and Asia*; vol. 2: *Europe, the Middle East and South Africa* (Westport: Praeger Security International, 2008).
48 Michael Warner, 'Building a theory of intelligence systems', in Treverton and Agrell, *National Intelligence Systems*, pp. 11–37. The review is Warner, '*Handbook of Global Security and Intelligence: National Approaches*', *Studies in Intelligence*, 53,2 (2008), https://www.cia.gov/library/center-for-the-study-of-intelligence/csi-publications/csi-studies/studies/vol53no2/handbook-of-global-security-and-intelligence.html, accessed 15 December 2011.

49 Hilsman, 'Intelligence and policy-making', p. 25. He answered his question: 'If our working model has a point, it is that the need is not for a separation of knowledge and action, but for an integration of the two. In rationally conducted foreign affairs, the relationship of knowledge and action should be one of continuous interplay; knowledge and action should interact, should condition and control each other at every point' (p. 42) We agree, and that is why we include action/power in our definition of intelligence.
50 Scott and Jackson, 'Study of intelligence', p. 150.
51 Christopher Dandeker, *Surveillance, Power and Modernity: Bureaucracy and Discipline from 1700 to the Present Day* (Cambridge: Polity, 1990); Anthony Giddens, *The Nation State and Violence* (Berkeley: University of California Press, 1985), pp. 181–92.
52 Michel Foucault, 'Governmentality', in Graham Burchell, Colin Gordon and Peter Miller (eds.), *The Foucault Effect: Studies in Governmentality* (London: Harvester Wheatsheaf, 1991), pp. 87–104.
53 Adda B. Bozeman, 'Knowledge and comparative method in comparative intelligence studies', in Bozeman, *Strategic Intelligence and Statecraft* (Washington, DC: Brassey's, 1992), pp. 198–205. James der Derian, 'Anti-diplomacy, intelligence theory and surveillance practice', *Intelligence and National Security*, 8,3 (1993), pp. 29–51 at 34–5.
54 David Lyon, *Surveillance Society: Monitoring Everyday Life* (Milton Keynes: Open University Press, 2001), p. 103. Cf. also der Derian, *Antidiplomacy*, p. 46; Reg Whitaker, *The End of Privacy: How Total Surveillance is Becoming a Reality* (New York: New Press, 1999).
55 Lyon, *Surveillance after September 11*.
56 Peter Gill, 'Intelligence, threat, risk and the challenge of oversight', *Intelligence and National Security*, 27,2 (2012), pp. 206–22.
57 Mark Phythian, 'Policing uncertainty: intelligence, security and risk', *Intelligence and National Security*, 27,2 (2012), pp.187–205.
58 E.g., David Strachan-Morris, 'Threat and risk: what's the difference and why does it matter?', *Intelligence and National Security*, 27,2 (2012), pp. 172–86.
59 Kent Center for Analytic Tradecraft, *Making Sense of Transnational Threats*, Sherman Kent School, Occasional Papers, 3,1 (2004), pp. 6–8.
60 John Scott, *Power* (Cambridge: Polity, 2001), pp. 6–12. Also Stewart R. Clegg, *Frameworks of Power* (London: Sage, 1989).
61 Richard W. Wilsnack, 'Information control: a conceptual framework for sociological analysis', *Urban Life*, 8 (1980), pp. 467–99. Cf. Scott, *Power*, pp. 16–25.
62 Carl J. Friedrich, *Man and His Government* (New York: McGraw-Hill, 1963), pp. 201–2.
63 As Jeremy Bentham wrote in relation to his original Panopticon concept: 'the more constantly the persons to be inspected are under the eyes of the persons who should inspect them, the more perfectly will the purpose of the establishment have been attained. Ideal perfection, if that were the object, would require that each person should actually be in that predicament, during every instant of time. This being impossible, the next thing to be wished for is, that, at every instant, seeing reason to believe as much, and not being able to satisfy himself to the contrary, he should *conceive* himself to be so' ('Panopticon Letters', in Bentham, *The Panopticon Writings* (London: Verso, 1995), p. 34). See also Michel Foucault, *Discipline and Punish: The Birth of the Prison* (London: Penguin, 1991), pp. 195–228.
64 For a summary of this debate see Michael Hill, *The Policy Process in the Modern State*, 3rd edn. (Hemel Hempstead: Harvester Wheatsheaf, 1997), pp. 98–126.
65 Fry and Hochstein, 'Epistemic communities', p. 20. For other views on the intelligence–policy relationship see Hilsman, 'Intelligence and policy-making', and Marrin, 'Intelligence analysis and decision-making'.
66 Sissela Bok, *Secrets: On the Ethics of Concealment and Revelation* (Oxford: Oxford University Press, 1986), pp. 6–7.
67 E.g., Chalmers Johnson, *Blowback: The Costs and Consequences of American Empire* (London:

Little, Brown, 2000); Christopher Simpson, *Blowback: America's Recruitment of Nazis and its Effects on the Cold War* (London: Weidenfeld & Nicolson, 1988).

68 Cf. Giddens, *Nation State and Violence*, pp. 10–11, regarding the 'dialectic of control' in social systems. See also Clegg, 'Power and authority, resistance and legitimacy', in Henri J. M. Goverde, Philip Cerny , Mark Haugaard and Howard Lentner (eds.), *Power in Contemporary Politics: Theories, Practices, Globalizations* (London: Sage, 2000), pp. 77–92.

69 Philip Cerny makes the point that the structural dominance of the nation-state is reflected throughout social science ('Globalization and the disarticulation of political power', in Goverde et al., *Power in Contemporary Politics*, pp. 17–86).

70 This might be compared with the approach in K. J. Holsti, *International Politics: A Framework for Analysis* (Englewood Cliffs, NJ: Prentice Hall, 1967), ch. 1. See also Barry Buzan, Ole Wæver and Jaap de Wilde, *Security: A New Framework for Analysis* (London: Lynne Riener, 1998), pp. 5–7.

71 Cf. levels as 'interwoven': Derek Layder, *New Strategies in Social Research* (Cambridge: Polity, 1993), pp. 71–106.

72 Of course, 'weak' states may be compared with 'strong' states in terms of the former's greater concern with *internal* security. Barry Buzan, *People, States and Fear*, 2nd edn. (Hemel Hempstead: Harvester Wheatsheaf, 1991), esp. pp. 96–107.

73 Sherman Kent, *Strategic Intelligence for American World Policy* (Princeton: Princeton University Press, 1966; first pub. 1949), p. 3.

74 Björn Müller-Wille, *For Our Eyes Only? Shaping an Intelligence Community Within the EU*, Occasional Paper 50 (Paris: Institute for Security Studies, 2004), www.isss-eu.org.

75 E.g., Jeffrey T. Richelson and Desmond Ball, *The Ties That Bind*, 2nd edn. (Boston: Unwin Hyman, 1990), on the UKUSA agreement; also Thorsten Wetzling, 'European counterintelligence intelligence liaisons', in Farson et al., *PSI Handbook*, vol. 2, pp. 498–529.

76 E.g., A. Walter Dorn, 'Intelligence-led peacekeeping: the United Nations stabilization mission in Haiti (MINUSTAH), 2006–07', *Intelligence and National Security*, 24,6 (2009), pp. 805–35.

77 See, e.g., Rolf Mowatt-Larssen, *Preventing Nuclear Terrorism: A Global Intelligence Imperative*, Report for Washington Institute for Near East Policy (April 2009), http://washingtoninstitute.org/templateC05.php?CID=3048.

78 Michael W. Eysenck and Mark T. Keane, *Cognitive Psychology: A Student's Handbook*, 4th edn. (Hove: Psychology Press, 2000), p. 54.

79 Ibid., *passim*. For consideration of these issues in the specific context of intelligence, see Kent Center, *Making Sense*, pp. 3–5.

80 R. Mayntz, 'Governing failures and the problem of governability', in Jan Kooiman (ed.), *Modern Governance: New Government–Society Interactions* (London: Sage, 1993), pp. 9–20.

81 Fred Halliday, 'The end of the Cold War and international relations: some analytic and theoretical conclusions', in Ken Booth and Steve Smith (eds.), *International Relations Theory Today* (Cambridge: Polity, 1995), pp. 38–61 at 38.

82 Danermark et al., *Explaining Society*, pp. 60–1; Layder, *New Strategies*, pp. 102–3.

83 Charles W. Kegley suggested four: describe, explain, predict and prescribe (*Controversies in International Relations Theory: Realism and the Neoliberal Challenge* (New York: St. Martin's Press, 1995), p. 8).

84 Johnson uses this approach in 'Bricks and mortar', though the general applicability of the propositions there could, we suggest, be enhanced by being rephrased more generally in terms of information and power.

85 E.g., Philip H. J. Davies, 'Intelligence culture and intelligence failure in Britain and the United States', *Cambridge Review of International Affairs*, 17 (2004), pp. 495–520.

86 Although, as Scott and Jackson rightly surmise, there is no guarantee that they will be listened to ('Study of intelligence', pp. 152–3). Cf. also Johnson, 'Preface', pp. 653–4.

CHAPTER 3 WHO DOES INTELLIGENCE?

1 Michael Fry and Miles Hochstein, 'Epistemic communities: intelligence studies and international relations', *Intelligence and National Security*, 8,3 (1993), pp. 14–28 at 22.
2 Peter Singer, *Corporate Warriors: The Rise of the Privatized Military Industry* (Ithaca: Cornell University Press, 2003), p. 18
3 Les Johnston and Clifford Shearing, *Governing Security: Explorations in Policing and Justice* (London: Routledge, 2002), pp. 144–8.
4 Michael Warner, 'Intelligence as risk shifting', in Peter Gill, Stephen Marrin and Mark Phythian (eds.), *Intelligence Theory: Key Questions and Debates* (London: Routledge, 2009), pp. 16–32 at 20.
5 Jennifer Frances, Rosalind Levačić, Jeremy Mitchell and Grahame Thompson, 'Introduction', in Grahame Thompson, Jennifer Frances, Rosalind Levačić and Jeremy Mitchell (eds.), *Markets, Hierarchies and Networks: The Co-ordination of Social Life* (London: Sage, 1991), pp. 1–19 at 14.
6 Manuel Castells, *The Rise of the Network Society*, 2nd edn. (Oxford: Blackwell, 2000), p. 445.
7 Cf. Loch K. Johnson, 'Bricks and mortar for a theory of intelligence', *Comparative Strategy*, 22 (2003), pp. 1–28.
8 Thompson et al., *Markets*.
9 Frank Leishman, 'Policing in Japan: East Asian archetype?', in R. I. Mawby (ed.) *Policing Across the World* (London: UCL Press, 1999), pp. 109–25 at 121–2.
10 Cf. Frances et al., 'Introduction', pp. 16–18.
11 David Knoke and James H. Kuklinski, 'Network analysis: basic concepts', in Thompson et al., *Markets*, pp. 173–82 at 173.
12 Peter K. Manning, 'Policing new social spaces', in James Sheptycki (ed.), *Issues in Transnational Policing* (London: Routledge, 2000), pp. 177–200.
13 Cf. Keith Dowding, 'Model or metaphor? A critical review of the policy network approach', *Political Studies*, 43,1 (1995), pp. 136–58; Jean-Paul Brodeur and Benoit Dupont, 'Will the knowledge workers put their act together?', *Policing and Society*, 16,1 (2006), pp. 7–26.
14 Jean-Paul Brodeur, *The Policing Web* (Oxford: Oxford University Press, 2010), p. 299.
15 Richard J. Aldrich, 'Global intelligence co-operation versus accountability: new facets to an old problem', *Intelligence and National Security*, 24,1 (2009), pp. 26–56 at 26–36.
16 Anthony McGrew, 'Conceptualizing global politics', in Anthony McGrew and Paul Lewis, *Global Politics* (Cambridge: Polity, 1992), pp. 1–28.
17 Peter Gill, *Rounding Up the Usual Suspects? Developments in Contemporary Law Enforcement Intelligence* (Aldershot: Ashgate, 2000), pp. 77–91; Brian Flood, 'Strategic aspects of the UK National Intelligence Model', in J. H. Ratcliffe (ed.), *Strategic Thinking in Criminal Intelligence* (Sydney: Federation Press, 2004), pp. 37–52.
18 Gill, *Usual Suspects?*, pp. 98–128; Michael Woodiwiss, *Organized Crime and American Power* (Toronto: University of Toronto Press, 2001), esp. pp. 362–89.
19 Home Office, *Guidelines on Special Branch Work in Great Britain* (London: Home Office, March 2004), para. 18.
20 HMIC, *A Need to Know: HMIC Thematic Inspection of Special Branch and Ports Policing* (London: Home Office Communications Directorate, January 2003).
21 Home Office, 'Anti-terrorist legislation must balance public protection with individual rights', press release 072/2004, 25 February 2004.
22 Peter Gill, *Policing Politics: Security Intelligence and the Liberal Democratic State* (London: Frank Cass, 1994), pp. 107–23.
23 www.acpo.police.uk/NationalPolicing/NCDENationalCoordinatorDomesticExtremism/Default.aspx, accessed 15 June 2011.

24 For a general discussion see Iain Cameron, 'Beyond the nation state: the influence of the European Court of Human Rights on intelligence accountability', in Hans Born, Loch K. Johnson and Ian Leigh (eds.), *Who's Watching the Spies? Establishing Intelligence Service Accountability* (Washington, DC: Potomac Books, 2005), pp. 34–53.
25 Security Service Act 1989, section 1(2–3).
26 Home Office, 'Anti-terrorist legislation'.
27 Christopher Andrew, *The Defence of the Realm: The Authorized History of MI5* (London: Allen Lane, 2009), pp. 799–829.
28 Tony G. Poveda, *Lawlessness and Reform: The FBI in Transition* (Pacific Grove: Brooks/Cole, 1990).
29 Thomas H. Kean and Lee H. Hamilton, *9/11 Commission Report: Final Report of the National Commission on Terrorist Attacks Upon the United States* (New York: Norton, 2004), pp. 209–10 (henceforward '*9/11 Commission Report*').
30 Office of the Inspector General, *The FBI's Efforts to Improve the Sharing of Intelligence and Other Information*, Report 04-10 (Washington, DC: Department of Justice, December 2003). See also Alfred Cumming and Todd Masse, *FBI Intelligence Reform since September 11, 2001: Issues and Options for Congress*, RL32336 (Washington, DC: Congressional Research Service, 2004).
31 *9/11 Commission Report*, p. 275.
32 Frederic F. Manget, 'Intelligence and law enforcement', in Loch K. Johnson (ed.) *The Oxford Handbook of National Security Intelligence* (Oxford: Oxford University Press, 2010), pp. 189–211.
33 Office of the Inspector General, *Review of the FBI's Investigations of Certain Domestic Advocacy Groups* (Washington, DC: Department of Justice, September 2010), www.justice.gov/oig/special/s1009r.pdf, accessed 16 June 2011.
34 D. C. McDonald, *Commission of Inquiry Concerning Certain Activities of the Royal Canadian Mounted Police*, Second Report, *Freedom and Security under the Law* (Ottawa: Minister of Supply and Services, 1981).
35 *9/11 Commission Report*, pp. 423–8.
36 Robert S. Mueller III, FBI Director, Statement before the Congressional Joint Inquiry, 17 October 2002.
37 Scott Shane and Lowell Bergman, 'FBI struggling to reinvent itself to fight terror', *New York Times*, 10 October 2006.
38 Cf. Harold M. Greenberg, 'Is the Department of Homeland Security an intelligence agency?', *Intelligence and National Security*, 24,2 (2009), pp. 216–35. For a more positive view of DHS intelligence, see Michael W. Studeman, 'Strengthening the shield: U.S. homeland security intelligence', *International Journal of Intelligence and Counterintelligence*, 20,2 (2007), pp. 195–216.
39 E.g., John Diamond, *The CIA and the Culture of Failure: U.S. Intelligence from the End of the Cold War to the Invasion of Iraq* (Stanford: Stanford University Press, 2008); Rhodri Jeffrey-Jones, *The CIA and American Democracy*, 3rd edn. (New Haven: Yale University Press, 2003); Kaeten Mistry (ed.), 'The CIA and U.S. Foreign Policy since 1947: reforms, reflections and reappraisals', special issue of *Intelligence and National Security*, 26,2-3 (2011); L. Britt Snider, *The Agency and the Hill: CIA's Relationship with Congress, 1946–2004* (Washington, DC: Center for the Study of Intelligence, 2008); Tim Weiner, *Legacy of Ashes: The History of the CIA* (London: Allen Lane, 2007).
40 E.g., Philip H. J. Davies, *MI6 and the Machinery of Spying* (London: Frank Cass, 2004); Stephen Dorril, *MI6: Fifty Years of Special Operations* (London: Fourth Estate, 2001); Keith Jeffery, *MI6: The History of the Secret Intelligence Service 1909–1949* (London: Bloomsbury, 2010).
41 E.g., Christopher Andrew and Oleg Gordievsky, *KGB: The Inside Story of its Foreign Operations from Lenin to Gorbachev* (New York, HarperCollins, 1991).

42 John J. Dziak, *Chekisty: A History of the KGB* (Lexington: Lexington Books, 1988).
43 Andrei Soldatov and Irina Borogan, *The New Nobility: The Restoration of Russia's Security State and the Enduring Legacy of the KGB* (New York: Public Affairs, 2010).
44 John Ranelagh, *The Agency: The Rise and Decline of the CIA* (New York: Simon & Schuster, 1987), pp. 385–90.
45 E.g., Amy Zegart, '"CNN with Secrets": 9/11, the CIA, and the organizational roots of failure', *International Journal of Intelligence and Counterintelligence*, 20 (2007), pp. 18–49.
46 See also James Bamford, *Body of Secrets: How America's NSA and Britain's GCHQ Eavesdrop on the World* (London: Arrow Books, 2002).
47 See also Richard J. Aldrich, *GCHQ: The Uncensored Story of Britain's Most Secret Intelligence Agency* (London: HarperPress, 2010).
48 Scott Ritter, *Iraq Confidential: The Untold Story of America's Intelligence Conspiracy* (London: Tauris, 2005), pp. 133–43.
49 Aldrich, *GCHQ*, pp. 532–9.
50 Joan M. Jensen, *Army Surveillance in America, 1775–1980* (New Haven: Yale University Press, 1991).
51 Marco Cepik, 'Structural change and democratic control of intelligence in Brazil', in Thomas C. Bruneau and Steven C. Boraz (eds.), *Reforming Intelligence: Obstacles to Democratic Control and Effectiveness* (Austin: University of Texas Press, 2007), pp. 149–69.
52 See discussion below in chapter 5. Also, more generally, Stephen Dycus, 'The role of military intelligence in homeland security', *Louisiana Law Review*, 64 (2004), pp. 779–807; Kevin D. Haggerty and Richard V. Ericson, 'The militarization of policing in the information age', *Journal of Political and Military Sociology*, 27 (1999), pp. 233–55.
53 Mark Mazzetti, 'Pentagon is expected to close intelligence unit', *New York Times*, 2 April 2008.
54 Mark Mazzetti, 'Military role in U.S. embassies creates strains, report says', *New York Times*, 20 December 2006.
55 Dana Priest and William M. Arkin, '"Top secret America": a look at the military's Joint Special Operations Command', *Washington Post*, 2 September 2011.
56 www.presstv.ir/detail/184774.html, accessed 15 July 2011.
57 www.defense.gov/home/features/2010/0410_cybersec/docs/CYBERCOM%20Fact%20Sheet%20to%20replace%20online%20version%20on%20OCT%2013.pdf, accessed 15 July 2011.
58 Rahul Roy-Chaudhury, 'India', in Stuart Farson, Peter Gill, Mark Phythian and Shlomo Shpiro (eds.), *PSI Handbook of Global Security and Intelligence: National Approaches*, vol. 1: *The Americas and Asia* (Westport: Praeger Security International, 2008), pp. 211–29 at 221–2. Hajime Kitaoka, 'Japan', in Farson et al., *PSI Handbook*, vol. 1, pp. 263–79 at 272–7.
59 Richard Best Jr., *The NIC: Issues and Options for Congress* (Washington, DC: Congressional Research Service, 2011), R40505.
60 A comparison of these systems is provided by Michael Herman, *Intelligence Power in Peace and War: Intelligence Services in the Information Age* (Cambridge: Cambridge University Press, 1996), pp. 257–79. See also Philip H. J. Davies, 'Intelligence culture and intelligence failure in Britain and the United States', *Cambridge Review of International Affairs*, 17 (2004), pp. 495–520.
61 John Scarlett, evidence to Hutton Inquiry, 26 August 2003 at 92–6 and 23 September 2003 at 78–9, www.the-hutton-inquiry.org.uk, accessed 19 December 2011.
62 Her Majesty's Government, *National Intelligence Machinery* (London: Stationery Office, 2010), p. 24.
63 Prime Minister, *Government Response to the Intelligence and Security Committee Inquiry into Intelligence, Assessments and Advice prior to the Terrorist Bombings on Bali 12 October 2002*, Cm 5765 (London: Stationery Office, February 2003), para. 11.

64 Her Majesty's Government, *National Intelligence Machinery*.
65 Ibid.
66 *9/11 Commission Report*, pp. 407–16.
67 E.g., Richard Best Jr., *Intelligence Reform After Five Years: The Role of the Director of National Intelligence* (Washington, DC: Congressional Research Service, 2010), R41295.
68 A snapshot of these in the US is provided in Gill, *Usual Suspects?*, pp. 40–54.
69 Corporations engage in a wide variety of 'business intelligence' or 'competitive intelligence' practices regarding their market share, development of new products and so on. We do not cover these here but concentrate on specifically 'security' intelligence activities.
70 Fred Schreier and Marina Caparini, *Privatizing Security: Law, Practice and Governance of Private Military and Security Companies*, DCAF Occasional Paper No. 6 (Geneva, March 2005), p. 39, http://dspace.cigilibrary.org/jspui/bitstream/123456789/27442/1/Privatising%20Security%20-%20Law,%20Practice%20and%20Governance%20of%20Private%20Military%20and%20Security%20Companies.pdf?1, accessed 19 December 2011.
71 Conor O'Reilly and Graham Ellison, '"Eye spy private high": re-conceptualising high policing theory', *British Journal of Criminology*, 46,4 (2006) pp. 641–60; James Mackay, *Allan Pinkerton: The First Private Eye* (New York: Wiley, 1996), pp. 137–60.
72 E.g., Clifford D. Shearing and Philip C. Stenning (eds.), *Private Policing* (London: Sage, 1987); Les Johnston, *The Rebirth of Private Policing* (London: Routledge, 1992); Les Johnston, *Policing Britain: Risk, Security and Governance* (Harlow: Longman, 2000); Mark Button, *Private Policing* (Cullompton: Willan, 2002).
73 Arthur S. Hulnick, *Fixing the Spy Machine: Preparing American Intelligence for the Twenty-First Century* (London: Praeger, 1999), pp. 151–71, provides a general survey of 'spying for profit' in the US; see also Gary T. Marx, *Undercover: Police Surveillance in America* (Berkeley: University of California Press, 1988).
74 www.G4S.com, accessed 21 June 2011.
75 www.securitas.com/en/Services, accessed 21 June 2011.
76 www.securitas.com/pinkerton/en/Services, accessed 21 June 2011.
77 www.mpri.com/web/index.php/content, accessed 21 June 2011.
78 Les Johnston, 'Transnational private policing: the impact of global commercial security', in James Sheptycki (ed.), *Issues in Transnational Policing* (London: Routledge, 2000), p. 34; Singer, *Corporate Warriors*, pp. 124–30; www.mpri.com/web, accessed 19 December 2011.
79 www.control-risks.com/Default.aspx?page=2, accessed 21 June 2011.
80 Jeremy Scahill, *Blackwater: The Rise of the World's Most Powerful Mercenary Army* (New York: Nation Books, 2007).
81 House Committee on Oversight and Government Reform, Report on Blackwater prepared by the Democratic majority staff, October 2007, http://graphics8.nytimes.com/packages/pdf/national/20071001121609.pdf.
82 See, e.g., Steve Fainaru and Saad al-Izzi, 'U.S. security contractors open fire in Baghdad', *Washington Post*, 27 May 2007; Oliver August, 'Iraqis speak of random killings committed by private Blackwater guards', *The Times*, 7 August 2007; and Ewen MacAskill, 'Iraq security firm denies trigger-happy charge', *Guardian*, 3 October 2007.
83 James Glanz and Andrew W. Lehren, 'Use of contractors added to war's chaos in Iraq', *New York Times*, 23 October 2010.
84 James Risen and Mark Mazzetti, 'Blackwater guards tied to secret CIA raids', *New York Times*, 10 December 2009.
85 Tim Shorrock, *Spies for Hire: The Secret World of Intelligence Outsourcing* (New York: Simon & Schuster, 2008), pp. 6 and 81–114.
86 www.fas.org/irp/world/para/index.html, accessed 31 July 2011.

87 Ronald J. Deibert, 'Deep probe: the evolution of network intelligence', *Intelligence and National Security*, 18,4 (2003), pp. 175–93.
88 Gill, *Usual Suspects?*, pp. 188–9.
89 Robert D. Steele, *The New Craft of Intelligence: Personal, Public and Political* (Oakton: OSS International Press, 2002), esp. pp. xiii–xviii.
90 Chris Strohm, 'Homeland Security to expand biometric visitor tracking system', 25 October 2005, www.govexec.com/?oref=topnav, accessed 19 December 2011.
91 Johnston, 'Transnational private policing', p. 38.
92 Deibert, 'Deep probe', p. 189.
93 E.g., Andrea Gimenez-Salinas, 'New approaches regarding private/public security', *Policing and Society*, 14,2 (2004), pp. 158–74; Johnston, *Policing Britain*, pp. 167–75; Trevor Jones and Tim Newburn, *Private Security and Public Policing* (Oxford: Clarendon Press, 1998).
94 John Philips, 'Up to 200 Italian police ran parallel anti-terror force', *Independent*, 5 July 2005.
95 Michael McClintock, *The American Connection: State Terror and Popular Resistance in El Salvador* (London: Zed Books, 1984); McClintock, *The American Connection: State Terror and Popular Resistance in Guatemala* (London: Zed Books, 1984).
96 David H. Bayley and Clifford D. Shearing, *The New Structure of Policing: Description, Conceptualization, and Research Agenda*, National Institute of Justice Research Report 187083 (Washington, DC: Department of Justice, 2001), www.ojp.usdoj.gov/nij, pp. 6–7, accessed 30 November 2005.
97 E.g., Robert W. Cox, 'The covert world', in Robert W. Cox with Michael G. Schechter, *The Political Economy of a Plural World* (London: Routledge, 2002), pp. 118–38.
98 Shorrock, *Spies for Hire*, p. 357.
99 Greenberg, 'Is the DHS an intelligence agency?', p. 233.
100 David Strachan-Morris provides an interesting account of the development of intelligence sharing between PSCs and military in Iraq in 'The future of civil–military intelligence cooperation based on lessons learned in Iraq', *Intelligence and National Security*, 24,2 (2009), pp. 257–74. Willis et al. discuss the problems of this in the context of homeland security in the US in Henry H. Willis, Genevieve Lester and Gregory F. Treverton, 'Information sharing for infrastructure risk management: barriers and solutions', *Intelligence and National Security*, 24,3 (2009), pp. 339–65.
101 Cf. Nicholas Dorn, 'Proteiform criminalities: the formation of organised crime as organisers' responses to developments in four fields of control', in Adam Edwards and Peter Gill (eds.), *Transnational Organised Crime: Perspectives on Global Security* (London: Routledge, 2003), pp. 227–40.
102 Gill, *Usual Suspects?*, pp. 54–7 and 246–9.
103 Walter J. M. Kickert and Joop F. M. Koppenjaan, 'Public management and network management: an overview', in Walter J. M. Kickert, Erik-Hans Klijn and Joop F.M. Koppenjaan (eds.), *Managing Complex Networks: Strategies for the Public Sector* (London: Sage, 1997), pp. 35–61.
104 Richard J. Aldrich, 'Transatlantic intelligence and security cooperation', *International Affairs*, 80,4 (2004), p. 732; Brodeur and Dupont, 'Will the knowledge workers put their act together?'; Björn Fägersten, 'Bureaucratic resistance to international intelligence cooperation: the case of Europol', *Intelligence and National Security*, 25,4 (2010), pp. 500–20.
105 Eliza Manningham-Buller, 'The international terrorist threat and the dilemmas in countering it', speech at the Ridderzaal, Binnenhof, The Hague, Netherlands, 1 September 2005, https://www.mi5.gov.uk/output/director-generals-speech-to-the-aivd-2005.html, accessed 19 December 2011.

106 Kristin Archick, *US–EU Cooperation Against Terrorism*, CRS Report (Washington, DC: Congressional Research Service, 2005), www.fas.org/irp, accessed 12 December 2011.

107 Belgian Standing Intelligence Agencies Review Committee, *Fusion Centres throughout Europe* (Antwerp: Intersentia, 2010).

108 Didier Bigo talks similarly of 'police archipelagos' in 'Liaison officers in Europe: new officers in the European security field', in Sheptycki, *Issues in Transnational Policing*, pp. 67–99 at 85. Similarly, Melanie Gutjahr, *The Intelligence Archipelago: The Community's Struggle to Reform in the Globalized Era* (Washington, DC: Joint Military Intelligence College, 2005).

109 See, e.g., Jean-Paul Brodeur, 'Cops and spooks: the uneasy partnership', in Tim Newburn (ed.), *Policing: Key Readings* (Cullompton: Willan, 2005), pp. 797–812, on the implications of co-operation between police and security.

110 See, e.g., *9/11 Commission Report*, pp. 416–19.

111 Jeffrey W. Seifert, *Data Mining: An Overview* (Washington, DC: Congressional Research Service, 2004), www.fas.org/irp, p. 1, accessed 12 December 2011.

112 Markle Foundation, *Creating a Trusted Information Network for Homeland Security*, 2nd Report of the Markle Foundation Task Force, December 2003, www.markle.org/publications/666-creating-trusted-network-homeland-security, accessed 19 December 2011.

113 National Research Council, *Protecting Individual Privacy in the Struggle against Terrorists: A Framework for Program Assessment* (Washington, DC: National Academies Press, 2008).

114 Russ Travers, 'The coming intelligence failure', *Studies in Intelligence* (1997), https://www.cia.gov/library/center-for-the-study-of-intelligence/csi-publications/csi-studies/studies/97unclass/failure.html, accessed 19 December 2011.

115 David L. Carter, *Law Enforcement Intelligence: A Guide for State, Local, and Tribal Law Enforcement Agencies* (East Lansing: Michigan State University and US Department of Justice Office of Community Oriented Policing Services, 2004), www.fas.org/irp/agency/doj/lei, accessed 19 December 2011.

116 Aldrich, 'Transatlantic intelligence and security cooperation', pp. 738–9.

117 Cf. O'Reilly and Ellison, 'Eye spy private high'.

CHAPTER 4 HOW DO THEY GATHER INFORMATION?

1 Cited in Charles E. Lathrop (ed.), *The Literary Spy* (New Haven: Yale University Press, 2004), p. 41.

2 E.g., Peter Gill, *Policing Politics: Security Intelligence and the Liberal Democratic State* (London: Frank Cass, 1994), pp. 153–4.

3 David Omand, *Securing the State* (London: Hurst, 2010), pp. 32–34.

4 E.g., Hans Born and Ian Leigh, *Making Intelligence Accountable: Legal Standards and Best Practice for Oversight of Intelligence Agencies* (Oslo: Parliament of Norway, 2005), pp. 55–63.

5 Peter Gill, *Rounding Up the Usual Suspects? Developments in Contemporary Law Enforcement Intelligence* (Aldershot: Ashgate, 2000), pp. 92–3 and 145; John Grieve, 'Developments in UK criminal intelligence', in J. H. Ratcliffe (ed.), *Strategic Thinking in Criminal Intelligence* (Sydney: Federation Press, 2004), pp. 25–36 at 34.

6 Harry Howe Ransom, *The Intelligence Establishment* (Cambridge: Harvard University Press, 1970), p. 81.

7 Loch K. Johnson, *Bombs, Bugs, Drugs and Thugs: Intelligence and America's Quest for Security* (New York: New York University Press, 2000), pp. 185–6.

8 Flood Report, p. 16.

9 Loch K. Johnson, *America as a World Power: Foreign Policy in a Constitutional Framework*, 2nd edn. (New York: McGraw-Hill, 1995), p. 273.

10 See, e.g., Tara Bahrampour, 'Internet helped Muslim convert from Northern Virginia embrace extremism at warp speed', *Washington Post*, 2 November 2010.
11 www.guardian.co.uk/world/us-embassy-cables-documents/219058, accessed 19 September 2011.
12 E.g., Oleg Penkovsky, *The Penkovsky Papers* (New York: Doubleday, 1965); Jerrold L. Schechter and Peter S. Deriabin, *The Spy Who Saved the World: How a Soviet Colonel Changed the Course of the Cold War* (New York: Scribner's, 1992); and Tom Mangold, *Cold Warrior: James Jesus Angleton: The CIA's Master Spy Hunter* (New York: Simon & Schuster, 1991).
13 Michael Herman, *Intelligence Power in Peace and War: Intelligence Services in the Information Age* (Cambridge: Cambridge University Press, 1996), pp. 62–3. See also Paul Henderson, *The Unlikely Spy: An Autobiography* (London: Bloomsbury, 1993); Richard Norton-Taylor, *Truth is a Difficult Concept: Inside the Scott Inquiry* (London: Fourth Estate, 1995).
14 See, e.g., the account in Victor Ostrovsky and Claire Hoy, *By Way of Deception: An Insider's Exposé of the Mossad* (London: Arrow, 1991).
15 Miles Copeland, *Beyond Cloak and Dagger: Inside the CIA* (New York: Pinnacle, 1975), p. 151.
16 Ibid., pp. 151–2.
17 Ronald Kessler, *The CIA at War* (New York: St. Martin's Press, 2004), p. 142.
18 Gabriele Kliem, 'The spy who loved her', *Guardian*, 18 November 2004.
19 Host governments are obviously alert to the practice. For an example, see Nick Paton Walsh, 'Russia accuses "spies" working in foreign NGOs', *Guardian*, 13 May 2005.
20 Greg Miller, 'Shades of cover', *Los Angeles Times*, 16 July 2005.
21 Richard Tomlinson, *The Big Breach: From Top Secret to Maximum Security* (Edinburgh: Cutting Edge, 2001), p. 176.
22 John M. Goshko, 'Annan: US spying charge could hurt disarmament', *Washington Post*, 3 March 1999.
23 BBC, 'Secrets, spies and videotape', *Panorama*, BBC1, 23 March 1999.
24 Ibid. See also the case of the CIA's 'Moe Dobbs' in Scott Ritter, *Endgame: Solving the Iraq Problem Once and For All* (New York: Simon & Schuster, 1999), ch. 10, expanded in Ritter, *Iraq Confidential: The Untold Story of America's Intelligence Conspiracy* (London: Tauris, 2005), esp. chs. 6 and 13.
25 Barton Gellman, 'Annan suspicious of UNSCOM role', *Washington Post*, 6 January 1999. The *Washington Post* had known of this since October, but had withheld it at the request of the US government. See also Gellman, 'Arms inspectors "shake the tree"', *Washington Post*, 12 October 1998.
26 Ian Williams, 'UNSCOM suffers a terminal blow', *Middle East International*, 15 January 1999.
27 Ellen Barry, '"Illegals" spy ring famed in lore of Russian spying', *New York Times*, 29 June 2010.
28 *United States of America v. Christopher R. Metsos, Richard Murphy, Cynthia Murphy, Donald Howard Heathfield, Tracey Lee Ann Foley, Michael Zottoli, Patricia Mills, Juan Lazaro and Vicky Pelaez*, Southern District of New York, 25 June, 2010, p. 5, www.justice.gov/opa/documents/062810complaint2.pdf, accessed December 19, 2011.
29 Ibid., p. 25.
30 Richard L. Russell, 'CIA's strategic intelligence in Iraq', *Political Science Quarterly*, 117,2 (2002), pp. 191–207 at 206.
31 On the links between sport and intelligence in the GDR, see Mike Dennis, *The Stasi: Myth and Reality* (Harlow: Longman, 2003), ch. 9.
32 See, e.g., Markus Wolf and Anne McElvoy, *Memoirs of a Spymaster* (London: Pimlico, 1998), p. 134.
33 *Economist*, 'Can spies be made better?', 19 March 2005.
34 Michael Sulick, 'Al Qaeda answers CIA's hiring call', *Los Angeles Times*, 10 July 2005. The

requirement raises the question posed by Richard K. Betts and which applies equally to other western national agencies: 'Should US intelligence trust recent, poorly educated immigrants for these jobs if they involve highly sensitive intercepts? How much will it matter if there are errors in translation, or wilful mistranslations, that cannot be caught because there are no resources to cross-check the translators?' ('Fixing intelligence', *Foreign Affairs*, 81,1 (2002), p. 47).

35 Kessler, *CIA at War*, p. 140.

36 On the question of trust, in relation to 9/11 and the post-9/11 'War on Terror' Richard Perle thought that 'one of the reasons why we're in trouble is we have depended too much on intelligence coming from friendly countries, some of whom are not entirely friendly and some of whom, even if they are friendly, have their own reasons for failing to share certain intelligence with us' (BBC Radio 4, *Spies R Us*, 6, 13 and 20 February 2003, www.bbc.co.uk/radio4/history/spies_cia.shtml, accessed 19 December 2011). In this respect, the question of trust in intelligence sharing has similarities with trust in the context of extended deterrence. See, e.g., Patrick M. Morgan, *Deterrence Now* (Cambridge: Cambridge University Press, 2003).

37 James Risen and David Rohde, 'A hostile land foils the quest for bin Laden', *New York Times*, 13 December 2004.

38 Barton Gellman, 'Secret unit expands Rumsfeld's domain', *Washington Post*, 23 January 2005.

39 David Ignatius, 'US, Pakistan could use a Muslim ritual to resolve Raymond Davis case', *Washington Post*, 2 March 2011.

40 See the detailed account of the experience of 'Officer A' in Tony Thompson, 'Inside the lonely and violent world of the Yard's elite undercover unit', *Observer*, 14 March 2010.

41 BBC, 'Subversive my arse', *True Spies* (BBC2, 27 October 2002, http://news.bbc.co.uk/1/hi/programmes/true_spies/default.stm, accessed 19 December 2011). On being informed that a former close colleague was a spy, one of the targets, Tariq Ali, commented: 'It is a bit distressing, especially as he must have been liked, he must have made friends. That is a form of fundamentalism for you, if you are prepared to subordinate everything else to what is your political aim or work aim. And I guess that's what spies are.'

42 Annie Machon, *Spies, Lies and Whistleblowers* (Lewes: Book Guild, 2005), p. 52.

43 Peter Cory, *Cory Collusion Inquiry Report: Patrick Finucane*, HC470 (London: Stationery Office, April 2004).

44 John Ware, 'Torture, murder, mayhem – the dirty war just got dirtier', *Guardian*, 12 May 2003.

45 Martin Ingram and Greg Harkin, *Stakeknife: Britain's Secret Agents in Ireland* (Dublin: O'Brien Press, 2004), p. 64.

46 Ibid., p. 81.

47 Michael Walzer, *Just and Unjust Wars*, 3rd edn. (New York: Basic Books, 2000), pp. 152–9. On the use of informers in Northern Ireland, see Jon Moran, 'Evaluating Special Branch and the use of informant intelligence in Northern Ireland', *Intelligence and National Security*, 25,1 (2010), pp. 1–23. See also Kevin Fulton, *Unsung Hero: How I Saved Dozens of Lives as a Secret Agent Inside the IRA* (London: John Blake, 2006).

48 Rosie Cowan, 'Unmasking leaves Provos seething with mutual suspicion', *Guardian*, 12 May 2003; Danny Morrison, 'The story of Stakeknife is full of holes', *Guardian*, 16 May 2003.

49 See, e.g., Henry McDonald, 'Revealed: five British spies inside IRA', *Observer*, 18 May 2003.

50 Stephen Dorril, *MI6: Fifty Years of Special Operations* (London: Fourth Estate, 2001), p. 789.

51 Henry McDonald, 'Northern Ireland police "face intelligence gap"', *Guardian*, 17 April 2010.

52 On the origins and evolution of the practice, see Jane Mayer, 'Outsourcing torture: the

secret history of America's "extraordinary rendition" program', *New Yorker*, 14 February 2005.

53 Key works include: Darius Rejali, *Torture and Democracy* (Princeton: Princeton University Press, 2009); Karen J. Greenberg (ed.),*The Torture Debate in America* (New York: Cambridge University Press, 2005); Alfred W. McCoy, *A Question of Torture: CIA Interrogation from the Cold War to the War on Terror* (New York: Owl Books, 2006); James P. Pfiffner, *Torture as Public Policy: Restoring US Credibility on the World Stage* (Boulder: Paradigm, 2010); Sanford Levinson (ed.), *Torture: A Collection* (New York: Oxford University Press, 2004); Bob Brecher, *Torture and the Ticking Bomb* (Malden: Blackwell, 2007); Yuval Ginbar, *Why Not Torture Terrorists? Moral, Practical, and Legal Aspects of the 'Ticking Bomb' Justification for Torture* (Oxford: Oxford University Press, 2010); Mirko Bagaric and Julie Clarke, *Torture: When the Unthinkable is Morally Permissible* (Albany: SUNY Press, 2007); Trevor Paglen and A. C. Thompson, *Torture Taxi: On the Trail of the CIA's Rendition Flights* (Cambridge: Icon Books, 2007); Stephen Grey, *Ghost Plane: The Untold Story of the CIA's Secret Rendition Programme* (London: Hurst, 2006); Asim Qureshi, *Rules of the Game: Detention, Deportation, Disappearance* (London: Hurst, 2009); Jane Mayer, *The Dark Side: The Inside Story of How the War on Terror Turned into a War on American Ideals* (New York: Doubleday, 2008); Clive Stafford Smith, *Bad Men: Guantánamo Bay and the Secret Prisons* (London: Weidenfeld & Nicolson, 2007); and Philippe Sands, *Torture Team: Uncovering War Crimes in the Land of the Free* (London: Allen Lane, 2008).

54 Ian Cobain, Stephen Grey and Richard Norton-Taylor, 'Destination Cairo: human rights fears over CIA flights', *Guardian*, 12 September 2005; Suzanne Goldenberg, 'More than 80,000 held by US since 9/11 attacks', *Guardian*, 18 November 2005. In November 2005 Spain launched a judicial inquiry into claims that its airports had been used for this purpose. Elizabeth Nash, 'Madrid begins inquiry into CIA "torture" flights', *Independent*, 16 November 2005.

55 Amnesty International, *Guantánamo and Beyond: The Continuing Pursuit of Unchecked Executive Power*, www.amnesty.org/en/library/info/AMR51/063/2005, accessed 6 March 2012.

56 John Hooper, 'Kidnap probe reveals CIA modus operandi', *Guardian*, 2 July 2005.

57 John Hooper, 'Italy demands US explanation over kidnapped cleric', *Guardian*, 1 July 2005; Tracy Wilkinson and Greg Miller, 'Italy says it didn't know of CIA plan', *Los Angeles Times*, 1 July 2005.

58 Tracy Wilkinson, 'Italy seeks former US diplomat in kidnapping', *Los Angeles Times*, 30 September 2005.

59 Dana Priest, 'CIA holds terror suspects in secret prisons', *Washington Post*, 2 November 2005; Daniel McGrory and Tim Reid, 'CIA accused of running secret jails in Europe for terrorists', *Independent*, 3 November 2005; Andrew Tyrie, Roger Gough and Stuart McCracken, *Account Rendered: Extraordinary Rendition and Britain's Role* (London: Biteback, 2011).

60 BBC News, 'Bush Admits to CIA Secret Prisons', 7 September 2006, http://news.bbc.co.uk/1/hi/world/americas/5321606.stm, accessed 19 December 2011.

61 George W. Bush, *Decision Points* (New York: Crown, 2010), pp. 168–9.

62 On the role of medical professionals, see Physicians for Human Rights, *Experiments in Torture: Evidence of Human Subject Research and Experimentation in the 'Enhanced' Interrogation Program*, June 2010, https://s3.amazonaws.com/PHR_Reports/Experiments_in_Torture.pdf, accessed 19 December 2011

63 George Tenet, *At the Center of the Storm: My Years at the CIA* (New York: HarperCollins, 2007), p. 241.

64 Bush, *Decision Points*, p. 171.

65 See, e.g., Richard Norton-Taylor and Ian Black, 'British deny George Bush's claims that

torture helped foil terror plots', *Guardian*, 9 November 2010. Moreover, unlike President Bush, the British government regarded waterboarding as a form of torture. See Haroon Siddique and Chris McGreal, 'Waterboarding is torture, Downing Street confirms', *Guardian*, 9 November 2010.

66 Jason Burke and Paul Harris, 'Bush aides claim torture helped search for Al-Qaeda's figurehead', *Guardian*, 4 May 2011.

67 Executive Order: Ensuring Lawful Interrogations, 22 January 2009, www.whitehouse.gov/the_press_office/EnsuringLawfulInterrogations, accessed 19 December 2011.

68 Charlie Savage and Eric Schmitt, 'US to prosecute a Somali suspect in civilian court', *New York Times*, 5 July 2011.

69 BBC News, 'MI5 "does not collude in torture"', 16 October 2009, http://news.bbc.co.uk/1/hi/8309919.stm, accessed 19 December 2011.

70 www.guardian.co.uk/uk/2010/oct/28/sir-john-sawers-speech-full-tex, accessed 19 December 2011.

71 The version of the document bearing this title is dated 2006.

72 Ian Cobain, 'Secret interrogation policy that could never be made public', *Guardian*, 5 August 2011.

73 Foreign and Commonwealth Office, *Annual Report on Human Rights 2008*, Cm 7557 (London: FCO, 2009), p. 15.

74 Martin Scheinin, *Report of the Special Rapporteur on the Promotion and Protection of Human Rights and Fundamental Freedoms while Countering Terrorism*, 4 February 2009, para. 55, http://daccess-dds-ny.un.org/doc/UNDOC/GEN/G09/106/25/PDF/G0910625.pdf?OpenElement, accessed 19 December 2011.

75 Hansard, 6 July 2010, col. 175.

76 See, e.g., Christopher Andrew, 'Conclusion: an agenda for future research', *Intelligence and National Security*, 12,1 (1997), pp. 224–33 at 228.

77 Interview with JIC official.

78 As far back as 1966, Senator Milton Young claimed that: 'As far as foreign policy is concerned, I think the National Security Agency and the intelligence it develops has far more to do with foreign policy than does the intelligence developed by the CIA' (cited in Matthew M. Aid and Cees Wiebes, 'The importance of signals intelligence in the Cold War', *Intelligence and National Security*, 16,1 (2001), pp. 1–26 at 7).

79 Ibid., p. 5.

80 A CIA officer cited in ibid., p. 6.

81 Paul Rogers, *Losing Control: Global Security in the Twenty-First Century* (London: Pluto Press, 2000), p. 32.

82 Jeffrey T. Richelson, *A Century of Spies: Intelligence in the Twentieth Century* (New York: Oxford University Press, 1995), pp. 385–7; Oleg Gordievsky, *Next Stop Execution* (London: Macmillan, 1995), p. 272. It is also worth noting that two 1984 NIEs concluded that the alert was intended to intimidate the west rather than represent a genuine scare. See Richelson, p. 386. It is worth noting because it appears to be wrong; see Rogers, *Losing Control*, p. 32. See also Robert M. Gates, *From the Shadows: The Ultimate Insider's Story of Five Presidents and How They Won the Cold War* (New York: Simon & Schuster, 1997), pp. 270–3.

83 Aid and Wiebes, 'Importance of signals intelligence', p. 15.

84 Loch K. Johnson, *America's Secret Power: The CIA in a Democratic Society* (New York: Oxford University Press, 1989), pp. 64–6.

85 On Echelon, see www.fas.org/irp/program/process/echelon.htm, and Patrick Radden Keefe, *Chatter: Dispatches from the Secret World of Global Eavesdropping* (New York: Random House, 2005).

86 Reportedly, by the mid-1990s the NSA 'was capable of intercepting the equivalent of the entire collection of the US Library of Congress (1 quadrillion Bits of information) every

three hours' (Matthew M. Aid, 'The time of troubles: the US National Security Agency in the twenty-first century', *Intelligence and National Security*, 15,3 (2000), pp. 1–32 at 17).

87 Kessler, *CIA at War*, p. 73.

88 John Ranelagh, *The Agency: The Rise and Decline of the CIA* (New York: Simon & Schuster, 1987), pp. 207–8.

89 Kessler, *CIA at War*, p. 74.

90 Martin Bright and Peter Beaumont, 'Britain spied on UN allies over war vote', *Observer*, 8 February 2004.

91 Clare Short, *An Honourable Deception? New Labour, Iraq, and the Misuse of Power* (London: Free Press, 2004), pp. 242–3.

92 Chief Surveillance Commissioner, *Annual Report to the Prime Minister and to Scottish Ministers for 2010–2011*, HC1111 (London: Stationery Office, 30 June 2011), paras. 4.4–4.5.

93 Regulation of Investigatory Powers Act, 2000, Part II.

94 Interception of Communications Commissioner, *Annual Report to the Prime Minister for 2010*, HC1239 (London: Stationery Office, 30 June 2011).

95 Leslie Cauley, 'NSA has massive database of Americans' phone calls', *USA Today*, 11 May 2006. For a detailed account of the NSA's efforts in this area, and its relationship with communications corporations, see James Bamford, *The Shadow Factory: The Ultra-Secret NSA from 9/11 to the Eavesdropping on America* (New York: Anchor Books, 2009).

96 Richard J. Aldrich, *GCHQ: The Uncensored Story of Britain's Most Secret Intelligence Agency* (London: HarperPress, 2010), p. 543.

97 BBC News, 'Giant database plan "Orwellian"', 15 October 2008, http://news.bbc.co.uk/1/hi/uk_politics/7671046.stm, accessed 19 December 2011.

98 Dominic Grieve and Eleanor Laing, *Reversing the Rise of the Surveillance State* (September 2009), www.conservatives.com/News/News_stories/2009/09/~/media/Files/Policy%20Documents/Surveillance%20State.ashx, accessed 19 December 2011.

99 See Misha Glenny, *Dark Market: Cyberthieves, Cybercops and You* (London: Bodley Head, 2011).

100 Richard Norton-Taylor and Julian Borger, 'Hague anger as Chinese cyber-spies penetrate Foreign Office computers', *Guardian*, 5 February 2011.

101 Peter Walker, 'China chief suspect as report reveals cyberspying on an industrial scale', *Guardian*, 4 August 2011.

102 Brian Krebs, 'Botnets: the democratization of espionage', *Computer World*, 22 January 2010, www.computerworld.com/s/article/9147538/Botnets_The_Democratization_of_Espionage_?source=CTWNLE_nlt_security_2010-01-25, accessed 19 December 2011.

103 Roland Dobbins of Arbor Networks, cited in Krebs, 'Botnets'.

104 See the comments of the retired four-star Navy admiral quoted in Seymour M. Hersh, 'The online threat: should we be worried about a cyber war?', *New Yorker*, 1 November 2010, www.newyorker.com/reporting/2010/11/01/101101fa_fact_hersh, accessed 19 December 2011.

105 Kessler, *CIA At War*, p. 70.

106 Jeffrey T. Richelson, *The Wizards of Langley: Inside the CIA's Directorate of Science and Technology* (Boulder: Westview, 2001), pp. 198–202 and 276.

107 For an example, see David E. Sanger, 'What are Koreans up to? US agencies can't agree', *New York Times*, 12 May 2005.

108 Robert Baer, *See No Evil: The True Story of a Ground Soldier in the CIA's War on Terrorism* (New York: Crown, 2002), p. xvii.

109 Loch K. Johnson, 'Spymaster Richard Helms: an interview with the former US Director of Central Intelligence', *Intelligence and National Security*, 18,3 (2003), pp. 24–44 at 32.

110 Dennis M. Gormley, 'The limits of intelligence: Iraq's lessons', *Survival*, 46,3 (2004), pp. 7–28 at 11–13.

111 This section is drawn from the Federation of American Scientists, 'Signals intelligence in the Gulf War', www.fas.org/spp/military/docops/operate/ds/signals.htm, accessed 6 March 2012. See also Richelson, *Wizards of Langley*, pp. 247–50.
112 Bob Woodward, *The Commanders* (London: Simon & Schuster, 1991), pp. 219–20.
113 Ibid, pp. 220–1.
114 Ibid.
115 John Simpson, *From the House of War* (London: Arrow, 1991), p. 41.
116 James Bloom, 'Way up there – and personal', *Guardian*, 28 January 2009. See the examples in the image gallery on the GeoEye website, www.geoeye.com/CorpSite.
117 Rahul Bedi, 'Mumbai attacks: Indian suit against Google Earth over image used by terrorists', *Daily Telegraph*, 9 December 2008.
118 Jeffery T. Richelson, 'MASINT: the new kid in town', *International Journal of Intelligence and Counterintelligence*, 14,2 (2001), pp. 149–92.
119 Charles Cogan, 'Hunters not gatherers: intelligence in the twenty-first century', *Intelligence and National Security*, 19,2 (2004), pp. 304–21 at 304.
120 Kessler, *CIA at War*, p. 127.
121 Cogan, 'Hunters not gatherers', p. 317.
122 Baer, *See No Evil*.
123 See Anne Applebaum, 'The torture myth', *Washington Post*, 12 January 2005. For a less negative assessment of the utility of torture, see the *Economist*, 'Torture: ends, means and barbarity', 9 January 2003.

CHAPTER 5 HOW IS INFORMATION TURNED INTO INTELLIGENCE?

1 *9/11 Commission Report*, p. 77.
2 See discussion in chapter 3.
3 Hibbert, 'Intelligence and policy', *Intelligence and National Security*, 5,1 (1990), pp. 110–28.
4 Robert Mandel similarly discusses (1) the personality and proficiency of officials, (2) the complexity of intelligence performance, (3) internal bureaucratic obstacles and (4) the external policy environment ('Distortions in the intelligence decision-making process', in Stephen J. Cimbala (ed.), *Intelligence and Intelligence Policy in a Democratic Society* (Ardsley-on-Hudson, NY: Transnational, 1987), pp. 69–83).
5 Kent Center for Analytic Tradecraft, *Making Sense of Transnational Threats*, Sherman Kent School, Occasional Papers, 3,1 (2004), p. 4.
6 Mark M. Lowenthal, *Intelligence: From Secrets to Policy*, 2nd edn. (Washington, DC: CQ Press, 2003), pp. 92–3.
7 Cf. James Sheptycki, 'Organizational pathologies in police intelligence systems', *European Journal of Criminology*, 1, 3 (2004), pp. 316–17.
8 *9/11 Commission Report*, p. 355.
9 Roberta Wohlstetter, *Pearl Harbor: Warning and Decision* (Stanford: Stanford University Press, 1962), p. 392; cf. also Sheptycki, 'Organizational pathologies', pp. 315–16.
10 Russell Bond, 'Methods and issues in risk and threat assessment', in Jerry H. Ratcliffe (ed.), *Strategic Thinking in Criminal Intelligence* (Sydney: Federation Press, 2004), pp. 119–28 at 120.
11 Peter Klerks, 'The network paradigm applied to criminal organisations: theoretical nitpicking or a relevant doctrine for investigators?', in Adam Edwards and Peter Gill (eds.), *Transnational Organised Crime: Perspectives on Global Security* (London: Routledge, 2003), pp. 97–113.
12 Mandel, 'Distortions', p. 70.
13 *9/11 Commission Report*, p. 92.
14 Mandel, 'Distortions', p. 73.

15 Cf. the 'digital divide' in Sheptycki, 'Organizational pathologies', pp. 313–14.
16 *9/11 Commission Report*, pp. 78–80. For discussion of the impact of 'the wall' in the USS *Cole* investigations see ibid., pp. 266–72.
17 Peter Gill, *Rounding Up the Usual Suspects? Developments in Contemporary Law Enforcement Intelligence* (Aldershot: Ashgate, 2000), p. 213.
18 Sheptycki, 'Organizational pathologies', p. 317; Gill, *Usual Suspects?*, pp. 212–15.
19 The term 'groupthink' was coined by Irving L. Janis. As he explained: 'The more amiability and esprit de corps among the members of a policy-making in-group, the greater is the danger that independent critical thinking will be replaced by group-think, which is likely to result in irrational and dehumanising actions directed against out-groups' (*Victims of Groupthink: A Psychological Study of Foreign Policy Decisions and Fiascos* (Boston: Houghton Mifflin, 1972), p. 13). For a discussion of its application in relation to the Iraq WMD failure, see Mark Phythian, 'The perfect intelligence failure? US pre-war intelligence on Iraqi weapons of mass destruction', *Politics & Policy*, 34,2 (2006), pp. 400–24.
20 Jack Davis, 'Why bad things happen to good analysts', in Roger Z. George and James B. Bruce (eds.), *Analyzing Intelligence: Origins, Obstacles and Innovations* (Washington, DC: Georgetown University Press, 2008), pp. 157–70, has good examples of perils facing analysts in 'normal' conditions at pp. 159–63.
21 Mandel, 'Distortions', p. 76.
22 *9/11 Commission Report*, pp. 344–8.
23 Foreign and Commonwealth Secretary, *Review of Intelligence on Weapons of Mass Destruction: Implementation of its Conclusions*, Cm 6492 (London: Stationery Office, March 2005).
24 See, e.g., the series of articles in *Intelligence and National Security* 23,3 (2008).
25 Gregory F. Treverton and C. Bryan Gabbard, *Assessing the Tradecraft of Intelligence Analysis* (Washington, DC: Rand, 2008), pp. xi–xii
26 E.g., William E. Odom, 'Intelligence analysis', *Intelligence and National Security* 23,3 (2008), pp. 325–6; Treverton and Gabbard, *Assessing the Tradecraft*, pp. 44–5.
27 Daniel Gressang, 'The shortest distance between two points lies in rethinking the question: intelligence and the information age technology challenge', in Loch K. Johnson (ed.), *Strategic Intelligence*, vol. 2: *The Intelligence Cycle* (Westport: Praeger Security International, 2007), pp. 123–42 at 135–6; Carmen A. Medina, 'The new analysis', in George and Bruce, *Analyzing Intelligence*, pp. 238–48 at 242.
28 Richards J. Heuer Jr., 'Computer-aided analysis of competing hypotheses', in George and Bruce, *Analyzing Intelligence*, pp. 251–65.
29 James B. Bruce, 'Making analysis more reliable: why epistemology matters to intelligence', in George and Bruce, *Analyzing Intelligence*, pp. 171–90 at 182–5.
30 Wilhelm Agrell, 'Intelligence analysis after the Cold War: new paradigm or old anomalies?', in Gregory F. Treverton and Wilhelm Agrell (eds.), *National Intelligence Systems: Current Research and Future Prospects* (New York: Cambridge University Press, 2009), pp. 93–114 at 98–102.
31 Ibid., p. 108.
32 Medina, 'New analysis', p. 239.
33 Carmen Medina and Rebecca Fisher, 'What the world economic crisis should teach us', *Studies in Intelligence*, 53,3 (2009), pp. 11–16 at 16.
34 E.g., Bridget Hutter and Michael Power, 'Organizational encounters with risk: an introduction', in Hutter and Power (eds.), *Organizational Encounters with Risk* (Cambridge: Cambridge University Press, 2005), pp. 1–32 at 18–19.
35 Stephen Marrin and Jonathan D. Clemente, 'Improving intelligence analysis by looking to the medical profession', *International Journal of Intelligence and Counterintelligence*, 18,4 (2005–6), pp. 707–29.
36 Lewis Shepherd, 'The purple history of Intelink', 13 December 2009, http://lewisshepherd.wordpress.com/2009/12/13, accessed 28 June 2011.

37 ODNI, *National Intelligence: A Consumer's Guide*, www.dni.gov/reports/IC_Consumers_Guide_2009.pdf, pp. 71–6, accessed 28 June 2011.

38 Matthew S. Burton, 'Connecting the virtual dots: how the web can relieve our information glut and get us talking to each other', *Studies in Intelligence*, 49,3 (2005), https://www.cia.gov/library/center-for-the-study-of-intelligence/csi-publications/csi-studies/studies/vol49no3/html_files/Intelligence_Networking_6.htm, accessed 19 December 2011.

39 Massimo Calabresi, 'Wikipedia for spies: the CIA discovers Web 2.0', *Time*, 8 April 2009; see also http://en.wikipedia.org/wiki/Intellipedia, accessed 28 June 2011.

40 Mark Drapeau, 'Government 2.0: intelligence renaissance networks', http://mashable.com/2008/09/22/government-intelligence-renaissance-networks, accessed 28 June 2011.

41 Rutrell Yasin, 'National security and social networking are compatible', *Government Computer News*, 23 July 2009.

42 ODNI, *Library of National Intelligence (LNI): Making Discovery Easier*, www.dni.gov/content/AT/LNI.pdf ; http://en.wikipedia.org/wiki/A-Space, accessed 28 June 2011.

43 Stella Rimington on whether she would, as MI5 Director General, have resisted Blair's request for a dossier: 'I can't say, as I don't know the circumstances . . . but I expect I would have thought: no good will come of this' (cited in Elizabeth Grice, 'Dossier a mistake – Rimington', *Daily Telegraph*, 12 June 2004).

44 Gill, *Usual Suspects?*, p. 226; Michael Herman, *Intelligence Power in Peace and War: Intelligence Services in the Information Age* (Cambridge: Cambridge University Press, 1996), p. 45.

45 Herman, *Intelligence Power*, p. 45.

46 Harold Lasswell, *Politics: Who Gets What, When, How* (New York: McGraw-Hill, 1936).

47 Sherman Kent, *Strategic Intelligence for American World Policy* (Princeton: Princeton University Press, 1966; first pub. 1949), pp. 7–8. According to the ODNI, the US intelligence community now publishes three overlapping levels of intelligence analysis: current intelligence, trend analysis and long-term assessment (*National Intelligence*, p. 14).

48 Abram N. Shulsky and Gary J. Schmitt, *Silent Warfare: Understanding the World of Intelligence*, 3rd edn (Washington, DC: Brassey's, 2002), pp. 57–8; *9/11 Commission Report*, pp. 90–1.

49 Herman, *Intelligence Power*, p. 235; Shulsky and Schmitt, *Silent Warfare*, p. 59.

50 *9/11 Commission Report*, pp. 344–8.

51 David Strachan-Morris, 'Threat and risk: what's the difference and why does it matter?', *Intelligence and National Security*, 27,2 (2012), pp. 172–86.

52 www.dhs.gov/files/publications/ntas-public-guide.shtm, accessed 4 July 2011.

53 Shulsky and Schmitt, *Silent Warfare*, pp. 60–1.

54 *9/11 Commission Report*, p. 342. See also Loch K. Johnson, 'Glimpses into the gems of American intelligence: the *President's Daily Brief* and the National Intelligence Estimate', *Intelligence and National Security*, 23,3 (2008), pp. 333–70.

55 Herman, *Intelligence Power*, p. 46.

56 Steve Coll, *Ghost Wars: The Secret History of the CIA, Afghanistan, and Bin Laden, from the Soviet Invasion to September 10, 2001* (New York: Penguin, 2004), pp. 149–50. White House Chief of Staff James Baker left a briefing book with President Reagan the day before the 1983 world economic summit. Seeing it untouched the following morning, Baker asked Reagan why he hadn't read the briefing. '"Well, Jim, *The Sound of Music* was on last night," Reagan said calmly' (Lou Cannon, *President Reagan: The Role of a Lifetime* (New York: Simon & Schuster, 1991), pp. 56–7).

57 Herman, *Intelligence Power*, p. 326; see also Harold L. Wilensky, *Organizational Intelligence: Knowledge and Policy in Government and Industry* (New York: Basic Books, 1967), pp. 42–8.

58 Bruce D. Berkowitz and Allan E. Goodman, *Best Truth: Intelligence in the Information Age* (New Haven: Yale University Press, 2000), pp. 96–8. In a similar vein, Herman argues that intelligence managers must convey entrepreneurial values as well as public service and scholarly ones (*Intelligence Power*, pp. 336–8).

59 *9/11 Commission Report*, p. 417.

60 E.g., Jeffrey T. Richelson and Desmond Ball discuss the history of intelligence co-operation between the UKUSA countries: UK, US, Canada, Australia and New Zealand (*The Ties That Bind*, 2nd edn (Boston: Unwin Hyman, 1990), esp. pp. 239–61).

61 *9/11 Commission Report*, pp. 353–60.

62 'Summary of the White House Review of the December 25, 2009 Attempted Terrorist Attack, January 7, 2010', www.whitehouse.gov/the-press-office/white-house-review-summary-regarding-12252009-attempted-terrorist-attack, p. 2, accessed 1 July 2011.

63 Ibid., p. 4.

64 Mark M. Lowenthal, 'Towards a reasonable standard for analysis: how right, how often on which issues?', *Intelligence and National Security*, 23,3 (2008), pp. 303–15 at 306.

65 Office of the Inspector General, *Follow-Up Audit of the Terrorist Screening Center*, Audit Report 07-41 (Washington DC: Department of Justice, September 2007), www.justice.gov/oig/reports/FBI/a0741/intro.htm, accessed 6 March 2012; Peter Baker and Carl Hulse, 'US had early signals of a terror plot, Obama says', *New York Times*, 30 December 2009.

66 'Summary of the White House Review', pp. 5–6.

67 See, e.g., *9/11 Commission Report*, p. 143; Lowenthal, *Intelligence*, pp. 100–1.

68 Butler Report, para. 45.

69 Ibid., para. 603.

70 Ibid., para. 45 fn.13.

71 Ibid., para. 604.

72 Foreign and Commonwealth Secretary, *Review*, paras. 29–30.

73 *9/11 Commission Report*, p. 265.

74 On the relationship between intelligence and the media, see Robert Dover and Michael S. Goodman (eds.), *Spinning Intelligence: Why Intelligence Needs the Media, Why the Media Needs Intelligence* (London: Hurst, 2009); David Leigh, 'Britain's security services and journalists: the secret story', *British Journalism Review*, 11,2 (2000), pp. 21–6.

75 John Sweeney, *Trading with the Enemy: Britain's Arming of Iraq* (London: Pan, 1993), pp. 169–71.

76 Lord Hutton, *Report of the Inquiry into the Circumstance Surrounding the Death of Dr. David Kelly C.M.G.*, HC 247 (London: HMSO, 2004), para. 255.

77 Ibid., para. 112.

78 Scott Ritter, 'How the British spy agency MI6 secretly misled a nation into war with Iraq', interview broadcast 30 December 2003, www.democracynow.org/2003/12/30/scott_ritter_how_the_british_spy, accessed 6 March 2012.

79 Butler Report, p. 90.

80 E.g., www.cia.gov, www.fbi.gov, www.csis-scrs.gc.ca/eng and www.mi5.gov.uk.

CHAPTER 6 WHAT DO THEY DO WITH INTELLIGENCE?

1 Michael G. Fry and Miles Hochstein, 'Epistemic communities: intelligence studies and international relations', *Intelligence and National Security*, 8,3 (1993), pp. 14–28 at 25.

2 Michael Warner, 'Intelligence and reflexivity: an invitation to a dialogue', *Intelligence and National Security*, 27,2 (2012), pp. 167–71.

3 *British Army Field Manual. Vol. 1 Part 10: Countering Insurgency*, October 2009, http://news.bbc.co.uk/1/shared/bsp/hi/pdfs/16_11_09_army_manual.pdf, paras. 5.16–5.25, accessed 31 July 2011.

4 Michael T. Flynn, Rich Juergens and Thomas L. Cantrell, 'Employing ISR: SOF best practices', *Joint Force Quarterly*, July 2008, www.dtic.mil/cgi-bin/GetTRDoc?Location=U2&doc=GetTRDoc.pdf&AD=ADA516799, p. 57, accessed 6 March 2012.

5 'Influence' is often used in the literature as a more general term than 'power' to discuss the social and political phenomenon in which we are interested – an early exponent was Robert A. Dahl, *Modern Political Analysis*, 5th edn (Englewood Cliffs: Prentice Hall, 1991), esp. pp. 12–48. Amitai Etzioni, *A Comparative Analysis of Complex Organisations: On Power, Involvement and Their Correlates* (New York: Free Press, 1961), p. 5; John Scott, *Power* (Cambridge: Polity, 2001), pp. 12–16. Dennis H. Wrong uses a similar classification of force, manipulation and persuasion in *Power: Its Forms, Bases, and Uses* (Oxford: Blackwell, 1988), pp. 21–34.

6 Loch K. Johnson provides a model of a 'ladder' of covert action in *Secret Agencies: US Intelligence in a Hostile World* (New Haven: Yale University Press, 1996), ch. 3, as does Mark M. Lowenthal, *Intelligence: From Secrets to Policy*, 2nd edn. (Washington, DC: CQ Press, 2003), p. 130.

7 Ch. 4 of the *9/11 Commission Report*, 'Responses to Al Qaeda's initial assaults', provides a detailed account that illustrates these combinations in practice (pp. 108–43).

8 Joseph S. Nye Jr., *Soft Power: The Means to Success in World Politics* (New York: Public Affairs, 2004).

9 An obvious exception to this is Israel, whose policies of targeted assassination and settlement construction are carried out entirely openly but contrary to successive UN resolutions and other prohibitions.

10 Len Scott, 'Secret intelligence, covert action and clandestine diplomacy', *Intelligence and National Security*, 19,2 (2004), pp. 322–41; Peter Taylor, *Brits: The War Against the IRA* (London: Bloomsbury, 2001).

11 A good example is Roy Godson, *Dirty Tricks or Trump Cards: US Covert Action and Counterintelligence* (Washington, DC: Brassey's, 1995).

12 Lowenthal, *Intelligence*, p. 131.

13 Canadian Security Intelligence Service Act 1984, s.12.

14 Security Service Act 1989, s.1(2).

15 Intelligence Services Act, 1994, section 7.

16 One form of action that police may take is to arrest people; this power is not available to MI5. The debate as to whether security agencies such as MI5 should or should not possess arrest powers forms an important part of the whole debate around the democratic control of security policing. The combination of special information gathering powers and powers of arrest are often seen as the ingredients for repressive forms of 'political policing'.

17 Thaddeus Holt, *The Deceivers: Allied Deception in the Second World War* (London: Weidenfeld & Nicolson, 2004), p. 2.

18 Michael Herman, *Intelligence Power in Peace and War: Intelligence Services in the Information Age* (Cambridge: Cambridge University Press, 1996), p. 55. As before, we see that Herman prefers to distinguish intelligence from operations (or policy); we would argue that this is unhelpful because it is impossible to distinguish the 'intelligence' and 'operational' role of the double agent.

19 One of the earliest CIA covert actions was providing financial and propaganda support to Christian Democrats in Italy after the Second World War in order to prevent the Communist Party taking power. John Ranelagh, *The Agency: The Rise and Decline of the CIA* (New York: Simon & Schuster, 1987), pp. 176–77; James Callanan, *Covert Action in the Cold War: US Policy, Intelligence and CIA Operations* (London: Tauris, 2010), ch. 2.

20 The Iran–Contra affair was the plot by Reagan Administration officials to sell arms covertly to embargoed Iran (then at war with Iraq) in the hope of securing the release of US hostages being held by Hezbollah in Lebanon, and to use the profits from the sales to arm the Contra guerrillas seeking to overthrow the Sandinista government in Nicaragua, despite the fact that Congress had blocked funding for any such support via the Boland

Amendment. See Theodore Draper, *A Very Thin Line: The Iran–Contra Affairs* (London: Chapmans, 1991); Ann Wroe, *Lives, Lies and the Iran–Contra Affair* (London: Tauris, 1992).

21 Luke Harding, 'Inside Putin's "mafia state"', *Guardian*, 2 December 2010. See also the account in David Leigh and Luke Harding, *WikiLeaks: Inside Julian Assange's War on Secrecy* (London: Guardian Books, 2011), pp. 216–18.

22 For brief accounts of the current interrelationships between Russian security and intelligence services, crime and corruption, see Misha Glenny, *McMafia: Crime Without Frontiers* (London: Bodley Head, 2008), pp. 61–86; Andrei Soldatov and Irina Borogan, *The New Nobility: The Restoration of Russia's Security State and the Enduring Legacy of the KGB* (New York: Public Affairs, 2010), pp. 75–82.

23 Steve Coll, *Ghost Wars: The Secret History of the CIA, Afghanistan, and Bin Laden, from the Soviet Invasion to September 10, 2001* (New York: Penguin, 2004).

24 Foreign Affairs Committee, *Sierra Leone*, 2nd Report, Session 1998–99, HC116-I, para. 26.

25 See Paul Henderson, *The Unlikely Spy: An Autobiography* (London: Bloomsbury, 1993); Tim Spicer, *An Unorthodox Soldier: Peace and War and the Sandline Affair* (Edinburgh: Mainstream, 2000); and the report of the official inquiry by Thomas Legg and Robin Ibbs, *Report of the Sierra Leone Arms Investigation* (London: Stationery Office, 1998).

26 Peter Singer, *Corporate Warriors: The Rise of the Privatized Military Industry* (Ithaca: Cornell University Press, 2003) pp. 114–15.

27 E.g., it occupies just one paragraph of Odd Arne Westad's *The Global Cold War: Third World Interventions and the Making of Our Times* (Cambridge: Cambridge University Press, 2005), despite its theme and Third World focus; see p. 205.

28 www.gwu.edu/~nsarchiv/news/20001113, accessed 20 December 2011.

29 Cited in Peter Kornbluh, *The Pinochet File: A Declassified Dossier on Atrocity and Accountability* (New York: New Press, 2004), pp. 1–2 and 36.

30 In addition to meetings with the coup plotters, the CIA smuggled in guns required for the kidnap operation, while the CIA Station authorized the payment of US$50,000 to the unidentified abduction team. Ibid., pp. 28, 29 and 73.

31 Indeed, elements within the CIA Station in Santiago even argued against covert support for opposition political parties in favour of a focus on developing 'the conditions which would be conducive to military actions', including support of extremist groups such as Patria y Libertad, so as to 'promote economic chaos, escalate political tensions and induce a climate of desperation in which . . . the people generally come to desire military intervention'. Ibid., p. 107.

32 On the role of the CIA in the 1973 Chilean coup, see also Jonathan Haslam, *The Nixon Administration and the Death of Allende's Chile* (London: Verso, 2005); and Lubna Z. Qureshi, *Nixon, Kissinger, and Allende: US Involvement in the 1973 Coup in Chile* (Lanham: Lexington Books, 2009). For an argument that the centrality of the CIA role has been exaggerated, see Kristian Gustafson, *Hostile Intent: US Covert Operations in Chile, 1964–1974* (Washington, DC: Potomac Books, 2007), and the review of Gustafson's book by Stephen G. Rabe, *Diplomatic History*, 34,2 (2010), pp. 447–53.

33 Examples of documents are included in Cathy Perkus (ed.), *COINTELPRO: The FBI's Secret War on Political Freedom* (New York: Monad Press, 1975).

34 Tony G. Poveda, *Lawlessness and Reform: The FBI in Transition* (Pacific Grove: Brooks/Cole, 1990), provides a good account of this shift.

35 E.g., Dan Eggen, 'FBI taps campus police in anti-terror operations', *Washington Post*, 25 January 2003.

36 Peter Gill, *Rounding Up the Usual Suspects? Developments in Contemporary Law Enforcement Intelligence* (Aldershot: Ashgate, 2000) pp. 232–6.

37 Mark Townsend and Tony Thompson, 'Undercover police cleared "to have sex with activists"', *Observer*, 23 January 2011.

38 Emily Apple, 'The traitor in our midst', *Guardian*, 11 January 2011.

39 Paul Lewis and Rob Evans, 'Kennedy unlawfully spied on climate activists, say judges', *Guardian*, 20 July 2011.

40 Peter Cory, *Cory Collusion Inquiry Report: Patrick Finucane*, HC470 (London: Stationery Office, April 2004), para. 1.293.

41 John Stevens, *Stevens Enquiry: Overview and Recommendations* (London: Stationery Office, 17 April 2003), para. 4.7. See also Stevens, *Not For the Faint-Hearted: My Life Fighting Crime* (London: Weidenfeld & Nicolson, 2005), pp. 171–6.

42 Rt Hon. Lord Maclean, *The Billy Wright Inquiry: Report*, HC431 (London: Stationery Office, 2010), webarchive.nationalarchives.gov.uk/20101210142120/www.official-documents.gov.uk/document/hc1011/hc04/0431/0431.asp, para. 1.33, accessed 10 August 2011.

43 Michael Morland, *Rosemary Nelson Inquiry: Report*, www.rosemarynelsoninquiry.org/, paras. 465–7, accessed 20 December 2011.

44 Peter Taylor, *Talking to Terrorists: A Personal Journey from the IRA to Al Qaeda* (London: HarperPress, 2011), ch. 13.

45 Nick Fielding and Ian Cobain, 'Revealed: US military's scheme to infiltrate social media with fake online identities', *Guardian*, 18 March 2011.

46 Dana Priest and William M. Arkin, '"Top secret America": a look at the military's Joint Special Operations Command', *Washington Post*, 2 September 2011.

47 Ewen MacAskill, 'Cyberworm heads off US strike on Iran', *Guardian*, 17 January 2011.

48 John Markoff and David E. Sanger, 'In a computer worm, a possible biblical clue', *New York Times*, 29 September 2010.

49 William Yong and Robert F. Worth, 'Bombings hit atomic experts in Iran streets', *New York Times*, 29 November 2010; Julian Borger and Saeed Kamali Dehghan, 'Covert war against Iran's nuclear goals takes a chilling turn', *Observer*, 5 December 2010.

50 On this, see Ward Thomas, 'Norms and security: the case against international assassination', *International Security*, 25,1 (2000), pp. 105–33.

51 See Paul McGeough, *Kill Khalid: The Failed Mossad Assassination of Khalid Mishal and the Rise of Hamas* (New York: New Press, 2009); Daniel Byman, *A High Price: The Triumphs and Failures of Israeli Counterterrorism* (New York: Oxford University Press, 2011). See also the official *Report of the Commission Concerning the Events in Jordan September 1997*, www.fas.org/irp/world/israel/ciechanover.htm, accessed 20 December 2011.

52 BBC News, 'Top Chechen killed in Qatar blast', 13 February 2004, http://news.bbc.co.uk/1/hi/world/europe/3485993.stm, and 'Chechen rebel chief Basayev dies', 10 July 2006, http://news.bbc.co.uk/1/hi/5165456.stm, both accessed 20 December 2011.

53 Sadie Gray, 'Russia backed dissident's poisoning', *Independent*, 8 July 2008. See also Martin Sixsmith, *The Litvinenko File: The True Story of a Death Foretold* (Basingstoke: Macmillan, 2007).

54 BBC News, 'Russia law on killing "extremists" abroad', 27 November 2006, http://news.bbc.co.uk/1/hi/world/europe/6188658.stm, accessed 20 December 2011.

55 Rosa Prince and Adrian Massie-Blomfield, 'Britain expels Mossad chief in row over Dubai assassination', *Daily Telegraph*, 24 March 2010.

56 Coll, *Ghost Wars*, p. 522.

57 On this, see the *9/11 Commission Report*, ch. 6.

58 Coll, *Ghost Wars*, p. 530.

59 Ron Suskind, *The One Percent Doctrine: Deep Inside America's Pursuit of Its Enemies Since 9/11* (New York: Simon & Schuster, 2006).

60 BBC News, 'Mapping US drone and Islamic militant attacks in Pakistan', 22 July 2010, www.bbc.co.uk/news/world-south-asia-10648909, accessed 20 December 2011.

61 CIA response to an American Civil Liberties Union (ACLU) Freedom of Information Act (FOIA) request relating to records concerning drones, 9 March 2010, www.aclu.org/files/assets/20100309_Drone_FOIA_CIA_Glomar_Response.pdf, accessed 6 March 2012.

62 Walter Pincus, 'Missile strike carried out with Yemeni cooperation: official says operation authorized under Bush finding', *Washington Post*, 6 November 2002.

63 Amnesty International, 'An extrajudicial execution by the CIA?', 18 May 2005, www.amnesty.org/en/library/asset/AMR51/079/2005/en/bcffa8d8-d4ea-11dd-8a23-d58a49c0d652/amr510792005en.html, accessed 6 March 2012.

64 See, e.g., Mary Ellen O'Connell, 'When is a war not a war? The myth of the global war on terror', *ILSA Journal of International and Comparative Law*, 12,2 (2006), pp. 535–9.

65 The following discussion draws on Mark Phythian, 'The problem of intelligence ethics', in Annika Bergman-Rosamond and Mark Phythian (eds.), *War, Ethics and Justice: New Perspectives on a Post-9/11 World* (London: Routledge, 2011), pp. 128–49.

66 www.newyorker.com/online/blogs/newsdesk/2009/10/jane-mayer-predators-drones-pakistan.html, accessed 20 December 2011.

67 ACLU, 'Rights groups file challenge to targeted killing by US', 30 August 2010, www.aclu.org/national-security/rights-groups-file-challenge-targeted-killing-us, accessed 20 December 2011.

68 Jane Mayer, 'The Predator war', *New Yorker*, 26 October 2009, www.newyorker.com/reporting/2009/10/26/091026fa_fact_mayer, accessed 20 December 2011. The CIA subsequently claimed that only Mehsud and his wife were killed in the strike. See Peter Finn and Joby Warrick, 'Under Panetta, a more aggressive CIA', *Washington Post*, 21 March 2010.

69 Mayer, 'Predator war'.

70 Joby Warrick and Pamela Constable, 'CIA base attacked in Afghanistan supported airstrikes against al-Qaeda, Taliban', *Washington Post*, 1 January 2010; Finn and Warrick, 'Under Panetta'.

71 See the discussion on this in Bob Brecher, *Torture and the Ticking Bomb* (Malden, MA: Blackwell, 2007), pp. 40–5.

72 Harold H. Koh, 'The Obama Administration and international law', speech to the Annual Meeting of the American Society of International Law, Washington, DC, 25 March 2010, www.state.gov/s/l/releases/remarks/139119.htm, accessed 20 December 2011.

73 Philip Alston, *Study on Targeted Killings*, UN General Assembly Human Rights Council, 28 May 2010, www2.ohchr.org/english/bodies/hrcouncil/docs/14session/A.HRC.14.24.Add6.pdf, p. 27, accessed 20 December 2011.

74 UN Office of the High Commissioner for Human Rights, press release: 'UN expert criticizes "illegal" targeted killing policies and calls on the US to halt CIA drone killings', 2 June 2010, www.unog.ch/unog/website/news_media.nsf/(httpNewsByYear_en)/73F4C83992E3BFB0C1257736004F8D41?OpenDocument, accessed 20 December 2011.

75 Cited in *9/11 Commission Report*, p. 189.

76 E.g., the barrister Geoffrey Robertson, 'Why it's absurd to claim that justice has been done', *Independent*, 3 May 2011. Robertson argued that: 'Killing instead of capturing Osama Bin Laden was a missed opportunity to prove to the world that this charismatic leader was in fact a vicious criminal, who deserved to die of old age in prison, and not as a martyr to his inhuman cause.'

77 E.g., Coll, *Ghost Wars*.

CHAPTER 7 WHY DOES INTELLIGENCE FAIL?

1 See, e.g., the 'Checklist of what can go wrong' in the intelligence cycle in Bruce D. Berkowitz and Allan E. Goodman, *Strategic Intelligence for American National Security* (Princeton: Princeton University Press, 1991), pp. 195–202.

2 Defense Department briefing, 12 February 2002, www.quotationspage.com/quote/30526.html, accessed 20 December 2011.

3 Richard K. Betts, 'Analysis, war and decision: why intelligence failures are inevitable',

World Politics, 31,1 (1978), pp. 61–89 (reprinted in Gill et al., *Intelligence Theory*, pp. 87–111) at 61. For Christopher Andrew: 'The historical record suggests . . . that the points at which the intelligence cycle most frequently breaks down are in the assessment process and the policy interface rather than in collection. How and why that breakdown occurs require far more research – and research, first and foremost, in archives' ('Intelligence, international relations and "under-theorisation"', *Intelligence and National Security*, 19,2 (2004), pp. 170–84 at 172).

4 Betts, 'Analysis, war, and decision', p. 61.

5 Betts notes that: 'A common reaction to traumatic surprise is the recommendation to cope with ambiguity and ambivalence by acting on the most threatening possible interpretations. If there is *any* evidence of threat, assume it is valid, even if the *apparent* weight of contrary indicators is greater' (ibid., p. 73). On the question of surprise more generally, see Michael I. Handel, 'Surprise in diplomacy', in Robert L. Pfaltzgraff Jr., Uri Ra'anan and Warren Milberg (eds.), *Intelligence Policy and National Security* (London: Macmillan, 1981), pp. 187–211; Abram N. Shulsky and Gary J. Schmitt, *Silent Warfare: Understanding the World of Intelligence*, 3rd edn (Washington, DC: Brassey's, 2002), pp. 62–73.

6 Amy B. Zegart, *Spying Blind: The CIA, the FBI and the Origins of 9/11* (Princeton: Princeton University Press, 2007), p. 4. See also Zegart, *Flawed By Design: The Evolution of the CIA, JCS, and NSC* (Stanford: Stanford University Press, 1999).

7 Zegart, *Spying Blind*, pp. 112–15.

8 BBC Radio 4, *Spies R Us*, 13 February 2003, www.bbc.co.uk/radio4/history/spies_cia.shtml, accessed 19 December 2011.

9 Ibid., 6 February.

10 Kevin Drum, 'Political animal', *Washington Monthly*, 1 September 2001, www.washingtonmonthly.com/archives/individual/2005_09/007023.php, accessed 20 December 2011.

11 Michael R. Gordon, 'Poor intelligence misled troops about risk of drawn-out war', *New York Times*, 20 October 2004. In the UK the intelligence regarding post-invasion planning in Iraq was considered by the Chilcot Inquiry.

12 For a more radical argument that the post-invasion chaos in Iraq was less the consequence of poor intelligence and planning than the result of a misguided neoconservative attempt to impose instant free-market capitalism on Iraq, see Naomi Klein, *The Shock Doctrine: The Rise of Disaster Capitalism* (London: Penguin, 2007), chs. 16–18.

13 Gordon, 'Poor intelligence'.

14 It concluded that 'The JIC may, in some assessments, also have misread the nature of Iraqi governmental and social structures. The absence of intelligence in this area may also have hampered planning for the post-war phase . . . We note that the collection of intelligence on Iraq's prohibited weapons programmes was designated as being a JIC First Order of Priority whereas intelligence on Iraqi political issues was designated as being Third Order' (Butler Report, para. 459, pp. 112–13).

15 Regarded as essentially an analytical failure. See Douglas J. MacEachin, *US Intelligence and the Confrontation in Poland, 1980–1981* (Philadelphia: Penn State University Press, 2002). See also Mark Kramer, 'US intelligence performance and US policy during the Polish crisis of 1980–81: revelations from the Kukliński files', *Intelligence and National Security*, 26,2–3 (2011), pp. 313–29.

16 Donald P. Steury, 'How the CIA missed Stalin's bomb', *Studies in Intelligence*, 49,1 (2005), https://www.cia.gov/library/center-for-the-study-of-intelligence/csi-publications/csi-studies/studies/vol49no1/html_files/stalins_bomb_3.html, accessed 20 December 2011. Steury cites explanations for the failure: 'it was not the overall intelligence *process* – with its focus on collection – that had failed to warn of the Soviet atomic bomb, but intelligence *analysis* – the ability to assemble, integrate, and derive meaning from the full range of information collected'.

17 Stephen Marrin, 'Preventing intelligence failures by learning from the past', *International Journal of Intelligence and Counter Intelligence*, 17,4 (2004), pp. 655–72 at 660.

18 Letter from Sir A. Gascoigne to Foreign Office, 5 July 1950, in H. J. Yasamee and K. A. Hamilton (eds.), *Documents on British Policy Overseas, Series II. Vol. IV: Korea June 1950–April 1951* (London: HMSO, 1991), pp. 31–2.

19 Douglas MacEachin, 'Predicting the Soviet invasion of Afghanistan: the intelligence community's record', https://www.cia.gov/library/center-for-the-study-of-intelligence/csi-publications/books-and-monographs/predicting-the-soviet-invasion-of-afghanistan-the-intelligence-communitys-record/predicting-the-soviet-invasion-of-afghanistan-the-intelligence-communitys-record.html, accessed 13 December 2011. Later in 1979 analysis suggested that the costs of an invasion would include 'the grave and open-ended task of holding down an Afghan insurgency in rugged terrain. The Soviets would also have to consider the likely prospect that they would be contending with an increasingly hostile and anti-Soviet population. The USSR would then have to consider the likelihood of an adverse reaction in the West, as well as further complications with Iran, India, and Pakistan. Moscow would also have to weigh the negative effects elsewhere in the Muslim world of a massive Soviet military presence in Afghanistan . . . A conspicuous use of Soviet military force against an Asian population would also provide the Chinese considerable political capital' (cited in ibid.).

20 Jack Davis, *Tensions in Analyst–Policymaker Relations: Opinions, Facts, and Evidence*, Sherman Kent Center for Intelligence Analysis Occasional Papers, 2, 2 (2003), https://www.cia.gov/library/kent-center-occasional-papers/pdf/OPV2No2.pdf p. 9, accessed 20 December 2011.

21 The full list of cases considered is as follows:

Case	Date
Likelihood of North Vietnam intervention in South Vietnam	1945–65
Likelihood of all-out Soviet support of Hanoi	1950–65
Cuba	1957
Sino-Soviet split	1959
1st Chinese nuclear test	1964
Soviet ALFA-class submarine	1969
Libya	1969
OPEC price increase of December 1973	1973
Ethiopia	1973
Afghanistan	1978
Iran	1978
Nicaragua: the nature of Somoza's opposition	1978

See H. Bradford Westerfield (ed.), *Inside CIA's Private World: Declassified Articles from the Agency's Internal Journal, 1955–92* (New Haven: Yale University Press, 1995), pp. 238–54.

22 Ibid., p. 254.

23 Douglas J. MacEachin, 'CIA assessments of the Soviet Union: the record versus the charges', *Studies in Intelligence* (2007), https://www.cia.gov/library/center-for-the-study-of-intelligence/csi-publications/books-and-monographs/cia-assessments-of-the-soviet-union-the-record-versus-the-charges/3496toc.html, accessed 20 December 2011.

24 Evan Thomas and Gregory Vistica, 'A troubled company', *Newsweek*, 13 November 1995.

25 On the importance of Gorbachev to the events of 1989 and 1990, see Archie Brown, 'Gorbachev and the end of the Cold War', in Richard K. Herrmann and Richard Ned Lebow (eds.), *Ending the Cold War: Interpretations, Causation, and the Study of International*

Relations (New York: Palgrave, 2004), pp. 31–57; Brown, *The Gorbachev Factor* (Oxford: Oxford University Press, 1996).

26 Gregory F. Treverton, *Reshaping National Intelligence for an Age of Information* (New York: Cambridge University Press, 2003), pp. 1–8.

27 George Perkovich, *India's Nuclear Bomb: The Impact on Global Proliferation* (Berkeley: University of California Press, 1999), pp. 417–18; Ronald Kessler, *The CIA at War* (New York: St. Martin's Press, 2004), pp. 210–12.

28 Kessler, *CIA at War*, p. 212.

29 Mark Mazzetti, 'Obama faults spy agencies' performance in gauging Mideast unrest, officials say', *New York Times*, 4 February 2011.

30 Loch K. Johnson, *America's Secret Power: The CIA in a Democratic Society* (New York: Oxford University Press, 1989), pp. 63–4.

31 On the specific case of forewarning about Operation Barbarossa, see David E. Murphy, *What Stalin Knew: The Enigma of Barbarossa* (New Haven: Yale University Press, 2005).

32 David S. Robarge, 'CIA analysis of the 1967 Arab–Israeli war', *Studies in Intelligence*, 49,1 (2005), https://www.cia.gov/library/center-for-the-study-of-intelligence/csi-publications/csi-studies/studies/vol49no1/html_files/arab_israeli_war_1.html, accessed 20 December 2011.

33 Chester L. Cooper, 'The CIA and decision-making', *Foreign Affairs*, 51,1 (1972), pp. 20–40 at 27.

34 For a recent analysis, see Michael Warner, 'US intelligence and Vietnam: the official version(s)', *Intelligence and National Security*, 25,5 (2010), pp. 611–37.

35 On Phoenix, see Dale Andradé, *Ashes to Ashes: The Phoenix Program and the Vietnam War* (Lexington: D. C. Heath, 1990).

36 Harold P. Ford, 'Unpopular pessimism: why CIA analysts were so doubtful about Vietnam', *Studies in Intelligence*, 1 (1997), https://www.cia.gov/library/center-for-the-study-of-intelligence/csi-publications/csi-studies/studies/97unclass/vietnam.html, accessed 20 December 2011.

37 Ibid.

38 Harold P. Ford, 'Revisiting Vietnam: thoughts engendered by Robert McNamara's *In Retrospect*', *Studies in Intelligence*, 39,5 (1996), https://www.cia.gov/library/center-for-the-study-of-intelligence/csi-publications/csi-studies/studies/96unclass/ford.htm, accessed 20 December 2011.

39 Ibid.

40 Bob Woodward, *Plan of Attack* (London: Simon & Schuster, 2004), p. 249. In April 2005, Tenet told an audience: 'Those were the two dumbest words I ever said.' Suzanne Goldenberg, 'Ex-CIA chief eats humble pie', *Guardian*, 29 April 2005. Tenet later claimed his comment had been taken out of context (Tenet, *At the Center of the Storm: My Years at the CIA* (New York: HarperCollins, 2007), ch. 19.

41 See Gary Sick, *All Fall Down: America's Tragic Encounter With Iran* (New York: Penguin, 1986), pp. 33–36.

42 BBC Radio 4, *Spies R Us*, 13 February. Nevertheless, there were inherent difficulties involved in estimating the likelihood of an uprising against the Shah. As a senior DDI analyst put it: 'We knew the Shah was widely unpopular, and we knew there would be mass demonstration, even riots. But how many shopkeepers would resort to violence, and how long would Army officers remain loyal to the Shah? Perhaps the Army would shoot down 10,000 rioters, maybe 20,000. If the ranks of the insurgents swelled further, though, how far would the Army be willing to go before it decided the Shah was a losing proposition? All this we duly reported; but no one could predict with confidence the number of dissidents who would actually take up arms, or the "tipping point" for Army

loyalty' (cited in Loch K. Johnson, *America as a World Power: Foreign Policy in a Constitutional Framework*, 2nd edn. (New York: McGraw-Hill, 1995), p. 277).

43 Harold P. Ford, 'The US government's experience with intelligence analysis: pluses and minuses', *Intelligence and National Security*, 10,4 (1995), pp. 42–3.

44 BBC Radio 4, *Spies R Us*, 13 February.

45 Ibid. See also Sick, *All Fall Down*, pp. 106–8; James A. Bill, *The Eagle and the Lion: The Tragedy of American–Iranian Relations* (New Haven: Yale University Press, 1988), ch. 10.

46 Robert Jervis, *Why Intelligence Fails: Lessons from the Iranian Revolution and the Iraq War* (Ithaca: Cornell University Press, 2010), p. 107.

47 Michael Donovan, 'National intelligence and the Iranian revolution', in Rhodri Jeffreys-Jones and Christopher Andrew (eds.), *Eternal Vigilance? 50 Years of the* CIA (London: Frank Cass, 1997), pp. 143–63 at 159.

48 Cited in ibid., p. 160.

49 Gregory F. Treverton, 'Intelligence analysis: between "politicisation" and irrelevance', in Roger Z. George and James B. Bruce (eds.), *Analyzing Intelligence: Origins, Obstacles and Innovations* (Washington, DC: Georgetown University Press, 2008), pp. 91–104 at 93–6.

50 Paul R. Pillar, 'Democratic Policy Committee hearing: an oversight hearing on pre-war intelligence relating to Iraq', 109th Congress, Second Session, 26 June, 2006, pp. 183–4, http://democrats.senate.gov/dpc/hearings/hearing33/pillar.pdf, accessed 30 September 2009.

51 Martin Petersen, 'The challenge for the political analyst', *Studies in Intelligence*, 47,1 (2003), https://www.cia.gov/library/center-for-the-study-of-intelligence/csi-publications/csi-studies/studies/vol47no1/article05.html, accessed 20 December 2011.

52 Ibid.

53 Avi Shlaim, 'Failures in national intelligence estimates: the case of the Yom Kippur War', *World Politics*, 28,3 (1976), pp. 348–80.

54 Cited in Davis, *Tensions in Analyst–Policymaker Relations*, p. 4.

55 Ibid., p. 7.

56 Seymour M. Hersh, *Chain of Command: The Road from 9/11 to Abu Ghraib* (London: Penguin/Allen Lane, 2004), p. 223.

57 Dafna Linzer, 'Two detail Bolton's efforts to punish dissent', *Washington Post*, 29 April 2005.

58 Seymour M. Hersh, 'The stovepipe', *New Yorker Online*, 27 October 2003, www.newyorker.com/archive/2003/10/27/031027fa_fact?currentPage=1, accessed 20 December 2011.

59 Hersh, *Chain of Command*, pp. 218–19.

60 Kenneth M. Pollack, *The Threatening Storm: The Case for Invading Iraq* (New York: Random House, 2003), pp. 248–80.

61 Michael Herman, 'Threat assessments and the legitimation of policy?', *Intelligence and National Security*, 18,3 (2003), pp. 174–8 at 177.

62 E.g., a survey of scientists employed by the US Fish and Wildlife Service revealed pressure to alter findings to suit either external customers or government policy preferences. Julie Cart, 'US scientists say they are told to alter findings', *Los Angeles Times*, 10 February 2005.

63 Elizabeth Drew, 'Pinning the blame', *New York Review of Books*, 23 September 2004, p. 6.

64 Richard A. Clarke, *Against All Enemies: Inside America's War on Terror* (London: Simon & Schuster, 2004).

65 *9/11 Commission Report*, p. 260.

66 Ibid., p. 263.

67 Ibid., pp. 262 and 277.

68 Stephen Marrin, 'The 9/11 terrorist attacks: a failure of policy not strategic intelligence analysis', *Intelligence and National Security*, 26,2–3 (2011), pp. 182–202 at 202.

69 E.g., Frank J. Cilluffo, Ronald A. Marks and George C. Salmoiraghi, 'The use and limits of US intelligence', *Washington Quarterly*, 25,1 (2002), pp. 61–74.

70 On the political dynamics of these inquiries, and inquiries into security and intelligence issues more broadly, see James P. Pfiffner and Mark Phythian (eds.), *Intelligence and National Security Policymaking on Iraq: British and American Perspectives* (Manchester: Manchester University Press, 2008); Stuart Farson and Mark Phythian (eds.), *Commissions of Inquiry and National Security: Comparative Approaches* (Santa Barbara: Praeger, 2011).

71 US SSCI, *Report on the US Intelligence Community's Prewar Intelligence Assessments on Iraq* (Washington, DC: GPO, June 2004), p. 8 (henceforward SSCI (2004)).

72 Ibid., pp. 5, 14 and 15.

73 Ibid., p. 11.

74 Sherman Kent, *The Law and Custom of the National Security Estimate: An Examination of the Theory and Some Recollections Concerning the Practice of the Art*, June 1975, https://www.cia.gov/library/center-for-the-study-of-intelligence/csi-publications/books-and-monographs/sherman-kent-and-the-board-of-national-estimates-collected-essays/5law.html, accessed 20 December 2011.

75 SSCI (2004), pp. 13 and 302.

76 Ibid., pp. 25 and 260.

77 Ibid., p. 14.

78 Ibid.

79 Ibid., p. 188.

80 Ibid., p. 187.

81 CIA, *Iraq's Weapons of Mass Destruction Programs*, https://www.cia.gov/library/reports/general-reports-1/iraq_wmd/Iraq_Oct_2002.pdf, p. 2, accessed 20 December 2011. See also p. 17.

82 SSCI (2004), pp. 188, 211 and 212–13. On 'layering', see pp. 22–3.

83 Ibid., p. 17.

84 E.g., the NIE stated that 'we judge that we are seeing only a portion of Iraq's WMD efforts, owing to Baghdad's vigorous denial and deception efforts. Revelations after the Gulf War starkly demonstrate the extensive efforts undertaken by Iraq to deny information' (ibid.).

85 Ibid., pp. 20, 163–4, 462, 230, 235, 226 and 236.

86 Woodward claims there were just four as late as 2002, and that these were located in ministries such as foreign affairs and oil that did not allow them access to the kinds of military intelligence most needed. Ironically, given the Butler Inquiry's subsequent discovery of the limited nature of UK HUMINT sources in Iraq at this time, DCI Tenet regarded UK sources as being superior to those of the US (Woodward, *Plan of Attack*, p. 107).

87 SSCI (2004), p. 21.

88 Similarly, the UK Butler Inquiry concluded that there was a 'tendency for assessments to be coloured by over-reaction to previous errors' (Butler Report, para. 458, p. 112).

89 www.dni.gov/press_releases/20071203_release.pdf, accessed 20 December 2011. A qualifying footnote suggested that, as critics claimed, the judgement should not have been so categorical. The footnote explained: 'For the purposes of this Estimate, by "nuclear weapons program" we mean Iran's nuclear weapon design and weaponization work and covert uranium conversion-related work; we do not mean Iran's declared civil work related to uranium conversion and enrichment.'

90 See, e.g., Henry Kissinger, 'Misreading the Iran Report: why spying and policymaking don't mix', *Washington Post*, 13 December 2007.

91 SSCI (2004), pp. 26, 27–8 and 128–9.

92 Ibid, pp. 160–1.

93 Ibid, p. 149. At p. 246, the number of these reports is put at 95.
94 Ibid, p. 149.
95 Ibid., pp. 248 and 249.
96 Ibid., p. 28. On this, see also Richard K. Betts, 'Fixing intelligence', *Foreign Affairs*, 81,1 (2002), pp. 43–59 at 55.
97 SSCI (2004), p. 29. See also p. 139.
98 Ibid., p. 2.
99 US SSCI, *Postwar Findings about Iraq's WMD Programs and Links to Terrorism and How They Compare with Prewar Assessments,* www.fas.org/irp/congress/2006_rpt/srpt109-331.pdf, accessed 6 March 2012; US SSCI, *The Use by the Intelligence Community of Information Provided by the Iraqi National Congress,* http://intelligence.senate.gov/phaseiiinc.pdf, accessed 6 March 2012.
100 Press release, 'Senate Intelligence Committee unveils final phase II reports on prewar Iraq intelligence', 5 June 2008, http://intelligence.senate.gov/press/record.cfm?id=298775, accessed 20 December 2011.
101 Jervis, *Why Intelligence Fails*, pp. 136 and 174.
102 Fulton Armstrong, 'The CIA and WMDs: the damning evidence', *New York Review of Books*, 19 August 2010, www.nybooks.com/articles/archives/2010/aug/19/cia-and-wmds-damning-evidence, accessed 20 December 2011. See also Robert Jervis and Thomas Powers, 'The CIA & Iraq: how the White House got its way: an exchange', *New York Review of Books*, 15 July 2010, www.nybooks.com/articles/archives/2010/jul/15/cia-iraqhow-white-house-got-its-way-exchange, and Thomas Powers, 'How they got their bloody way', *New York Review of Books*, 27 May 2010, www.nybooks.com/articles/archives/2010/may/27/how-they-got-their-bloody-way, both accessed 20 December 2011. See also Scott Lucas, 'Recognising politicization: the CIA and the path to the 2003 war in Iraq', *Intelligence and National Security*, 26,2–3 (2011), pp. 203–27.
103 On this, see Brian Jones, *Failing Intelligence: The True Story of How We Were Fooled into Going to War in Iraq* (London: Dialogue, 2010).
104 Butler Report, pp. 107–8, para. 436.
105 Ibid., p. 114, para. 466.
106 Ibid., p. 159, para. 63. Blair's subsequent appointment of William Ehrman as chair of the JIC failed to meet this requirement. See Richard Norton-Taylor and Michael White, 'New intelligence chief fails to meet Butler guidelines', *Guardian*, 17 July 2004.
107 Butler Report, p. 16, para. 58.
108 BBC 1, 'The Hutton inquiry', *Panorama*, 21 January 2004.
109 Jason Bennetto, 'Predicted bomb attacks reveal intelligence gaps on al-Qa'ida', *Independent*, 8 July 2005.
110 Richard Norton-Taylor, 'Security services face worst scenario', *Guardian*, 13 July 2005.
111 Frank Gregory and Paul Wilkinson, *Riding Pillion for Tackling Terrorism is a High Risk Policy*, ISP/NSC Briefing Paper 05/01 (Chatham House, July 2005), http://image.guardian.co.uk/sys-files/Politics/documents/2005/07/18/Chathamreport.pdf, accessed 20 December 2011.
112 Cited in Michael Meacher, 'Britain now faces its own blowback', *Guardian*, 10 September 2005.
113 ISC, *Annual Report 2001–2002*, Cm 5542, June 2002, http://isc.independent.gov.uk/committee-reports/annual-reports, p. 24, accessed 20 September 2011.
114 ISC, *Annual Report 2003–2004*, Cm 6240, June 2004, http://isc.independent.gov.uk/committee-reports/annual-reports, pp. 11–12, accessed 20 September 2011.
115 Meacher, 'Britain now faces its own blowback'.
116 Elaine Sciolino and Don Van Natta Jr., 'June report led Britain to lower its terror alert', *New York Times*, 19 July 2005.

117 Crispin Black, 'Intelligence got it wrong', *Guardian*, 8 July 2005.

118 ISC, *Could 7/7 Have Been Prevented? Review of the Intelligence on the London Terrorist Attacks on 7 July 2005*, Cm 7617 2009, http://isc.independent.gov.uk/committee-reports/special-reports, para. 84, accessed 6 March 2012.

119 Coroner's Inquests into the London Bombings of 7 July 2005, *Report*, May 2011, http://7julyinquests.independent.gov.uk/docs/orders/rule43-report.pdf, para. 99, accessed 6 March 2012.

120 Ibid., paras. 71–88 and 118; see also ISC, *Could 7/7 Have Been Prevented?*, paras. 171–2.

121 In the context of 7/7, see Richard Norton-Taylor, 'There's no such thing as total security', *Guardian*, 19 August 2005.

122 ISC, *Could 7/7 Have Been Prevented?*, para. 212; Coroner, *Report*, para. 15.

CHAPTER 8 CAN INTELLIGENCE BE DEMOCRATIC?

1 Various authors have pointed to the risk of official exploitation of fear, including Corey Robin, *Fear: The History of a Political Idea* (New York: Oxford University Press, 2004); Joanna Bourke, *Fear: A Cultural History* (London: Virago, 2005); Mark Phythian, 'Still a matter of trust: Post-9/11 British intelligence and political culture', *International Journal of Intelligence and CounterIntelligence*, 18,4 (2005–6), pp. 653–81; Adam Curtis, 'Fear gives politicians a reason to be', *Guardian*, 24 November 2004; Robert Shrimsley, 'The bogeyman and the fearmongers are out to get you', *Financial Times*, 22 October 2004.

2 In one episode of *The Simpsons*, Homer Simpson turns vigilante, leading his daughter, Lisa, to ask, 'If you're the police, who will police the police?', to which he replies, 'I don't know, the Coast Guard?' *Homer the Vigilante*, fifth season, Fox Network.

3 Speaking in 1971, US Senator John Stennis reflected a common view when he said: 'Spying is spying. You have to make up your mind that you are going to have an intelligence agency and protect it as such, and shut your eyes and take what is coming' (cited in Charles E. Lathrop (ed.), *The Literary Spy* (New Haven: Yale University Press, 2004), p. 236.

4 Throughout this chapter we are concerned with the general principles by which elected representatives may control permanent intelligence officials rather than precise differences between, say, presidential and parliamentary systems. Therefore we use the terms 'legislative' and 'parliamentary' interchangeably.

5 Cf. Loch K. Johnson, 'Lawmakers and spies: Congressional oversight of intelligence in the United States', paper given to the Annual Meeting of International Studies Association, Hawaii (2005), pp. 4–6.

6 The relevant government memos 2001–4 and reports concerning abuses at Abu Ghraib and Guantánamo are compiled in Karen L. Greenberg and Joshua L. Dratel (eds.), *The Torture Papers: The Road to Abu Ghraib* (Cambridge: Cambridge University Press, 2005).

7 R. N. Berki, *Security and Society: Reflections on Law, Order and Politics* (London: J. M. Dent, 1986), pp. 1–43.

8 'Oversight' has another dictionary meaning, that is, an omission or failure to notice. This may also be significant in the governance of intelligence as it reflects the sentiment, expressed by John Stennis (see n. 3) that politicians may prefer not to know about the actions being taken in their name by security agencies. Also, although some literature refers just to 'democratic control', we think it important to distinguish control from oversight while noting that both are required. Cf., e.g., Thomas C. Bruneau and Steven Boraz, 'Intelligence reform: Balancing democracy and effectiveness', in Bruneau and Boraz (eds.), *Reforming Intelligence: Obstacles to Democratic Control and Effectiveness* (Austin: University of Texas Press, 2007), pp. 1–24 at 14.

9 This section is drawn from Peter Gill and Michael Andregg, 'Comparing the democratisation of Intelligence', *Intelligence and National Security*, forthcoming.
10 Eduardo Estevez, 'Comparing intelligence democratization in Latin America: The cases of Argentina, Peru, and Ecuador', *Intelligence and National Security*, forthcoming.
11 Cf. Charles Tilly, *Democracy* (Cambridge: Cambridge University Press, 2007) on 'de-democratisation', pp. 51–79.
12 Peter Gill and Lee Wilson, 'Intelligence and security sector reform in Indonesia', in Kristian Gustafson and Philip Davies (eds.), *Intelligence Elsewhere: The History and Practice of Non-Western Intelligence Services* (Washington, DC: Georgetown University Press, 2012).
13 Greenberg and Dratel, *Torture Papers, passim*. See John Yoo, *War By Other Means: An Insider's Account of the War on Terror* (New York: Atlantic Monthly Press, 2006), from an architect of the Bush policy. Cf. Jane Mayer, *The Dark Side: The Inside Story of How the War on Terror Turned into a War on American Ideals* (New York: Doubleday, 2008) and Philippe Sands, *Torture Team: Uncovering War Crimes in the Land of the Free* (London: Allen Lane, 2008) for critical accounts.
14 Hans Born and Ian Leigh, *Making Intelligence Accountable: Legal Standards and Best Practice for Oversight of Intelligence Agencies* (Oslo: Parliament of Norway, 2005). The following summary of legal principles draws on this except where otherwise stated. See also Aidan Wills, *Guidebook: Understanding Intelligence Oversight* (Geneva: DCAF, 2010).
15 Helen Fenwick, *Civil Liberties*, 2nd edn. (London: Cavendish, 1998), pp. 78–82.
16 D. C. McDonald, *Commission of Inquiry Concerning Certain Activities of the Royal Canadian Mounted Police*, Second Report, *Freedom and Security under the Law* (Ottawa: Minister of Supply and Services, 1981), esp. pp. 407–11.
17 Born and Leigh, *Making Intelligence Accountable*, pp. 37–42.
18 Michael Herman, 'Ethics and intelligence after September 2001', *Intelligence and National Security*, 19,2 (2004), pp. 342–58 at 343.
19 Toni Erskine, '"As rays of light to the human soul?" Moral agents and intelligence gathering', *Intelligence and National Security*, 19,2 (2004), pp. 359–81.
20 See Michael Walzer, *Just and Unjust Wars*, 3rd edn. (New York: Basic Books, 2000), pp. 151–9.
21 Erskine, 'As rays of light', pp. 371–2.
22 Ibid., p. 363.
23 Phillip Knightley, *The Second Oldest Profession: The Spy as Patriot, Bureaucrat, Fantasist and Whore* (London: André Deutsch, 1986).
24 E.g., Special Committee of the Senate on the CSIS, *Delicate Balance: Security Intelligence Services in a Democratic Society* (Ottawa: Minister of Supply and Services, 1983).
25 This argument is developed in detail in Laurence Lustgarten and Ian Leigh, *In From the Cold: National Security and Parliamentary Democracy* (Oxford: Clarendon Press, 1994), pp. 3–35.
26 'Agency policy on liaison with overseas security and intelligence services in relation to detainees who may be subject to mistreatment', unpublished leaked memo; see Ian Cobain, 'Revealed: Britain's secret policy on overseas torture', *Guardian*, 5 August 2011.
27 Clearances themselves exist in ascending order of access, e.g., from 'confidential' through to 'top secret'.
28 E.g., Stuart Farson, 'Old wine, new bottles and fancy labels', in Gregg Barak (ed.), *Crimes by the Capitalist State* (Albany: SUNY Press, 1991), pp. 185–217.
29 Born and Leigh, *Making Intelligence Accountable*, pp. 110–12.
30 Ibid., pp. 77–9, provides a useful comparison of arrangements in seven countries.
31 Respectively, ISC, *Annual Report 2001–2002*, Cm 5542, June 2002, and *Annual Report 2010–11*, Cm 8114, July 2011, p. 12, http://isc.independent.gov.uk/committee-reports/annual-reports, p. 15, accessed 20 September 2011.
32 Steven Aftergood, 'Total intelligence budget for 2007–2009 disclosed', www.fas.org/blog/secrecy/2011/03/mip_disclosures.html, accessed 8 August 2011.

33 E.g., '88, count 'em', editorial, *New York Times*, 9 January 2010.

34 United States Code, Title 50, section 413b; Intelligence Services Act 2001, s.30 (Australia); Intelligence Services Act 1994 (UK); Born and Leigh, *Making Intelligence Accountable*, pp. 91–3; Peter Gill, 'Reasserting control: Recent changes in the oversight of the UK intelligence community', *Intelligence and National Security*, 11,2 (1996), pp. 313–31.

35 Alfred Cumming, *'Gang of Four' Congressional Intelligence Notifications* (Washington, DC: Congressional Research Service, 18 March 2011); Cumming, *Sensitive Covert Action Notifications: Oversight Options for Congress* (Washington, DC: Congressional Research Service, 6 April 2011).

36 Eleanor Hill, *Joint Inquiry Staff Statement*, part 1, 18 September 2002, www.fas.org/irp/congress/2002_hr/091802hill.html, accessed 1 December 2005.

37 SSCI and House Permanent Select Committee on Intelligence, *Report of Joint Inquiry into Intelligence Activities Before and After the Terrorist Attacks of September 11, 2001* (107th Congress, 2nd Session), December 2002, p. 2.

38 Michael Mates, speaking on *Newsnight*, BBC2, 19 May 2009.

39 ISC, *Report into the London Terrorist Attacks on 7 July 2005*, Cm 6785, 2006, http://isc.independent.gov.uk/committee-reports/special-reports, accessed 20 December 2011.

40 ISC, *Could 7/7 Have Been Prevented? Review of the Intelligence on the London Terrorist Attacks on 7 July 2005*, Cm 7617 2009, http://isc.independent.gov.uk/committee-reports/special-reports, para. 11, accessed 6 March 2012.

41 http://7julyinquests.independent.gov.uk/hearing_transcripts/index.htm, accessed 10 August 2011.

42 Cf. Johnson, 'Lawmakers and spies'.

43 Reg Whitaker, 'The Bristow affair: A crisis of accountability in Canadian security intelligence', *Intelligence and National Security*, 11,2 (1996), pp. 279–305.

44 Stuart Farson and Mark Phythian, 'Toward the comparative study of national security commissions of inquiry', in Farson and Phythian (eds.), *Commissions of Inquiry and National Security: Comparative Approaches* (Santa Barbara: Praeger, 2011), pp. 1–12. This book includes case studies from Australia, Canada, the EU, Israel, Latin America, Scandinavia, South Africa, Spain, the UK and the US.

45 Federation of American Scientists, *Secrecy News*, 91 (2002), 19 September, www.fas.org.

46 David Firestone and James Risen, 'White House, in shift, backs inquiry on 9/11', *New York Times*, 21 September 2002.

47 Philip Shenon, 'Bush names former New Jersey governor to 9/11', *New York Times*, 17 December 2002. Initially it was announced that the Commission would be headed by Henry Kissinger. He shortly declined on the grounds that he was unwilling to disclose his international consulting clients as required by federal law. For detailed accounts of the operation of the 9/11 Commission, see Thomas H. Kean and Lee H. Hamilton, *Without Precedent: The Inside Story of the 9/11 Commission* (New York: Knopf, 2006); Philip Shenon, *The Commission: The Uncensored History of the 9/11 Commission* (London: Little, Brown, 2008).

48 E.g., 'Wrestling for the truth of 9/11', *New York Times*, 9 July 2003; 'The mystery deepens', *New York Times*, 3 April 2004.

49 E.g., Dan Eggen and Walter Pincus, 'Ashcroft's efforts on terrorism criticized', *Washington Post*, 14 April 2004; Pincus and Eggen, 'Al Qaeda unchecked for years, panel says Tenet concedes CIA made mistakes', *Washington Post*, 15 April 2004. The staff reports and testimony are available at www.9-11commission.gov, accessed 6 March 2012.

50 The issues are discussed in more detail in Peter Gill, 'Inquiring into dirty wars: A "huge smokescreen of humbug"?', in Farson & Phythian, *Commissions of Inquiry*, pp. 78–97.

51 Rt Hon. Lord Maclean, *The Billy Wright Inquiry: Report*, HC431 (London: Stationery Office, 2010), webarchive.nationalarchives.gov.uk/20101210142120/www.official-documents.gov.uk/document/hc1011/hc04/0431/0431.asp, , esp. ch. 6, accessed 10 August 2011.

52 *Statement by the Police Ombudsman for Northern Ireland on Her Investigation into the Circumstances Surrounding the Death of Raymond McCord Junior and Related Matters*, 22 January 2007, pp. 11–13, www.policeombudsman.org/modules/investigation_reports/index.cfm/reportId/162, accessed 6 March 2012.

53 Marny Requa, 'Truth, transition, and the Inquiries Act 2005', *European Human Rights Law Review*, 4 (2007), pp. 404–26.

54 Declan McCullagh, 'Report: Anti-terror efforts pinch privacy', *CNET News*, 3 September 2002, http://news.com.com, accessed 1 June 2003. EPIC publishes regular reports on the impact of counterterrorist laws in the US: www.epic.org/reports.

55 A systematic review of the impact of media in the security sector is provided by Marina Caparini (ed.), *Media in Security and Governance* (Münster: Nomos Verlagsgesellschaft, 2004).

56 One indicator of the unhappiness at the Iraq fiasco in parts of the Whitehall intelligence machinery is the number of documents leaked to the press after 2003 – press briefings were common before then but leaked documents far less so and certainly less than in the US.

57 Richard Norton-Taylor, 'Court attacks US refusal to disclose torture evidence', *Guardian*, 23 October 2008.

58 Richard Norton-Taylor, 'MI5 officer escapes charges over Mohamed torture case', *Guardian*, 18 November 2010.

59 Jonathan Evans, 'Conspiracy theories aid Britain's enemies', *Daily Telegraph*, 11 February 2010, www.telegraph.co.uk/news/uknews/terrorism-in-the-uk/7217483/Jonathan-Evans, accessed 12 February 2010.

60 The Queen on the Application of Binyam Mohamed and Secretary of State for Foreign and Commonwealth Affairs, EWCA Civ 65, February 2010, paras. 55–7, www.judiciary.gov.uk/media/judgments/2010/binyam-mohamed-judgments, accessed 6 March 2012.

61 Richard Norton-Taylor and Ian Cobain, 'Law must change to prevent Guantánamo payments happening again, says Clarke', *Guardian*, 17 November 2011. ISC, *Annual Report 2010–11*, para. 211, gives half a million documents.

62 Owen Bowcott, 'Supreme Court bans secret evidence in torture trials', *Guardian*, 14 July 2011.

63 www.official-documents.gov.uk/document/cm81/8194/8194.pdf, accessed 7 March 2012.

64 ISC, *The Handling of Detainees by UK Intelligence Personnel in Afghanistan, Guantánamo Bay and Iraq*, Cm 6469, March 2005, http://isc.independent.gov.uk/committee-reports/special-reports, accessed 20 September 2011.

65 ISC, *Alleged Complicity of the UK Security and Intelligence Agencies in Torture or Cruel, Inhuman or Degrading Treatment*, 17 March 2009, www.cabinetoffice.gov.uk/media/143156/090317_alledged.pdf, accessed 24 March 2009.

66 Hansard, 18 March 2009, col. 55WS.

67 Michael Mates, 'Untwisting facts on MI5', *Guardian*, 19 February 2010.

68 ISC, *Annual Report for 2010–2011*, paras. 238–44.

69 ISC, *Handling of Detainees*, para. 47.

70 Human Rights Watch, *No Questions Asked: Intelligence Cooperation with Countries that Torture*, 29 June 2010, www.hrw.org/reports/2010/06/28/no-questions-asked-0, pp. 9–10, accessed 20 December 2011. The arguments on the interpretation of 'complicity' are rehearsed in Joint Committee on Human Rights, *Allegations of UK Complicity in Torture*, 23rd Report Session 2008–9, HL paper 152/HC230, 12–19 August 2009.

71 ISC, *Handling of Detainees*, para. 60.

72 Ibid., paras. 64–5.

73 Ibid., paras. 123 and 101.

74 Cited in Foreign Affairs Committee, *Human Rights Annual Report, 2008*, 7th Report of 2008–9, July 2009. These earlier guidelines were published by the *Guardian* on 4 August 2011. www.guardian.co.uk/law/interactive/2011/aug/04/mi6-torture-interrogation-policy-document?INTCMP=SRCH, accessed 5 August 2011.
75 Richard Norton-Taylor, 'Boycott by rights groups over lack of openness', *Guardian*, 5 August 2011.
76 Ian Cobain, 'UK investigations into torture and rendition: a guide', *Guardian*, 13 February 2012.
77 Hansard, 7 July 2009, cols. 940–5, on which this account is based. See also Human Rights Watch, *Cruel Britannia: British Complicity in the Torture and Ill-Treatment of Terror Suspects in Pakistan* (New York: Human Rights Watch, 2009), www.hrw.org/sites/default/files/reports/uk1109web_0.pdf, pp. 3–34, accessed 20 December 2011.
78 'Agency policy', paras. 13–14.
79 ISC, *Rendition*, Cm 7171, 2007, http://isc.independent.gov.uk/committee-reports/special-reports, para. 173, accessed 20 December 2011.
80 Ian Cobain, 'What terror jury was not told', *Guardian*, 19 December 2008.
81 Cf. Richard J. Aldrich, 'International intelligence cooperation in practice', in Hans Born, Ian Leigh and Aidan Wills (eds.), *International Intelligence Cooperation and Accountability* (London: Routledge, 2011), pp. 18–41 at 21; see also Ian Leigh, 'Accountability and intelligence cooperation: Framing the issue', in ibid., pp. 3–17 at 3–4.
82 Philippe Hayez, 'National oversight of international intelligence cooperation', in ibid., pp. 151–69 at 153–4.
83 Leigh, 'Accountability', p. 10.
84 Aidan Wills and Hans Born, 'International intelligence cooperation and accountability', in Born et al., *International Intelligence Cooperation*, pp. 277–308 at 284.
85 Andrea Wright, 'Fit for purpose? Accountability challenges and paradoxes of domestic inquiries', in ibid., pp. 170–98 at 182.
86 David Leigh and Rob Evans, 'A cover-up laid bare: Court hears how SFO inquiry was halted', *Guardian*, 15 February 2008; Leigh and Evans, 'Britain powerless in face of Saudi threats, court told', *Guardian*, 16 February 2008.
87 Dick Marty, *Secret Detentions and Illegal Transfers of Detainees Involving Council of Europe Member States*, Second Report (Strasbourg: Council of Europe Committee on Legal Affairs and Human Rights, 2007), http://assembly.coe.int, para. 168, 30 June 2008.
88 Mayer, *Dark Side*, pp. 320–1.
89 E.g., a letter from Prime Minister Blair to the ISC on 26 March 2007. See ISC, *Rendition*, para. 197.
90 Richard Norton-Taylor and Julian Borger, 'Embarrassed Miliband admits two US rendition flights refuelled on British soil', *Guardian*, 22 February 2008.
91 John Stevens, *Stevens Enquiry: Overview and Recommendations* (London: Stationery Office, 17 April 2003), para. 3.4.
92 Wills and Born, 'International intelligence cooperation', p. 291.
93 Commission of Inquiry into the Actions of Canadian Officials in Relation to Maher Arar, *Analysis and Recommendations* (Ottawa: Public Works and Government Services Canada, 2006), http://publications.gc.ca, p. 77, accessed 10 May 2007.
94 Commission of Inquiry into the Actions of Canadian Officials in Relation to Maher Arar, *A New Review Mechanism* (Ottawa: Public Works and Government Services Canada, 2006), http://publications.gc.ca, pp. 582–91, accessed 10 May 2007.
95 ISC, *Annual Report 2010–11*, paras. 275–82.
96 Anne-Marie Slaughter, 'Disaggregated sovereignty: Towards the public accountability of global government networks', in David Held and Mathias Koenig-Archibugi (eds.), *Global Governance and Public Accountability* (Oxford: Blackwell, 2005), pp. 35–66 at 47.

97 Belgian Standing Intelligence Agencies Review Committee, *Activity Reports 2006, 2007: Investigations and Recommendations* (Antwerp: Intersentia, 2008), p. x.

98 Belgian Standing Intelligence Agencies Review Committee (ed.), *Fusion Centres Throughout Europe* (Antwerp: Intersentia, 2010).

99 Review Committee on the Intelligence and Security Services, *Annual Report 2010–11* (The Hague: CTIVD, 2011), www.ctivd.nl, p. 29, accessed 20 December 2011.

100 Richard J. Aldrich, 'Global intelligence co-operation versus accountability: new facets to an old problem', *Intelligence and National Security*, 24,1 (2009), pp. 26–56 at 36–7.

101 Cf. Hayez, 'National oversight' pp. 162–3.

102 Amnesty International, *Below the Radar: Secret Flights to Torture and 'Disappearance'*, 5 April 2006; *State of Denial: Europe's Role in Rendition and Secret Detention*, June 2008, both at www.amnesty.org; Stephen Grey, *Ghost Plane: The Untold Story of the CIA's Secret Rendition Programme* (London: Hurst, 2006); www.extraordinaryrendition.org, accessed 20 December 2011; Andrew Tyrie, Roger Gough and Stuart McCracken, *Account Rendered: Extraordinary Rendition and Britain's Role* (London: Biteback, 2011).

103 The story is told by Steve Wright, 'The ECHELON trail: An illegal vision', *Surveillance and Society*, 3,2/3 (2005), pp. 198–215.

104 Part of the Blair government's 2002 WMD dossier and Powell's presentation to the UN in February 2003 was that Iraq had been discovered attempting to buy raw uranium 'yellow cake' from Niger. It emerged quite quickly that the allegations were based on forged documents, although the British government insisted they had independent verification. Aldrich, 'Global intelligence co-operation', pp. 39–40.

105 Wright, 'Fit for purpose?'

106 Cf. Gill, 'Inquiring into dirty wars', pp. 91–3.

107 Marty, *Secret Detentions*.

108 Dana Priest, 'CIA holds terror suspects in secret prisons'. *Washington Post*, 2 November 2005.

109 Hans Born and Aidan Wills, 'International responses to the accountability gap: European inquiries into illegal transfers and secret detentions', in Born et al., *International Intelligence Cooperation*, pp. 199–227.

110 E.g., Richard J. Aldrich, 'US–European intelligence co-operation on counter-terrorism: Low politics and compulsion', *British Journal of Politics & International Relations*, 11,1 (2009), pp. 122–39; Thorsten Wetzling, 'European counterintelligence intelligence liaisons', in Stuart Farson, Peter Gill, Mark Phythian and Shlomo Shpiro (eds.), *PSI Handbook of Global Security and Intelligence: National Approaches*, vol. 2: *Europe, the Middle East and South Africa* (Westport: Praeger Security International, 2008), pp. 498–529.

111 E.g., Silvia Borelli, 'Rendition, torture and intelligence cooperation', in Born et al., *International Intelligence Cooperation*, pp. 98–123; Leigh, 'Accountability', pp. 6–8.

112 Thorsten Benner, Wolfgang H. Reinicke and Jan Martin Witte, 'Multisectoral networks in global governance: Towards a pluralistic system of accountability', in Held and Koenig-Archibugi, *Global Governance*, pp. 67–86 at 75–6.

113 See, e.g., Aldrich, 'Global intelligence co-operation'.

114 Mathieu Deflem, *Policing World Society* (Oxford: Oxford University Press, 2002).

115 Cited in Hayez, 'National oversight', p. 157.

116 Wills and Born, 'International intelligence cooperation', pp. 285–6.

117 Born and Leigh, *Making Intelligence Accountable*.

118 Aldrich, 'US–European intelligence co-operation'.

119 Mayer, *Dark Side*, pp. 295–312.

120 Ian Leigh, 'National courts and international intelligence cooperation', in Born et al., *International Intelligence Cooperation*, pp. 231–51 at 245–6.

121 Craig Forcese, 'The collateral casualties of collaboration: The consequences for civil and human rights of transnational intelligence sharing', in ibid., pp. 72–97 at 91.
122 Wright, 'Fit for purpose?', pp. 189–90.
123 Hayez, 'National oversight', p. 161, points out that in Europe only Luxembourg requires its foreign intelligence agency to inform its oversight committee of relations with foreign agencies.
124 Cf. Leigh, 'Accountability', pp. 9–10.
125 Cf. Benner et al., 'Multisectoral networks', p. 74; cf. also Born and Wills, 'International responses', p. 220.
126 David H. Bayley and Clifford D. Shearing, *The New Structure of Policing: Description, Conceptualization, and Research Agenda*, National Institute of Justice Research Report 187083 (Washington, DC: Department of Justice, 2001), www.ojp.usdoj.gov/nij, pp. 32–3, accessed 15 June 2003. See also Mark Button, *Private Policing* (Cullompton: Willan, 2002), pp. 118–30; Fred Schreier and Marina Caparini, *Privatizing Security: Law, Practice and Governance of Private Military and Security Companies*, DCAF Occasional Paper No. 6 (Geneva, March 2005), pp. 110–23, http://dspace.cigilibrary.org/jspui/bitstream/123456789/27442/1/Privatising%20Security%20-%20Law,%20Practice%20and%20Governance%20of%20Private%20Military%20and%20Security%20Companies.pdf?1, accessed 19 December 2011.

CHAPTER 9 INTELLIGENCE FOR A MORE SECURE WORLD?

1 Bernard Porter, *Plots and Paranoia: A History of Political Espionage in Britain 1790–1988* (London: Unwin Hyman, 1989), p. 234.
2 Reg Whitaker, 'A Faustian bargain? America and the dream of total information awareness', in Kevin D. Haggerty and Richard V. Ericson (eds.), *The New Politics of Surveillance and Visibility* (Toronto: University of Toronto Press, 2005), pp. 141–70.
3 Greg Miller and Julie Tate, 'CIA shifts focus to killing targets', *Washington Post*, 2 September 2011. See also the discussion in chapter 3.
4 See, e.g., Mark Danner, 'After September 11: Our state of exception', *New York Review of Books*, 13 October 2011.
5 Shlomo Shpiro, 'Conclusions', in Stuart Farson, Peter Gill, Mark Phythian and Shlomo Shpiro (eds.), *PSI Handbook of Global Security and Intelligence: National Approaches*, vol. 2: *Europe, the Middle East and South Africa* (Westport: Praeger Security International, 2008), pp. 651–4.
6 Miller and Tate, 'CIA shifts focus'.
7 George Tenet, *At the Center of the Storm: My Years at the CIA* (New York: HarperCollins, 2007), p. 321.
8 On this risk, see Corey Robin, *Fear: The History of a Political Idea* (New York: Oxford University Press, 2004), esp. pp. 1–25.
9 Paradoxes of intelligence are discussed in Peter Gill, 'Theories of intelligence: where are we, where should we go and how might we proceed?', in Peter Gill, Stephen Marrin and Mark Phythian (eds.), *Intelligence Theory: Key Questions and Debates* (London: Routledge, 2009), pp. 208–26 at 211–12.
10 Kevin Drum, 'Political animal', *Washington Monthly*, 1 September 2001, www.washingtonmonthly.com/archives/individual/2005_09/007023.php, accessed 20 December 2011.
11 The initial proposal was made in the *9/11 Commission Report*, section 13.2.
12 http://projects.washingtonpost.com/top-secret-america/articles/methodology, accessed 30 September 2010. See also Dana Priest and William M. Arkin, *Top Secret America: The Rise of the New American Security State* (New York: Little, Brown, 2011).

Selected Further Reading

The three journals listed provide a regular diet of historical and topical articles on intelligence issues. The first two are academic and published by Taylor & Francis and the third is in-house at the CIA. The listed books and articles include references that we believe to be particularly useful and, in the main, recent. The edited collections will provide access to a large number of chapters, some reprinted journal articles, some written on specific issues or providing detailed country studies. We have not identified any specific websites – there are now so many – but many agencies now have their own websites, national archives of many countries provide access to historical intelligence documents, and the quality media provide a trove of past and current material. The Internet is a wonderful resource but must be used with great care – intelligence is a field of study that sees more than its fair share of garbage housed on obscure websites.

Intelligence and National Security
International Journal of Intelligence and Counterintelligence
Studies in Intelligence, https://www.cia.gov/library/center-for-the-study-of-intelligence/csi-publications

Aldrich, Richard, 'Global intelligence co-operation versus accountability: new facets to an old problem', *Intelligence and National Security*, 24,1 (2009), pp. 26–56.

Aldrich, Richard, *GCHQ: The Uncensored Story of Britain's Most Secret Intelligence Agency* (London: HarperPress, 2010).

Andrew, Christopher, *The Defence of the Realm: The Authorized History of MI5* (London: Allen Lane, 2009).

Andrew, Christopher, Richard Aldrich and Wesley Wark (eds.), *Secret Intelligence: A Reader* (London: Routledge, 2009).

Bergman-Rosamond, Annika and Mark Phythian (eds.), *War, Ethics and Justice: New Perspectives on a Post-9/11 World* (London: Routledge, 2011).

Betts, Richard, *Enemies of Intelligence: Knowledge and Power in American National Security* (New York: Columbia University Press, 2007).

Born, Hans, Loch Johnson and Ian Leigh (eds.), *Who's Watching the Spies? Establishing Intelligence Service Accountability* (Washington, DC: Potomac Books, 2005).

Born, Hans, Ian Leigh and Aidan Wills (eds.), *International Intelligence Cooperation and Accountability* (London: Routledge, 2011).

Bruneau, Thomas C. and Steven Boraz (eds.), *Reforming Intelligence: Obstacles to Democratic Control and Effectiveness* (Austin: University of Texas Press, 2007).

Cogan, Charles, 'Hunters not gatherers: intelligence in the twenty-first century', *Intelligence and National Security*, 19,2 (2004), pp. 304–21.

Dover, Robert and Michael Goodman (eds.), *Spinning Intelligence: Why Intelligence Needs the Media, Why the Media Needs Intelligence* (London: Hurst, 2009).

Dover, Robert and Michael Goodman (eds.), *Learning from the Secret Past: Cases in British Intelligence History* (Washington, DC: Georgetown University Press, 2011).

Farson, Stuart, Peter Gill, Mark Phythian and Shlomo Shpiro (eds.), *PSI Handbook of Global Security and Intelligence, National Approaches*, vol. 1: *The Americas and Asia*; vol. 2: *Europe, the Middle East and South Africa* (Westport: Praeger Security International, 2008).

Farson, Stuart and Mark Phythian (eds.), *Commissions of Inquiry and National Security: Comparative Approaches* (Santa Barbara: Praeger, 2011).

Fry, Michael and Miles Hochstein, 'Epistemic communities: intelligence studies and international relations', *Intelligence and National Security*, 8,3 (1993), pp. 14–28.

George, Roger and James Bruce (eds.), *Analyzing Intelligence: Origins, Obstacles, and Innovations* (Washington, DC: Georgetown University Press, 2008).

Gill, Peter, Stephen Marrin and Mark Phythian (eds.), *Intelligence Theory: Key Questions and Debates* (London: Routledge, 2009).

Goldman, Jan (ed.), *Ethics of Spying: A Reader for the Intelligence Professional* (Lanham: Scarecrow Press, 2006).

Grey, Stephen, *Ghost Plane: The Untold Story of the CIA's Secret Rendition Programme* (London: Hurst, 2006).

Herman, Michael, *Intelligence Power in Peace and War* (Cambridge: Cambridge University Press, 1996).

Herman, Michael, *Intelligence Services in the Information Age* (London: Frank Cass, 2001).

Hughes, R. Gerald, Peter Jackson and Len Scott (eds.) , *Exploring Intelligence Archives: Enquiries into the Secret State* (London: Routledge, 2008).

Jeffery, Keith, *MI6: The History of the Secret Intelligence Service 1909–1949* (London: Bloomsbury, 2010).

Jervis, Robert, *Why Intelligence Fails: Lessons from the Iranian Revolution and the Iraq War* (Ithaca: Cornell University Press, 2010).

Johnson, Loch K. (ed.), *Handbook of Intelligence Studies* (Abingdon: Routledge, 2007).

Johnson, Loch K. (ed.), *The Oxford Handbook of National Security Intelligence* (Oxford: Oxford University Press, 2010).

Johnson, Loch K., *National Security Intelligence: Secret Operations in Defense of the Democracies* (Cambridge: Polity, 2012).

Marrin, Stephen, *Improving Intelligence Analysis: Bridging the Gap between Scholarship and Practice* (London: Routledge, 2011).

Omand, David, *Securing the State* (London: Hurst, 2010).

Pfiffner, James and Mark Phythian (eds.), *Intelligence and National Security Policymaking on Iraq: British and American Perspectives* (Manchester: Manchester University Press, 2008).

Priest, Dana and William Arkin, *Top Secret America: The Rise of the New American Security State* (New York: Little, Brown, 2011).

Ratcliffe, Jerry, *Intelligence-Led Policing* (Cullompton: Willan, 2008).

Scott, Len and Peter Jackson, 'The study of intelligence in theory and practice', *Intelligence and National Security*, 19,2 (2004), pp. 139–69.

Shorrock, Tim, *Spies for Hire: The Secret World of Intelligence Outsourcing* (New York: Simon & Schuster, 2008).

Steele, Robert, *The New Craft of Intelligence: Personal, Public and Political* (Oakton: OSS International Press, 2002).

Treverton, Gregory and Wilhelm Agrell (eds.), *National Intelligence Systems: Current Research and Prospects* (Cambridge: Cambridge University Press, 2009).

Zegart, Amy, *Spying Blind: The CIA, the FBI and the Origins of 9/11* (Princeton: Princeton University Press, 2007).

Index

Individual intelligence agencies are listed under their home country.